Mysticism and Meaning

Multidisciplinary Perspectives

edited by

Alex S. Kohav

Three Pines Press
PO Box 530416
St Petersburg, FL 33747
www.threepinespress.com

9 8 7 6 5 4 3 2 1

First Three Pines Press Edition, 2019
Printed in the United States of America

⊗ This edition is printed on acid-free paper that meets the American National Standard Institute Z39.48 Standard.
Distributed in the United States by Three Pines Press.

Cover art: "Turquoise Honey River," by Alex Shalom Kohav, 1990, 80 x 128 inches, acrylic on linen.

Library of Congress Cataloging-in-Publication Data

Names: Kohav, Alex S., 1948- editor.
Title: Mysticism and meaning : multidisciplinary perspectives / edited by Alex S. Kohav.
Description: First [edition]. | St Petersburg : Three Pines Press, 2019. | Includes index.
Identifiers: LCCN 2019014833 | ISBN 9781931483407 (alk. paper)
Subjects: LCSH: Mysticism. | Experience (Religion) | Meaning (Philosophy)--Religious aspects.
Classification: LCC BL625 .M8854 2019 | DDC 204/.22--dc23
LC record available at https://lccn.loc.gov/2019014833

Contents

Preface ix

1. Alex S. Kohav 1
Introductory Essay: The Problem, Aporia, and Mysterium of Mysticism

PROLOGUE: MYSTICISM'S BREADTH OF MANIFESTATION

2. Jeff Warren 23
The Anxiety of the Long-Distance Meditator
What is the distinction between religious dogmas versus practitioners' real experience? In some Western Buddhist circles, the taboo against discussing one's mystical "attainments" is being overturned by rigorous descriptions of the phenomenology of advanced meditation practice. This essay offers a brief taste of one such account.

3. Gregory M. Nixon 29
Breaking out of One's Head (and Awakening to the World)
Nixon recounts a life-changing, harrowing mystical occurrence in his life when he found his "*being* as part of the living world and not in [his] head, discovering [his] perspectival center to be literally everywhere."

4. Jack Hirschman 58
The Mystical Essay: Kabbala, Communism, and Street-Level Café Poiesis
The author, an academic-turned-poet, relates his personal journey to prominence as a "street poet" in San Francisco, where he subsequently becomes that city's official poet laureate. The journey intrinsically and intimately parallels Hirschman's close involvement with mystical experiences and texts.

PART I: RELIGIONS AT BIRTH, IN PERPETUITY, AND IN FLUX

5. Livia Kohn 71
Oneness with Heaven and Earth: Mysticism in the Chinese Tradition
Mysticism has permeated the different aspects of the Chinese tradition and is present as much in Confucianism and Buddhism as in Daoism. How does the Chinese mystical tradition differ from comparable Western and Indian systems?

6. Alex S. Kohav 91
God of Moses versus the "One and All" of Egypt: From Magic of Hypostatized Spirituality to Discriminating Paradigm of Non-Idolatry
Ancient Egyptian religious approach exemplifies what amounted to a ritualized imbuing of objects-as-symbols and conceptions with magical significance. The essay argues that ancient Israelite religion markedly defined itself through a rejection of magical consciousness.

7. Harry T. Hunt 125
Toward an Existential Understanding of Christianity: Phenomenologies of Mystical States as Mediating between Kierkegaard's Christian Dogmatics and Early Gospel Accounts
Transpersonal psychology is applied to selected Gospel narratives as a step toward a reconstruction of specific numinous states implied within early Christianity. The Christian doctrines are seen as amplifications of the phenomenology of inner forms of here-and-now consciousness.

PART II: PHILOSOPHY & MYSTICISM: CONJOINED AT SOURCE?

8. Ori Z. Soltes 153
Convergent Paths along the Via Spinoza: Philosophy and Mysticism from Socrates to Ibn' Arabi and the Ba'al Shem Tov
Like Plato—and unlike Descartes—Spinoza presents himself as hostile to mystical (and general religious) thought. But like Plato's thought, and in part in close if unconscious alignment with an important thread of mystical thought extending from Ibn' Arabi to the Baal Shem Tov, Spinoza's thinking shares significant ground with panhenotheistic mysticism.

9. Jacob Rump 177
Not How the World Is, but That It Exists: Wittgenstein on the Mystical and the Meaningful
Wittgenstein's conception of the mystical should not be understood as referring to a realm of fundamental but ineffable facts or truths. Rather, it is a marker of that which makes facticity and truth possible. Questions of fundamental value ascription are beyond the reach of scientific or logical analysis.

PART III: PSYCHOLOGICAL, LINGUISTIC, & SEMIOTIC TURNS

10. Brian ("Les") Lancaster 201
Mystical Maps and Psychological Models: States of Consciousness in the Language Mysticism of the *Zohar*
A study of the states of mystical consciousness as depicted in the *Zohar*, the central text of kabbalah. The essay explores the characteristics of three mystical states of consciousness portrayed in the latter and identifies their possible neurocognitive correlates.

11. Louis Hébert 228
Becoming a Buddha: A Semiotic Analysis of Visualizations in Tibetan Buddhism
This essay analyzes certain aspects of Vajrayana Buddhism using François Rastier's theory of anthropic zones. *Sādhana* texts are examined, in which complex visualizations are used to invite the practitioner to be progressively transformed into an enlightened being, or Buddha.

CODA: A NEW AGE FOR THE MYSTICAL?

12. Richard H. Jones 249
Mysticism in the New Age: Are Mysticism and Science Converging?
Jones discusses the New Age contention of the convergence of scientific and mystical claims about reality. The issues addressed include the differences in mystical and scientific approaches to reality; how mysticism and science might intersect in principle; how mysticism and science might be reconciled—but are not; and the insubstantiality of the alleged convergences.

POSTSCRIPT: SOUL-FREE HOMO SAPIENS?

13. Burton H. Voorhees 279
Fragments from Records of the First Information Age
In the year 2392, a chance discovery offers a rare glimpse of what remains of the archives of the secular regime that collapsed in the cyber-spiritual revolution of 2136-43. The net-link and personal memory files for the academic known as Ted Sy-Ex2 were corrupted, and what remains regarding this interesting character and his implanted personal assistant/manager Jeeves (who was martyred by erasure) is the exchange reproduced in this chapter.

Contributors 287
Index 293

To

Ziony Zevit

&

In Memory of My Father,

Moses Stern (1921-2015)

Do you think anyone is ever going to grant
that a person who is altering is the same person
as he was before the altering began?
—Plato, *Theaetetus*

There is indeed the inexpressible.
This shows itself; it is the mystical.
—Wittgenstein, *Tractatus Logico-Philosophicus*

Preface

Mysticism and Meaning: Multidisciplinary Perspectives explores the question of the meaning of mystical phenomena and, conversely, attempts to articulate unexplored aspects of the category "meaning," via insights suggested by mystical experiences. The book as a whole endeavors to answer the question, Can progress be made in our understanding of the meaning of mystical phenomena?

While previous generations of researchers emphasized the historical-ethnographic and linguistic manifestations of mysticism, this volume deemphasizes them or reorients and updates earlier investigations. It brings ancient, major religions such as Judaism and Christianity "in line" with those other traditions that have never doubted their mystical origins, for example, Buddhism and ancient Chinese traditions. Linguistic approaches to mysticism are both supplemented or in some cases supplanted by the cognitive and semiotic "turns." A renewed and expanded philosophical and cognitive-psychological scrutiny of mysticism is provided, with implications for philosophy itself. The book closes with a look at a remarkable resurgence of mysticism in recent decades in its more popular and less clear manifestation known as the New Age. Thus the volume's reach extends to realms largely disregarded or unidentified by earlier investigators of mysticism.

In its attempt to address the crucial question of mysticism's meaning through pertinent interdisciplinarity, the volume brings together researchers from such disparate fields as philosophy, psychology, history of religion, cognitive neuroscience, and semiotics.

One strand within the volume provides a framework for identifying the fertile source of the continuing fascination of mysticism. Two contributions within this strand showcase ancient Egypt's engrossment with alterations of consciousness analogous to magic, and the influence of mystical praxis on Judaism's and Christianity's origins (chapters 6 and 7); two other chapters highlight mysticism's formative presence in Chinese traditions (chapter 5) and Tibetan Buddhism (chapter 12).

Another discernable, forceful strand in the volume concerns multidisciplinary analyses of the phenomenon of mysticism, specifically, via philosophical, psychological, cognitive, and semiotic explorations. These chapters are supplemented by three poignant personal accounts of significant mystical experiences in the prologue which serve as the volume's lead-in, setting the tone for what follows through intimate, first-person impressions that cannot be readily conveyed by detached, neutral academic analysis. The book concludes with a sobering postscript that envisions a future without things mystical.

The book took six years to prepare. Considering its enigmatic subject; the disciplinary diversity of its thirteen chapters, the work of twelve contributors hailing from Canada, England, and the United States; and its level of investigation aimed at giving the reader a broad, discerning account of things mystical, such a time frame does not seem excessive.

Chapter 1, the editor's "Introductory Essay: The Problem, Aporia, and Mysterium of Mysticism," addresses the following two, at first glance naive questions: Why do most efforts at theorizing mysticism remain ineffectual? And what is it that often marks mysticism as such an objectionable topic and issue? The approach taken in the chapter rests initially on a distinction between "problem" and "aporia" drawn by Jacques Derrida and applied here to the question of mysticism. The discussion shows why this distinction, important in and of itself, nonetheless fails to capture fully mysticism's authentic nature. There is, the essay finds, a more basic aspect of mystical phenomena, one that the paradigmatic terms "problem" and "aporia" will not satisfactorily encompass. The essay argues that identifying and naming this more-fundamental mystery that is implicated and the way to approach its significance should be via a distinct and germane designation: it proposes the term *mysterium* (which is the Latin cognate of mystery). *Mysterium* (and, at its most sublime, *mysterium tremendum*) is to aporia what aporia is to the problem, and it is not associated with either the logoic "intellection" or intuition. The essay proposes that the exceedingly uncommon epistemic "faculty" associated with *mysterium* be named "illumination."

The prologue, titled "Mysticism's Breadth of Manifestation: Three Contemporary Examples," includes three chapters that exemplify contemporary instances of how mysticism is viewed, practiced, and experienced today, in the midst of our complex twenty-first-century lives.

Jeff Warren, author of chapter 2, "The Anxiety of the Long-Distance Meditator," is a Toronto-based journalist and meditation teacher who is also the author of *The Head Trip: Adventures on the Wheel of Consciousness* (Random House, 2007). In his discussion, Warren offers a short experiential account of his personal attempt to attain "initial enlightenment" (or "stream entry," as it is known in Buddhism) during a thirty-day solitary retreat in rural Alabama. He conveys how, "under the guidance of a contemporary meditation teacher . . . [he moved] along what is known as the 'Progress of Insight,' a sequence or map of meditative states and shifts described in classic Buddhist texts such as the *Visuddhimagga* and the *Abihidharma* and updated in the early twentieth century by a Burmese Vipassana teacher named Mahawsi Sayadaw." As Warren notes, "Vipassana—also known as mindfulness meditation—has become increasingly popular in the West, yet there is very little discussion about where these practices may lead, and how they may shift the practitioner's perspective, identity, and sense of suffering."

Chapter 3 continues the experiential aspect of explorations in mind alteration, in this case not by following tenets of a tradition such as Buddhism but spontaneously. In "Breaking Out of One's Head (and Awakening to the World)," another Canadian, Gregory M. Nixon of the University of Northern British Columbia in Prince George, recounts the life-changing, harrowing mystical occurrence when he found his "*being* as part of the living world and not in [his] head, discovering [his] perspectival center to be literally everywhere." Now a researcher of consciousness known among fellow critics of the so-called pure consciousness hypothesis as the one who memorably raised the "hermeneutic objection,"[1] in this introspective and movingly personal essay Nixon writes: "Since awakening to the world takes one beyond thought and language and thus also beyond the symbolic construction of time, it is strange to place this event and its aftermath as happening long ago in my life. It is forever present."

He notes, "Ironically, the memory itself with its facade of knowledge may prevent me from a new, unexpected mystical experience. Only by forgetting can I hope to leave a crack in the verbal armament of self, so the world soul may break through and free me once again." His stirring, courageous chronicle concludes with the following: "My linear march into aging and death inexorably continues, yet it seems somehow unreal, worth a smile as the inevitable changes ensue. Still, I write of the events leading up to my time out of mind and then review the serious repercussions that followed. . . . I close by looking back with theories that might explain what happened."

Nixon's first-person, emotional yet analytical, reasoned account is followed by chapter 4, "The Mystical Essay: Kabbala, Communism, and Street-Level Café *Poiesis*," which is also of a decidedly autobiographical nature. Its author, Jack Hirschman,[2] is an academic-turned-poet who is the fourth poet laureate of the City of San Francisco, and considered by some to be the most important living American poet. In this chapter, he relates why and how his journey as a poet intrinsically and intimately parallels close involvement with mystical texts and mysticism.

We learn of numerous other poets and writers of his generation in the United States who, in their search for self-discovery and transformation, have sought means that often included kabbalah and other mystical traditions and sources. "Whether it is Kabbala or [Haitian vodun mysticism], I take these elements as fundamentally active linguistic tropes, part of a poet's arsenal of inter-

---

[1] Gregory Nixon, "A 'Hermeneutic Objection': Language and the Inner View," in *The View from Within: First-Person Approaches to the Study of Consciousness*, ed. F. J. Varela and J. Shear, 257–67 (Thorventon, UK: Imprint Academic, 2000). Originally published in *Journal of Consciousness Studies* 6, nos. 2–3 (1999): 257–67.

[2] Hirschman's magnum opus is *The Arcanes*, two large volumes published by Multimedia Edizioni, Salerno, Italy, in 2006 and 2016.

ests," avers Hirschman. The essay begins with his pithy definition of mysticism, one that is remarkable in that it originates from a self-declared dedicated communist: "There are many definitions of mysticism, I suppose, but generally speaking the attainment of the knowledge of the existence of, or identification with, or receptivity to God (and the various means to do so, i. e., ritual, prayer, ecstasy, trance) approaches the core of such a definition. Underlying all the words in that dynamic is the unspoken one: inwardness. And if we are talking of inwardness and/or as soul, then—at least as far as I am concerned—we are talking about poetry."

Hirschman's discussion has a singular effect on the reader as it conveys, in his intellectually feverish way, the manner in which a whole generation of American poets, writers, and artists have searched for, and often found, inspiration and energies in ancient, near-extinct mystical texts, often in tongues other than English and thus in need of new, if not first-ever translations. I encountered this colorful, intensely diverse sediment of American culture—or more accurately, its anticulture—when I first arrived to the United States more than four decades ago.[3]

Next, Part 1, "Religions at Birth, in Perpetuity, and in Flux," attempts to capture the enormous presence, indeed dominance of religions in the story of humanity. The section's three chapters focus on the intimate and causative connection to mystical manifestations found in several ancient religious traditions.

Chapter 5, "Oneness with Heaven and Earth: Mystical Attainment in the Chinese Tradition," takes us to ancient China. In this masterful survey essay, Boston University's Livia Kohn,[4] a foremost American scholar of Daoism, details how mysticism "has permeated the different aspects of the Chinese tradition and is present as much in the dominant school of Confucianism and in the foreign religion of Buddhism as it is in Daoism, the indigenous higher religion of China."

Kohn addresses the following specific questions: "How does the Chinese mystical tradition differ from comparable Western and Indian systems? What

---

[3] Thus the personal references to me in Hirschman's essay, which would be difficult to excise without altering the flow of his thought and narrative. Shortly after my arrival in San Francisco in early 1976, Jack translated my long poem, *The Orange Voice*, into English, and we jointly translated a collection of "transrational," or *zaum*, poems by the remarkable Russian Futurist poet Alexei Kruchenykh, eventually published as *Suicide Circus* (Green Integer, 1999). My sporadic but earnest attempts to enlighten Jack about the exceedingly awful truth of the Soviet reality served, it seemed, only to amplify his fascination with Russia—and with communism.

[4] Livia Kohn's many publications include *Introducing Daoism* (Routledge, 2008); *Sitting in Oblivion: The Heart of Daoist Meditation* (Three Pines Press, 2010); and *Science and the Dao* (Three Pines Press, 2016), and *Guides to Sacred Texts: The Daode jing* (Oxford UP, 2098).

are some of its fundamental characteristics?" The chapter explicates that "Chinese mysticism in its various forms always focuses on the attainment of oneness with Heaven and Earth, is centered on the body-mind of the living individual, has a strong social and political dimension, and relates to an underlying force of multiple divinities rather than a single creator god." By the "divinities," however, Kohn does not mean to imply any transcendent entities: "There is no entity completely beyond the world, no transcendent other, no 'thou' to a this-worldly 'us,' no power that will never cease and never change. Rather, the Chinese tradition sees its ultimate in the Dao, a divine force so immanent that it is even in the soil and tiles; so much a part of the world that it cannot be separated from it."

In chapter 6, "God of Moses versus the 'One and All' of Egypt: From Magic of Hypostatized Spirituality (Egypt) to Discriminating Paradigm of Non-Idolatry (Israel)," I portray a dimension that, as the chapter asserts, is at the core of civilizational "tectonic" shifts, then—in early antiquity—as much as now: Magic and magical consciousness as religious experience versus, or contrasted with, religious experience of mysticism proper, one that would determinedly reject magical consciousness.

Egyptian priestly praxis involved significant alterations of consciousness reflecting worship of numerous diverse-scale deities and preternatural powers. It presented a magic-saturated theology and worldview that oversaw ritualized imbuing of multiple objects-as-symbols with magical significance. Ancient Israelite religion, to the contrary, has defined itself from its inception through refutation of magical cognizance vis-à-vis the world. This included a forceful refusal to idolize objects, entities, and persons, opting instead for a relationship with a highest-scalar agent conceivable who henceforth would not be confused with—nor seen as infusing—either the material or the mental realities. At the same time, ancient Israelite religion opted for alphabet-based, ideationally fecund language with mimetic capabilities; the latter supplied and sustained a vastly expanded range of semiotic resources giving rise to a priestly initiation tradition based on direct, *mysterium tremendum*-kind mystical experiences.

Part I concludes with chapter 7, "Toward an Existential Understanding of Christianity: Phenomenologies of Mystical States as Mediating between Kierkegaard's Christian Dogmatics and Early Gospel Accounts," by a key theorist of mystical phenomena, Harry T. Hunt (Brock University in Ontario, Canada).[5] It engages a foremost world religion originating in late antiquity, Christianity, from the standpoint of the present volume's overall focus on mysticism and

---

[5] Harry T. Hunt is the author of *On the Nature of Consciousness: Cognitive, Phenomenological, and Transpersonal Perspectives* and *The Multiplicity of Dreams: Memory, Imagination, and Consciousness* (both from Yale University Press, 1995 and 1991), as well as *Lives in Spirit: Precursors and Dilemmas of a Secular Western Mysticism* (SUNY Press, 2003).

specifically from "existential-phenomenological perspective [that] is shown to be broadly congruent with the contemporary transpersonal psychology of higher states of consciousness."

As Hunt—a leading authority on meditative and transpersonal states of consciousness—frames it, "a more directly experiential understanding of the doctrines of Christian redemption, loving compassion, and eternal life reveals them as amplifications of the phenomenology of the inner forms of ordinary here and now consciousness, within which they are already foreshadowed." Referencing philosophers such as Martin Heidegger, Max Scheler, and Søren Kierkegaard and mystics such as Meister Eckhart and Saint Paul, the essay tracks and develops a connection between "felt experience of presence" and "numinous qualities in the New Testament" and early Christianity.

The above chapters depict mystical foundations of indigenous ancient Chinese religions (Confucianism and Daoism), ancient Egypt, ancient Israel, as well as the mystical origins of Christianity. As the volume unfolds its multidisciplinary investigation of mystical phenomena, the reader additionally encounters Tibetan Buddhism (chapter 12), medieval Judaism's kabbalah (chapter 10), and aspects of Islamic-Sufi mysticism (chapter 8). The book does not, however, seek to cover most or even many religions but rather to highlight exemplary instances that afford valuable insights.

As the title of Part 2, "Philosophy and Mysticism: Conjoined at Source?," suggests, the study now turns to yet another ancient symbiosis, one between mysticism and philosophy. Chapter 8, "Convergent Paths along the *Via Spinoza*: Philosophy and Mysticism from Socrates to Ibn 'Arabi and the Ba'al Shem Tov," by Ori Z. Soltes of Georgetown University,[6] demonstrates that contrary to some disciplines' endemic prejudices against mysticism, philosophy is hardly averse to it: "Like Plato's thought, and in part in close if unconscious alignment with an important thread of mystical thought extending from Ibn' Arabi to the Baal Shem Tov, Spinoza's thinking has significantly more in common with panhenotheistic mysticism, in spite of his intense rationalism—and, paradoxically, in spite of how antithetical to 'religion' in its traditional shape his thinking is—than he or we might suppose."

One might add that at philosophy's dawn, the Pre-Socratics were on track to trade the *mythos* paradigm for rationality, or *logos*, yet they themselves were often practicing mystics whose philosophical breakthroughs are often indistin-

[6] Ori Z. Soltes is an unusually prolific investigator whose research interests cover a wide area. He has authored over 275 books, articles, catalogs, and essays, ranging from philosophy and religious studies to art criticism and poetry. Soltes's most recent book is his magisterial *Magic and Religion in the Greco-Roman World: The Beginnings of Judaism and Christianity* (Academia-West Press); he is also the coeditor, with Alex S. Kohav, of "A Paradise of Paradoxes: Resolute Perplexities of Israel's Inscrutable Edenic Trees and Ineffable God" (forthcoming).

guishable from mystical visions. Pythagoras is an outstanding example, also Empedocles (easily a "shaman"), the prophet-like Heraclitus, as well as Parmenides, what with his personal shamanic journey (unmistakably portrayed in a key surviving fragment) and his proto-Einsteinian reality-as-endless-sphere conceptualization. Philosophy then tended to focus on the question of human self-realization (including, in some cases, God-realization), thus identifying with the goals of many mystical traditions. Constructing a self, one suitable for philosophical inquiry, was often seen as necessarily tied to ascetical, that is to say, mystical, practices—thus reinforcing the impression of the conjoined-at-birth, fraternal bonds of philosophy and mysticism.

Chapter 9, "Not How the World Is, but That It Exists: Wittgenstein on the Mystical and the Meaningful," by the young American philosopher Jacob Rump, effectively examines the relationship between the mystical and meaning in Ludwig Wittgenstein's early work, especially his celebrated and still-controversial *Tractatus Logico-Philosophicus.* While some readers of Wittgenstein to this day routinely misconstrue his position vis-à-vis mysticism (specifically, that he was hostile to the latter), Rump's essay cogently demonstrates that "Wittgenstein's remarks concerning the mystical are . . . an attempt to persuade us of the persistence—even if merely indirect or symbolic—of such ultimate value and meaning. And he recognized, like few others before or since, that such a guarantee could not be made in ignorance of logic, language, and the facts of the world, but only by looking first through and then *beyond* them to find what is greater."

In Part 3, "Psychological, Semiotic, and Linguistic-Epistemic Turns," the discussion shifts to more-specific explorations of mysticism's manifestations that will then be continued in subsequently in the book.

Chapter 10, "Mystical Maps and Psychological Models: States of Consciousness in Language Mysticism of the *Zohar*," is by Manchester, England–based Les Lancaster.[7] His chapter explores language mysticism, which "is of interest," he states, "because of the central role played by language in relation to the self and the individual's construction of reality." Lancaster introduces a valuable notion of "mapping, or modeling, mind processes and states of consciousness [which] is identified as a key area of consonance between psychology and mysticism. Broadly similar goals are advanced by these two areas of human inquiry using complementary methods."

He also discusses states of mystical consciousness depicted in the *Zohar*, a central text of kabbalah. "The first state entails perceptual intensification and intuition of supernormal meaning. It may relate to hyperactivation of recurrent perceptual neural systems interacting with feedforward pathways and concomi-

---

[7] Brian L. Lancaster's publications include *Approaches to Consciousness: The Marriage of Science and Mysticism* (Palgrave Macmillan, 2004) and *The Essence of Kabbalah* (Chartwell Books, 2005).

tant attenuation of systems generating the normal self-construct. The second state is characterized by an all-knowing sense, whereby the mystic is, as it were, in rapport with the pattern underlying all things. This state points to increased awareness of normally preconscious associative functions whereby current sensory input triggers diverse memory engrams. The final state is one in which there is no awareness of form, only 'light.' It is proposed that this state be understood in terms of phenomenality in the absence of intentionality."

Chapter 11, "Becoming a Buddha: A Semiotic Analysis of Visualizations in Tibetan Buddhism," is an essay by Louis Hébert of Quebec, Canada, who specializes in textual and visual semiotics and interpretive semantics.[8] The essay analyzes certain aspects of Vajrayana Buddhism applying François Rastier's theory of anthropic zones. Hébert's chapter—originally written in French for this volume and then translated into English—examines *sādhana* texts, in which complex visualizations "invite the practitioner to be progressively transformed into an enlightened being, or Buddha."

The author—whose work throughout the years has focused on semiotics' ability to uniquely foreground crucial meaning—explains that "the practitioner travels in his mind . . . from the identity zone to the distal zone, and this is done through the mediation of a Buddhist deity that functions as an idol." The deity is the practitioner's teacher, "a fellow creature. . . . In taking the form of the practiced deity Avalokiteśhvara in the visualization, he becomes an idol who represents transcendence and makes its attainment possible."

The Coda—entitled "A New Age for the Mystical?—contains chapter 12, "Mysticism in the New Age: Are Mysticism and Science Converging?," by Richard H. Jones. [9] Jones discusses the New Age contention of the convergence of scientific and mystical claims about reality.[10] The issues addressed in the chapter include the differences between mystical and scientific approaches to reality; how mysticism and science might intersect in principle; and how mysticism and science might be reconciled—but are not.

Specifically, Jones discusses "the differences in mystical and scientific subjects (i. e., the 'beingness' of things or their ontological source versus under-

---

[8] Louis Hébert is coeditor with Lucie Guillemette of two volumes: *Intertextualité, Interdiscursivité et Intermédialité* (2009) and *Performances et Objets Culturels: Nouvelles Perspectives* (2011), both published by Presses de l'Université Laval.

[9] Richard H. Jones is the author of numerous books, among them the recently published, groundbreaking *Philosophy of Mysticism: Raids on the Ineffable* (SUNY Press, 2016).

[10] New Age is a term, used since about 1971, that refers to "an eclectic group of cultural attitudes arising in late 20th century Western society that are adapted from those of a variety of ancient and modern cultures, that emphasize beliefs (such as reincarnation, holism, pantheism, and occultism) outside the mainstream, and that advance alternative approaches to spirituality, right living, and health" (Merriam-Webster.com).

standing how things work); the different intents of mysticism and science (i. e., soteriological goals versus disinterested understanding); the differences between mystical awareness and scientific observations; the misuse of science and the misunderstanding of Asian mysticism leading to distortions in New Age comparisons; and the overall insubstantiality of the alleged convergences. Examples include the different meanings of 'emptiness' in mysticism and in science, the role of consciousness in quantum physics, and whether the Buddha can be classified as a 'scientist.'" The chapter's conclusion is stern but, it would seem, justified: "Seeing mysticism and science converging is no doubt a desideratum in New Age thought: it would give the imprimatur of science to New Age spirituality. However, New Age claims to convergence do not pan out."

This book's finale, however, has not been reached unless we endure the perversely disturbing pleasure of reading chapter 13, "Fragments from Records of the First Information Age," by Burton H. Voorhees.[11] The chapter serves as the volume's postscript—with the latter's subtitle querying the following still-inconceivable question: "Soul-Free Homo Sapiens?" Yes, the time has arrived to ask such once-rhetorical questions, but this time without the rhetorical intent. Voorhees—an American physicist and mathematician based in Canada and Tucson, Arizona, who is active in consciousness studies—bluntly portrays a *possible*, and perhaps even likely, future awaiting human beings.

The pleasure remarked on above pertains to the inimitable manner in which Voorhees's piece forcibly takes one into what we might refer to as the soulless future. The futuristic, whimsical chronicle from the time-to-come—the year 2392—forewarns us that when such things as mystical insights and visions—or the spiritually, intellectually, and artistically sublime—are "erased" from one's "personal memory files" (to use the chilling language of the postscript essay), we can safely conclude, echoing Tom Wolfe's "Sorry, but Your Soul Just Died," that we are no longer quite human.

* * *

---

[11] Burton Voorhees has published in the disciplines of relativity theory (in which he is known for the "Voorhees solutions" of the Einstein equations), mathematical biology, applied mathematics, psychology, systems theory, philosophy of science, and consciousness studies, authoring over eighty publications, including *Computational Analysis of One-Dimensional Cellular Automata* (World Scientific, 1995). His research encompasses incompleteness, undecidability, and strong AI; origins of self-consciousness; epistemology of complex systems; scientific reasoning and the foundations of logic; and cellular automata and substitution systems.

I would like to acknowledge the enormous fortitude that the contributors to this volume have shown, in spite of the extent of time and effort that it took. We have "lost" three potential contributions, one due to illness, another due to youthful impatience (the essay was to come from Italy, after all!), and the third because its would-be author has decided to change his research focus entirely. Life happens. This has also been an effort that in some cases required a total rewrite of the initial drafts; I am humbled to recall that these sometimes senior scholars have uniformly been thankful for the definitive result. We have had, too, the benefit of the always-skillful input from Barb Wojhoski in Atlanta, who copyedited most of the chapters; I want to thank Barb for her ability to field the large differences in styles and content, not to mention the idiosyncrasies, either personal or disciplinary, among the essays.

I dedicate this book, first, to Ziony Zevit, who bravely took a chance on following my dissertation research as a supportive committee member, however much my approach radically differed from that of his biblical studies' colleagues; and to the memory of my father, who passed away at ninety-four just when the book was approaching its final form. As a friend warned me at the time, it has been a "slow burner" ever since.

Alex Kohav
Boulder, Colorado
March 2019

1. Introductory Essay

The Problem, Aporia, and Mysterium of Mysticism

Alex S. Kohav

Abstract

What is it that often marks mysticism as such an objectionable topic and issue? The approach taken in the essay rests, initially, on a distinction between "problem" and "aporia" drawn by Derrida and applied specifically to the question of mysticism. There is, however, a more inexplicable core experienced in mystical phenomena, one that concepts such as *aporia* let alone "problem" are not able to account for. If *problematizing* altered states of consciousness, among them the various mysticisms, reduces them to *logos*-based rationalizations; and if positing *aporias*—by bringing into play intuition—also falls short of grasping the inscrutabilities encountered; then a widening of contextual ground from which one attempts to perceive these phenomena is called for.

The mystics themselves, throughout millennia, have offered names for certain capabilities of the human mind that, as they typically claim, not only reach beyond instinct as well as reason and reasoning but also get past intuition (which is the highest Spinozist "knowledge level"). Invariably, to describe the achieved mind-states, they invoke such terms as "illumination," "enlightenment," "*samadhi*," "*satori*," "nirvana," "beatitude" or "blessedness," and so on.

The essay proposes the Latin term, *mysterium*, for designating both the phenomenon of mystical alteration of consciousness and the manner which investigators must adopt when researching mysticism. As the essay argues, *mysterium*—and, at its most sublime, *mysterium tremendum*—is to aporia what aporia is to the problem, and thus is not associated with either the logoic "intellection" or intuition. If a *problem* is that which burdens our need to know and explain albeit not necessarily to understand; and if aporia is our concession to that which our rational understanding fails to fathom due to the inscrutability of a problem we may have encountered, then *mysterium* is that which must and can only be approached by way of a relevant firsthand experience—not by way of a mental deliberative (when seen as a problem) or contemplative (vis-à-vis aporia) effort. The inimitable cognitive-epistemic capabilities often accompanying the *mysterium*—to distinguish from instinct, imagination, intellect, and/or intuition their nature, praxes that they entail, and the attendant, attainable mental states—the essay designates as illumination.

> There, in sum, in this place of aporia, there is no longer any problem. . . . Can one speak—and if so, in what sense—of an experience of the aporia? An experience of the aporia as such? Or vice versa: Is an experience possible that would not be an experience of the aporia?
> —Jacques Derrida, *Aporias*

What is it that often marks mysticism as such an unacceptable topic and issue?[1] Putting together a shortlist of key "bewildering" or otherwise perplexing features or aspects of things mystical has turned out to be not too difficult. Without claiming either comprehensiveness or success in encapsulating the principal complications, or even that the topics I chose to address are the most important among such contentious characteristics, I initially planned to discuss four prickly, hard-to-sidestep issues:

(1) The notion of "transcendence"
(2) The question of pathology such as hallucinations and delusions
(3) The role of mysticism in (the history of) philosophy and human thought in general
(4) The likely reasons why most attempts at theorizing mysticism are often less than helpful and usually rapidly become obsolete

In the end, however, only the last issue receives a detailed analysis in this essay, with the remaining three concerns being put off until another occasion.

With regard to the selected issue, the approach taken for discovering the reasons why theorizing about mysticism is such a weighty stumbling block—in terms of achieving explanatory coherence and efficacy—will rest, first, on a key distinction between "problem" and "aporia" drawn by Jacques Derrida in his short book *Aporias*. As we shall see, Derrida's distinction is categorically valid—and thus should be brought into any discourse pertaining to some fundamental aspect of human beings' quest for authentic and comprehensive meaning, a discourse that seeks to understand as opposed to being content with "explaining away."

Yet there is a further, crucial aspect of mystical phenomena, one that even the term *aporia* will not be adequate to account for. If problematizing altered states of consciousness—among them the various mysticisms—reduces these to logos-based rationalizations that inevitably prove to be futile for the task; and if the far more sophisticated appreciation of the complexities involved, by positing aporias and introducing intuitions, nonetheless still falls short of the goal of grasping the inscrutabilities typically encountered; then a further expli-

---

[1] I want to express my thanks to Richard Jones who read through the initial draft of this essay and offered numerous helpful suggestions for improvement. Jones is a contributor to the present volume.

cation, a further deepening of the thought and widening of the ground, from which one attempts to perceive these mysteries of the mind, is called for. The mystics themselves, throughout millennia, have offered names for such alleged capabilities of the human mind that, it is usually claimed, go beyond mere reason and reasoning, and beyond both instinct and intuition. Invariably, they have invoked such terms as "illumination," "enlightenment," "*samadhi*," "*satori*," "nirvana," "beatitude" or "blessedness," and so on. It would seem that positing of some such term as, for example, "illumination" is necessary.

The more ordinary or customary faculties of the mind such as reason/reasoning, imagination, instinct, or even intuition, simply are not and cannot be helpful in elucidating mystical phenomena, since the latter go significantly beyond the ordinary states of consciousness, where such faculties are usually barely relevant and often inappropriate. Mystical phenomena, as was always claimed by the mystics themselves, of diverse historical and geographic traditions, typically achieve alterations of consciousness that necessitate introduction of new terms, for naming new, often vastly expanded or heretofore-unknown, new faculties or powers of the human mind.

I. *Problēma* of Playing Fields

"To approach a symbol, myth or archaic practice as the expression of an existential situation is already to recognize that it has human dignity and philosophical meaning." Mircea Eliade immediately adds to these discerning words the following observation, which to me is alarming in its implications: "This attitude would have seemed laughably absurd to a 19th-century scholar. For him 'savagery' or 'primordial stupidity' could represent only an embryonic and consequently 'a-cultural' phase of humanity."[2] If Eliade is in the wrong here, it is only because the attitude expressed in this passage would in fact *continue* to seem "laughably absurd" well beyond the 19th century, all throughout the twentieth, and also in our own, the 21st century.

This essay endeavors to address what many consider to be a foremost and possibly the principal mystery of the story of the human being, namely, the enigma of mysticism. This mysterious conundrum unfolds from the dim primordial origins of hominids and continues down into our own day, just now beginning to position itself to take center stage in our still-groping exploration of a related enigma, consciousness. And throughout this progression, the mystery in question typically implicates some of the most precious, most hard fought, most significant of human attainments, as well as the most consequential markers of difference in human evolvement and civilization. It also implicates much of the fusion of thought/feeling with the sacred/ sublime/ mean-

---

[2] Mircea Eliade, *The Two and the One*, trl. J. M. Cohen (New York: Harper & Row, 1969), 12.

ingful-and-treasured. Obviously, such an outsized as well as counterintuitive claim must be substantiated. But while the mystery itself is the essay's subject, it would be a task proper to a historian of ideas to trace and justify the broader claims apropos this mystery's central role in human civilization, including its less than delightful aspects when the mysterious takes on frighteningly malevolent roles.

The mystery under consideration here pertains to a notion only partially captured by a word that etymologically is encompassed within the linguistic family of "mystery." The tag "mysticism" itself is an umbrella term for a significant range of mental phenomena that are as diverse as they are riveting and, in any case, mystifying (the latter term is a member of the same linguistic family).[3] However, one has to cast a broader net if one is to capture several related consciousness-bending phenomena, all entailing alteration of consciousness to one degree or another. It is the latter notion, I propose, that must be seen as the sole, or at least most salient common thread connecting all such propensities. It promises to account for all varieties of mysticism, deriving from a recently emerged composite academic field known as consciousness studies (even if apropos the definitive nature of consciousness per se there is, as of yet, no scholarly consensus).

Should one attempt to define mysticism right at the outset, to avoid any misunderstanding early on? If one considers, however, that more than a century ago a writer on mysticism was able to list "26 different definitions of 'mysticism,'"[4] one's reluctance to commit too soon, for the fear of prejudging that which one is investigating, becomes understandable. Nonetheless, as Don Cupitt observes, "We can . . . *indicate* what is usually meant by 'mysticism.'"[5]

> In the monotheistic faiths at least, it is a tradition of devotional writing which commonly uses the vocabulary of Plato and the neoplatonists, and is rather consciously paradoxical. It discourses at length about the Ineffable, uses erotic metaphors to describe matters purely spiritual, and speaks in visual terms about the Invisible.[6]

---

[3] As Don Cupitt avers, "In classical Greece one said '*Mu, mu*,' meaning 'Sh! Sh!,' keep *mum*. *Muein* meant to close the lips or eyes, and *musteria*, mysteries, were esoteric, occult, or secret religious practices such as the Eleusinian mysteries. A *mystic* then became a person initiated into a higher and secret form of knowledge," *Mysticism after Modernity* (Oxford: Blackwell, 1998), 23.

[4] Jerome Gellman, *Mystical Experience of God: A Philosophical Inquiry* (Aldershot, England: Ashgate, 2001), 3, referring to W. R. Inge, *Christian Mysticism* (New York: Scribner's, 1899).

[5] Cupitt, *Mysticism after Modernity*, 25, emphasis added.

[6] Ibid.

Students of Kabbalah, for example, might recognize a similar formulary in the *Zohar* or within Lurianic mysticism, with their compulsion to employ erotic metaphors and to render that which is supposed to be invisible in expressly visual language. Further,

> In mystical experience, we learn, the subject-object distinction is transcended; yet such experience is always described as noetic. How can there be *knowledge*, where there is no longer any distinction between the knower and the known? And for that matter, how can the mystic or anyone else draw "nearer" to God, when theology says that God is already omnipresent in his whole being and power at every point in space and time? Everything and everyone, whether holy or sinful, is already as "close" to God as it is possible to be. God is always and everywhere already coincident with each and every human self. And, by the way, how is mystical experience able to be "simultaneously" "timeless" and "transient"?[7]

These are just some of the oddities and paradoxes one habitually encounters while reading mystical reports and their scholarly elaborations. If even as perceptive a writer as Cupitt speaks of such notions as "mystical experience" in the singular—thus inevitably mixing together the often incompatible or incongruent features that different types of mystical experience possess—then is it any wonder that, apart from the inevitable and necessary paradoxes, one is typically forced to deal also with unnecessary agglomerations of confusions?

Let us recognize at the outset that not all alterations of consciousness are or have been created equal, and not all mystical experiences lead to the same outcome—quite the contrary. Some are decidedly malevolent; some do cross the very thin divide between, on the one hand, the sublime, the consciousness-expanding, the enabling of penetrating understanding and the loftiest energies that inspire and empower, and, on the other, the pathological. If one begins to examine the mystery of mysticism in the customary manner—considering its outlandish, often bizarre contentions and contents *a problem* or, still more problematically (pun intended), several *compound* problems—then one will, necessarily I think, find oneself confronting a maze or even multiple mazes at once. Everything about this topic is going to be questionable, unpredictable, and, to fully capture the zeitgeist involved, *non-ordinary*. Almost from the outset the would-be investigator is assailed with otherwise rarely encountered, curious notions such as "ineffability," "supramundane" or "ultimate" realities,[8] or such entities as supernatural agents, for instance, God or gods, along with a panoply

---

[7] Ibid.

[8] Mark Webb, "Religious Experience," *Stanford Encyclopedia of Philosophy* (2011): 1-19, pp. 3, 10.

of uncanny beings or, somewhat more accurately, existences or presences whose very actuality—sans corporeality—can never be ascertained independently in a parallel research facility halfway around the globe (as is routinely done in physics and other "hard" sciences).

Why shouldn't an investigator consider mysticism a "problem"? How else to approach its tantalizing and at the same time, on the face of it, preposterous—or at least aberrant—manifestations? To begin to answer this question, it would be helpful to recognize one obvious and palpable yet slippery feature of mystical phenomena: they invariably entail crossing boundaries. A mystical experience is indeed non-ordinary—which is another way of suggesting that certain critical dividing lines, certain boundaries may have been crossed, in this case those "lines" that demarcate normalness or ordinariness from the zone or zones situated beyond the latter. Jacques Derrida elaborates on such crossings:

> The crossing of borders always announces itself according to the movement of a certain step—and of the step that crosses a line. An indivisible line. And one always assumes the institution of such indivisibility. Customs, police, visa or passport, passenger identification—all of that is established upon this institution of the indivisible. . . . Where the figure of the step is refused to intuition, where the identity or individuality of a line . . . is compromised, the identity to oneself and therefore the possible identification of an intangible edge—the crossing of the line—becomes a *problem*.[9]

We instinctively know what a problem, any problem, is. More often than not, it is something one must or wishes to attend to, a quandary; yet either one does not know how or does not see any good solution to it. A problem is also that which one tackles when trying to find an explanation for or the meaning or significance of something. Mysticism, for any sympathetic scholar determined to solve the problem it represents, is of the latter variety. One hopes to account for the most blatant, observable, or typically reported of mysticism's features; one sets up some kind of classificatory array that would allow distinguishing between the cases of most divergence from a type seen as the most conspicuous; one is compelled to expand or invent new or additional vocabulary in order to name that which hasn't yet been named; finally, one may attempt some explanatory relief to mysticism's problem, coming up with this hypothesis or that, one theory or another. It is precisely the situation one generally encounters within the ample, though hardly enormous literature on mysticism of the past several decades.

With a few examples that follow, I wish to show that such earnest as well as ostensibly blameless scholarly efforts—ostensibly because they, if anything,

---

[9] Derrida, *Aporias*, 11, emphasis in original.

keep to a rather standard academic procedure of classification of types, clarification of terms, and development of conceptual apparatus and accounts—often only manage to further obfuscate their problematic subject. Consider the single most important such effort a full generation ago, the series of four books on mysticism edited by Steven Katz.[10] To consider the positive side first, publications such as these have played a considerable role in making the subject of mysticism somewhat more respectable in academic circles. And they do offer varied and interesting explanations along the lines described above, often polemically engaging rival hypotheses that have sprung up just in time to make the whole discussion stimulating. What more could one desire or, framing it as before, what is it that would make an approach that sees mysticism *as a problem* to be explained, inadequate?

Bruce Janz expresses the difficulty generated by such approaches: "We need an account that deals with mysticism as *understanding* at its most basic level, not as knowledge that has been *constructed* from some raw data."[11] He refers here to the well-known debate between the so-called constructivists (represented by Katz, this position advocates for the crucial role of religious traditions in "constructing" a mystical experience); the essentialists or perennialists (represented by Huston Smith, this approach asserts an essential unity of or identical core in all mystical experiences); and the purists (those who, like Robert Forman,[12] argue for the existence of "pure" or contentless mystical experiences). Janz notes a key misunderstanding that plagues this debate: "Confusing the two issues of purity and unity has led to misconstruing Katz's position."[13] He concludes: "The problem for both Katz and most of his critics is that they forget the metaphor. Is the mystical experience *really* primitive or is it *really* constructed? This is a false dichotomy, brought on by the metaphor of sensation. Like [the experience of reading a] novel, the mystical experience can be both."[14] We need not delve here into the details of Janz's effectual arguments; tellingly, a generation later these debates already seem quite dated. However, the debates failed because of a deeper flaw than merely engaging erroneous or unsuitable positions—an issue I turn to in the next section.

---

[10] Steven T. Katz, ed. *Mysticism and Philosophical Analysis* (New York: Oxford University Press, 1978); idem, *Mysticism and Religious Traditions* (New York: Oxford University Press, 1983); idem, *Mysticism and Language* (New York: Oxford University Press, 1992); idem, *Mysticism and Sacred Scripture* (New York: Oxford University Press, 2000).

[11] Bruce Janz, "Mysticism and Understanding: Steven Katz and His Critics," *Studies in Religion/Sciences Religieuses* 24, no. 1 (1995): 77-94, here 88-89, emphasis added.

[12] Robert K. C. Forman, "Mysticism, Constructivism, and Forgetting," in *The Problem of Pure Consciousness: Mysticism and Philosophy*, ed. Robert K. C. Forman (New York: Oxford University Press 1990).

[13] Janz, "Mysticism and Understanding," 84.

[14] Ibid., 92.

While Janz does not explicate what he means by "understanding" (when he states that "we need an account that deals with mysticism as understanding at its most basic level, not as knowledge that has been constructed from some raw data"),[15] the idea behind this is perhaps illuminated by another theorist, the historian Yuval Noah Harari. Writing about "the Sapiens" in his panoramic view of the history of human beings, the subject of his recent book, Harari remarks that

> in order to *understand* how Sapiens behave, we must describe the historical evolution of their actions. Referring only to our biological constraints would be like a radio sportscaster who, attending the World Cup football championships, offers his listeners a detailed description of the playing field rather than an account of what the players are doing.[16]

What are "the players" doing while undergoing mystical experiences? More urgent for this discussion, however, is the issue we have been pursuing: Why is seeing something as a problem, a problem? Mysticism certainly seems problematic, as well as different, puzzling, erratic.

II. Aporia as Experience of a Nonpassage

Why would any proliferation of concepts, born of the reflexive need to "explain the problem," anticipate solving it? Why is this so in the case of something as significant and as mystifying as the behavior of Homo Sapiens, including when affected by something that we call, with a more than a hint of distaste, "mysticism"? Why does this lead to inept accumulations of "knowledge"—but not to understanding?

> *Problēma* can signify *projection* or *protection*, that which one poses or throws in front of oneself, either as the projection of a project, of a task to accomplish, or as the protection created by a substitute, a prosthesis that we put forth in order to represent, replace, shelter, or dissimulate ourselves, or so as to hide something unavowable—like a shield (*problēma* also means shield, clothing as barrier or guard-barrier) behind which one guards oneself *in secret* or *in shelter* in case of danger. Every border is *problematic* in these two senses.[17]

---

[15] Ibid., 88-89.

[16] Yuval Noah Harari, *Sapiens: A Brief History of Humankind* (New York: HarperCollins, 2015), 39, emphasis added.

[17] Derrida, *Aporias*, 11-12, emphasis in original.

There is much in this passage by Derrida that makes clear the reasons for the habitual obfuscatory *problem*-atic that is nearly unavoidable if one consults the typical literature on mysticism. Perhaps the most edifying is the phrase "so as to hide something unavowable." Avowable is a synonym of "unashamed"; unavowable thus is Derrida's Freudian bid to note something that we would be loath to address, or unwilling to acknowledge, or averse to recognize—or even to genuinely examine. Could mysticism represent the kind of problem that some people, perhaps especially academic investigators, would be ashamed of? Could it be the reason, too, for the avoidance of the "players" (still using Harari's metaphor) and focusing instead solely on the "playing field"? In point of fact, *what are* "the players" doing? The innocent-sounding question is far trickier than it seems: many a thinker of oversized mentation has bared himself or herself to ridicule on this one.

If "*problēma* can signify projection or protection," that is, "a prosthesis that we put forth in order to represent, replace, shelter, or dissimulate ourselves, or so as to hide something unavowable," then it is *aporia*, that "tired word of philosophy and logic" that Derrida proposes for cases of "not knowing where to go":[18]

> It ha[s] to be a matter of the nonpassage, or rather from the experience of the nonpassage, the experience of what happens and is fascinating in this nonpassage, paralyzing us in this separation in a way that is not necessarily negative: before a door, a threshold, a border, a line, or simply the edge or the approach of the other as such. It should be a matter of what, in sum, appears to block our way or to separate us in the very place where *it would no longer be possible to constitute a problem*, a project, or a projection, that is, at the point where the very project or the problematic task becomes impossible and where we are exposed, absolutely without protection, without problem, and without prosthesis, without possible substitution, singularly exposed in our absolute and absolutely naked uniqueness, that is to say, disarmed, delivered to the other, incapable even of sheltering ourselves behind what could still protect the interiority of a secret. There, in sum, in this place of aporia, *there is no longer any problem.*[19]

It would seem that Derrida here, intentionally or not, captures the meaning of at least one major category of mystical experience, a theistic kind apropos which Rudolf Otto has coined the now-indispensable terms *mysterium tremendum* and "wholly other."[20] As a naked Adam or Eve, one stands before "the

---

[18] Ibid.

[19] Ibid., emphasis in original.

[20] Rudolf Otto, *The Idea of the Holy*, trl. John Harvey, 2nd ed. (1923; Oxford: Oxford University Press, 1950).

other," the Ultimate Other epitomizing the *mysterium tremendum* that is "wholly other." We stand "exposed, absolutely without protection, without problem, and without prosthesis, without possible substitution, singularly exposed in our absolute and absolutely naked uniqueness, that is to say, disarmed, delivered to the other, incapable even of sheltering ourselves behind what could still protect the interiority of a secret." There, adds Derrida, "in this place of aporia, there is no longer any problem." The project, or the projection of a strictly speculative-conceptual sort undertaken in order to "resolve a problem" but which, in effect, allows one to hide behind the largely superfluous mental constructs accordingly erected, is hardly what one needs if one's goal is the meaning of the mystery or its understanding, instead of a manufactured explanation.[21]

Next consider a much celebrated passage that portrays as well as any such attempt the mystical experience *as an aporia*—as a mystery, as a spontaneous, massively engaging, awesome happening that is like no other, a surprise like no other surprise, an entry into a realm one never suspect exists. The passage depicts just one kind of mystical experience, yet, in a deep sense, it is highly evocative of mysticism's extraordinary nature in general—most likely in an unrivaled way. The master who authored it is Jorge Luis Borges, and while this excerpt, as Borges says there, may be "contaminated by literature, by fiction," it vivifies and expressly exemplifies the *aporia* that is mysticism (as opposed to having anything to do with the *problem* of mysticism).

III. Mystical Experience "Contaminated" by Fiction

"O joy of understanding, greater than the joy of imagining, greater than the joy of feeling!"[22] Conceptual knowledge is not specifically mentioned in this anaphora, as being inferior to understanding, but it is to understanding that Borges sings his ode. We may appreciate *why* after "taking in" the following extended excerpt from Borges's *The Aleph*:

> Then I saw the Aleph.
>
> I arrive now at the ineffable core of my story. And here begins my despair as a writer. All language is a set of symbols whose use among its speakers assumes a shared past. How, then, can I translate into words the limitless Aleph, which my floundering mind can scarcely encompass? Mystics, faced

---

[21] Cf. Mark Johnson: "Meaning is not just a matter of concepts and propositions, but also reaches down into the images, sensorimotor schemas, feelings, qualities, and emotions that constitute our meaningful encounter with our world" (*The Meaning of the Body: Aesthetics of Human Understanding* [Chicago: University of Chicago Press, 2007], xi).

[22] Jorge Luis Borges, *Collected Fictions*, trl. Andrew Hurley (New York: Viking, 1998), cited in Maria Kodama, "Introduction: Jorge Luis Borges and the Mystical Experience," in *Jorge Luis Borges: On Mysticism*, ed. Maria Kodama, vii-xvii (New York: Penguin, 2010), xi.

with the same problem, fall back on symbols: to signify the godhead, one Persian speaks of a bird that somehow is all birds; Alanus de Insulis, of a sphere whose center is everywhere and circumference is nowhere; Ezekiel, of a four-faced angel who at one and the same time moves east and west, north and south. (Not in vain do I recall these inconceivable analogies; they bear some relation to the Aleph.) Perhaps the gods might grant me a similar metaphor, but then this account would become contaminated by literature, by fiction.

Really, what I want to do is impossible, for any listing of an endless series is doomed to be infinitesimal. In that single gigantic instant I saw millions of acts both delightful and awful; not one of them occupied the same point in space, without overlapping or transparency. What my eyes beheld was simultaneous, but what I shall now write down will be successive, because language is successive. Nonetheless, I'll try to recollect what I can.

On the back part of the step, toward the right, I saw a small iridescent sphere of almost unbearable brilliance. At first I thought it was revolving; then I realized that this movement was an illusion created by the dizzying world it bounded. The Aleph's diameter was probably little more than an inch, but all space was there, actual and undiminished. Each thing (a mirror's face, let us say) was infinite things, since I distinctly saw it from every angle of the universe. I saw the teeming sea; I saw daybreak and nightfall; I saw the multitudes of America; I saw a silvery cobweb in the center of a black pyramid; I saw a splintered labyrinth (it was London); I saw, close up, unending eyes watching themselves in me as in a mirror; I saw all the mirrors on earth and none of them reflected me; I saw in a backyard of Soler Street the same tiles that thirty years before I'd seen in the entrance of a house in Fray Bentos;

I saw bunches of grapes, snow, tobacco, lodes of metal, steam; I saw convex equatorial deserts and each one of their grains of sand; I saw a woman in Inverness whom I shall never forget; I saw her tangled hair, her tall figure, I saw the cancer in her breast; I saw a ring of baked mud in a sidewalk, where before there had been a tree; I saw a summer house in Adrogué and a copy of the first English translation of Pliny—Philemon Holland's—and all at the same time saw each letter on each page (as a boy, I used to marvel that the letters in a closed book did not get scrambled and lost overnight);

I saw a sunset in Querétaro that seemed to reflect the color of a rose in Bengal; I saw my empty bedroom; I saw in a closet in Alkmaar a terrestrial globe between two mirrors that multiplied it endlessly; I saw horses with flowing manes on a shore of the Caspian Sea at dawn; I saw the delicate bone structure of a hand; I saw the survivors of a battle sending out picture postcards; I saw in a showcase in Mirzapur a pack of Spanish playing cards; I saw the slanting shadows of ferns on a greenhouse floor; I saw tigers, pistons, bison, tides, and armies;

> I saw all the ants on the planet; I saw a Persian astrolabe; I saw in the drawer of a writing table (and the handwriting made me tremble) unbelievable, obscene, detailed letters, which Beatriz had written to Carlos Argentino; I saw a monument I worshipped in the Chacarita cemetery; I saw the rotted dust and bones that had once deliciously been Beatriz Viterbo; I saw the circulation of my own dark blood; I saw the coupling of love and the modification of death; I saw the Aleph from every point and angle, and in the Aleph I saw the earth and in the earth the Aleph and in the Aleph the earth; I saw my own face and my own bowels;
>
> I saw your face; and I felt dizzy and wept, for my eyes had seen that secret and conjectured object whose name is common to all men but which no man has looked upon—the unimaginable universe.[23]

IV. Stopping Thinking—a Philosophical Desideratum?

As noted earlier, many conceptual constructions concerning mysticism detail the "playing field"—itemizing, particularizing, specifying, hypothesizing as well as speculating not a little—and they do so frequently in a manner that promptly gives rise to contrary views *and* to associated further, additional conceptual constructs. The still-larger issue, as I have argued, is trivializing a complex, seemingly inscrutable phenomenon into a "problem"—to be solved, as is the usual intent of the otherwise well-meaning theorists, via conceptual, mental constructions (whether reductive or not). Invoking Philo Judaeus, the ancient Alexandrian philosopher, Erwin Goodenough explains that it is in the nature of the mental-conceptual, or "the light of human thought," to be the very stumbling block for achieving "the Light of Being" that a mystic strives for:

> All categories and classifications are, as Philo said, illusions, false perceptions. The mystic achieves his end when every one of his own formulations lose value, and in the complete nothing of human categories he finds the all and only of reality. As Philo said, the Light of Being can come to us only *when the light of human thought is extinguished.*[24]

Without question, such a condition for achieving mystical ends, whatever they may be, will strike even the most open-minded, sympathetic readers as being unreasonable—since indeed it is, quite literally, un-*reason*-able. In this regard, Bertrand Russell's impression, upon sojourning in Holland with Wittgenstein

---

[23] Excerpted from Jorge Luis Borges, *El Aleph*, trl. Norman Thomas Di Giovanni, in collaboration with the author (1945). http://www.phinnweb.org/links/literature/borges/aleph.html, accessed August 15, 2015.

[24] Erwin Ramsdell Goodenough, *The Psychology of Religious Experiences* (New York: Basic Books, 1965), 158, emphasis added.

for a week of tête-à-tête discussions pertaining to the latter's *Tractatus*, is bound to give one pause: "[Wittgenstein] has penetrated deep into mystical ways of thought and feeling, but I think (though he wouldn't agree) that what he likes best in mysticism is its power to make him stop thinking."[25] Disregarding what Wittgenstein himself has thought apropos Russell's grasp of the *Tractatus*—Russell's introduction to the *Tractatus*, wrote Wittgenstein, amounted to "superficiality and misunderstanding"[26]—what matters for us here is that a subtle mind such as that of Bertrand Russell perceived Wittgenstein's mystical endeavors as that which had the power to make him "stop thinking." At this juncture of our inquiry, it does not really matter that this is actually the other way around (that is, one needs to stop thinking, so to speak, in order to achieve the mystic's ends, in Goodenough's phrasing of Philo's stance). It seems "thinking" has "got to go."

This notion, especially when involving philosophers such as Philo and especially ones on the scale of Wittgenstein, must be seen as extraordinary, given that *thinking* is the sine qua non of the Western idea of philosophy. Yet I would be opening the proverbial can of worms if I were to ask now what exactly is meant by thinking. Even disregarding the busy activities of the overwhelming majority of human beings that, according to Spinoza's classification, only lead to the thoroughly false First Level of Knowledge—which the masses acquire via "imagination," states Spinoza's *Ethics*—and focusing on his Second ("intellect") and Third Level ("intuition"), one may wonder what it is that is meant by "stopping thinking" were we to superimpose such a notion on Spinoza's epistemic taxonomy. Spinoza's "intellect" can be straightforwardly identified as the activities of *logos*, which, ever since the Western philosophical project proper was launched in ancient Greece, has always been the single most important, most vital facet of both the human mind and rationality. Aristotle famously defines the human being as an "animal with *logos*," and this otherwise extremely versatile term can be safely assumed to refer to discourse in general and logical, argument-based critical discourse in particular. *Logos* is reason, as well as "reasoning made flesh," so to speak. It is "reason," then, which, above and beyond reasoning per se, also executes its parallel burden of incessantly "thinking." According to Philo, this thinking, whatever it stands for, seems to be the very obstacle to entering a mystical state.

I have yet to discuss the final Spinozist Knowledge Level, the third level that he designates as based on "intuition." Perhaps we have failed to notice the following in the excerpt from Derrida cited earlier: "Where the figure of the

---

[25] Bertrand Russell, "Letter to Lady Ottoline Morrell," 20 December 1919, cited in Russell Nieli, *Wittgenstein: From Mysticism to Ordinary Language* (Albany: State University of New York, 1987), vi.

[26] Ray Monk, *How to Read Wittgenstein* (New York: W. W. Norton, 2005), 33.

step is refused to intuition, where the identity or individuality of a line . . . is compromised, the identity to oneself and therefore the possible identification of an intangible edge—the crossing of the line—becomes a problem."[27] Derrida here brings up intuition as part of his elaboration of the matter of crossing of borders. Yet neither Derrida nor Spinoza clarifies what exactly they mean by intuition (even though it is unlikely that either of them thought that the notion of "intuition" needs no explanation) or how to engage intuition for one's aim, for example, how to cross the "line" into the Spinozist Third Knowledge level.

Just as I have written the above, one of my intellectual sparring partners has emailed a well-timed question. (Only insensitivity would deny this being a case of "synchronicity" or else of some stealthy serendipity!) "Had an interesting thought," wrote my interlocutor, "after reading a discussion of how Western philosophy had been limited by Descartes. I put it into a contemplation of: The cogito and the Burning Bush. Any thought on that?"[28] "Cogito ergo sum" is of course the Latin of "I think, therefore I am [or: exist]." David Woodruff Smith weighs in as follows: "What kind of certainty does the experience of thinking give one about one's thinking and about one's existence? What *form of inference* is the cogito, and what is the source of its validity and soundness?"[29] When one presses this question to its conscientious end, he further says, "the source of certainty for one's knowledge of one's own existence—and even for the validity of the cogito inference—is not *logical* but *phenomenological* (to use a term not yet available in Descartes's day)."[30]

We are in fact back to where Wittgenstein found himself almost a century ago: logic—and thus *logos*—is of little use when one is trying to ascertain that which lies beyond the walls signifying the limits of language's reach (and language is one of the fundamental aspects of *logos*). Is there anything which language—and thus *logos*—cannot possibly express? Well, yes; that would be the inexpressible, the unspeakable, the mystical: "There is indeed the inexpressible. This *shows* itself; it is the mystical."[31] And what exactly is this inexpressible "mystical"? It may be inexpressible as such, but perhaps one can identify what is meant here. Wittgenstein states this succinctly: "Not *how* the world is, is the mystical, but *that* it is. The contemplation of the world sub specie aeterni is its contemplation as a limited whole. The feeling of the world as a limited whole is

---

27 Derrida, *Aporias*, 11.

28 Burton Voorhees, personal communication. Voorhees is a contributor to the present volume, see chapter 13.

29 David Woodruff Smith, "The Cogito circa A.D. 2000," in *Mind World: Essays in Phenomenology and Ontology*, 42-75 (Cambridge: Cambridge University Press, 2004), 42, emphasis added.

30 Ibid., 47, emphasis in original.

31 Ludwig Wittgenstein, *Tractatus Logico-Philosophicus*, trl. C. K. Ogden (Mineola, NY: Dover, 1999), 107 (6.522), emphasis in original; originally published by Routledge & Kegan Paul, 1922.

the mystical feeling."[32] Note that the mystical is what Wittgenstein describes as a "feeling," hardly a rigorous philosophical classification, but it is enough for us here to see that the mystical is not related to cogito, that is, to the logoic.

So far, so good, since this accords with both Philo's directive and Wittgenstein's apparent wish to "stop thinking" (as reported by Russell). Can we attempt to ascertain a more precise connotation of Wittgenstein's "feeling," as it pertains to his sense of the mystical? At this point, the Spinozist and Derridean emergent but unspecified invocations of "intuition" ought to suggest themselves for consideration, because intuition is the basis of Spinoza's ultimate Third Knowledge. And Derrida argues that when intuition is not employed apropos "the identity or individuality of a line," the crossing of which would signify one's being transferred to the mystical—that is, if intuition is not recognized as the operative mode here as opposed to a logoic one—in such cases attempting to understand what has been transpiring during "crossing of the line . . . becomes a problem."[33] Mysticism becomes *a problem*—rather than aporia—when one is "attempting to understand what has been transpiring" all the while thinking hard via language-based logos. The "problem," as we saw at such a juncture, is typically tackled via mental-conceptual constructs that necessarily would represent rapidly fading modi vivendi—that is, at each occurrence but a temporary and therefore passing and inadequate mental accommodation, a "practical compromise; *especially*: one that bypasses difficulties."[34] Such a rationalizing account of the question of mysticism, that is, of that which is intrinsically of a nature beyond the powers of logos to grasp, is, in the end, worse than pointless: it (inadvertently) obfuscates and thus can lead to delays or even at times hopelessness vis-à-vis prospects for real understanding.

Back to the question regarding the burning bush and the cogito. We all would readily agree that neither Moses nor anyone else could have *reasoned* his way to what he is confronting now, namely, a "burning" bush that doesn't burn, out of which speaks the Voice. A situation of this nature must be seen as an unmistakable example of a human being encountering the *mysterium tremendum* epitomized and, simultaneously, as that which on a biomedical level is a hallucination,[35] but which, from cognitive-scientific and psychological perspec-

---

[32] Wittgenstein, *Tractatus*, 107 (6.44 and 6.45), emphasis in original.

[33] Derrida, *Aporias*, 11.

[34] "Modus Vivendi," *Merriam-Webster OnLine*, accessed December 21, 2015, www.merriam-webster.com.

[35] "Hallucination: A sensory experience of something that does not exist outside the mind. A person can experience a hallucination in any of the five senses." One of close to a dozen similar descriptions at *The Free Dictionary*, accessed December 21, 2015, http://medical-dictionary.thefreedictionary.com/hallucination.

tives, must be seen, rather, as an *altered state of consciousness*.[36]

Crucially, mystical alteration of consciousness cannot be coerced or obtained by way of logical inferences and propositions. When viewed as "a problem" that a would-be theorist wishes to account for, mysticism's complexity and mystery are reduced to explanations, that is, habitually irrelevant or futile rationalizing attempts to "explain away." A common case in point in our discussion of "the cogito and the Burning Bush" is an almost irresistible compulsion to explain away the entire "burning bush" episode as being merely an instance of hallucination, *and in particular*, a hallucination of a kind generated by hallucinogenic plants or other such substances (other terms in use are "psychotropic," "psychedelic," and "entheogens"). It is likely, states psychologist Benny Shanon, that "the recourse [to] powerful psychoactive plants and preparations . . . has been at the very heart of shamanic practices all over the globe." Further, "psychoactive plants and substances also played a key role in the religions of the old world."[37]

Shanon cites such cases as the use of the "*Soma*, the magical nectar of the Hindu Vedas"; the *Homa* or *Haoma* of ancient Zoroastrianism; and the "psychoactive brew . . . containing ergot alkaloids" purportedly used in the Eleusinian mysteries in Greece."[38] From this, Shanon proposes, by his own admission in the article's subtitle, "a speculative hypothesis" (but which also is a logical fallacy in that it infers that if many or even most ancient traditions availed themselves of psychoactive substances, then so did ancient Israel): "The an-

---

[36] By "altered state of consciousness" is usually meant alteration of the epistemic and cognitive frameworks of the experiencer or to indicate any noticeable alteration of the "baseline" or "normal waking" consciousness. A. Dittrich's influential "APZ" or "5D-ASC" questionnaire for assessing altered states of consciousness lists the following general characteristics of ASCs: "1. ASCs represent a marked deviation in the subjective experience or psychological functioning of a normal individual from her/his usual waking consciousness. 2. This deviation represents not only changes in mood or motor activity (as under alcohol or tranquilizers) but also an unusual experience of oneself and one's surroundings. Time and space as fundamental categories of human experience are changed. 3. As opposed to psychiatric diseases, ASCs normally last only a few hours. 4. ASCs are self-induced or may occur in the 'normal way of life.' They are not the result of illness or adverse social circumstances. 5. ASCs are considered 'irrational,' 'abnormal,' 'exotic,' or 'pathological' by the social norms of the mainstream of present western society." A. Dittrich, "The Standardized Psychometric Assessment of Altered States of Consciousness (ASCs) in Humans," *Pharmacopsychiatry* 31 (1998): 80-84, here 80. While a few specifics in this list can be contested (e. g., some ASCs may last for months rather than a few hours), these formulations, it would seem, represent the widest possible array of ASCs, which also includes mystical phenomena. Importantly for our discussion, Dittrich's 5D-ASC questionnaire clearly distinguishes between "psychiatric diseases" and the ASCs.

[37] Benny Shanon, "Biblical Entheogens: A Speculative Hypothesis," *Time and Mind: The Journal of Archaeology Consciousness and Culture* 1, no. 1 (2008): 51-74, p. 52.

[38] Ibid., 52-54.

cient Israelite religion was associated with the use of entheogens (mind-altering plants used in sacramental contexts)."[39] Shanon puts forward his own distinction marking the hallucinatory: a "false judgment on the part of the cognitive agent."[40] For example, he writes of the *ayahuasca* substance's effect on himself on one occasion:

> I saw an enchanted city, all constructed of gold and precious stones. It was of indescribable beauty. The scene that I was seeing appeared to be in front of my eyes and, at the same time, separated from me—just as a scene in the theatre would be. Every now and then I would turn my head aside and away from the scene of the vision. Returning my gaze, I would come back to the same visionary scene I had inspected before this turn.[41]

This description, by depicting a radically different phenomenon from the one that Genesis describes—for example, via the "ringstraked, speckled, and spotted" flocks of Jacob—helps one see the difference: if Jacob's experience is of a hallucinatory nature, it is not the kind that Shanon describes in that no "false judgment on the part of the cognitive agent" is involved: the spots and streaks do not create any "fundamental" or "structural" nonexistent visual content in the surrounding world (such as the "enchanted city") that distorts reality in a fundamental way. No theatrical-like scene apart from the experiencer's immediate visual reality is involved. Moses's burning-bush episode likewise seems to be of the same "natural" kind as Jacob's spotted and streaked visual phenomena, since it is indicated that "the bush burned with fire, and the bush was not consumed" (Exod. 3:2 KJV): crucially, the bush *is* real even if the fire may have been hallucinatory in nature.[42]

What was going on in Moses's mind as he viewed the bush? As the text tells us, Moses was about to be addressed by . . . who? Or what? At first, a nameless addresser but later disclosing such names as "I Am That I Am" and "I Will Be That I Will Be" and, ultimately, "YHWH," this literally and fearfully awesome *mysterium tremendum* personified cannot possibly be encountered by way of the cogito—that much is clear. One cannot hope to ever arrange such an encounter by way of logoic discourse or reasoning, whether with others or with oneself, or by way of, say, a petitionary or some other kind of prayer. And it is equally obvious that Moses has not *intuited* the mystery that now affects him down to every cell of his body and that is also more fearsome than any-

---

39 Ibid., 51.

40 Benny Shanon, "Hallucinations," *Journal of Consciousness Studies* 10. 2 (2003): 3-31, p. 5.

41 Ibid., 8.

42 For a more detailed discussion, see my *The Sôd Hypothesis: Phenomenological, Cognitive, Semiotic, and Noetic-Literary Recovery of the Pentateuch's Embedded Inner-Core Mystical Initiation Tradition of Ancient Israelite Cultic Religion* (MaKoM, 2013).

thing he could possibly have *imagined.* Thus, it is not an enigmatic aporia that Moses has encountered, nor is it a *problem* that he needs to scrutinize by way of reasoning, and neither is it a product of his imagination, that is to say, his creative faculty engaged in a bit of fantasizing. Rather, what confronts Moses is a *mysterium*—in Moses's case of theistic mysticism, *mysterium tremendum* per se.

What exactly is that which *mysterium* signifies? If a *problem* is that which burdens our need to know and explain albeit not necessarily to understand; and if aporia is our concession to that which our rational understanding fails to fathom due to the inscrutability of a problem we may have encountered, then *mysterium* is that which can be approached only by way of a relevant firsthand experience—not by way of a mental deliberative (when seen as a problem) or contemplative (vis-à-vis aporia) effort. Nor will descriptions of such experiences by others do, nor will constructions of possible explanations be of any meaningful utility. Why is this necessarily so when it comes to mystical phenomena? Why must the would-be investigator of mysticism have had firsthand experience of such phenomena?

Edmund Husserl, the founder of an influential 20th-century branch of philosophy called phenomenology, which is devoted to "the study of structures of consciousness as experienced from the first-person point of view,"[43] has attributed three essential aspects, or parts and distinct functions, to all intentional acts: *hyle*, noema, and noesis. The *hyle* "are experiences which we typically have when our sense organs are affected. . . . They form a kind of boundary condition for the kind of noesis we can have in acts of perception."[44] Noesis, in turn, is how one would express both what one has experienced as the *hyle* and its mental content, its meaning (viz., the noema). If the hyletic experiences "form a kind of boundary condition for the kind of noesis we can have," it becomes clear that anyone who wants to investigate mysticism and hopes to understand it conceptually (noema) and then to express his or her findings as a scholarly work (noesis) without personal, firsthand experience of at least some of mysticism's varieties will inevitably be outside the mental boundaries that the experience under investigation would have set up—but did not, if the investigator never went through such an experience.

The issue in question—i. e., the absolute necessity of *hyletic* experiences for grasping mystical phenomena—can also be framed semiotically, as follows: "Index" is one the three categories in one of Charles Peirce's typologies of signs, namely, icon, index, symbol. It is indexicality, in the sense of the "inter-

---

[43] David Woodruff Smith, "Phenomenology," *The Stanford Encyclopedia of Philosophy, ed. Edward N. Zalta,* Winter 2016, https://plato.stanford.edu/archives/win2016/entries/ phenomenology/, accessed Dec. 1, 2016.

[44] Dagfinn Føllesdal, "The Thetic Role of Consciousness," in *Husserl's Logical Investigations Reconsidered,* ed. D. Fisette, 11-20 (Dordrecht, Netherlands: Kluwer Academic, 2003), 12-13.

actants hav[ing] perceptual-motor (indexical) access to the phenomena of experience,"[45] that is paramount in a religious experience. In contrast, "symbolic semiosis does not necessarily entail that interactants have perceptual-motor (indexical) access to the phenomena of experience."[46]

V. Conclusion: Not a Problem or Aporia but *Mysterium*

We are invited to experience a revelation of our own. The "aporia of mysticism," it would seem, is an already reduced and thus further obfuscating view of mysticism, since no mere intuition—normally the only means for contending with an aporia—can be of help here. Aporia here is merely a conventional name-holder for one's genuine puzzlement and related disorientation. In addition to the aporetic perspective apropos mysticism, equally if not more incommensurate with the difficulties one faces when attempting to come to terms with mystical phenomena is the problematizing reason, the logoic reasoning. The latter is an inappropriate, misplaced stratagem here, one that tends to produce reductive conceptualizations of mysticism, cerebral ersatz mock-ups that more often than not entirely miss both the point and the phenomenal genuineness of mystical experiences. At its most sublime and most ineffable, the puzzling, apparent aporia of mysticism is, as one possible outcome, a most awesome experience of the *mysterium tremendum*. Yet the *mysterium tremendum* is to aporia what aporia is to the problem, and it is not associated with either the logoic "intellection" or the intuition required for contending with aporias.

This rarefied capacity of the human consciousness is a step "higher" in the ability of consciousness to alter itself. Whether we call the result achieved, or the manner of achieving it, "inspiration," "illumination," "at-one-ment," or some other such cryptic designation depends on the specific religious-spiritual tradition in question and the initiation system it entails. It is apropos this capacity of the human mind or consciousness to *alter itself*—whether spontaneously or with the aid of some organized system of practices including innumerable esoteric and religious traditions throughout human history and around the world—that the term "mystery" must still be resorted to, since it is signaling its distance not only from the "problem of mysticism" but also from the aporia of mysticism. Mystery's Latin cognate is *mysterium*, and it is a term on which I depend for designating both the phenomenon of mystical alteration of consciousness and the manner that investigators—if they are keen to avoid either

---

[45] Paul J. Thibault, "Body Dynamics, Social Meaning-Making, and Scale Heterogeneity: Reconsidering Contextualization Cues and Language as Mixed-Mode Semiosis," in *Language and Interaction: Discussions with John J. Gumperz*, ed. S. L. Eerdmans, C. L. Prevignano, and P. J. Thibault, 127-47 (Amsterdam: John Benjamins), 146.
[46] Ibid.

the problematics or the aporias with which all mysticisms are riddled—might wish to adopt at the outset of their research. *Mysterium*'s attendant state of mind—in what appears to be the human mind's unique, additional faculty or potential faculties—is such that it necessitates designations that distinguish them from the conventional ones. If instinct + imagination + intellect + intuition (roughly following here Spinoza's epistemic taxonomy, i.e., his tripartite knowledge levels mentioned earlier but adding instinctual knowledge) are the functional terms for the increasingly sophisticated epistemic grades, then "illumination," it would seem, is as good a designate as any for capturing the mind's transmutation into a post-logoic as well as post- or trans-intuitive epistemic capability or faculty. Here even, or perhaps especially, "imagination" has also been thwarted from affecting that which has been designated by the term *mysterium*. It, the *mysterium*, is generated and sustained by alteration of our conventional conscious awareness and, in consequence, also results in altering our perspective on "consensus reality."

Prologue

Mysticism's Breadth of Manifestation

Three
Contemporary
Experiential
Examples

2. The Anxiety of the Long-Distance Meditator

Jeff Warren[1]

Abstract

What does the 21st century spiritual quest actually look like in practice? "The Anxiety of the Long-Distance Meditator," originally published December 2012 in *The New York Times* online editorial pages, is a short experiential account of the author's attempt to attain "initial enlightenment" (or "stream entry" as it is known in Buddhism, from the Pali "*sotāpanna*") over the course of an intense 30-day solitary Vipassana retreat in rural Alabama. Under the guidance of a contemporary meditation teacher named Daniel Ingram - who in 2008 published a controversial underground book called *Mastering the Core Teachings of the Buddha* - the author moves along what is known as the "Progress of Insight," a sequence or map of meditative states and shifts described in classic Buddhist texts such as the *Visuddhimagga* and the *Abihidharma* and updated in the early 20th century by a Burmese Vipassana teacher named Mahawsi Sayadaw. Vipassana - also known as mindfulness meditation - has become increasingly popular in the West, yet there is very little discussion about where these practices may lead, and how they may shift the practitioner's perspective, identity, and sense of suffering. What is religious dogma vs. practitioners' real experience? What is the nature of "progress" in meditation? In some Western Buddhist circles the taboo surrounding discussions of one's mystical "attainments" is being overturned by rigorous descriptions of the phenomenology of advanced meditation practice. "The Anxiety of the Long-Distance Meditator" is a brief taste of one such account.

"You want to cultivate the crackling intensity of the ninja," Daniel Ingram told me. Ingram made a living as an emergency doctor, but his real passion was teaching advanced meditation. It was day one of a 30-day solitary retreat, and this was my first meditation instruction. We were sitting in Ingram's straw bale guesthouse, a squat round building next to the main house at the end of a long country road in rural Alabama. Behind the house a thick forest buzzed with insect life.

I learned about "stream entry," a Buddhist term for initial enlightenment, and I wanted it.

---

[1] Previously published by *The New York Times*, on Dec. 18, 2012. Reprinted with permission.

Ingram stood and began to walk, arms outstretched and eyes shock-widened, as though his entire body was communing with the humid air, which it probably was. "Feel the weirdness and wonder of everything." He took a step in slow motion. "Notice the moving, the physicality, the contact with the ground, the air on your skin, your joints balancing, the planning of the next step, the room shifting around you." He made strange guttural clicks as he moved, like the bionic man. "It's the same when you sit — notice every detail of the sensation of breathing in the abdomen, as fast as you can, as many frames a second as possible. If you notice everything from the moment you wake to the moment you sleep, there will come a time when everything congeals into a single 360-degree fluxing field of awareness."

He opened his hands and clapped them together so forcefully that I started in my seat. "At this point you'll get stream entry. That's how it works."

"Stream entry," is a Buddhist term for initial enlightenment — a shift in perspective where the practitioners' mind flips inside-out and for a split-second recognizes its own inseparability from the rest of the natural world. Everything is different after this; there has been, in Ingram's language, a "breach in continuity." Meditators reported dramatic reductions in personal suffering, although more mature commentators also discussed a commensurate increase in heartbreak and vulnerability. For better or for worse, they have now entered the undulating stream of true spiritual practice.

I wanted stream entry. Seven years ago I started meditating because I was in agony. I had nothing ostensibly wrong with me — I was healthy, I had friends and romance and interesting work. The problem was in my mind. I felt trapped behind a spinning barrier of rumination. I couldn't connect — not in a real way, not in an intimate reassuring way. It had gotten so bad that I could hardly look people in the eye, convinced they could see the shadows of my anxieties and my alienation flickering behind my gaze. It made me desperate — panicked — as though I were strapped to a bomb I could neither explain nor get rid of.

I tried everything to fill the hole: sex, drugs, exercise, creative expression, psychotherapy, even, for a few grim weeks, ADD medication. Nothing worked. I made a living writing about the mind — mostly the science — but I had read enough Eastern philosophy to recognize that my condition was probably spiritual in origin. The meditators and practitioners who delved deep into the mind all reported the same thing: each anxiety is descended from the original anxiety of separation, the perceived gap between self and world, a gap that could apparently be closed. This wasn't a religious fantasy. It was an empirical observation, one that in today's culture of information-sharing and transparency, more and more practitioners were speaking openly about.

~~~
~~~

I began attending week-long meditation retreats in different traditions and as I did things began to shift. For long periods of time I felt calmer and more expansive, but also more sensitive, more tender. Yet always the alienation and the anxiety returned.

Then I came across a book by Ingram, already an underground classic in some Buddhist circles. Published in 2008, "Mastering the Core Teachings of the Buddha" is a lurid first-person account of what is known as the Buddhist "progress of insight" — a map of sequential contemplative shifts that unfolds when practitioners adhere rigorously to a single technique. Hard working meditators, Ingram writes, can "attain" to stream entry in two or three months of hard practice, an accomplishment that should cleave a large chunk of suffering from their lives.

It's an audacious claim — most Western Buddhist teachers are far more restrained. And yet it's a claim an increasing number of practitioners are corroborating in articles and podcasts and online forums. Ingram himself professes to be living proof. He signs the book "The Arahat Daniel M. Ingram" — a Buddhist term for a fully enlightened being.

The only way to know for sure was to see for myself. I knew that Ingram had hosted a single meditator at his home the past couple of summers. I contacted him and he agreed. The retreat would be entirely self-policed, based on a rigorous Burmese monastic schedule: up at 4:30 a.m., to bed at 10:30 p.m. Alternately sit for an hour, and then walk for an hour. Thirty minutes for breakfast, an hour for lunch, no dinner. No writing, no reading, no leaving the house except for a lunchtime shower. Eighteen hours of practice a day. I would get out of it what I put into it. Ingram would check in on me every other day.

The first days were a struggle, my mind unruly and distracted. Half my walking sessions degenerated into me crawling around on my hands and knees looking for tics in the floorboards. Sitting, my attention would drift to the groan of the metal roof, or I'd find myself reviewing, again and again, my microwave lunch options. They were stacked in the freezer — 3 piles of 10 — arranged by preference and cuisine type. Kashi all-natural Mayan Harvest Bake, Amy's Light and Lean Spinach Lasagna. I pondered the apparent advances in microwave food technology.

Outside the window I watched the trees move in the breeze, and looked forward to my short lunchtime walks, when I got to move in the open air. Sometimes I exchanged a silent nod with Ingram's wife Carol, an artist who worked in a studio next to the main house. I questioned my decision then. It seemed perverse that, seeking connection, I had placed myself in such isolation. At night in my little cubby-hole bed I thought about my friends and family at home. The days passed very slowly.

Then one afternoon perhaps a week into the retreat I realized that, actually, things were fine. Better than fine. I felt as though I had atomic vision. My attention was zingy; electric. I noticed everything — bap, bap, bap — flickers of intention before each movement, a vibrating topography of tensions and fluctuations under my belly skin, even my own keenly observant self. Such a good noticer. I noticed my ambition, my self-satisfaction, my disappointment that there was no one around to brag to about my progress ("You wouldn't believe how hard I can look at that tree").

This was a well-known progress of insight stage — the machine-like acceleration of mental noticing. Nothing can escape my highly-calibrated attentional precision, I thought, still walking in circles, although rather briskly and dispassionately now, like that liquid cyborg thing from "Terminator 2."

Ingram was encouraging but also somewhat ambivalent. He seemed to have some reservations. I soon found out why: the next day everything fell apart. My mind jangled like a live wire — old fears and insecurities, the heartbreak of an unhappy love affair — images and judgments tortured me for hours and then for days on end. I dreaded the meditation now — it was like sticking my attention into an electrical socket.

My schedule collapsed. I couldn't sit, and the prospect of walking around the room pretending to be a wonder-struck bionic ninja was agonizing and ridiculous. Instead, feeling guilty, I went for long walks in the 100-degree heat, accompanied by the sinister hum of cicadas. People went on retreats for months — years even —- yet the thought of being confined for three more weeks terrified me. There was a Greyhound station in Huntsville, a 20-mile hike. Filled with self-loathing, I decided to leave the next day at dawn, before Ingram could convince me otherwise.

I plugged in the guesthouse phone and called a friend, looking for comfort. Ingram happened to make his visit then; as he entered I quickly put down the phone. He arched an eyebrow. "If you're gonna blow the retreat, we have free long distance up at the house."

It turned out that this too was part of the process. It was on the map: fearfulness, dejection, the desire for deliverance. "Dark Night" in the popular meditative vernacular. Ingram was reassuring. "It's normal. Once the insight machine starts it eventually boomerangs back and starts to work on your core issues. You can't stop the machine. This is progress."

Was I doing the technique correctly? Was I deluding myself with magical thinking? I remembered a technique for dealing with anxiety taught to me by the Buddhist teacher Shinzen Young — "divide and conquer," he called it. One by one, I teased my fears into their constituent parts — the body feeling, the imagery, the inner talk. If the full sensory gestalt was overwhelming, each piece on its own was manageable. I found a friendliness in my attention. "Just like listening to an old friend repeat that same old story at a dinner party," I told myself. "No need to get uptight."

More long days passed and I persevered. Eventually on about day twelve, a strong equilibrium overtook me. This too was on the map — "knowledge of equanimity." Everything was clean and undramatic. I could sit for hours now, my heartbeat slowed way down. Concentration was easy, almost unnecessary. There was only the world, the view from the window, my own breath so silky smooth and consoling in in its ordinariness. I stared at my face in the bathroom mirror, shining now like a newborn's. Nothing needed to be any different than it was.

Ingram was excited. "You're on the verge of stream entry," he said. "The danger is you'll get complacent. This is the equanimity trap. Keep noticing — notice the way everything changes, the slight tension in things, the way each sensation is devoid of any "thing" called a self. Notice and let go."

How do you notice and let go? A low-level anxiety returned. Occasionally I felt as though I were sliding into a kind of inversion, but as soon as I did my journalist mind seized on the moment with nerdy analytic curiosity. My equanimity ebbed.

I began experimenting with different techniques: wondrous states of absorption, mantras that echoed choir-like in my mind, paradoxical "nondual" cognitive reframing exercises. I pretended these would help but I knew I was only distracting myself, avoiding a piece of work I couldn't quite identify.

Days passed and I lost all sense of progress. I became stressed, obsessed; instead of meditating I dug out my meditation books and guiltily read them in the corner of the room, pouring over the maps, looking for clues, trying to organize my vacillating experience. At this point Ingram was checking in almost every day. I engaged him relentlessly in intellectual discussions, recording each talk. He indulged me, but it was clear he was losing faith in my abilities as a meditator. "You think too much," he said, "you're more interested in writing about your experiences than having them. If you don't stop strategizing you'll blow this opportunity."

But I couldn't let go. I wanted to problem-solve my own liberation and the more I did the further away it got. I cycled up and down more wildly than ever, one moment beatifically clear, the next confused. Thus, my retreat ended.

I was both relived and shamed. I knew I had not had the strength or the faith to see things through, but I also wasn't sure what I might have done differently. Ingram was sympathetic but distant. He too was disappointed — he had wanted to show me what the world was like from his perspective. I realized then that Ingram too was lonely. Even in his enlightenment.

~~~
~~~

Before I went on retreat I asked another Buddhist teacher — a friend of Ingram's named Hokai Sobol — how he would describe the stages of contemplative development. He paused for a long time, because unlike Ingram, he didn't think that progress was quite so linear or predictable. When he finally answered he said he had noticed 3 flavors. The first flavor, he said, is bitter — the bitterness of effort, of beginning to recognize the depth of the contraction and the alienation and the subsequent struggle to address it. If you are sincere, he said, then you are rewarded with a second flavor: a sweetness. The sweetness of surrender, of opening. A new tenderness. This is what most spiritual practitioners crave, and it is delicious when we find it.

But ultimately, even this doesn't last. The final flavor, he said, is bittersweet. It is marked by a recognition that both effort and surrender are ways of re-tracing the basic illusion, the first that there is a self that need to get somewhere, the second that there is some "other" to surrender to. True devotion, he said, is not having faith in something or someone. It is a vehicle of questioning, and in that questioning our consolations are impossible to sustain.

It has been five months since my retreat ended. I keep meditating. My anxiety has lessened, although I don't know how long this will last. I stay curious, certain only that things will keep changing.

3. Breaking out of One's Head (and Awakening to the World)

Gregory M. Nixon[1]

Abstract

Herein I review the shattering moment in my life when I awoke from the dream of self to find *being* as part of the living world and not in my head, discovering my perspectival center to be literally everywhere. Since *awakening to the world* takes one beyond thought and language and also beyond the symbolic construction of time, it is strange to place this event and its aftermath as happening long ago in my life. It is forever present. This fact puts into question the reality of my daily journey from dawn to dusk with all the mundane tasks I must complete. My linear march into aging and death inexorably continues, yet it seems somehow unreal, worth a smile as the inevitable changes ensue. Still, I write of the events leading up to my time out of mind and then review the serious repercussions that followed when I was drawn back into ego only to find I did not have the conceptual tools or the maturity to understand what had occurred. I close by looking back with theories that might explain what happened. I am now ready to allow the memory to sink into peaceful oblivion and reference it from within my mind no more. Ironically, the memory itself with its facade of knowledge may prevent me from a new, unexpected mystical experience. Only by forgetting can I hope to leave a crack in the verbal armament of self, so the world soul may break through and free me once again.

> [O]ne of the things we scholars of mysticism lack are good, healthy autobiographical descriptions of mystical phenomena. We find ourselves often trying to tease our phenomenological description from a source's very complex interpretations, and it makes our work that much trickier. . . . Autobiographical reports are stronger "raw material" for the explorations of philosophers, scholars, mysticists (scholars of mysticism), and psychologists.
> —Robert K. C. Forman[2]

> I'm in words, made of words, others' words. —Samuel Beckett[3]

---

[1] Previously published in the *Journal of Consciousness Exploration & Research* (JCER), vol. 2-7 (2011): 1006-34. Reprinted with permission.

[2] Robert K. C. Forman, *Mysticism, Mind, Consciousness* (Albany: State University of New York Press, 1999), 139.

The Call

The call began in discontent, a sense of purposelessness that drained all meaning from my life at that time, even though I was, to all appearances, running over with intense experiences. I had a strong sense that I was playing a role in someone else's movie, that life was an illusion. Such anomie may have been merely a sign of the times, but I lived the illusion to the hilt.

I'm going to tell this story without filters, without shame, and without bravado, so you can believe me when I tell you that in my final high school years I was a robust and lusty youth who was somewhat wild in the country. In Alberta, Canada, the youth revolution of the late sixties was late in arriving, so I was still doing all the things an eighteen-year-old male in the fifties ethos that preceded the hippy ethos would be expected to be doing. I had a regular girlfriend, "Ellen," with whom I was at last having sex as often and as long as possible. Naturally enough, I cheated on her with any other girl who would accommodate me. I was an athlete who won the grand aggregate in track and field; I played on the high school football team as the fullback and jokingly called myself "The King" even though my actual touchdowns were few indeed. Ironically, I also hung out at a tough pizza joint on the north side of town called The King's Inn. The joke spread, and soon the other students were greeting me with, "Hi, King," in the hallways. Our northside "gang" would raid the south side and get into memorable brawls, or we would defend our territory should any southsiders dare to enter the King's Inn. I had a *rep*, but I was mostly well liked because I liked to fight loudmouth bullies but was not one myself (at least not the latter). Fights were fists and sometimes boots, but weapons were unthinkable. However, I got drunk at least every weekend, sometimes during the week, and my schoolwork, sports, family life (such as it was), and relationship suffered. This noisy life was about implode.

No doubt much of this bravado was overcompensation for my shy childhood in a village on the prairies of Saskatchewan. I was a hypersensitive kid who went into shock when the bigger boys shot a sparrow from a shed roof and it fell dead at my feet. I was especially attuned to animals, but all suffering caused me anguish. I would drive my bicycle into the hills alone and spend hours among the trees by the river where we were forbidden to go, just to be near the rustle of life happening. I was never still for very long, however, and loved to play rough with other boys in town, but when the big, stupid farm boys failed to pass their grades and were added to our younger class, I experienced real cruelty that surpassed anything called *play*. I was bullied mercilessly until a growth spurt in grade 8 and the release of pent-up rage showed me that

---

[3] Samuel Beckett, *The Unnamable*, in *Three Novels by Samuel Beckett* (New York: Grove Press, 1958), 386.

bullies really are cowards inside. Now in high school in a new city, I was playing the extrovert game and much enjoying the attention.

But I still felt unease; a despairing empty place within seemed always ready to consume me. Despite being *king* of my little world, I knew it was all a show, and a sad one at that. The king saw no future and wondered at the hatred in the world. I was lost, a corona of activity around an empty center. I yearned for adventure, to be sure, but also somehow felt that what the world was offering me had no real importance. I desired trial and breakthrough, not conquest or fame, but fucking and fighting were ends of their own and good ways to laugh in the face of adult society. The wild life put me in with a crowd who were in the nonacademic stream or already out of school in the world of work. I still did acceptably well in school in the matriculation (academic) stream (my mother pushed me), but the only subjects that held any interest were English and social studies, both containing stories of people who did extraordinary things. I had emotionally divorced myself from home life, I thought, since my parents never got along and were soon to be divorced themselves. I disdained the few long-haired guys appearing in our town, the messy chicks with them, and the whispers of "drugs" that surrounded them.

Everything changed when an acquaintance from class—let's call him Jake—invited me to smoke some hashish with him. I loved alcohol intoxication, so I was excited at trying a new way to achieve it. Such hash was far from the rough pot that was being smoked at that time with its seeds and twigs. It was Red Lebanese hashish, pressed flat in tinfoil and sent in an envelope to Jake from his hippy Hare Krishna sister now living in East Germany. We skipped school, went to my empty family apartment nearby, and smoked up in a pipe made with a simple spool, one open end blocked with a broken off piece of pencil. Jake had made a pipe bowl in the middle of the spool, covered tightly with a needle-perforated tinfoil to hold the drug while the other end of the spool was plugged with a hollow pen barrel that became the pipe stem through which we inhaled the smoke. A match was lit and the cinnamon-brown chunk glowed as air was drawn over it. The little toke of hash caught fire as I inhaled fire onto it. Jake blew out the flame, yet the lump continued to glow like a coal and release its rich pungent smoke. I quickly learned to inhale slow and steady right into my lungs, enjoying the heavy yet spicy-sweet flavor. I held my breath and tingles ran from my lungs up into my brain. The effect was nearly instantaneous. This was not like drinking at all! The room tilted, and the world seemed to be made of chuckles. Everything was suddenly brighter. I felt giddy and went with it while more-experienced Jake mumbled on about listening to music and tasting apples while high, though he too chuckled with pleasure. Suddenly I realized what a good guy this quiet, thoughtful neighbor from my classes was. It was the beginning of an eventful pothead friendship.

Jake became my main smoking partner, and it wasn't long until we had hooked up with other *heads* around town and bought a head-shop hookah—a water pipe—to which we added almond extract to flavor the smoke. I was graduating high school and had finally discovered what the hippies and the burgeoning counterculture were talking about: there was another way to be conscious! This way was open, laid back, and absorbed in sensual experience, especially music and psychedelic images (a far cry from the chaotic liberation of drink). We youth were bound together by our discovery that what the social mainstream called a crime was in fact a gateway to warm friendship and higher consciousness. I felt I could see that my sense of meaninglessness was from living society's big lie. Mistrust of the establishment "plot" (which I could now clearly see) led many to abandon their old friends, schooling, or employment and *turn on, tune in, and drop out*, as Timothy Leary suggested. I liked the scene, and I did drop many of my old friends, but I also entered university and hesitated to step fully into the new conformism of being a hippy. However, within months of entering university, I had new friends, a new way of dressing, had given up all sports, rarely got drunk and never violent, but was continuing to mess up my academic career by smoking the weed and even experimenting with soft-core psychedelics. Ellen showed no interest in pot or higher consciousness or the youth movement, so we saw less of each other. Our coupling became less frequent but, with the THC enhancement, more sensuous and slow, not to mention experimental.

Threshold

The lure of . . . *something* had me in thrall. I can look back now and call it higher consciousness (or at least more of it), and there's no doubt truth in that, but what we were after at the time was not exactly clear.[4] Jake and I would hit the library intent on reading up on eastern religions, meditation practices, or exotic rituals that were said to lead to *transcendence*, a new word I found compelling. Most often, however, we ended up finding good stuff on various forms of psychedelics or more physical drugs that we had not yet tried, so we learned about them instead. Most of our education was in the streets, of course, and in the secret places where everyone shared what they had and all got high with good vibes in the air along with Janis Joplin, the Beatles (post-*Revolver*), or the Jefferson Airplane. Of course, everyone had the fear of being caught, of *the man* bursting in upon us and locking us up like animals forever. It was obvious at the time that the police really did hate the counterculture, as it represented the freedom and disorder they most despised. In some people, this fear of "the

[4] "There's something happening here. / What it is ain't exactly clear...." Steven Stills, "For What It's Worth," recorded with Buffalo Springfield and released as a single, 1967.

pigs" developed into a form of paranoid mistrust of the establishment *conspiracy* that interfered with the good vibes of the love generation. But no matter to me; I had crossed the threshold.

I did various psychedelics and a lot of *weird things happened* to me and to others, sometimes simultaneously, but in retrospect, it was never truly *transcendent*, just weird. (So many tell stories of such altered states including hallucinations, mind reading, or moments of insight and with the afterglow of hindsight declare that, oh yeah, they were *one with the all*, mystically realized, but such declarations are most often memory pink-clouding simply being tripped out—not at all the same thing.) My high school friend, "Jarot" (from both football and The King's Inn), and the little Japanese-Canadian girl, "Naoko," who always seemed to follow him around with moony eyes, joined our group of high-flying, antiestablishment explorers who often shared our *weird things happening* tales. At the end of my first university year in April, everyone I knew seemed to go somewhere out of town; there were a lot of hippy meccas drawing heads to them like Haight-Ashbury in San Francisco or, closer to home, Gastown in Vancouver or the mountain town of Nelson. The highways were crowded with hitchhikers, and Jake and I made our way among them to the big city of Calgary, where we lodged in a cheap skid row, cockroach-infested room. I quickly screwed up my job as an encyclopedia salesman (my official reason for going there), and we fell in with local tripsters.

We dropped acid in a suburban house one night, and this guy came in with his buxom young girlfriend in a tight white dress. "Tell her she's got big boobs," someone whispered to me. "She really likes that." So I told her, she giggled a lot, and then followed me around afterward. As we all slouched quietly around the living room listening to The Doors, I saw her watching me so looked boldly back at her through my ever-present red shades. The vibe we exchanged as we looked at each other was overtly carnal. I had big can of apple juice on my lap and made of use of it by staring intently right at the girl's dress while slowly ripping the paper in strips down the sides of the can. Her eyes widened, and she asked no one in particular, "What's he *doing*?" But she never looked away. Something real began to happen between us along the lines of ectoplasmic sexual intercourse, if you'll forgive the corny expression. The sexual vibe was electric, in motion, going forth and back between us. I could see shadows in the air intermingling. I would say it was all in my mind, but the girl felt it too, glowing deeply red and moaning low, moving her body lasciviously. I felt myself growing tense and nearing some kind of apex when I noticed that several people, including her boyfriend, were agog, watching the invisible exchange between us. I felt like a thief, so abruptly rose and left the room, breaking the spell. The girl came after me, but I waved her off. A friend whispered, "It's not cool to take another guy's girl, man." *What just happened?* I wondered.

Confused and guilty, I left the back of the house and went up on the big hill behind the house that seemed to overlook the whole city. Below the roads and buildings looked like a vast tree inhabited by . . . What monkeys we are! Weird as the exchange below had been, my slow awakening awe at the city laid out before me soon overwhelmed its memory. *What is really going on here?* I wondered to myself, thinking of all the people living their lives like busy insects in the hive below me. *What are we*? For the first time in memory (it may have occurred in childhood before strong memories formed), I felt a tingling above me, like a doorway in the air beginning to open. My breathing slowed almost to a stop, then held. I felt a blissful anticipation—something big was about to happen. Then a thought intruded: *Dare I go through?* The doorway seemed to withdraw and close. *To think is to fear*. The moment passed. I felt remorseful yet excited and hyperaware as I walked back to the house around through the neighborhood. I had never heard of such a doorway opening for anybody, so I felt I ought not to share the experience (or near-experience).

Suddenly, a police car pulled up and asked me to get in. I grew tense but kept my cool when they asked me what I was doing on the hill. Neighbors had complained. I told them—in the sincere tones of a young man alone—that I was looking for work in the city and had just been viewing the city wondering about my future. I saw them glance at each other in approval; I was glad my hair was short. They nodded sympathetically and spoke encouraging words and dropped me off at the house I indicated. The car drove off as I went inside and, to my surprise, was greeted like some sort of hero. The police car had apparently stopped in front previously and freaked out everyone to the core of their trembling souls; they were deeply relieved that I had, in their eyes, saved them all from eternal imprisonment.

I mention this trip not because it has any deep significance but because it was the first time something completely *other* beckoned to me (at least the first time I had consciously noted it), something far beyond "weird things happening" (like the apple juice can incident). Though I had not gone through, I could not forget the *edge-of-miracle* anticipation sense. Later, I did tell others about it, and they pretended they knew all about it ("It's nirvana, man"), but Jake was the only one who listened. I wondered, afterward, if the opportunity for what I imagined must be transcendence had occurred because I had shown compassion by being, for once, unselfish and keeping my distance from someone else's girl, or perhaps it occurred because I had already begun an out-of-body experience. Not likely, to both, I decided. But I also clearly saw that we crowded humans were just animals, blindly running about, like any other. Finally, who knows? Ordinary events are linked. Extraordinary events need not be; they may not be caused at all.

Later, I returned to my small-city home, and Dad informed me that he had found me a job on the Great Slave Lake in the Northwest Territories as a deckhand. It seems a Department of Transport (DOT) official from Hay River had stopped by his barbershop and, upon hearing of my lack of employment (and likely my *waywardness*), had offered to hire me immediately as a deckhand on a DOT boat that put in buoys and light towers and kept the shipping lanes open for commercial transport on the big northern lake. The season up there was just getting started as it was the end of May, so I shipped out on the Greyhound bus to Edmonton, whence I was flown to Hay River on the shores of the huge, cold lake and put aboard *The Dumit*, a DOT construction boat hauling a long work barge. I was excited by this new adventure (and a true adventure it was, trials and tribulations galore, though it won't be told here), yet felt let down because so much was happening in the urban world to the south. I was going on one adventure at the cost of postponing another.

I need not have worried. By early July, I had been fired for drunkenly sleeping through my turn at night watch. The first mate, who took me into town and got me drunk, would not speak up for me, and I could not get myself to apologize to the cranky old Scots skipper, who hinted if I did so I could keep my job. We were deep down the Slave River at that time, and it took nearly a month to get back upriver to our landing station on the Great Slave, so I had time to think about my choices. There was much I had seen and done in that short time, certainly grown stronger and richer compared with the year spent sitting around and smoking pot, but I was anxious to check in on my friends, who, I had heard, were living in cheap cabins in the forest by the Strait of Georgia on Vancouver Island. That quest still beckoned.

I arrived back in my city just long enough to make rash, passionate love for two days to my still-abiding girlfriend, Ellen, since the apartment was empty while Mother taught school. Ellen certainly noticed that I had not been so eager or vigorous during the past year in the pot haze of university. Then, with the callousness of youth, I left Ellen behind and caught a ride in a crowded little car with a group of heads that took me right to Vancouver Island and even down from the highway on a curving gravel road to a little colony of cabins near the beach. Jarot, Naoko, and Jake were there in one cabin. Bill and Jay, two American draft-dodging pot dealers, occupied the cabin nearby but were temporarily away *on a mission*.

"Well, Nixon is here. Now we can head down to California, right?" Jarot drawled as I arrived. It was nice to hear I had been awaited, but I had the vague intention of returning to university after the summer. After warm greetings and hugs, they dug out their bag of weed, which was great after the dry months in the territories, but nothing compared with hashish. I sensed some tense distance between Jake and Jarot that neither had with me, and I noticed how sexy Naoko looked in her skimpy outfits. Jarot, however, hardly paid her any attention. We smoked up, felt great, had *deep talks*, laughed a lot, but soon ran out of weed. Now what? I was the only one with money and I was willing to use it, but my friends only scored their weed from Bill and Jay who were not around. "*I know where their private stash is,*" Jake offered in low tones, as though he could not believe the words coming out of him. After intense discussion, we agreed that it *might* be okay if we took just a little bit out and left some money in the bag.

Needless to say, we smoked most of it, and Bill and Jay were not happy dealers when they returned and found cash instead of their primo bud. "Cash ain't grass, man," Bill said mournfully, his long moustaches hanging in his coffee. But it really was incredible smoke, since, as I recall, I went on a walk alone in the woods with my brain singing and zinging, the twigs crunching beneath my feet, and the squirrels darting from tree to tree. Suddenly everything went silent. Even my brain activity paused. I stood still with that hair-raising feeling that something was about to happen. I heard the noise, low and far off at first, then the wind picked up volume and appeared, seeming to soar right through me. A small thing to describe, but I was shaken. It was as though I were being given notice that there was more here than meets the eye; the uncanny was afoot.

Bill and Jay eventually forgave us, and we set up a bonfire on the beach that night. Jake and Jarot talked passed each other in quiet disagreement about *our* direction. Jarot confided in me what a pain it was to have Naoko always hanging around. Jake confided in me how hot he thought she was. Across the fire, I misunderstood Naoko's inward gaze, thinking she was looking at me with sexual challenge. I tried to lie down with her, pulling her to me. She pushed me away in shock, and I, just as much in shock, returned to my spot. Neither Jarot nor Jake stirred one iota but gazed steadily at the flames throughout.

Later, Bill and Jay brought us hits of blotter acid that we cut into little squares, one for each of us, and we tripped out in our cabins. Only one memorable thing remains from that trip, but it was evidence of the rising tide against the gates of the normal *me.* We dropped the blotters, time went by, but nothing happened. Nothing happened and it showed; it felt heavy. We all withdrew into ourselves and busied ourselves with this or that, scrabbling around with a spot on the floor or absently turning pages in a picture book. Jarot scratched and yawned. We were waiting. *When is something going to happen?* We waited for the excitement to begin and in so doing became agitated and discontent. I watched everyone, Jake, cross-legged with his full black beard pawing away at something on the floor, big-shouldered Jarot looking around nervously, and Naoko trying to hum and move to some rhythm only she could hear. I felt on edge: there was a thought approaching that I was trying to resist. It kept coming closer and closer until it was on the edge of my mind. I resisted the apperception and sunk nervously into myself, but it would not be denied, so I opened my mind's eye: As clearly as anything I've ever seen in my life, the obvious was revealed to me, and I felt the trapdoor of light invisibly crack open and shine upon me: "We're animals!" I burst out with relief. Everyone looked at me startled. "Don't you see? We're animals, here in this room, on this floor, *we're just animals*!"

"Yeah? So what?" Jarot said. My revelation was obviously not as profound to my fellow tripsters. "Is that a bad thing?" Naoko asked. "We know that already," Jake said, but then as his mental antenna opened up he added, "Don't we?" Jake and Naoko looked vaguely hurt and Jarot confused, so they all three returned to their mundane, inwardly focused preoccupations. I was very excited and felt like a science fiction tractor beam was pulling me up toward that invisible trapdoor. "Don't you feel it?" I asked trembling. Blank looks. "What?" Jake asked. "Don't you feel the . . ." I paused shaking my hands in frustration at the lack of words: "Don't you feel like something is gonna happen—something *big*?" Now they all three looked intrigued. I tried to explain what I was experiencing, but neither then nor now do I have the words. "It's like a door is opening, just above me . . ." I attempted, "Like, like it's beckoning, and I really want to go through!" "Why doncha?" Jarot asked. Was there malicious curiosity in his eyes? "What's on the other side?" asked Naoko. "What's stopped you?" Jake. "I dunno. I'm afraid . . ." I managed, but even saying that word *afraid* made the intensity of the moment lessen. I tried to get it back. "I don't know what will happen. It's big. I might blow my mind, or die." There, I had said it. I named the guardian fears on either side of the doorway, both involving ultimate loss of self.

With that, the opportunity began to fade. To get it back, I went from person to person, talking right to them. "Do you feel it?" I would ask. When we connected, the air seemed to lighten and the promise of paradise hinted again. Jarot had the least patience for me, though we did briefly link. "I don't feel anything," he said finally, looking away. Naoko and I linked right away as she looked at me and listened to my words, but the link had some sharp edges, and she broke it off immediately. Obviously, the strain of my imposition on her person by the fire was still with her, and understandably so. I talked to Jake, and his eyes widened as he felt the connection that wasn't just between us two: the world seemed to be looking in on us. "Watch," I said, and turned away and the world immediately turned away too—energy lapse like music slowing on a turntable. "Do you see?" Energy return, a lightening and pleasure. "Wow," he said (an expletive heard often in those days). Perhaps at that point, I needed more being, another source. There was nowhere to go with this, I soon realized, and walked out into the forest again, which itself seemed about to awaken. The feeling faded, and soon I was left just walking and thinking about it but realizing that I had nothing concrete (no-thing) to think about.

Days went by in stonerville with an oyster bake consisting of oysters stolen from a nearby farm and an incident when we all showered in a private campground and I had to pay off the irate owner to prevent him from calling the RCMP. Bill and Jay arrived back from United States (the country whose draft they were dodging) with a kilo of marijuana wedged between their radiator and the grill, as well as a "surprise for the weekend." We had already lost track of when weekends were, but in a couple of days they told us in whispered tones that they had "purple microdot acid, man. One thousand fucking micrograms of lysergic acid dia-something or other in each hit.[5] First thing tomorrow." Naoko and the chicks the Americans brought back with them immediately began to plan dinner, as though tomorrow was some sort of special gathering, like a hoedown.

Awakening

"Attainment," which I originally called this section, is all wrong, for what happened on the trip was not really *attained*, that is, it was not an event that took place along the timeline of daily events. It is not my achievement, for it had little to do with my sense of self at all, so it was not even "mine." *Awakening* might be better term, for awakening is not part of the dream narrative from which one awakens. It is the end of the dream, just as it brings this narrative to a sudden stop

This is where the story ends. Up to this point, I have been telling a condensed tale, with varied settings and characters and, I hope, with something of a suspenseful plot. However, here the narrator exits so that the narrative must be left hanging. For how can I go on when I, myself—this writer, this narrator, this teller of tales, this self—was superseded by his own source? I can say, *time stood still*, but what can that really mean in a narrative since narrative is made of time as we know it? Both time and narrative have a beginning, a middle, and an end, and both contain events that cause further events and so on creating a linear unfolding as time progresses. Words will simply fall short, yet I must make an attempt with the poor metaphors of language to suggest my awakening from the dream of the language-enclosed self.

We each took what looked like a purple Sen-Sen (tiny licorice candy seeds), and the guys went outside to a shady spot at the edge of the evergreen forest overlooking the strait below while the girls stayed around the cabins. We chatted, kept busy, but, really, *waited*. Eventually, "O wow" things began to be noticed or claimed, but the *weird things happening* were just events of the imagination, and I knew it. "Wow, my mind just flew down this hill to the bay. I mean

[5] The microgram (μg) levels were never confirmed, of course, but 1000 μg is *very* high. See the Erowid site http://www.erowid.org/chemicals/lsd/lsd_dose.shtml, in which anything over 400 μg is *heavy*. Ram Dass claims to have given his guru in India 10,000 μg of LSD with no discernible effects, showing that the guru was already transcended. Ram Dass, *Be Here Now* (New York: Three Rivers Press, 1971).

I *was* the bay, man!" I settled into a spot with a view. I thought a bit, wondering where my trapdoor was, but then my thoughts trickled off and went utterly silent. Everything within was still, but instead of ascending or awakening, I began a descent. I didn't notice it at first; I just felt heavy, drawn into the earth. "What a thin shell is the ground," I thought vaguely, and the fragility of the surface presented itself to me. Irrationally, I began to feel I was about to break through the ground and fall helplessly into the depths. I held tightly to my spot, for the surface was in motion, wrinkling and cracking. Vertigo dizzied me. Just holding on, I began to shake. This went on for quite some time without anybody noticing. My terror slowly subsided but was replaced by utter abjection; a deep feeling of hopelessness expanded in my brain. I heard a whispered couplet from a disembodied voice, "Drifting shadows desert the night, bringing darkness to the light," and felt dead inside.

Jake appeared, "What's happening, man?" "I think I've lost my soul," I heard myself say flatly. "That's not good," he said, putting his hand on his chin somewhere beneath his thick black beard. He squatted down beside me, saying, "You can't just give up. There's got to be some way . . ." His words drifted off, and we remained in silence while in the distance Bill and Jarot talked of American submarines that were said to move under these waters. "There's no hope for me," I said, and in that context it seemed to make perfect sense. "But I'll go on. I might as well live for others." "Live for others . . ." Jake repeated thoughtfully, then suddenly looked up.

A bird cried. Jake, who never moved quickly, stood bolt upright with his index finger pointing up. I didn't know what he was doing as he walked quickly out of our shady spot and up a nearby hillock into the sunlight. He beckoned me, the darkness dissipated, and I felt the tingling all around me suddenly begin again. I *ran* up that hillock, I ran into the light, and then everything, literally, *happened at once.*

Remember, this did not take time, yet there was enough of me the observer present to recall that tingling flickers of light, like tiny sparks—more felt than seen—formed an invisible whirlpool right over my head. I felt, not *my self*, but my life energy, being pulled up into it. I tried to think, to comprehend, to warn myself, but the thoughts entered the inverted whirlpool until they were spinning too fast for me to catch. I could not block myself this time. I recognized the whirling thoughts as originating from the outside, from others. These thoughts transformed from concepts into feelings (for that's what they really are), also learned from others; and every feeling spun itself around a core to which it was attached—a vertical vortex pulling the me-fragments back into it. All thoughts and feelings were spinning, recombining back into their source. I may have been thinking, but I could not catch up to such cognitive speed. It was too overwhelming, too powerful and happened too fast for me to resist. Those *feelings* returning to core awareness, I know today, were the essence of my self-identity—all the conditioned inhibitions as well as the elements of vanity on which ego thrived. In an instant the thoughts that were feelings were pulled back into core *being*, and psychic energy reached such a point of intensity that in a jarring, orgasmic spasm of release, like a drowning swimmer surfacing, the awareness that had been contained by me broke free, *out of my head* becoming centered in the world around.

Only much later did I discover D. E. Harding's description of his startlingly similar moment of awakening while walking in the Himalayas: "I had lost a head and gained a world."[6] This was life-altering momentous. It was sudden, miraculous, dramatic, and it was definitely categorizable as a *transformational transcendent singular event* (TTSE).[7] Later when trying to write about it, I referred to the breakthrough as "The Cosmic Hammer," as it had metaphorically split my head wide-open and freed natural awareness from the house of mirrors of the socially constructed self. It came apart—and suddenly together—and I was bursting through.

Such a harsh, sundering ecstasy *hurt*—then with an echoing shudder I was through, the anguish was gone, and I was sublimely calm. But, ah, these words won't do; no words will. *Who* was sublimely calm? The sense of "I" was left behind, so why am I stuck with the first-person pronoun? *All was calm* yet vibrantly animated. As you can see, it is impossible to describe. I can only say that, for once, or for the first time in a long, long time, I burst free of the interior isolation of learned selfhood. My senses awoke—and perhaps other senses of which I had been only subliminally aware—and with an orgasmic thud, my being ecstatically escaped from my skull. At once, each worldly entity was preternaturally lit from within and glowing with life, and each thing was enmeshed in the golden web of all things. It was the most extraordinary and wondrous moment of this little life, and perhaps of other lives. I turned and saw Jake's eyes shining with joy as he looked in awe around him. He had awakened too!

Jake and I *recognized* each other, and in unfettered joy we opened our arms and leaped toward each other for a soul embrace. But Jake, a shy guy in ordinary life, suddenly froze. He looked at me in shock before we could even touch. "I can't do it," he said, pulling back. "What?" "I can't . . . *What does it mean*?" he asked. The words sounded distant and hollow to me, and they did not seem to matter. The wind tore across me, and I remained ecstatic. "What

[6] D. E. Harding, *On Having No Head* (New York: Harper & Row, 1972), 24. I was not aware of this coincidence of titles until coming across Harding's book during rewrites.

[7] Phil Wolfson, "A Longitudinal History of Self-Transformation: Psychedelics, Spirituality, Activism and Transformation," *Journal of Consciousness Exploration & Research* 2, no. 7 (2011): 982. Wolfson, a psychiatrist and veteran researcher into altered states of consciousness, drew up an insightful chart of various transformations of consciousness. The TTSE – singular and dramatic – is rare compared to transcendental transformations that happen gradually or more subtly.

does what mean? What are you afraid of?" I asked. "You know what I'm afraid of," he said. I clearly saw his inhibitions, but they seemed so foolish. "Of what, *love*?" Jake looked hopeful for a second, then his face fell, "What kind of love?" "What does it matter? We're here!" I cried. I could see he was afraid that hugging another man in such a state of joyful release implied homosexuality, but all such terms meant nothing to me at moment. "It doesn't *mean*, it's *here*!" I said and went spinning around to see the 360° panorama of the light, the wildflowers, and the forest around us. Jake wilted: "But I don't want. . . that." I couldn't wait for him and began to wander off; in retrospect, there was a slight diminishment to the intensity, but the wind blew through a bush full of quivering blossoms and I wandered off. I wish I had chosen my words more carefully, but at that moment words were just that, meaningless icons of ego.

I cannot describe the next hour or two, or however long we measure eternity, but I simply wandered about, part of everything—*of* it, not within it. This is not a metaphor: I merged with everything I observed in any sense or all senses. Corny as it sounds, butterflies paused near me, and birds kept singing even as I approached. I *was* those butterflies, I *was* that singing bird, and I *was* the bramble bush that took such pleasure (a pleasure I shared) in scratching my calves as I ambled by. Especially memorable was the wind. It blew with laughter wherever my attention went; it blew right through me, through my body. Today I still have no doubt: The wind was alive and playing with me, guiding me, though I realize that such a statement will cause a derisive smirk from the skeptical. I felt invisible presences who took delight in my joining them. I did not *do* anything during that period. Nothing crossed my mind, in general, though I did have one clear thought: *I am not going to forget this. I know in the future my own mind will cast doubt on this experience, but I am going to resist. I will keep this moment alive.* And so I have.

How was my experience so different from that of my tripper pal, who had earlier declared he *was* the bay below? For one thing, I would have been incapable of making the declarations I am now making. To even use the word *I* was not thinkable. I was no longer observing the world; *the world was observing itself through me.* I sensed my body, my power of movement, though not from *within* it. I was not me. My living body had become a sensorium through which the natural world could experience itself, to its joy and my bliss. According to a well-known writer on mysticism, Ken Wilber,[8] I experienced a lower level of mystical experience—the sense of atonement (at-one-ment) or unity with Nature, which is realized as alive and responsive. This is our natural condition, according to David Abram, and falling under the spell of the sensuous had liberated me from linguistic enclosure: "We can perceive things at all only because

[8] Ken Wilber, The Eye of Spirit: An Integral Vision for a World Gone Slightly Mad 3rd ed. (Boston: Shambhala, 2001).

we ourselves are entirely a part of the sensible world that we perceive! We might as well say that we are organs of this world, flesh of its flesh, and that the world is perceiving itself *through* us."[9]

I really don't know about this notion, but I have been something of a pantheist ever since, even though I sometimes need reminding. Panpsychism is a more secular choice, but how small bits of consciousness could combine into larger wholes resists explanation, so pantheism, with its hint of a natural, perhaps sacred, teleology, maybe better describes my experience. The whole thing is not an object of knowledge to me, just a strange interlude. I will speculate further in the last section.

At some point, Jake found me. His brow was creased and he had apparently been thinking furiously for the past hour. "So what about death?" he asked me out of the blue. "What about it?" I said. "It's nothing to think about." "What? What?" he asked. "Doesn't matter," I smiled, but Jake was totally confused. He could not grasp the meaning in my simple words. I had nothing to say, it's true, but we soon discovered it was as though I suddenly spoke another language. Before I got to the end of the sentence, he interrupted because he could not follow me. We were on different wavelengths, so to speak. Our rapport was broken, and at this point, communication was impossible. Later, with others, I discovered that my inability to speak sensibly to their understanding continued, but for the first time, I seemed to hear what others were really speaking to me.

We walked back down the path to the cabins and were met by Naoko. I saw and felt a warm glow of affection rise in me. "Hi," she said, and I gently took her hand. She was pleased and as natural as could be we walked hand-in-hand while she said something about the cabbage rolls being ready. Once we got there, I found that I wouldn't know what an appetite was if it was explained to me. I could not eat. I did, however, take great pleasure in every person I saw. I knew them. I loved them. I identified with them. There was nothing else to think about. My mind was still silent, but I found that certain people began talking to me and could not stop themselves, as though there was just something they had to communicate or some wound they had to reveal. It happened several times, sometimes taking only minutes for the speaker to be satisfied. I uttered hardly a word. To speak engaged a part of me that was just a sideshow, not the being who I was. Later, after dark, Naoko began a long, long talk about her dissatisfaction or frustration with something or other and the way she felt others' expectations on her but could not quite get to the point. Bill sighed from the shadows, "You're just afraid to be a woman." "No!" she snapped, then added after a pause, "Well, maybe." She left.

---

[9] David Abram, *The Spell of the Sensuous: Perception and Language in a More-Than-Human World* (New York: Pantheon, 1996), 68.

Jake appeared again, even more haggard then before, eyes all red-rimmed. He had a big revelation to tell me: "I'm a virgin," he whispered hoarsely, as though his secret might unhinge the masses. "That's why I didn't trust myself." He ran off again. It got confusing after that. I ran into Jarot, and we had nice heart-to-heart. I was surprised to feel the heavy sadness he carried within him. He smiled with pleasure and only a little confusion when I told him that I loved him and understood his pain, less from my words than my attention. We went back to our cabin. In a while, Naoko and Jake came in all bedraggled. We later learned Jake had told his terrible secret to Naoko, so they had found a place in the woods and managed, with some difficulty, to do something about it.

Somewhere toward morning I awoke. I was thinking again, already trying to grasp the fading impressions. Later, I made my way back to my home city, but even before the fall term at university began, I found myself the bewildered subject of a relentless interrogation by that same self. The objective self (perhaps *ego* is a more accurate term) that could not speak or think while my core subjective self (perhaps *soul* is a more accurate term) had escaped from its grip now demanded an explanation.

The Revenge of Ego

I call this penultimate section "The Revenge of Ego," for that is inevitably what occurred and continued for several years. What should have been my reintegration into my social self and society instead turned out to be my disintegration. It is not a pleasant tale, though not without gallows humour.

It took time for the objective self (the ego self) to reveal its antagonism to what had occurred, but soon everything changed for me. I returned to university that fall and, driven by a need I did not have before, began to take thoughtful courses more seriously. I—the culturally constructed self that says, "I"—needed to deal with what had happened. On the bright side, I sought explanations in literature, philosophy, and sometimes other people. I began my lifelong journey into learning. I found no answers in philosophy, of course, but did learn how to ask better questions. Something wonderful had been revealed to me, and I wanted to learn how it fit in my life, how to explain it, and perhaps how to return to that state, but my own obsessive thinking became my trap. I dug myself into a hole and hoped to get out by continuing to dig. I did not realize that thought cannot think its way out of a conundrum that thought has constructed. "No one can jump over his own shadow," as the enigmatic Heidegger expressed it.[10] I am still trying, however.

---

[10] Martin Heidegger, *An Introduction to Metaphysics*, trans. Ralph Manheim (New Haven, CT: Yale University Press, 1987), 199.

My obsessive thinking and reading found a new outlet in philosophy. I adopted it as my major. Philosophy gave me no answers, but it taught me how to question the given and to think with concepts I would have formerly found too abstract to understand. Metaphysical ideas became a searchlight into the unknown. Such words or ideas, I realized, did not have self-contained definitions that could be learned from a dictionary. Abstract thoughts were themselves creative explorations in which the amorphous shapes of nonconscious experience could be made conscious; one could *come to terms* with the unknown. My GPA soared.

On the dark side, however, I began to feel self-conscious in a whole new way. Since I have claimed that all human consciousness is self-consciousness (since all our experience is filtered through self-awareness), I suppose I became self-conscious of my self-consciousness. I felt different from others. All their chatter and concerns suddenly seemed so pointless, so random to me. I had no interest in idle conversation (which remains true to this day) or in partying. Most strangely, I began to feel uncomfortable smoking marijuana, unlike before. I no longer trusted spontaneity. I watched myself interact with others, and pot made the consciousness of self even more debilitating. When I smoked alone, thoughts arose that did not seem to come from me; they denied my own natural flow of cogitation. I do not mean they were *voices*; the negative thoughts mocked my inner monologues, in which, like most people, I often envisaged a bright, successful future. The dark thoughts told me that there was no longer any hope of a normal life in an abnormal world without mutual recognition or self-transcendent love. Dwelling darkly that now I was changed, that I was unlike anyone else, I concluded I must be crazy, for how could I love *everyone*? I found that when I talked, stoned or sober, most people did not understand me. My intensity sometimes intrigued but more often unnerved them. Not that much has changed, but now I sometimes get to finish my sentences and take a thought to its completion, like I'm doing right here.

The proud, extroverted young man I had been was gone. In his place was a nervous introvert who spent most of his time reading or looking into himself. My posture even changed. I felt rejected, lost, and, to say it outright, *guilty*.

I began to abandon my friendships, preferring to vegetate in the basement of my mother's apartment, where I lived. Ellen stuck by me and, in many ways, held me together. I became less interested in sex, but she understood. I tried to explain to her what was happening, and though her response was incomprehension, it was also compassionate. In this period, my intense inwardness grew manic. I could no longer sleep at night. The thoughts would come and grind on beyond my control. They most often used the pronoun "I," but if it was *me* thinking, why could I not shut the thoughts off at will? *I* accused myself of weakness in coming back to society, and I accused myself of arrogance for daring to transgress its constraints. I worried that maybe, in ignoring Jake's fears of sexuality, I had in fact accepted what he feared. I had my own life as evidence to the contrary, but ego accused nonetheless. I wondered about returning to the *state of nature* that I had apparently experienced, and sometimes I wondered if death was the only way back. The thoughts were like an ingrown hair that continued to work itself deeper. The only way I could manage them was to think thoughts of my own, that is, think the thoughts inspired by philosophic or literary discussion or to write another rambling academic paper. Philosophy, mad as it is, was my one respite from madness, but thinking in any form would not let me sleep.

There were physical repercussions, too, and I refer to more than sunken physique and general nervousness. My arms and ankles began to itch, and I scratched at them furiously, thinking the little purple lesions might be pustules. Eventually both my forearms were covered with scabs, as were my ankles. Job would have understood. The doctor misdiagnosed me first with hives, then psoriasis, but finally sent me to a dermatologist who, after some research, discovered I had lichen planus, a noncommunicable itchy inflammation that revealed itself in little purple lesions or bumps with cause and cure both unknown, apparently related to a mistake of the auto-immune system. The itching was maddening. I still have it, but it is now under control with corticosteroids. Was this self-loathing? Or had the purple microdots come back to laugh at me?

Exhausted and feeling that I was about to go over the edge, I told my regular doctor, who suggested he make me an appointment with a psychiatrist. My sensible side was very much against doing this. It meant going to the establishment for help with something that had begun by escaping the establishment and escaping much enculturation, too. "Once they get their hands on you, they won't let you go," a troubled young man with experience in such things had once told me. It turned out he was right, but what else could I do? I wanted a magical cure, a return to bliss.

My first session with Dr. Earloom lasted all of ten minutes, since he had an appointment at the hospital. I told him I could not stop thinking, and he asked me if I was hearing voices. "No," I said, "not voices. But it's not like me thinking them. They won't stop." "Do they accuse you or belittle you?" I admitted they did. "Ah," he nodded, satisfied. He briefly explained that the brain is a complex piece of electrical machinery. Sometimes wires get crossed, and things in the mind go haywire, too. When I asked why the wires get crossed, he admitted he did not know, but he assured me that they had the pharmaceuticals and, if needed, the *medical interventions*, to straighten things out. I admit I was somewhat relieved to hear this explanation and that I could be fixed so easily. He wrote me a prescription for some sort of antipsychotic drug that came in a very big pill and told me to take about five every day, and that I should "expect to be sleepy, at first." Sleep sounded *soooo* good. As I left after my ten-minute diagnosis, I asked him what I had. "Schizophrenia," he said with a shrug and rushed out passed me

To make a dreary story short, the drugs, whatever they were, worked wonderfully for sleep. I slept all through the night; in fact, I began to sleep all the time. I nodded off in class. I found isolated lounges on campus where I could go completely out. People walked around me unconcerned. There were a lot of layabouts in those days. However, whenever I tried stopping the pills, the sleeplessness and mental agitation came back. I got so tired it's amazing I kept up with my schoolwork at all. If I took a drink of alcohol, I would nod off. Papers became harder to write, but I had put my trust in medical science. I was caught in a trap.

By the next summer, after two years in university, Dr. Earloom, who occasionally talked to me just to make conversation, would occasionally refer to my "delusional experience" but generally avoided anything *psychological* (which he abhorred). When I insisted my self-transcendence had not been delusional, he decided my therapy was not progressing fast enough. He recommended electroshock treatment. I would not agree, but my father and one of my so-called *mature* friends thought it would be a good idea. Ellen did not know what to think but did want me back as I was before. It involved spending ten days in the hospital psyche ward and receiving the treatment once a day while I was under total anesthesia. The rest of the day we were to participate in group therapy (run by a woman) and rest. I resisted, but I had no will. *I just wanted to be clear again.* I was assured it was not like the electroconvulsive therapy depicted in the movies, for a much more gentle current was sent through my brain. In short, I went through it, making friends with a quite few girls who were doing group therapy for "suicidal impulses," every one of them a young, unmarried mother left on her own. I found my sense of humor appeared again, and I made them feel good about things. The therapist encouraged me to keep coming after my ten days were up. Ellen and I even once managed to make out behind the white curtains around my bed—and got caught, of course. Jarot and I drank wine in the chapel and laughed about life. Each morning when they administered the knockout anesthesia, I would crack a joke and try, unsuccessfully, to get a rise out of the anesthesiologist while I went under. She was unmoved, expressionless.

I'll never know whether the daze I was in for the next several years came from my dis-integrated self or from the medical treatment I was given for it. I know that today I have very vague recollections of my childhood years compared to other people, but I cannot know if there were any other repercussions. In my final year of university, I continued on the antipsychotic drugs and was sleepy all the time. I took a compressed course load, so that I could complete my degree early. I'm amazed I managed, but topics like "The One and the Many" (in a metaphysics course), "Love: Personal or Transpersonal?" (an independent study), and "The Universe as a Mind" (a nonmathematical quantum physics course for arts majors) continued to fire my imagination and give me direction. By my last semester, Ellen read assigned chapters aloud to me, then used the shorthand she had learned in business school to record my dictated essays, which she would later type up into presentable form. Without her, I may not have finished my major papers and graduated. Part of the bachelor's degree I finally got should have gone to her. In any case, I graduated, worked part time in the local brewery, then at the end of the summer took off for Europe with Jake and another pal, Brin.

Before leaving, Ellen pressured me for the engagement ring I had promised her, but when the time came, that is, when we were actually standing outside the jewelry store, I found I could not go through with it. There was no one in my life at the time to whom I owed so much, but I knew that by buying that ring I was committing myself to the sort of life everyone else seemed to be living, but, dozy as I was, I still felt sure there was still some great mystery out there for me to pursue (or perhaps a great mystery "in here" for me to reawaken). So in an attempt to rediscover selflessness in what was perhaps the most selfish act of my life, I refused to buy the ring and in a week had left for the postbaccalaureate European tour. (Hate me, if you must, dear reader. Writing this I feel I deserve it.)

The trip for the three of us was a bust. I was a drag on everyone, so after England and Amsterdam, the three of us went our separate ways in Düsseldorf, Germany. Brin went to Spain, Jake to East Germany (yes, to see his sister and bro-in-law), and me toward Greece. I ran out of my antipsychotics somewhere hitchhiking through Austria, continued to sleep well, and have never used them again. In Greece—my land of dreams since falling under the spell of Greek mythology in grade school—I experienced something of a hard-won renaissance. I spent a year there, mostly failing at everything I attempted, but, eventually, I learned to socialize again. I had trouble relating to old friends once I returned to Canada and the same old city (where Ellen let me know I still had a chance), so I left for Edmonton, Alberta's capital. Strangely, Naoko and I took up with each other at that time and went through a short, disastrous marriage. I rarely used marijuana or psychedelics again, though other, harder recreational pharmaceuticals like cocaine or oxycodone held brief appeal for me in the eighties and nineties. Slowly, my career path took over, such as it was, so, ever-watchful of judgment, I confined my energies to teaching (I have no other skills), first in high schools, then in universities, and in writing philosophical research. The irony never escapes me: How can I teach when I still have so very much to learn? My life has hardly been that of straight arrow since then, for I never forsook the belief that one should be willing to abandon everything if the right door—the door to awakening or vital life experience—swings open.

Aftermath

I am no longer the hero of this life story. This writer, this me, now reflecting on a life that was unfolding in vigorous but predictable ways until being humbled by the cosmic hammer, is not the same me who lived that reflected life. (Obviously, I still had the same genetics or soul and the same childhood experiences, but the crisis meant that the deck of possibilities had been reshuffled; I now faced a different reality, so the choices that seemed open to me were entirely different.) Pre-crisis, I was just learning mastery and becoming the hero of my own life; I was a seeker but probably more of the conquistador seeking *treasure* (something tangible) than the saint seeking self-negation. The explosive awakening of a more profound and timeless awareness shattered that nascent, heroic ego, and all that remained was the wreckage of my imploded social self, the fallen hero as Icarus. I who write am the outsider who emerged from the collapse of that social self, but I am more of a witness who reports these events from the sidelines of memory than the proverbial *doer of deeds*. After returning from Greece and becoming a professional, my life energy mostly returned and my time abused by the psychiatric industry was mostly forgotten. I became a sexual being again, but in all honesty, I must admit that I discovered a new taste in me for allowing myself to be easy prey to strong, sexual women.

I am unable to truly forget the events that undid my former self since the tale you have just read remains at the silent core of all my thought today. Beyond this recounting, however, I do not dwell on the transformation. In fact, I consider this writing a final closing of the door on such conscious memories lest such memories themselves bar the way to the possibility of a return to the state of selfless awareness. Looking for a way to return to that state very likely makes such a return impossible, for I can't help but project thoughts before me, thinking I know what to look for. However, it seems to me that such reified concepts lead one only to frustration, fantasy, or nostalgia, making authentic experience beyond words impossible.[11] For me, the romantic and tragic memory of that LSD-inspired miracle dies *now*, so that awakened—sacred—life may again spontaneously break through to disrupt my existence.

Certain questions remain that I have only limited space to touch on here (though I have addressed them in considerable detail in other essays).[12] Includ-

---

[11] This is why I tend to distrust religions, gurus, and perhaps even meditation practices that promise to guide the seeking soul on the path to higher awareness. In all fairness, some of these practices, less burdened with extraneous ritual or doctrine, promise no such rewards, only the loosening of the bonds of ego, which may or may not lead to breakthroughs into higher planes of awareness.

[12] The most complete rendering of my philosophy of mind to be found in one place is: "Hollows of Memory: From Panexperientialism to Individual Consciousness—Featuring Gregory M. Nixon's Work with Commentaries & Responses," *Journal of Consciousness Explora-*

ed among these, is, *What is the nature of the reality to which I was awakened?* And another is, *Why me?*

I will limit myself here to objective consideration of these events and experiences of so very long ago in the attempt to avoid applying conclusions to which I came much later as the result of immersion in the field of memory and consciousness studies and the cognitive contortions of phenomenologists like Heidegger and Merleau-Ponty. I will not be citing every author who has written on each idea I suggest. This way, I can focus on what this inadvertent experiment reveals or seems to reveal to me today and avoid fine-point dissection of well-known philosophical issues or speculation on the great unknowns that are only hinted at here. This is not too much of a limitation since much of my thinking has sprung from these primal experiences, even though my understanding has radically shifted over the years as the result of study, research, and philosophical disputation. One thing I have learned by now is that I am far from alone in experiences of such a mystical nature.

What worldview is this that allows for mystical experiences that transcend one's daily sense of identity? It's notable that the fact that I had no cultural knowledge to help me understand what was happening to me is both indicative of my youth and of a culture without a wisdom tradition and without any sacred sense of daily life. Yes, the libraries are full of writings on such arcane topics, but I, a twenty-year-old man in a small central city, had no exposure to their contents, and I only gained somewhat more once I switched my major to philosophy. The closest I came to understanding was the smatterings of "eastern thought" that had been filtered through the hippy sub-culture and the psychedelic wonder-world of those gurus of LSD like Timothy Leary. It was quite an affirmation when I discovered the writings of rare geniuses like Aldous Huxley, who used all sorts of psychedelics, and Joseph Campbell, who used none but noted that the path to awakened mind is no longer the possession of particular cultures but is instead the *creative* journey of the modern individual. Through them, I discovered the *perennial philosophy*, of which Huxley presents but one version.[13] The reality of such experiences is strong evidence that the conscious sense of self is largely learned, that is, it is a product of cultural construction. Since such realizations do not happen to everyone but are often the result of choosing to live in such a way as to make such transpersonal consciousness events more likely, it appears that we not merely externally deter-

---

tion & Research 2, no. 3 (2010): 213-401. This focus issue includes three essays, "From Panexperientialism to Conscious Experience" (216–233), "Hollows of Experience" (234-288), and "Myth and Mind: The Origin of Human Consciousness in the Discovery of the Sacred" (289-337), followed by seventeen commentaries from others on these works and my responses to each of them.

[13] Aldous Huxley, *The Perennial Philosophy*, 1st ed. (London: Chatto & Windus, 1946).

mined products of particular cultures and relationships, but that we have a certain degree of free or at least creative will.

So the first truth I learned is that I—my *self*, the interior lens through which I filtered all my experience and isolated the world *out there*—was made of a complex of feelings, too many to count and many of them conditioned by culture. Moreover, I learned that this complex of feelings that were self-referenced by the word "I" was almost entirely made of words. Every feeling that had shaped or conditioned me was originally a phrase or a sentence that I had internalized to become who I am. "I'm in words, made of words, others' words, what others, the place too, the air, the walls, the floor, the ceiling, all words, the whole world is here with me," as the mournful existentialist Samuel Beckett once wrote.[14] I know this with special clarity, for I *saw* all the words of my mind unite into a whirling vortex of feelings, just before I was catapulted through them.

But what was on the other side? My sense of an inner self (as opposed to an outer world) both enables me as a social being and inhibits me as a natural being, so what would I be without it? It seems clear that the experience was not atavistic in any way. I did not become a speechless prehuman animal again, free to release my natural instincts on the world. As noted, I was still capable of speech, though it felt artificial and seemed to communicate with few. Furthermore, I had no active animal instincts or drives of which to speak; I was neither hungry nor horny, angry nor placid, neither fearful nor desirous. Besides, the earlier awakening moment in the cabin when I realized that we were all animals somehow freed me from that incarnate limitation. Once I returned to society after the experience, learning to be an animal again (even a socialized animal) was one of the most difficult projects. So I would have agree with Jean Gebser,[15] an important proponent of integral consciousness, that transcendence is not a romantic return to Nature (as imagined, for example, by David Abram, who believes becoming animal is our highest attainment),[16] though its concomitant immanence is profoundly natural.

It would seem that such transpersonal awareness is indeed "ever-present," as Gebser suggests, but it is not common to daily human experience. Gebser has called this transcendent state the integral state, a term Ken Wilber later appropriated.[17] It has of course been called by many, many other names in the various world traditions, perhaps going all the way from *unity with God* to the *void consciousness* of Zen satori, the former implying the All, and the latter

---

[14] Beckett, *Unnamable*, 386.

[15] Jean Gebser, *The Ever-Present Origin*, trans. Noel Barstad (Athens: Ohio University Press, 1985).

[16] David Abram, *Becoming Animal: An Earthly Cosmology* (New York: Pantheon, 2010).

[17] Wilber, *The Eye of Spirit.*

expressing ultimate nothingness. The Chinese Flower Garland (Hua-yen) school indicated that everything in existence is mutually embedded, so it is equally true to say either that everything causes everything (pratityasamutpada) or that nothing (śunyata) exists, since each term is the obverse of the other.[18] Heidegger[19] referred to the trans-subjective state as *Dasein* (being-in-the-world), to avoid even mentioning the word *consciousness*, and Merleau-Ponty[20] called it the *chiasm*, to indicate the intertwining of the subjective and the objective but going beyond both.

I know nothing of the ultimate truth of these things, only that I awoke and felt myself *as the natural world*, no longer a distinct entity but a joyful expression and perhaps a witness or a conduit for that natural dynamism. I cannot imagine a higher or deeper state of consciousness, but I admit that I could not imagine the state of consciousness to which I was awakened until it was revealed to me. Still, if there is a PCE (pure consciousness event), as explained, for example, by Forman[21] and beautifully expressed in various eastern traditions, sometimes as nirvana or moksha, it must be also ever-present, and perhaps the visible Nature to which I refer is wrapped within its invisible embrace. It is by definition, however, empty of content (*śunyata, basho*); that is, it is awareness-without-an-object-of-awareness, so it neither has content that can be later recalled nor includes the self-as-observer to do the remembering. In this sense, the PCE is indeed nothing but may well hint at the timeless, spaceless ultimate awareness that preexists being, if you can follow this logical contortion. "It" is present as background during existence, and continues to "exist" when natural existence ceases, that is, in and after death.[22]

As I say, I can only know of my own experience—even granting all the illusions and interpolations created via interpretation through speech. I know the experience had content, I knew vast awareness, but I also felt myself not to be present as primary actor, or at least, not as a presence central to the experience. If we view the stages of consciousness as evolving from the flickering spasms of microorganisms to the self-conscious awareness of human beings, why would such transpersonal consciousness have evolved? I can only say with Gebser that, if the transcendent has always been present, it did not evolve (go-

---

[18] Khalil Atif, "Emptiness, Identity and Interpenetration in Hua-yen Buddhism". *Sacred Web: A Journal of Tradition and Modernity* 23, 49-76. Online, accessed Jan 11, 2019: http://dharma-rain.org/wp-content/uploads/2016/02/Hua_Yen_Buddhism_Emptiness_Identity_Inte.pdf

[19] Heidegger, *An Introduction to Metaphysics.*

[20] Maurice Merleau-Ponty, *The Visible and the Invisible, followed by Working Notes*, trans. Alphonso Lingis (Evanston, IL: Northwestern University Press, 1968).

[21] Forman, *Mysticism, Mind, Consciousness.*

[22] See various viewpoints on this most ultimate of questions in Gregory M. Nixon, ed., *Theories of Consciousness & Death: Journal of Consciousness Exploration & Research* 7 (11), Dec 2016. Online:www.academia.edu/30690806/Theories_of_Consciousness_and_Death_JCER_7_11

ing beyond panpsychism). If human consciousness has shown a tendency to move toward this higher state of awareness that involves such feelings as unity and love and selflessness, it may be that Nature is seeking awareness of itself. In this way, evolution can be seen has having a teleology, as analytical philosopher Thomas Nagel has recently expressed this idea of natural purpose (as opposed to the purpose of a divine designer or deity).[23] He does not give due credit to Henri Bergson, who formulated a similar theory earlier.[24]

That's as far as analytical philosophy dare go, it seems. However, the phenomenologists saw what we call the subjective and its presumed opposite, the objective, as a primordial unity in which the two are inextricably intertwined. After a schism, probably the schism of experience becoming conscious of itself in stages via language, we began to imagine the two as distinct—the subjective self within the head, behind the eyes and between the ears, while objective reality became, by default, "the world" out there. In the age of science, the world out there is the ultimate reality from which the mind in here derives. However, those with a spiritual bent see the subjective mind as a soul originating in the ultimate subjectivity, God, who created the objective world.

The phenomenologist says neither one is possible: you cannot have a subject without an object, just as you cannot have an object without a subject. In this way, picturing planet earth before there were observers is an illusion created by the imaginative act of picturing, which is an observation. Absolute (unobserved) objectivity is an illusion. In the same way, speaking of a pure consciousness event (PCE) that is entirely without content or even an observing self is the illusion of absolute subjectivity (which can have nothing to do with intentional consciousness, which requires memories or purposes). For the phenomenologist, it is the phenomenon itself that more nearly approximates the ultimate ground of being. What is the phenomenon? It is the ever-present event of an experienced world coming into being, a process that unites the observer and the observed (or the experiencer and the experienced) in an eternal dance of creation.[25] It needs hardly be added that the dynamic dance of reality creation is a vital, living process, as intimated by such luminaries as Whitehead[26] and Merleau-Ponty.[27]

---

[23] Thomas Nagel, *Mind and Cosmos: Why the Materialist Neo-Darwinian Conception Is Almost Certainly False* (Oxford: Oxford University Press, 2012).

[24] Henri Bergson, *Creative Evolution*, trans. Arthur Mitchell (1911; repr. Lanham, MD: Holt, 1983).

[25] It is perhaps worth noting that the controversial observer effect in quantum physics indicates the same strange notion—that to be is to be observed—but I won't go into that here.

[26] Alfred North Whitehead, *Process and Reality: An Essay in Cosmology*, corrected ed., ed. David Ray Griffin and Donald W. Sherburne (1929; New York: Free Press, 1978).

[27] Merleau-Ponty, *Visible and the Invisible.*

From my awakening and my observations since then, it is clear to me that the world and everything in it is indeed alive, and there is no real distinction between subject and object, between being in one's head or in the world. However, this unity has by now been largely relegated to the unconscious. In our cultural sphere (which is today assuming global proportions), we reduce reality to materialism. This worldview implies that we (feelings, experience, life) are separate from the objective world and that the objective world, in this sense, is virtually dead, not a direct part of our lives. My experience gave the lie to this worldview. That the world is alive and somehow aware (perhaps *aware through us*) is neither materialism nor subjective transcendence but more attuned to phenomenology, as ground to both. As I mention above, an alive, mystically participating world suggests panpsychism or, better, *pantheism*. The latter suggests divinity rather than merely mind; the presence of the sacred that immersed me and threw me out of my self was a form of divinity, though it was multiple, playful and exuberant, more suggesting the invisible forest gods of Grecian Arcadia than the weighty holiness of omnipotent deity. The big question is, if we have access to such a joyful, timeless, sacred level of awareness, why do we do everything in our power to hide from it, even to demonize it?

This leads me to the second question that I shall briefly approach here, "Why me?" or "How did I cause this to happen?" The most honest answer is I do not know, but I might also express the thought that since such transpersonal awareness is ever-present, it does not need to be caused, and opening to it may be as random as where a leaf in a storm may land or the path waters take to the sea. If Nature is seeking self-awareness, it may be that I happened to be just the right vessel for this process at that moment. I was, after all, a reckless, reasonably intelligent, open-minded young man who was at that time intensifying his mind with massive doses of lysergic acid diethylamide. And there I was amid some of the most awesome natural landscapes on the planet. Of course, this explanation won't quite do, as many, many people have used various psychedelics or entheogens, and as many of them claim to have had mystical experience as have suffered the sort of breakdowns I myself later may have experienced. The many people who have told me about their self-transcendent or mystical experiences, whether via psychedelics or meditation, with a shrug of "been there, done that," leave me totally unconvinced. A mystical experience is not something one "has done" and then left behind as if it were nothing more than a neat happening. If the experience is truly self-transcendent, it will remain a *presence*, whether acknowledged or not, the rest of one's days. Furthermore, these claimants often describe how they became aware of their time of mystical union only in retrospect.[28] "Oh yes, I can see now that back then I was *there*."

---

[28] Forman (*Mysticism, Mind, Consciousness*) admits that one realizes one has experienced a pure consciousness event only after the fact since the event itself has no content. My "event" was

"I know I had a PCE because I have two hours of blank memory!" Very few people, aside from the great mystics of the eastern tradition or certain western saints, claim to have experienced a sudden, unexpected moment when everything changed. Richard Bucke,[29] who coined the term *cosmic consciousness*, experienced the phenomenon as uncaused, unexpected, and sudden. For me, the cosmic hammer defines that moment; it happens all at once or not at all (though it may last from minutes right on up to a lifetime for those few realized individuals).

For me it lasted about ten hours with moments of return in various follow-up acid trips. It is no longer with me, but I am still changed, and I still feel the presence of the greater reality around me through the permeable wall of self. I know *there is more here than meets the eye*. Which brings up a final corollary of the *why me* question: *What happened to me afterward?*

I feel we are most truly in touch with soul when we transcend our daily selves, and that may occur in moments of crisis, during intensely creative action, or, perhaps most importantly, when love overwhelms common sense. We cannot culturally avoid moments of crisis, but we are constantly training ourselves to quickly and effectively contain them, so whatever awakening the moment of crisis has released is quickly dissipated in orderly routines. Creative action we seem to encourage, but every culture has developed ways to guide those impulses down socially acceptable channels that soon narrow into convention. Love, however—not romantic love but the unhindered energy of universal love that I felt sear through me like that animated fire we call *wind*—has been most effectively repressed and transmogrified by the forces of cultural domestication. Aside from the containment in family, tribal, or national groups mentioned above, we have developed organized religions and a whole culture of caregivers and charities, both of which offer sanctimonious substitutes for the transcendence of real love. But the most effective counter to the life force of love within us has been the constructed self, the individual ego that confines us within acceptable attitudes and supplies us with social roles that in subtle ways specify generic appropriateness. If one dares transgress such roles, one had better have a ready support group or at least mindful conceptualizations at hand to help soul to reintegrate itself. The use of LSD may have rushed me through to reality when I was not yet ready to deal with it. As Roland Cichowski wrote:

> Such a forced breaking of the veil . . . often leaves the experiencer shattered and in some ways dysfunctional if the mental thought patterns that might al-

---

rich with content, and *I*, the witness, was part of this content. Subject and object were merged but not obliterated.

[29] Richard M. Bucke, *Cosmic Consciousness* (New York: Innes & Sons, 1905).

> low you to accept such a revelation have not had cause to develop, and are not in place. Even when they are partially there, as may have been the case with me, you can fear for your sanity as I did. It is not for nothing that the spiritual traditions that use drugs require the guidance of an experienced shaman or guide.[30]

Clearly, in my youth, I did not know how to live with what I had found or, perhaps, who I had found I was.[31] When I returned, I not only lacked the conceptions to explain my experience to others; I lacked even the cognitive tools to explain it to myself. I certainly encountered no one of wisdom who could smile with understanding at my confusion and offer me words of insight, which I so desperately needed to retain a solid sense of self-identity. Perhaps I was like Plato's seeker who is thrown into the direct sunlight of truth too quickly and, as a result, is blinded by light. As I wandered confused but unbound among my still-bound but ordered countrymen, always facing ahead, is it any wonder my tales were rejected and, through repressive drugs and electricity, subjected to banishment? Is it any wonder that by treating me as insane I was very nearly driven so?

My final suggestion is that current self-consciousness originally emerged out of unbearable fear, and that is to what I returned. I doubt that our reductive materialist culture originated this fear, but it may have exacerbated it through its morbid attachment to technology and weapons and its denial of inner experience. What fear is this? It can only be the fear of death. When our ancestors achieved enough language to gain foresight into the inevitable destiny that waits for each of us, there must have been a truly existential crisis as word of undeniable mortal knowledge spread. Why struggle to live when death awaits us in any case? This primordial knowledge must have been more unbearable then than it seems to be now. Is it any wonder that we hid mortal knowledge under all sorts of guises to give us hope for a future that surpassed or denied it? This creation of culture for the sake of denying death has been a theme of several important authors, and some of them see in such denial an inherent denial of life. Ego, the creation of individual self-identity within a culture of denial, must also be built of the same primary emotions. To overcome one's culturally

---

30 Roland Cichowski, "Self-Transcendence as a Developmental Process in Consciousness," *Journal of Consciousness Exploration & Research* 2 (7), Gregory M. Nixon, ed., 2011: 976.

31 However, many innocent minds suffered trauma from the overthrow or transcendence of the ego-self during LSD or other psychedelic trips (or the return to it afterward) because of ignorance at that time, others today see serious psychedelic research as currently undergoing a renaissance. See, e.g., Thomas B. Roberts, *The Psychedelic Future of the Mind: How Entheogens Are Enhancing Cognition, Boosting Intelligence, and Raising Values* (South Paris, ME: Park Street Press, 2013); Ben Sessa, *The Psychedelic Renaissance: Reassessing the Role of Psychedelic Drugs in 21st Century Psychiatry and Society* (London: Muswell Hill Press, 2012).

constructed ego flies in the face of the greatest (and most repressed) cultural terror we bear, the fear of death. We fear those who make us face our fear. So when I came back from rejecting my fearful ego, it should be no surprise to find that fears arose all around me like shadows in the night in the attempt to make sure I never ventured such boundary-breaking again.[32]

But the other thing the fear of death protects us from is the secret realization of oneself in another. If we opened ourselves to the realization that we find our most intimate self in the world and in other people, we have to bear the burden of unconditional love. Even toward the end of my fateful trip, I wondered whether I dared live with the absolute love I felt while listening intently yet with a heart wide open to the needs of others. As I neared sleep, I concluded that such an open heart would almost certainly lead to martyrdom. Bleeding hearts are killed, I thought vaguely, and remembered with comfort my previous life. Later, on the shallow emotional level of the self, I was simply afraid that what I had discovered was dangerous to my sanity, perhaps even too lovey-dovey for my concept of masculinity, and certainly to any success I might wish for in life. Of course, back then in my "return" I had twisted everything backward. Today I know since I have managed to think through it: *The walls of ego are made of fear.*

Self-transcendence is very real—more real than the moment I write this and you read it—and, as indicated by the Zen master D. T. Suzuki, such transcendence takes us back *into* the world, not beyond it. It is indeed the "discovery or the excavation of a long lost treasure."[33] However, there is a price to be paid for this treasure, and it is the price of the self we each believe we are. Before we find ourselves amid the light of the *anima mundi*, we have to enter a dark night of the soul (and, in my case, maybe return to it). Our assumptions about nature, world, love, and being may have to die before we can be reborn, that is, reawakened to being.

Words twist again: I now realize that this will never happen again to me alone. In fact, it never did happen to me. *Dynamic being* itself broke into awareness by breaking through my sole ego-self. I now know that one is not truly an

---

[32] Well-known authors with this perspective include Ernest Becker, *The Denial of Death* (New York: Free Press, 1973); Norman O. Brown, *Life Against Death: The Psychoanalytic Meaning of History* (Middletown, CT: Wesleyan University Press, 1959); Ajit Varki and Danny Brower, *Denial: Self-Deception, False Beliefs, and the Origins of the Human Mind* (New York: Twelve, Hatchette Book Group, 2013); and, less known, my own essay, "Myth and Mind: The Origin of Human Consciousness in the Discovery of the Sacred," *Journal of Consciousness Exploration & Research* 2 (3), 2010: 289–337.

[33] Daisetz T. Suzuki, "The Awakening of a New Consciousness in Zen," in *Man and Transformation: Papers from the Eranos Yearbooks*, ed. Joseph Campbell, Bollingen Series, vol. 30, no. 5 (Princeton, NJ: Princeton University Press, 1964), 179–202, here 179. Original published in *Eranos-Jahrbücher* 23 (1954).

isolated being, so it cannot happen *to me* again. Being is always happening; somehow, we have become isolated from it. Awakening to Being is the dream that needs to come true for all humanity, for all life, and it is likely to happen since dynamic Being, not conflicted selves, is the Reality we cannot contain forever—unless we choose self-destruction, of course.

4. The Mystical Essay

Kabbala, Communism, and Street-Level Café *Poiesis*[1]

Jack Hirschman

Abstract

The author, an ex-UCLA academic-turned-poet, relates his personal journey to prominence in San Francisco as a "street poet" with communist ideological preferences. He becomes a conspicuous presence at the city's poetry scene and eventually San Francisco's official poet laureate. This journey intrinsically and intimately parallels Hirschman's close involvement with mysticism and mystical texts.

The essay portrays numerous other poets and writers of his generation in the United States who, in their search for self-discovery and transformation, have sought out means that often included kabbalah and other mystical traditions and sources. Beginning with his encounter and translation of the *Sepher Yetzira* and publication of his *YOD*, Hirschman details how kabbalah and Haitian vodun mysticism have affected his life and thus his poetry. In particular, Abraham Abulafia's medieval Kabbalistic method of word creation through combinations of Hebrew letters inspires him.

This interest has led to his translation of Abulafia's *Path of the Names* and eventually his conception of a monumental series of poems linked by their joint title, *The Arcanes.* "Whether it is kabbala or vodun, I take these elements as fundamentally active linguistic tropes, part of a poet's arsenal of interests," he states in the essay. "Indeed it's as if in me, this year, the Angel of Rilke's great work, the Angel Raziel of Abulafia's verbal dexterities, and the Angel of Love that inspires the poems of Rumi have set up a strong and wonderful camp in this time of so many needless wars and willful lies, to resist with great poetry the devastation of the body and soul in these abundantly destitute days."

[1] This essay has been abridged, to include only the most relevant sections.

1.

There are many definitions of mysticism, I suppose, but generally speaking the attainment of the knowledge of the existence of, or identification with, or receptivity to God (and the various means to do so, i.e. ritual, prayer, ecstasy, trance) approaches the core of such a definition. Underlying all the words in that dynamic is the unspoken one: inwardness. We are talking soul here. And if we are talking of inwardness and/or as soul, then—at least a far as I am concerned—we are talking about poetry. And thus of language.

The first significant experience I had with language and inwardness—excluding of course responses to the music of poems read to me as a child or the poems we as kids made up in the street—was when I was almost 19. In the library of the City College of New York where I was a student, I discovered the English translation in 5 volumes of *The Zohar*, the bible of the kabbala, or Jewish mysticism.

Now some years before, when I was 12, I had the misfortune of studying for my "confirmation" as a man, or bar-mitzvah, with a sadistic rabbi who would whack my knuckles with a ruler till the knuckles bled if I erred in reading the *alephbais* or text.

I hated that guy. He finished me off for religion from that time forward and long before I was found by revolutionary Marxist thought I thought of myself as an atheist. And yet, while this essay is not going to be a "circumcision of the foreskin of the heart" or a return to religion, it was a linguistic if not poetic revelation to me when, in reading *The Zohar* I read how each of the letters of the alphabet appears before God asking to be the first letter of the first word of the Bible.

And why the first letter of the first word of the Bible is B, for Bereshith (In the beginning).

And what then is the letter A?

In short, for me, language as poetry (I had been writing prose for the most part till then, even for newspapers) was coming to birth in me. Little wonder then, when Dylan Thomas gave his last public reading of poetry at City College in 1953, I was in attendance. Thomas of course was a poet-shaman, a magician of words whose poems—at least many of them—still continue to enthrall people allover the world.

As I had precociously signed up to study James Joyce's *Finnegans Wake* for my baccalaureate degree, I heard and felt the music of both these poets as central to my belief that a poem was grounded in a sounding of the depths of the soul, like a charge that exploded truths that both stripped the heart naked and consoled its grievings with the music it verbalized.

If Thomas and Joyce—and Mallarme, Neruda, Eluard and Lorca, all read in translation—represented the magic of the Word, there was another revelation that I experienced during that period.

I discovered the *Duino Elegies* of Rainer Maria Rilke. This book of poems, which I subsequently read twice every year for the next 20 years, had the "feel" of mysticism through and through for me. It was grounded in the heights of philosophical and religious sentiment and its existential and ontological lyricism was breathtaking, and still is. Please remember that the Angel evoked by Rilke in these Elegies is not the judeo-christian one but the Angel closer to the Islamic world view.

The *Duino Elegies* is the first book of poems of a modern poet which convinced me that a poet's inwardness was communicable to other inwardnesses and moreover could strengthen the latter in times of war and stress. That is the essential meaning of *The Arcanes* begun 20 years after I first read Rilke's great book. And in fact in one of the (now) 75 Arcanes I have continued writing after the publication of *The Arcanes* in 2006, "The Dasein Arcane," I say to Rilke:

> you did not so much make
> me a poet as reveal what
> poetry really is, and how
> its resonance streams
> all the way down into
> the profounds of the
> foundation of inwardness.

2.

For the next 11 years (from 1955-1966) I was part of the cultural corporation, or the academy of the U.S., as a student-teacher of English at Indiana University, an instructor at Dartmouth College and an assistant professor at UCLA, where I was terminated. Until then my relation to poetry had been tied to the mystery of language and sounds.

Yes, I would now and then read a text on kabbala after having read the signature work on the subject, Gershom Scholem's *Major Trends in Jewish Mysticism.* That book contained a chapter on Abraham Abulafia, a figure who is to play an important part in my life with respect to mysticism, and politics (about whom more will be forthcoming in the third section of this essay). For the most part, however, I was writing poetry and getting excited by the new American trends in writing, ie., the emergence of the Beats as an antennae into the Civil Rights movement (the last great movement of the people until the global Occupy movement), and the manifestation of the Black Mountain school of poets. These were the years of John Kennedy as well.

In Indiana (1955-59), in the university library, I one day found a text in French of a basic kabbalistic book, the *Sepher Yetsira*. And sometime between 1959-1961 when I was in Hanover, New Hampshire, teaching at Dartmouth College, I made a translation of that book. I did so for my own interest and didn't think of publishing it and in fact soon found out that there were a couple of English translations of that book in print.

I indicate this memory simply to point to an interest in mysticism that continued in the academic period of my life. This aspect came to a point (no pun intended) of concentration when, on a sabbatical in Europe to complete the gathering of materials for the City Lights edition of works of the French poet Antonin Artaud, and included stays in Paris, the island of Hydra, Greece, and London (1964-65), I met in London, after many years, a childhood friend of my family and sort of a young uncle to me, the poet Asa Benveniste. He'd lived a couple of streets from me in The Bronx, was the brother of one of my parents' best friends, had fought in WW2 and decided to live in Europe. Asa, the poet co-editor of Zero (with View, Merlin and Tiger's Eye), one of the most avant-garde literary magazines of the'50s and early 60's, had a press now, called Trigram Press which operated out of King's Cross Road in London.

It can be said that the phrase in Allen Ginsberg's *Howl*, "bop kabbala" (which probably referenced poet Bob Kaufman) also applied to Asa Benveniste. He knew a great deal about mysticism, Jewish and otherwise, the Tarot, etc., and was inspirational in getting me to write/draw the pages of a concentrated meditation on the smallest letter—Yod—of the Hebrew alphabet, the shape of a spermatozoa (from which all the other letters of that alphabet are formed), which he then silk-screened each page of, and published in an extraordinary edition called *YOD*. It can be said that its publication in 1966, the year I was expelled from teaching, is the beginning of my beginning as a kabbalist and communist.

3.

During the years in Los Angeles after my expulsion (1967-72), I lived in the Venice Beach area and in Topanga Canyon, and many things "mystical" textured my poetical and political life: I translated from French a book by a Haitian poet and intellectual, Rene Depestre, called *A Rainbow for the Christian West.* It featured, in verse form, an invasion by the pantheon of Vodun gods into the southern and most racist part of the U.S. (The Vietnam War had begun in 1965 and was daily raging.) That translation, from French, changed my life in a political way. After it, I always spoke of myself as a communist as a poet. I do so to this day.

Looked at objectively, the Haitian people are the finest example of what revolutionaries of today call the New Class, though the Haitian multitudes have never NOT known poverty and desolation. Technology in the people's hands could create the paradise on earth that everyone deserves, but which in the hands of the capitalists will lead—notwithstanding giving everyone the opposite illusion—to, more and more unemployment, starvation, disease, wars and disasters. Only the New Class of globeletariats can change that situation.

So in fact it was a mysticism (vodun) that also is the indigenous culture of the Haitian people that spoke to me in the late '60's and continues to, to this day.

During that period as well—when I lived at the end of Venice Beach, close to the ocean, in great isolation,—a correspondence developed between myself and a poet who lived in San Francisco at the time, David Meltzer.

Meltzer, like Benveniste in London, belonged to a loose circle of poets and artists who were interested or influenced by Jewish mysticism. In Meltzer's case, he'd lived in Los Angeles prior to moving north and had met in the north an artist who then moved back to Los Angeles where he'd been born and raised. That artist was Wallace Berman who was an early mentor of Meltzer's and who became a good friend of mine as well in those Los Angeles years. Berman was the hippest artist I ever knew. A foto-montagist in the tradition of John Heartfield and Hannah Hoch, he loved—as I did—the shapes of the letters of the Hebrew alphabet, and he would include words he invented of Hebrew letters in his verifax montages. With Wally and his circle of friends, including artists Bob Alexander, George Herms, artist-actors Dean Stockwell and Russ Tamblyn and poets Michael McClure, Robert Duncan and Stuart Perkoff, —and in the tradition of Heartfield and George Grosz—messages went through the mails pretty continuously: a poem, a snippet of insight, a graphic, on cards or cardboard cut-ups. More a cabal than a kabbala, these missals through the mails nonetheless knitted the sensibilities in those heady days and nights of the '60s.

And Meltzer was central to it all in the North. He'd founded not mere a press for poetry, Tree Books, but also an anthology called *Tree* which he edited and which was entirely devoted to kabbalistic texts in the contemporary sense as well as translations of Jewish mystic texts from the past.

David was indeed, from the point of view of the written word, the central force for the publication of kabbalistic texts. He was a contemporary poet, recognized as one of the "New American" poets who emanated a national image out of New York. Yet his central obsession was the kabbala.

Our correspondence north to south and south to north was obsessive. We are both punographers and love the dooblah and treblah meanings of words ever since we were "Wake'd up", so to speak. I also know a few other languages and so translated kabbalistic texts from French, Spanish, German, Italian and Yiddish for through the years of the anthology in the '70s and David published a couple of books of my own kabbalistic poems as well as the translations.

It was through his project with *Tree* that I was led to discover that a text of Abraham Abulafia was available in Hebrew. This was revelation some 42 years ago. I got a photocopy of it made and, because I didn't know the Hebrew language beyond the alphabet (those early knuckings by that sadist rabbi had had a wicked effect on me), I asked an artist friend, Bruria Finkel, to translate it for Tree Books and I would put her translation into good Amer-English. She agreed and *The Path of the Names* is the result.

Abulafia, who lived in the 13th century, is perhaps the most important mystic of medieval kabbala. He was at heart a poet and his insistence upon *tseruf* or the making of new words by combining letters of the Hebrew alphabet—which technique he regarded as the highest modes of achieving not merely a reception of ecstatic kabbala and prophecy but an identification with the Divine that borders on blasphemy, —is why both orthodox Judaism and the Catholic Church persecuted and imprisoned him.

He furthermore said: "Every man his own messiah," which belongs with the most pre-revolutionary Marxist statements of medieval times.

The *tseruf* technique reminded me of course of Wallace Berman's playing with Hebrew letters and words Hebrew, or even with Finnegans Wake. Indeed Abulafia to my way of thinking, linguistically is as contemporary as any 21st century poet. He experimented with letters not merely to receive God's word, but even to surpass—in outrageous heredicness—the Divinity.

Now the letters of the word kabbala, KBL, mean: to, receive, and of course ALL creative works are receptions of mind, heart or soul spirit.

Yes, say most of us, and that goes without saying.

Abulafia said it, however, wrote books and manuals about it and, in that sense, is a linguistic master who can open any potential poet to new possibilities of language.

I'm reading the great scholar Moshe Idel's *The Mystical Experience in Abraham Abulafia* for the third time as I write this essay and it confirms previous beliefs that Abulafia, ironically involved thoroughly in prophecy, forgot to elaborate that he himself would turn out to be among the great poetical experimenters some 800 years later!

During the years 1967-72—while writing and translating poets of the social and political dimension of those days, and writing a chapbook essay called *Kabbala Surrealism*—I also was involved in other occult strands. For example, in the light of the political assassinations especially of 1968 I became fascinated with the figure of Le Comte de St. Germain, an Hungarian mystic, composer, poet and political figure too, especially known for appearing—magically—in different centuries, like a reincarnation phenomenon. I discovered the book he supposedly authored, *The Most Holy Trinosophia*, from which I took notes, as I did about another Christian kabbalist, Athanasius Kircher, the mystical linguist of the 17th century who is the first man to project an image from what would later be developed as a moving picture camera.

In the winter of 1972, in the Echo Park section of Los Angeles, at the home of the Italian-American poet Paul Vangelisti and his then wife Margaret, who had left me their place as I was in the process of separating from my own wife of 18 years, I began *The Arcanes*. I wrote the beginning of the first Arcane and because one of the books I referenced in it was *The Most Holy Trinosophia*, I would call it *The Arcane of Le Comte de St Germain,* as if he were the persona I was going to use for future works. The 12 parts that comprise that Arcane is actually the first of the 126 Arcanes in the 2006 edition.

This brings me to the San Francisco days and the profound changes that would occur linguistically and politically in my life.

4.

Unquestionably one of the very central events in my adult life has been my meeting with Alexander Kohav in 1975. Earlier that year I had begun translating from Russian poetry in the light of the confusion, ignorance and hatred of things Russian which occurred among many Americans after the Vietnam War concluded, related to the Soviet Union's support of North Vietnam.

I had by then been pretty much a street poet and I was a communist in word and spirit, though I did not belong to any Party. And I wasn't ideologically militant at that time and so welcomed "Sasha" Kohav's poetry into my translating dominion. I translated three very fine books of his, his language coming from the Futurist/Soviet process, rather than from the traditional Russian/Anglo process manifested by poets like Mandelstam and Brodsky whose dissidence was nonetheless similar to Kohav's.

A year after Sasha's arrival, one fine day, I began to write poems in Russian on the streets of San Francisco! That day, the most important lyripolitical day of my life, led me to write one poem a day in Russian for the next 11 years. (I would usually write a poem in American, then one in Russian, which I would spontaneously translate to people I read it to, and then another poem in American.

In this period as well, I wrote a still unpublished book of notations which I call *Kabbala Cyrillicism*, in essay form. This was an extension of the earlier *Kabbala Surrealism* which I'd written in Venice, California some years earlier. The later work concerns certain kabbalistic techniques—influenced by my reading and translating with Bruria Finkel of the work of Abraham Abulafia—but transferred to the Russian alphabet and language.

For example, the use and play of initial letters of names to make new words or names was one technique. There were also Russian poets who used the Cyrillic alphabet as subject matter of poems. These alphabetic fancies were part of those years when I was drawing closer to the communist movement itself. I must admit that in those years mystical thought or theosophical philosophy was no priority to me. The word play and letter combinations were what I loved most, and they resonated in me to my early involvement with James Joyce's *Finnegans Wake*; for between the mid-70s and the new Millennium I would now and again write a prosodic group of lines inspired by Joyce in his final book, pages that I did not publish but which I actually thought of as contemporary kabbalistic writing.

At the same time I began in 1976 to create an agit-prop form of verbo-visuality I called Talking Leaves (after the great American genius and creator of the Cherokee syllabary, Sequoia), though its real roots lay in the agitpropagatings of the Soviet poet, Vladimir Mayakovsky: on a sheet of paper, or cardboard, or paper I would scavenge, or napkin I would make (1) a graphic gesture, (2) write a word in Russian, (3) above that word write the word AMERUS in Russian, (4) under that word write the word communist in Russian, (5) on one side of the sheet write a solidarity, ie., Solidarity Haiti or solidarity United Auto Workers, in American, (6) on the other side of the sheet write No Nazis or No Klan in American, (7) write the name of literary or political or artistic figure as Presente or Present, ie., Abraham Abulafia present, and (8) write in American a haiku or should poem.

Between 1976 and 1987, I made and gave more than 100,000 of the Talking Leaves to people of all walks of life. The kabbala and especially Abulafia's *tseruf* techniques were instrumental in helping me produce such works.

5.

In 1980, a year after Sasha Kohav had left San Francisco and upon my return from Sicily and Greece, I joined the Communist Labor Party, a small but principled Marxist-Leninist party. I worked militantly for it for the next dozen years, when comrades agreed to auto-dissolve the Party, but I have continued working with communist revolutionaries in its succeeding non-Party formations, including the present League of Revolutionaries for a New America (LRNA). The Communist Labor Party was one that refused NOT to read and study the works of Joseph Stalin and so was thought of and called a "Stalinist" Party.

Having studied dialectics and understood in my own studential way that material development vis-a-vis the law of nature casts doubt on the mystical dimension because the question of God's existence as something objective to the human mind is itself impossible to recognize as anything more than something intended to imprison people in the Penitentiary of Religion and absoluteness rather than a process that is more accurately and dialectically reflective of the unwritten laws of development in nature. Of course in mysticism there are the dramas of light and darkness, of revelation and concealment, and the like. But the image of God him/her/it-self as the origin of everything, and therefore the form which rules human motion and change makes it impossible for one to believe that human beings can change anything in life.

To my communist way of thinking, the God-figure was an obstacle to change and progress made by human beings.

Yet in the 33 years since I had last spoken to Sasha Kohav—a full generation!—, years in which I worked rather militantly for the communist movement, not simply by going table to table in cafes and door to door in homes with the CLP's newspaper, *The People's Tribune*; going also to factory gates and—in the '90s, and the Millennium's first decade—to lines of homeless workers; going to jail at times for being active on issues of homelessness, hunger, and anti-war demonstrations; and culturally organizing an international journal—*Compages*—which published translations (and original languages) of revolutionary poetry from all over the world, translated American revolutionary poems into different languages, and sent copies to different revolutionary organizations and or unions of writers in different countries around the world; and at the same time developing in extension the orchestrated poem I call an Arcane, which contains a mixture of politics and mysticism, or rather a mysticism and poesy that is transformed in the process of creation into an event for the strengthening of the reader's inner life in recognition that the politically fascist (corporation) world exists and yet must be resisted not merely by physical demonstrations and actions but by a strength of soul that (hopefully) my Arcanes might help provide.

For example, concerning mystical techniques, in "The Proletarian Arcane," using a name-transfer gleaned from Abraham Abulafia, I wrote an Arcane about Norma Jean Baker (the real name of Marilyn Monroe) dedicating the poem to General Baker, a comrade of mine in the Communist Labor Party who was running for a political office in the Michigan state elections. In "The Jonestown Arcane" (synchronically I am writing these words on the 34th anniversary of that tragedy, November 18, 2012) I begin each strophe of that poem with two lines in Russian made up of words which don't mean anything—they are a glossolalia- mantra from the 19th century Khlysty, a flagellation sect whose most famous adherent was Rasputin.

Other Arcanes are, for example, "The Golem Arcane," "The Zimzum Arcane," "The Kavvana Arcane"—all whose titles and contents come from readings in kabbala that went on amid my heavy political activity. Through the 126 Arcanes that comprise the 2006 edition, there are many works referencing or being imbued with kabbalistic ideas, especially from Abulafia, but also from the 16th century revolutionary mystic, Isaac Luria; and in "The Assasuicide Arcane," written about the 9/11 event and its extenuations, I evoke the so-called false messiah of the Jews, Sabbatai Tsvi, who led a kabbalistic revolution in 1666 and then, threatened with arrest and death by the Turkish sultan, he converted to Islam while remaining a kabbalist revolutionary within. He is the most interesting political figure in all of kabbala for me, and my Arcane presents his image as an ongoing and living revolutionary one.

In this sense elements from "mystical" life have been an essential part of my politically driven Arcanes but in no way are those elements presented in a manner so as to suggest mystical or religious resolutions. If there is any *devequt* (or cleaving to create an identity-with and ultimately a "union"), it is to unite with the communist movement through the exposing of the forces of evil and oppression that are linked with the capitalist system, economically and politically. Whether it is kabbala or vodun (which is also an important part of my "occult" study—ie., ecstasy underlying both) I take these elements as fundamentally active linguistic tropes, part of a poet's arsenal of interests, especially if the poet is interested in "sects" that have been oppressed by the law (as Abulafia was persecuted by both rabbis and the Catholic church; as vodunists are still being persecuted today in Haiti; as were the Narodniki in Russia in the 19th Century i.e., sects like the Khlysty, the Skopzi and the Molokans whose rebelliousness led Lenin to call them the precursors of the Bolshevik Revolution: (the 5th Arcane in my book is "The Narodnik Arcane").

Thus, mystical and political justice go hand in hand in my work with the economic and social struggle to end the capitalist system of exploitation. I am for example convinced that Abulafia'a letter-combining to create new words makes him, of the 13th century, a 21st century poet; that Luria's theory of zimzum is a revolutionary idea in the most modern way of affirming human responsibility in the unfolding drama of existence, and I believe that the contradictory elements in sabbateanism are precisely what are necessary to see in the light of the only thing that can solve the Israeli-Palestinian crisis—a communist Palisrael.)

At the outset of this essay I wrote of the inwardness that was necessary to the life of the poet and mystic both and I mentioned that the discovery of the *Duino Elegies* of R.N. Rilke was the essential work in my early studential years. Now at the age of 79, I have in my 78th year "discovered" another poet who has restored my faith in the inner life of the Word. An anecdote must be told in relation to this discovery:

At a Wednesday night table in Specs Café in North Beach, San Francisco, where I have been meeting with the publisher of Left Curve magazine, Csaba Polony, with whom I have worked for 30 years to bring that annual Mayday magazine into print, a table which now is a gathering place for many other writer, artists and intellectuals, one evening in a joking way, I asked: "Who's the finest poet in the United States?" To both perplexed and slightly scornful looks on many faces there I said: "Well, they say that the translations of Jelalludin

Rumi's poetry made by Coleman Barks are not translations. If they're not translations, then Coleman Barks is the finest poet in the U.S."

It was a joke of course, but with an accuracy too. Coleman's great versions of Rumi, I discovered full-force again in 2012, have reaffirmed the greatness of poetry as the greatest affirmation of the beingness of inner life and inner strength. That he wrote in Farsi about Jews like Moses and Abraham, Joseph, Jacob and Jesus as brothers in the light of the Love that galvanizes every word of Rumi's should put to rest the chauvinistic myopias that separate beings from one another. ANYONE can recognize the greatest of Rumi's lyric wisdom as he is a poet of love in the most profound sense of the word and his mystical *sorbhets* or conversations with Shams of Tabriz or with you yourself are among the deepest expressions of human beingness.

Indeed it's as if in me, this year, the Angel of Rilke's great work, the Angel Raziel of Abulafia's verbal dexterities, and the Angel of Love that inspires the poems of Rumi have set up a strong and wonderful camp in this time of so many needless wars and willful lies, to resist with great poetry the devastation of the body and soul in these abundantly destitute days.

Part I

Religions at Birth,

in Perpetuity,

and in Flux

5. Oneness with Heaven and Earth

Mysticism in the Chinese Tradition

Livia Kohn[1]

Abstract

Chinese mysticism has a long and varied history, from the early thinkers of thea Axial Age through various permutations in the middle ages to modern versions of both theory and practice. Mysticism permeated the different aspects of the Chinese tradition and was present in the dominant school of Confucianism and the foreign religion of Buddhism as in Daoism, the indigenous higher religion of China. How does the Chinese mystical tradition differ from comparable Western and Indian systems? What are some of its fundamental characteristics? Can we pinpoint commonalities and differences among its main indigenous forms, Confucianism and Daoism? What are these traditions? How do they understand wisdom, the self, mystical training, and the ideal human, and envision mystical union?

Main Features of the Chinese Tradition

The first fact one notices when looking at Chinese religion in general and the mystical tradition in particular is that the Chinese tradition does not have a single creator deity or focus on a monotheistic god. There is no entity completely beyond the world, no transcendent other, no "thou" to a this-worldly "us," no power that will never cease and never change. Rather, the Chinese tradition sees its ultimate in Dao, a divine force so immanent that it is even in the soil and tiles; so much a part of the world that it cannot be separated from it.[2] Oneness or union with Dao is the birthright of every being, not a rare instance

---

[1] An earlier version of this essay, entitled "Merging with Heaven and Earth: Mystical Attainment in the Chinese Tradition," appeared in *ARC: The Journal of the Faculty of Religious Studies at McGill University* 35 (2008), 17-41. Reprinted with permission.

[2] The entire early philosophy of China focuses on Dao and how best to live in and with it. Thus, A. C. Graham named his discussion of early Chinese thought *Disputers of the Tao: Philosophical Argument in Ancient China* (La Salle, Ill.: Open Court Publishing Company, 1989).

of divine grace. It is natural to begin with and becomes only more natural as it is realized through practice.[3]

The Chinese mystical experience of oneness with Dao, as a consequence, is astounding only in the beginning. It represents a way of being in the world different from ordinary perception, which is determined by the senses and the intellect, but not essentially alien or completely other. The longer the mystic lives with the experience, the more he integrates it into his or her life and being and the less extraordinary it becomes. Being at one with Dao, joining Heaven and Earth, is the natural and original state of humanity, which is recovered through mystical practice.[4] Thus, neither is the experience itself the central feature of the tradition, nor is there a pronounced "dark night of the soul," a desperate search for a glimpse of the transcendent divine. Dao is here and now, residing right within oneself. The main difficulty Chinese mystics face in realizing Dao is the scatterbrained and pleasure-seeking nature of their ego-centered self. This, in turn, is amply discussed in the texts, together with varied techniques to overcome it.[5]

Still, even there the Chinese go their own way. They do not envision the ego-centered self in a dualism of body versus divine soul or rational mind. Rather the human being—body, mind, and spirit, plus everything else that exists in the universe—consists of *qi*, vital cosmic energy, the concrete, material aspect of Dao.[6] There is only one *qi*, just as there is only one Dao; already the ancient thinker Zhuangzi emphasizes that human life is the accumulation of *qi* while death is its dispersal. After receiving a core potential of primordial *qi* at birth, people throughout life need to sustain it. They do so by drawing postnatal *qi* into the body from air and food, as well as from other people through sexual, emotional, and social interaction. But they also lose *qi* through breathing bad air, overburdening their bodies with food and drink, and getting involved

---

[3] Mystical practice can thus be seen as the intensification and perfection of ordinary life. See Livia Kohn, *Early Chinese Mysticism: Philosophy and Soteriology in the Taoist Tradition* (Princeton: Princeton University Press, 1992), 11.

[4] Kohn, *Early Chinese Mysticism*, 23.

[5] Some of these techniques involve the conscious reorganization of thinking and perception in a meditation practice known as "observation." Adapted from Buddhist insight meditation, it forms an important part of a seven-step program to Daoist realization. See Livia Kohn, *Sitting in Oblivion: The Heart of Daoist Meditation* (Dunedin, Fla.: Three Pines Press, 2010)

[6] Livia Kohn, *Health and Long Life: The Chinese Way* (Cambridge, Mass.: Three Pines Press, 2005), 11. Further discussions of *qi* are found in Stephen Chang, *The Complete Book of Acupuncture* (Berkeley: Celestial Arts, 1976); Ted Kaptchuk, *The Web that Has No Weaver: Understanding Chinese Medicine* (New York: Congdon & Weed, 1983); and Donald E. Kendall, *Dao of Chinese Medicine: Understanding an Ancient Healing Art.* (New York: Oxford University Press, 2002).

in negative emotions and excessive sexual or social interactions. Body, mind, and soul are part of one and the same continuum of *qi*.[7]

Rather than by overcoming a body that is a prison or hindrance to the soul, the Chinese accordingly find mystical attainment through creating an utmost harmony of *qi*-flow, a perfect balance of patterns and forces, a subtlety and refinement of vital energy. Once they have reached such a balance, they continue their practice and gradually transform their *qi*, which is both personal and universal at the same time, into a finer cosmic energy known as spirit (shen).[8] A subtle dimension of *qi*, this serves as the guiding vitality behind all its other forms; it is the active, organizing force and transformative influence in the individual that connects him or her to Heaven and the underlying oneness with Dao. Within the person it is individual awareness and mental direction; it resides in the heart and is related to the mind and the emotions.[9]

As mystics attain their realization of personal *qi*-subtlety, they not only gain physical health, mental well-being, and a sense of oneness with Dao. They also contribute to harmony and health in the larger universe: in nature, where *qi*-balance appears as regular weather patterns and the absence of disasters; in society, where it is found in the peaceful coexistence among families, clans, villages, and states; and in the greater world in the state of Great Peace, the great cosmic harmony of all.

This outflowing dimension of mystical attainment means that in the Chinese tradition the mystic is not one to leave society behind and stay away from all involvement. On the contrary, the accomplished mystic is always a social being who would spread and radiate his qualities throughout the world. Placed at the pinnacle of society, the mystic is the sage and also the ideal ruler, a continuation of the ancient Chinese ideal of the shaman-king as the chief intermediary between humanity and the cosmos.[10] Mysticism in China thus was never isolated from society but always had a strong political dimension.[11] The tradi-

---

[7] Kohn, *Health and Long Life*, 12.

[8] A powerful discussion of *shen* in Chinese medicine is found in Manfred Porkert, *The Theoretical Foundations of Chinese Medicine* (Cambridge, Mass.: MIT Press, 1974). An examination of the notion in ancient Chinese and Daoist thought appears in Harold D. Roth, "The Early Taoist Concept of *Shen*: A Ghost in the Machinery?," in *Sagehood and Systematizing Thought in the Late Warring States and Early Han*, edited by Kidder Smith (Brunswick, Maine: Bowdoin College, 1990), 11-32.

[9] Kaptchuk, *The Web That Has No Weaver*, 58.

[10] This notion is already a central feature of the thought of the ancient *Daode jing*. See Benjamin Schwartz, "The Worldview of the *Tao-te-ching*," in *Lao-tzu and the Tao-te-ching*, edited by Livia Kohn and Michael LaFargue (Albany: State University of New York Press, 1998), 189-210. On the spiritual dimensions of rulership in ancient China in general, see Roger T. Ames, *The Art of Rulership: A Study in Ancient Chinese Political Thought* (Honolulu: University of Hawaii Press, 1983).

[11] Kohn, *Early Chinese Mysticism*, 172.

tion as a whole is much more immanent, body-focused, and socially responsible than what one might expect from comparative Western and Indian models.

The two main indigenous traditions of China that have both brought forth active mystical traditions are Confucianism and Daoism. Both arose around 500 BCE with dominant thinkers that form part of the Axial Age, had their founders divinized under the Han dynasty around the beginning of the Common Era, underwent serious transformations under Buddhist influence in the middle ages, and have survived actively in modern forms to the present day.

Confucianism and Daoism

Confucianism goes back to the thinker Confucius, Kongfuzi or "Master Kong" (551-479 BCE), the illegitimate son of the ruler of Lu, a small state in eastern China (modern Shandong). Trained in elementary feudal arts as well as to read and write, he became a minor functionary in the state's administration, then developed certain ideas of his own as to the causes of his country's problems and their remedy.[12] In an effort to see his ideas put into practice, he left his employment and traveled through China, presenting himself as a potential prime minister to many local rulers. However, no ruler employed Confucius, and so he returned home and began to teach interested disciples in private, soon establishing a name for himself and his ideas.[13] The disciples later collected his sayings into a volume known as the *Lunyu* (Analects).[14]

The main concept of early Confucianism is the idea of ritual formality or etiquette (*li*) in alignment with the overarching universal power of Heaven.[15] The character represents the image of a ritual vessel and indicates the proper behavior in all social and religious situations: in society, government, and ritual. Socially, *li* means proper behavior among people of different rank and status, defined through hierarchical relationships that always incluce a senior and a junior person, and each has obligations toward the other, expressed in the so-called Confucian virtues which foster the positive, heavenly nature in people: benevolence, righteousness, filial piety, and loyalty. According to Confucius and his followers, if everyone knew his or her personal and social position at any

---

[12] For the role of Confucius and his thought, see Herbert Fingarette, *Confucius: The Secular as Sacred* (New York: Harper & Row, 1972).

[13] Biographical studies of Confucius include Raymond Dawson, *Confucius* (New York: Hill and Wang, 1982); Betty Kelen, *Confucius in Life and Legend* (New York: T. Nelson, 1971); and Wu-chi Liu, *Confucius, His Life and Time* (New York: Philosophical Library, 1955).

[14] For translations of the *Analects*, see Arthur Waley, *The Analects of Confucius* (New York: Vintage Books, 1989 [1938]); D. C. Lau, *The Analects* (New York: Penguin, 1979); and Roger T. Ames, *The Analects of Confucius: A Philosophical Translation* (New York: Ballantine, 1998).

[15] See Robert Eno, *The Confucian Creation of Heaven: Philosophy and the Defense of Ritual Mastery* (Albany: State University of New York Press, 1989).

given moment and acted fully in accordance with it, society would be fully harmonious.[16]

The same idea also applies to government organizations, which should act in proper accordance with their specific duties and not infringe upon or compete with each other; and also to religious rituals, where it is important to honor the ancestors and the local and cosmic deities with proper formalities, offering sacrifices of food and drink. Everybody under Heaven should participate in this ideal Confucian world of li to their best ability, and while some may have a stronger natural inclination toward it than others, everyone can learn. In fact, learning in ancient Confucianism and for the Chinese throughout history has been the key method of attaining the proper feeling for li in all given situations, and good behavior that creates social harmony is at first a learned response, which becomes natural after many years of training.[17] Social harmony, moreover, as formulated most expressively in the "Daxue" (Great Learning) chapter of the *Liji* (Book of Rites), begins with the individual and radiates outward, to create an overarching sense of oneness and balance throughout the world.[18]

In the Song dynasty (960-1260), Confucianism underwent a revival and transformed to include various Buddhist elements. Its thinkers began to encourage a more internal realization of "bright virtue," the inherent power of the individual that could make the self one with Heaven and Earth and bring Great Peace to the world. They supported meditation methods such as quiet-sitting and lauded a spontaneous connection to Heaven known as "innate knowledge," thus giving rise to a mystical tradition in their own right.[19]

Unlike the Confucian preoccupation with society, the proponents of the cosmic "Way" (Dao) proposed a return to naturalness, spontaneity, and organic so-being. Their ideas were first represented in the *Daode jing* associated the

---

[16] On Confucian thought and social relevance, see David Hall and Roger T. Ames, *Thinking through Confucius* (Albany, State University of New York Press, 1987).

[17] For the development and role of Confucianism in Chinese society over the millennia, see John H. Berthrong, *Transformations of the Confucian Way* (Boulder, Col.: Westview Press, 1998); Jennifer Oldstone-Moore, *Confucianism: Origins, Beliefs, Practices, Holy texts, Sacred Places* (New York: Oxford University Press, 2002).

[18] A translation of this, with other Confucian documents, appears in Wing-tsit Chan, *A Source Book in Chinese Philosophy* (Princeton: Princeton University Press, 1963). For a complete rendition of the *Liji*, see James Legge, *The Li Ki—Book of Rites* (Delhi: Motilal Bernasidass, 1968 [1885]). A discussion of the role of ritual in ancient China is found in Joseph P. McDermott, *State and Court Ritual in China* (Cambridge: Cambridge University Press, 1999).

[19] On the development of Confucianism since the Song dynasty, see William Theodore De-Bary, *The Unfolding of Neo-Confucianism* (New York: Columbia University Press, 1975); and *Neo-Confucian Orthodoxy and the Learning of the Mind-and-Heart* (New York: Columbia University Press, 1981). For its modern vision and relevance, see Wei-ming Tu, *Humanity and Self-Cultivation: Essays in Confucian Thought* (Berkeley: Asian Humanities Press, 1979).

thinker Laozi, the Old Master, a largely legendary figure who allegedly served as an official at the royal Zhou court and instructed Confucius about the rites.[20]

The text consists of about five thousand characters and is commonly divided into eighty-one chapters and two parts, one on Dao (chs. 1-37), and one on De (chs. 38-81).[21] It is written in verse—not a rhyming, steady rhythmic kind of verse, but a stylized prose that has strong parallels and regular patterns—and contains sections of description contrasted with tight punchlines.[22]

The *Daode jing* has been transmitted in several different editions, three of which are most important today. The first is the so-called standard edition, also known as the transmitted edition. Handed down by Chinese copyists over the ages, it is at the root of almost all translations of the text. It goes back to the 3rd century, to the erudite Wang Bi (226-249) who edited the text and wrote a commentary on it that Chinese since then have considered inspired. It has shaped the reception of the text's worldview until today.[23]

The second edition is called the Mawangdui edition, named after a place in south China (Hunan) where a tomb was excavated in 1973 that dated from 168 BCE. It contained an undisturbed coffin surrounded by numerous artifacts and several manuscripts written on silk, mostly dealing with cosmology and medicine.[24] Among them were two copies of the *Daode jing*. The Mawangdui version differs little from the transmitted edition: there are some character variants which have helped clarify some interpretive points, and the two parts are in reversed order, i.e., the text begins with the section on De, then adds the

---

[20] As A. C. Graham has shown, Laozi was associated with a growing "Daoist" community in the 4th century BCE and credited with longevity and even immortality under the Qin. See "The Origins of the Legend of Lao Tan," in *Studies in Chinese Philosophy and Philosophical Literature*, edited by A. C. Graham (Albany: State University of New York Press, 1990), 111-24.

[21] The *Daode jing* is one of the world's great works. For a comprehensive outline of its history, thought, and reception both in China and the West, see Livia Kohn, *Guides to Sacred Texts: The Daode jing*. New York: Oxford University Press, 2019.

[22] The particular style of *Daode jing* poetry is closely related to that of the *Shijing* (Book of Songs), a collection of ancient local songs and poems that date back to around 500 B.C.E. For a discussion, see William H. Baxter, "Situating the Language of the *Lao-tzu*: The Probable Date of the *Tao-te-ching*," in *Lao-tzu and the Tao-te-ching*, edited by Livia Kohn and Michael LaFargue (Albany: State University of New York Press, 1998), 231-54.

[23] On the creation of the standard edition and commentary by Wang Bi, see Alan Chan, *Two Visions of the Way: A Study of the Wang Pi and the Ho-shang-kung Commentaries on the Laozi* (Albany: State University of New York Press, 1991). A translation of the commentary appears in Paul J. Lin, *A Translation of Lao-tzu's Tao-te-ching and Wang Pi's Commentary* (Ann Arbor: University of Michigan, Center for Chinese Studies Publications, 1977); Ariane Rump and Wing-tsit Chan, *Commentary on the Lao-tzu by Wang Pi* (Honolulu: University of Hawaii Press, 1979).

[24] A detailed study of the Mawangdui finds and a complete translation of the medical works is found in Donald Harper, *Early Chinese Medical Manuscripts: The Mawangdui Medical Manuscripts* (London: Wellcome Asian Medical Monographs, 1998).

section on Dao.[25] The manuscripts are important because they show that the *Daode jing* existed in its complete form in the early Han dynasty, and that it was considered essential enough to be placed in someone's grave.

The third edition was discovered in 1993 in a place called Guodian (Hubei). Written on bamboo slips and dated to about 300 BCE, the find presents a collection of various philosophical works of the time, including fragments of Confucian and other texts. Among them are thirty-three passages that can be matched with thirty-one chapters of the *Daode jing*, but with lines in different places, and considerable variation in characters. Generally, they are concerned with self-cultivation and its application to questions of rulership and the pacification of the state. Polemical attacks against Confucian virtues, such as those describing them as useless or even harmful, are not found; instead negative attitudes and emotions are criticized.[26] This Guodian find of this so-called "Bamboo Laozi" tells us that in the late 4th century BCE the text existed in rudimentary form, and consisted of a collection of sayings not yet edited into a coherent presentation. Another text found at Guodian, the *Taiyi sheng shui* (Great Unity Creates Water), gives further insights into the growing and possibly even "Daoist" cosmology of the time, as does a contemporaneous work on self-cultivation, the "Neiye" (Inward Training) chapter of the *Guanzi*.[27] It appears that, gradually, a set of ideas and practices was growing that would eventually develop into something specifically and more religiously Daoist.

The *Daode jing* has often been hailed as representing the core of the Daoist worldview and the root of Daoist mysticism. But it is in fact a multifaceted work that can, and has been, interpreted in many different ways, not least as a manual of strategy, a political treatise on the recovery of the golden age, a guide to underlying principles, and a metalinguistic inquiry into forms of prescriptive discourse. It can be read in two fundamentally different ways: as a document of early Chinese culture or as a scripture of universal significance.

It outlines the ultimate power and reality of Dao, the underlying source and power of the universe, the way the world functions, a mystical power of universal oneness. Benjamin Schwartz describes it as "organic order"—"organic" in the sense that it is part of the world and not a transcendent other as in Western religion, "order" because it can be felt in the rhythms of the

---

25 See Robert Henricks *Lao-Tzu: Te-Tao ching* (New York: Ballantine, 1989).

26 A translation of the Guodian text appears in Robert Henricks, *Lao Tzu's Tao Te Ching: A Translation of the Startling New Documents Found at Guodian* (New York: Columbia University Press, 2000). A collection of essays on the texts is found in Sarah Allen and Crispin Williams, eds., *The Guodian Laozi* (Berkeley: Institute of East Asian Studies, 2000).

27 A detailed discussion and translation of this early Daoist mystical text, which represents a practical supplement to the *Daode jing*, is found in Harold D. Roth, *Original Tao: Inward Training and the Foundations of Taoist Mysticism* (New York: Columbia University Press, 1999).

world, in the manifestation of organized patterns.[28] Dao is at the root of creation—tight, concentrated, intense, and ultimately unknowable, ineffable, and beyond conscious or sensory human attainment—and also present in the world, in the patterned cycles of life and visible nature. The way to be with Dao is through nonaction (*wuwei*) and naturalness (*ziran*), which means letting go of egotistic concerns and passions and desires, finding a sense of where life, nature, and the world are headed on the social level, and abstaining from forceful and interfering measures in the political realm. The person who has realized Dao to the utmost is the sage, in the *Daode jing* ideally the ruler, to whom the treatise was originally addressed.[29]

In the course of history, Laozi was divinized as a personification of Dao and began to appear in ecstatic visions to selected seekers.[30] These seekers founded various organized schools that proposed specific celestial realms to attain, moral rules to follow, rituals to observe, and a plethora of mystical practices to master, from basic physical refinements of *qi* through diets, exercises, breathing, and sexual control to advanced meditations of all different kinds: quietistic concentration, Buddhist-inspired insight meditation, intricate visualizations of the gods, and the still-active practice of internal alchemy.[31]

We will not be able to go into all these details, but will have to limit ourselves to pointing out the main common points and unique features of the two main mystical traditions of China.

Common Points

A first common point among Confucianism and Daoism is the belief in what perennialists call the "Ground," an underlying power or force that creates and supports the universe.[32] Described as Dao or "Way" in both, it is known more

---

[28] Schwartz, "The Worldview of the *Tao-te-ching*, 192.

[29] The original setting and structure of the *Daode jing* are particularly explored in Michael LaFargue, *The Tao of the Tao-te-ching* (Albany: State University of New York Press, 1992).

[30] On the growth of Laozi into a god and one of the key deities of the Daoist religion, see Anna Seidel, *La divinisation de Lao-tseu dans le taoïsme des Han* (Paris: Ecole Française d'Extrême-Orient, 1969); Livia Kohn, *God of the Dao: Lord Lao in History and Myth* (University of Michigan, Center for Chinese Studies, 1998).

[31] On the various practices involved in Daoist cultivation, see Livia Kohn, ed., *Taoist Meditation and Longevity Techniques* (Ann Arbor: University of Michigan, Center for Chinese Studies, 1998); *Daoist Body Cultivation: Traditional Models and Contemporary Practices* (Magdalena, NM: Three Pines Press, 2006).

[32] The notion of the Ground appears in discussions of the perennial philosophy, a term coined by the German philosopher Leibniz and more extensively formulated by Aldous Huxley in *The Perennial Philosophy* (New York: Harper & Brothers, 1946). Among mysticism studies, it is most clearly present in F. C. Happold, *Mysticism: A Study and an Anthology* (Baltimore: Penguin, 1970).

specifically as the Nonultimate among the Confucians. This is depicted as an empty circle, from which the Great Ultimate arises, depicted as the classic diagram of yin and yang. The Great Ultimate, in turn, is the core of the existing universe, and as such gives rise to the three forces (Heaven, Earth, Humanity) and the five evolutive phases (wood, fire, earth, metal, water), which in different combinations appear in everything that exists.[33]

In Daoism, at least in its classical form, Dao similarly is said to give rise to the One, the core of creation and existence that is part of chaos yet also contains the universe in seminal form. This unfolds in a dividing movement to produce the two, the two forces yin and yang, which in their turn unite to form the three, described as yin and yang plus "yin and yang in harmony." These three, then, characterize everything created in the world, and are accordingly said to "produce the myriad beings."[34]

Within this overall cosmogonic framework and common reliance on the universal Ground, both Confucian and Daoist mysticism further rely heavily on traditional Chinese cosmology of yin-yang and the five phases and their complex correspondences. All beings actively participate in the cosmic cycles. They have the power to either go along with them smoothly or distort them at their will. The ordinary consciousness of people, typically governed by passions and desires, and their actions in society are then understood as forms of distortion, which cause self and world to be out of balance. The mystical endeavor in both traditions as a result aims not only at the restoration of cosmic harmony but at its conscious and active realization within the individual who is then able to live as long as Heaven and Earth.

From this arises a third common point: the understanding that every part of the world is closely interrelated with every other part and that the macrocosm and microcosm mirror each other to perfection. The world here is seen as a series of concentric circles, which are isomorphic structurally and in their energy makeup. They begin with the body on the microcosmic level, then proceed through the family, the community or society, and the natural world to the cosmos as visible in the movements of the stars and planets. Each level is the exact replica of the next, and impulses in one have inevitable responses in all others. Mystical realization, as a result, means the perfection of the whole, beginning with the smallest entity and extending toward the larger universe. The mystic in China, whether Confucian or Daoist, is therefore never socially sepa-

---

[33] While this cosmology is already part of the ancient *Yijing* and appears in Han-dynasty commentaries to the text, it is most explicitly formulated in early Neo-Confucian documents, notably the works of Zhou Dunyi (1017-1073). A translation of the full document is found in Wing-tsit Chan, *A Source Book in Chinese Philosophy* (Princeton: Princeton University Press, 1963), 463-64.

[34] *Daode jing*, ch. 42.

rate and his realization has highest relevance for the perfection of human life as a whole.

These points appear in the "Great Learning" chapter of the *Liji* and are formulated strongly in the philosophy of resonance or "impulse and response" (ganying) in the Han dynasty,[35] and later taken up vibrantly in Ming dynasty Neo-Confucianism, notably in the thought of Wang Yangming.[36] In Daoism, they form part of the vision of Great Peace but are also pervasively present in the understanding of the body and the role of humanity in the greater universe.

Another aspect both traditions share is their indebtedness to Buddhism, Daoism since the Six Dynasties period (ab. 406-489) and Confucianism since the Song dynasty.[37] In Daoism, Buddhism contributed the monastic setting of its practice, the doctrine of karma and retribution (including punishments in the hells), the belief in popular savior figures and techniques of insight meditation.[38] Neo-Confucianism owes to the religion especially its understanding of the difference between principle and affairs, the underlying essence of the world and its manifestation in reality, as well as its meditation of quiet-sitting, which goes back to the practice of zazen.[39] Buddhism, a highly sophisticated system of doctrines, meditations, and monastic organization, thus contributed significantly to the shaping of the Chinese mystical tradition, even in its indigenous forms.

Historical Unfolding

These four points common to both Confucianism and Daoism—the belief in the Ground, the application of five-phases cosmology, the correspondence of macro- and microcosm, and the adaptation of Buddhist concepts—have their root in the historical development of the traditions, which is highly parallel and reflects the overall unfolding of Chinese religion. Typically, this development is

---

[35] For a discussion of the concept of resonance, see Charles Le Blanc, "Resonance: Une interpretation chinoise de la réalité," in *Mythe et philosophie a l'aube de la Chine impérial: Etudes sur le Huainan zi*, edited by Charles Le Blanc and Remi Mathieu (Montreal: Les Presses de l'Universite de Montreal, 1992), 91-111.

[36] On the thought of Wang Yangming, see Julia Ching *To Accumulate Wisdom: The Way of Wang Yang-ming* (New York: Columbia University Press, 1976).

[37] On the transmission and adaptation of Buddhism in China, see Kenneth Ch'en, *The Chinese Transformation of Buddhism* (Princeton: Princeton University Press, 1973); Erik Zürcher, *The Buddhist Conquest of China: The Spread and Adaptation of Buddhism in Early Medieval China* (Leiden: E. Brill, 1959); Zenryu Tsukamoto and Leon Hurvitz, *A History of Early Chinese Buddhism* (Tokyo: Kodansha, 1985).

[38] Erik Zürcher, "Buddhist Influence on Early Taoism," *T'oung Pao* 66 (1980), 84-147.

[39] For Buddhist influence on Neo-Confucianism, see Carsun Chang, *The Development of Neo-Confucian Thought* (New York: Bookman Associates, 1962); Rodney Taylor, *The Cultivation of Selfhood as a Religious Goal in Neo-Confucianism* (Missoula, Mont.: Scholars Press, 1978).

divided into three periods: a classical that reaches from the ancient philosophers to the Han dynasty (206 BCE-220 CE); a medieval that lasts from the Three Kingdoms (221-265) to the Tang (618-907); and a modern that begins with the Song dynasty in 960 and goes all the way through late imperial China (Ming and Qing dynasties, 1368-1644, 1644-1911) to the present.[40]

Each of these periods has its specific tendencies and overall marks. The classical is characterized by a high emphasis on philosophical speculation and the emergence of a systematic cosmological base; the medieval evolves under the strong influence of Buddhism and sees the emergence of sophisticated concepts of body and mind as well as complex methods of meditation and mystical attainment; the modern recovers the classical models and integrates them in a new and farther reaching synthesis that allows a broad vision of practice and realization.

More specifically, in the classical period we have the key thinkers of the two traditions, Confucius and Mencius in Confucianism, Laozi and Zhuangzi in Daoism. While none of them wrote anything himself, their words were considered important enough to be transmitted through generations of disciples and committed to bamboo and silk around the 3rd century BCE. Even the vagaries of changing dynasties and the notorious book- burning of 214 did not lessen either their intactness or importance for Chinese culture.[41] Classics in the true sense of the word, they were used for governmental as much as personal guidance, cited frequently and interpreted ever anew, and in both their overall outlook and particular phrasing gave the two traditions their unique foundations. In addition, the classical period saw the emergence of the five-phases cosmology with its complex correspondence system and its vision of the universe as concentric circles of parallel layers and its postulation of an intimate interrelation between all levels of life.

The medieval period of about seven hundred years is commonly divided into an early and a high phase, the boundary being set in the 6th century when the country was reunified after a long stretch of division. The early medieval period is characterized by an unprecedented dynamic, especially in Daoism, which saw the emergence of its major schools (Celestial Masters, Highest Clarity, Numinous Treasure) under the heavy influence of Buddhism, which was sponsored particularly by the Central Asians in north China. The period saw the divinization of the philosopher Laozi, who was venerated as a personifica-

---

[40] For a discussion of periodization issues in Chinese religion and Daoism, see Russell Kirkland, "The Historical Contours of Taoism in China: Thoughts on Issues of Classification and Terminology," *Journal of Chinese Religions* 25 (1997), 57-82.

[41] On the burning of the books and other radical measures under the first Chinese imperial dynasty, see Derk Bodde, Derk, *China's First Unifier: A Study of the Ch'in Dynasty as Seen in the Life of Li Ssu, 280?-208 B.C.* (Leiden: E. Brill, 1938).

tion of Dao and became increasingly like the Buddha in character. It also saw the formulation of Daoist mystical attainment through ecstatic journeys to the stars and the realization of mental detachment.[42]

Confucianism, the more dominant creed of the south, was less affected, but still had to engage in debates with a growing number of Buddhists and gradually began to incorporate Buddhist ways of thinking into its worldview. The high medieval phase, next, saw a consolidation of the new forms of thinking, actively integrating Buddhist visions into indigenous Chinese systems and creating the sophisticated mystical systems of the mid-Tang. These systems were carried largely by Daoists, Confucianism being relegated to state-supporting doctrine at the time.

This changed in the Song dynasty when an overall recovery of Chinese roots and the ancient classics took place. This recovery followed upon two hundred years of confusion and civil war, beginning in 755 with the rebellion of An Lushan, a general of Central Asian descent, and ending only with the founding of the Song in 960. With much of high culture and social infrastructure in ruins, the new dynasty engaged both in the eager collection of lost materials (turning the Song into the great age of Chinese encyclopedias) and in the return to ancient models that were more Chinese and less Central Asian or Indian. As a result, Confucianism was greatly revived and turned, in its Neo-Confucian form as formulated especially by the great Zhu Xi (1130-1200), into a form of mystical self-cultivation, giving rise to a rich and varied tradition that had its own form of meditation (quiet-sitting), its own centers of learning (academies), and its own specific vision of the world (as issuing from the Great Ultimate and relying on universal principle).[43]

Daoism, at this time much less important than Confucianism, reformulated its doctrines in the integrated system of inner alchemy, which applies alchemical metaphors and the symbols of the *Yijing* (Book of Changes) to express a vision of immortality highly patterned on the Buddhist attainment of nirvana. In addition, its new leading school of Complete Perfection imitated the Chan (Zen) tradition in many ways, organizationally, doctrinally, and in methods of transmission and asceticism. Both traditions have continued to the present day along the patterns established in the Song dynasty, evolving new forms of interpretation and new modes of practice but leaving the overall framework of worldview and mystical vision unchanged. While both suffered under Communist rule in China and are today recovering, Confucianism in addition was also heartily adopted in Korea and Japan and has a rich extended environment for its modern unfolding.

---

[42] For an overview of Daoist history, see Livia Kohn, *Daoism and Chinese Culture* (Cambridge, Mass.: Three Pines Press, 2001).
[43] See Wing-tsit Chan, *Chu Hsi: New Studies* (Honolulu: University of Hawaii Press, 1989).

Unique Characteristics

Having seen the overall commonality and historical parallels of the two traditions, we shall now turn to their distinct and unique characteristics, understanding how they differ in mystical worldview, location, and practice.

Creation. To begin, in their vision of the ultimate Confucians posit a relationship between humanity and the cosmos that is direct and immediate, with harmony and virtuous order the key factors in the attainment of oneness and mystical vision. The same holds true for classical Daoism, the teachings of the ancient thinkers Laozi and Zhuangzi, but is vastly different in the religion, where Dao gives rise to the One, which unfolds into three *qi* or cosmic energies, called the mysterious, beginning, and primordial. These, in turn, coagulate to bring forth the first god, the deity Laozi, personification of Dao.

Coagulating further, the same energies also produce a series of nine heavens, a number of other deities (as, for example, the Queen Mother of the West as representative of pure yin), and a canon of sacred scriptures which contain, in essential and celestial form, the teachings the world will need to be created. Before, therefore, the world ever comes into existence, there is a level of manifest divinity, found in the heavens, the gods, and the scriptures, which are neither beyond sensory experience and verbal expression as Dao itself nor yet manifest in the world. Mediating chaos and creation, they represent a pure level of Dao-existence, from which human life springs and to which it will return. Dao, as apparent on this mythical level, is a willful agent that is no longer a spontaneous "flow of life" but gives a soteriological dimension to the creation. The mystical quest accordingly goes beyond the attainment of harmony with the cosmos, however encompassing, to the transcendence of the world in a state of immortality in the celestial realm.[44]

Wisdom. Wisdom in the classical texts and later interpretation of the two traditions appears similarly different. Confucians emphasize the acquisition of wisdom through learning and its practical realization in benevolence and social harmony, striving for the perfect equilibrium of forces and energies.[45] They begin with inherent intelligence, whose training leads to sincerity. Sincerity in turn brings forth an equilibrium, which results in an overarching harmony that radiates brilliantly from the person to the community and into the world, bringing "happy order" to Heaven and Earth. Daoists, on the contrary, find Heaven and Earth in their own body and see the five phases of the larger universe as spirits in the five *qi*-storing organs (liver, heart, spleen, lungs, kidneys). Practic-

---

[44] Kohn, *Daoism and Chinese Culture*, 89-90.

[45] Ching, *To Accumulate Wisdom*, 15.

ing controlled breathing, they balance the different powers on a microcosmic level and find the One in themselves to then reach out to the celestial spheres.[46]

As wisdom and a sense of harmony in Confucianism are acquired through learning, an intellectual effort that is based on the classics, the goals and means of the practice are always described in words. The tradition acknowledges that some words are better than others but never reaches the point of denying their potential or use. Not so the Daoists. They, in both the classical and religious traditions, place a high emphasis on the ineffability of Dao. Zhuangzi in his famous chapter on "Making All Things Equal" even denies any applicability of words whatsoever.[47] Words to Daoists are just sounds, made meaningful only by convention. Dependent on opposites, they are eternally relative and therefore nowhere near the truth. Valuing silence highest, Daoists describe their creed as the "teaching without words," and follow the statement of the *Daode jing*: "Who speaks does not know, and who knows does not speak."[48] As a result, the state of oneness with Dao is explained in paradoxes and by redefining words in spiraling circles, taking the adept's consciousness to ever more formless and ineffable levels, until is dissolves in utter serenity.[49]

The Self. The self in mystical experience is similarly verbalized and conscious in the Confucian tradition and ineffable and formless in Daoism, where mythological figures are called upon to replace words in giving expression to its transformation.[50] An individualized aspect of the Great Ultimate, the self in Neo-Confucianism is linked to the origins in its inherent "mind of Heaven," which has to be freed from attachments to externals and focused back on stillness and sincerity. As Confucian auto-biographies document, this process is a conscious search that takes place as part of a government career which leaves room for serious practice after hours and between official posting and never necessitates the complete withdrawal from society. Inspired by readings and verbal teachings, the conscious mind is led to give certain interpretations to the

---

[46] Livia Kohn, "Taoist Visions of the Body." *Journal of Chinese Philosophy* 18 (1991), 227-52.

[47] See Burton Watson, *The Complete Works of Chuang-tzu* (New York: Columbia University Press, 1968), 41.

[48] *Daode jing*, ch. 81.

[49] A good example of the mystical use of language in Daoism is found in the medieval *Xisheng jing* (Scripture of Western Ascension), which purports to contain Laozi's oral instructions at the time of *Daode jing* transmission. For a translation and study, see Livia Kohn, *Daoist Mystical Philosophy: The Scripture of Western Ascension* (Albany: State University of New York Press, 19991).

[50] A study of the different aspects of the self is found in Livia Kohn, "Selfhood and Spontaneity in Ancient Chinese Thought," In *Selves, People, and Persons,* edited by Leroy Rouner (South Bend, IN: University of Notre Dame Press, Boston University Series in Philosophy and Religion, vol. 13, 1992), 123-38.

world, as for example, "in reality there is not a single thing," and accordingly finds harmony in its social environment.[51]

The Daoist self, on the other hand, is transformed into celestial dimensions after it is first seen as consisting of several contradictory forces—seven material or yin souls matching three spiritual or yang souls, plus various celestial deities of the pure Dao and demonic parasites known as the three worms—which pull it into opposite directions, yin toward instinct satisfaction, sensuality, and darkness; yang toward intellectual endeavors, spirituality, and light.[52] Through control of the yin impulses and the destruction of inner demons, the adept's inner nature is changed into pure yang. Then the celestials, notably the Three Ones, can come to occupy all thinking and feeling by being constantly visualized in the energy centers or elixir fields of head, chest, and abdomen.[53] The body, a microcosm of the created world, is transformed into a replica of the heavens, the gods, and the scriptures that reside before the creation of the material universe. Adept in the process become denizens of the empyrean, leaving behind the perfection of naturalness in the attainment of celestial purity.

Mystical Training. Mystical training differs accordingly. Centered on the five virtues (honesty, propriety, wisdom, benevolence, and righteousness) and their proper feelings, Confucians are guided to see the inherent principle of universal oneness in their body and mind, and from there expand it into the family, community, and wider world.[54] As the virtues, among which humanity or benevolence is first, are realized, all selfish impulses are overcome and the mind becomes identical with the impartiality of Heaven. A harmonious life in the world is possible, and the world itself finds perfect balance.[55]

Daoists, in their turn, undertake mystical training not within family and society but in a monastic setting that separates them from the concerns of everyday life. They live in establishments tucked far away in remote mountain areas and set up to replicate the wondrous world of the immortals, wear formalized ritual garments, adapt a simple vegetarian diet combined with regular peri-

---

[51] See Rodney Taylor, "The Centered Self: Religious Autobiography in the Neo-Confucian Tradition," *History of Religions* 17 (1978), 255-283; *The Religious Dimensions of Confucianism* (Albany: State University of New York Press, 1990).

[52] A discussion of the various souls and their impact on the body-mind in Daoism appears in Livia Kohn, "Yin and Yang: The Natural Dimension of Evil," in *Philosophies of Nature: The Human Dimension*, edited by Robert S. Cohen and Alfred I. Tauber (New York: Kluwer Academic Publishers, Boston Studies in the Philosophy of Science, 1997), 89-104.

[53] The specific method of visualizing the Three Ones, with a detailed description of their looks and garb and the incantations necessary for their activation is translated in Poul Andersen, *The Method of Holding the Three Ones* (London: Curzon Press, 1980).

[54] A detailed discussion of the virtues in Confucian self-cultivation is found in Wing-tsit Chan, *Neo Confucian Terms Explained* (New York: Columbia University Press, 1986), 177-79.

[55] See Philip J. Ivanhoe, *Confucian Moral Self-Cultivation* (New York: Peter Lang, 1993).

ods of fasting, and follow a strict ritual schedule that denies normal patterns of waking and sleeping.[56] They vow to obey sets of precepts that also include Confucian values, but rather than cultivating specific virtues, they strife for an overall harmony with the natural forces. In their practice, moreover, they think less of the social impact—although that will eventually follow—but focus on their physical bodies, which they see as the primary residence of the gods, nurturing them with herbal remedies instead of the rich foods of the world. In place of man-made structures, they engage actively with physical nature, close to mountains and streams, boulders and grottoes, while yet maintaining a strong cosmic awareness and visualizing celestial palaces both in the body and in the stars.

Ethics and Community. Directly related to this aspect of mystical training is the nature of community and ethics, being highly hierarchical and family-centered in Confucianism, and more egalitarian and universal in Daoism. Confucian specialist communities, preparatory to life in society, are academies where the classics are read and thoughts are developed in active contemplation. Their rules include proper reverence for elders, awareness of hierarchies, and abstention from harmful social actions. As the Neo-Confucian thinker Dai Zhen (1723-1777) says: "When a person is neither selfish nor beclouded, his mind is pure and clear; this is a state of supreme illumination. When a mind is still and does not move, it is pure and attains the perfection of heavenly virtue."[57]

Daoist communities, in comparison, are religious organizations, dedicated under Mahayana influence to the universal salvation of all beings. Thus community rules here imitate the Buddhist precepts, emphasizing the restraint of baser appetites, and often focus on the purity of the body attained through the retention of the gods within. In addition, they guide adepts to give proper veneration to sacred locations and objects and threaten punishments in mythological form as tortures in the various hells.

As regards the practice that goes on in these centers, Confucians aside from reading the classics and pondering the oneness of the universe, engage in a form of meditation called quiet-sitting, essentially contemplation that aims at stilling the mind and making it into a mirror that reflects but does not act on its own.[58] Without cutting off social relationships and responsibilities, practitioners

---

[56] See Livia Kohn, *Monastic Life in Medieval Daoism: A Cross-Cultural Perspective* (Honolulu: University of Hawaii Press, 2003).

[57] Chung-ying Cheng, *Tai Chen's Inquiry into Goodness* (Honolulu: East-West Center Press, 1971), 106. For more details on Confucian rules for mystical training, see the Korean interpretation of Zhu Xi's guidelines translated in Michael Kalton, *To Become a Sage: The Ten Diagrams on Sage Learning by Yi T'oegye* (New York: Columbia University Press, 1988).

[58] For an outline of traditional Confucian practice, see Chan, *Neo Confucian Terms Explained.* For contemporary forms of Confucian meditation, see Rodney Taylor, *The Confucian Way of*

develop a pure and reflecting mind and thereby lose all selfish impulses in favor of a calm and impartial response to the world. Anger and happiness in this context are accepted as part of the natural response and encouraged to occur at right times.

Daoists, again more Heaven-oriented, have a much larger variety of practices. They begin with a change in diet and daily habits, then perform various physical and breathing exercises to open up the *qi*-channels in the body and activate the energy centers in the five organs. These practices tend to combine slow body movements with deep breathing, and a keen mental awareness. They go back far; in Chinese they are nowadays known under the name of Qigong.[59]

Beyond that, Daoists engage in more cosmically centered meditations, visualizing the five cosmic energies as they appear in their characteristic colors in the five organs and thus relating the body actively to the heavenly spheres. They also imagine deities in the body such as the Three Ones who, often in the form of infants and clad in luscious brocades, reside in the inner palaces and bestow health, harmony, and celestial empowerment on the practitioner. Externalizing these gods, Daoists further visualize them as outside entities, from whom they can acquire valuable knowledge or celestial energies. In yet another form of Daoist practice, adepts refine their bodies to heavenly purity in a quasi-alchemical process, seeing the yin and yang energies of the body as the lead and mercury of the crucible and concocting a cinnabar elixir, the pearl of immortality, within. This pearl eventually grows into an immortal embryo, the spirit alter ego of the practitioner, allowing him or her to leave the body behind and traverse the heavens in utter freedom. As the body falls away in death, this spirit entity survives and the practictioner becomes a celestial being, living forever and attaining a celestial form of oneness with Dao.

The Ideal Human. Anyone having attained the goal of the tradition becomes a master, an ideal human being in the Confucian tradition and a celestial sage or heavenly perfected in the Daoist vision. The Confucian gentleman (*junzi*) is characterized as highly virtuous and eminently learned, a paragon of benevolence and filial piety, who knows all about ceremonies and music and can explain the truth of cosmic harmony with ease and simplicity. As described in a Neo-Confucian document, "he is as pure as pure gold, and as mild and

---

Contemplation: Okada Takehiko and the Tradition of Quiet-Sitting (Columbia: University of South Carolina Press, 1988).

[59] A good overview of Qigong as practiced today is found in Kenneth S. Cohen, *The Way of Qigong: The Art and Science of Chinese Energy Healing* (New York: Ballantine, 1997). Traditionally it goes back to a practice called *daoyin* (lit. "guiding the *qi* and stretching the body"), discussed in depth in Livia Kohn, *Chinese Healing Exercises: The Tradition of Daoyin* (Honolulu: University of Hawaii Press, 2008). The martial art of Taiji quan is often also practiced in a similar healing and self-awareness manner and has been adopted in many Daoist establishments today. For a discussion, see Kohn, *Health and Long Life*, 191-202.

lovable as excellent jade. Liberal but not irregular, he maintains harmony with others but does not drift with them. His conscientiousness and sincerity penetrate metal and stone, and his filial piety and brotherly respect influence all beings.[60]

The Daoist sage (*shengren*) or perfected (*zhenren*) has similarly characteristics but more dominantly is a heavenly being with no explicit teachings who acts in complete nonaction among people. Moving along with the currents of the world, he or she neither supports nor hinders but gives free rein to the currents of life and lets things take their natural course. Never claiming to know or be able to do anything, the accomplished Daoist simply floats through in the world as a ray of pure heavenly light, shining widely and transforming all without active intention.[61] As the *Daode jing* says: "The sage does not act and so does not ruin; he does not grasp and so does not lose;"[62] and: "He always helps people and rejects none; always helps all beings and rejects none."[63] This is called practicing brightness.

Despite these differences, both traditions emphasize the importance of microcosmic perfection in macrocosmic reality and claim the transformative powers of the accomplished mystic in society at large. The goal, however much the Daoists may emphasize Heaven, is ultimately the transformation of earth, seen here as the establishment of a celestial kingdom on earth, a state that both contains and transcends the happy order of Confucianism.

Mystical Union. Mystical union, finally, as celebrated in the traditions, reflects once more their fundamental difference as inherent versus transcendent. Confucians hope to "regard Heaven, Earth, and the myriad things as one body, the world as one family and the country as one person." They come to "form one body with Heaven, Earth, and the myriad beings," seeing "all people as their brothers and sisters, and all things as their companions." [64] The underlying oneness of the cosmos is fully realized in the mystics'mindsas they become impartial and pure in their relationship to all. Joining all creatures in celestial oneness, they have empathy for all and give selflessly everywhere. Their own person one with the family, the community, the world, and the cosmos,

---

[60] Wing-tsit Chan, *Reflections on Things at Hand: The Neo-Confucian Anthology Compiled by Chu Hsi and Lü Tsu-ch'ien* (New York: Columbia University Press, 1967), 299.

[61] See Livia Kohn, "The Sage in the World, the Perfected without Feelings: Mysticism and Moral Responsibility in Chinese Religion," in *Crossing Boundaries: Essays on the Ethical Status of Mysticism*, edited by G. William Barnard and Jeffrey J. Kripal (New York: Seven Bridges Press, 2002), 288-306.

[62] *Daode jing*, ch. 64.

[63] *Daode jing*, ch. 27.

[64] Wing-tsit Chan, *Instructions for Practical Living and Other Neo-Confucian Writings by Wang Yang-ming* (New York: Columbia University Press, 1963), 272-74.

they naturally radiate bright virtue, spreading benevolence and goodness wherever they go.

Daoist mystics, on the contrary, after living out an extended lifespan as sages or perfected on earth, find complete realization in a triumphant ascent to the heavens. Having realized the cosmos within, they ride into the empyrean on cloudy chariots drawn by a quadriga of dragons, encountering pure divinities of Dao and joining splendid banquets in the celestial palaces.[65] As the Tang poet Wu Yun (d. 778) has it:

> The emperor of the Great One settles in my heart;
> As streaming light pours from my elixir field.
> The gods, like Non Radiance and Lord Peach,
> Chant brightly from the chapters of long life.
> My six viscera glow with luminous morning light;
> My hundred joints are like a net of purple mist.
> My whirlwind carriage traverses endless space:
> Slow and steady, I rise on light itself.[66]

Watching phoenixes and unicorns dance to spheric music, they enjoy the eternal freedom of the pure spirit; at one with Dao in its first creative stage and partaking of its powers, they can live forever, appear and disappear at will, be in numerous places at once, and reverse the course of nature.[67] Still dedicated to universal salvation, they then use their new power and position to administer celestial justice and, almost in bodhisattva fashion, aid humanity in its plight. Having become gods, Daoist mystics are beyond the world and yet for it, personifications of the purity of Heaven and the creative powers of Dao.

Conclusion

Chinese mysticism in its various forms always focuses on the attainment of oneness with Heaven and Earth, is centered on the body-mind of the living individual, has a strong social and political dimension, and relates to an underly-

---

[65] Poetic descriptions of the ecstatic flight of the Daoist mystic are first found in ancient shamanic songs, then in medieval poetry. See David Hawkes, *Ch'u Tz'u: The Songs of the South* (Oxford: Clarendon Press, 1959); Donald Holzman, *Poetry and Politics: The Life and Works of Juan Chi (210-263)* (Cambridge: Cambridge University Press, 1976).

[66] Wu Yun, *Buxuci* (Songs on Pacing the Void, author's rendition. See Edward H. Schafer, "Wu Yün's 'Cantos on Pacing the Void'," *Harvard Journal of Asiatic Studies* 41 (1981), 377-415.

[67] Detailed descriptions of ideal Daoists, their activities and powers are found in a collection of immortals' biographies from the 4th century. See Robert F. Campany, *To Live As Long As Heaven and Earth: A Translation and Study of Ge Hong's Traditions of Divine Transcendents* (Berkeley: University of California Press 2002).

ing force of multiple divinities rather than a single creator god. In its indigenous mode, it comes in two major traditions: Confucian and Daoist, which have undergone parallel phases of historical development, are deeply indebted to Buddhism, and served Chinese society widely with their vision.

Classified traditionally in the complementary system of yin and yang, Confucian self-realization is the more outward-going, society-oriented, politically active form, achieved through conscious learning and the steadfast practice of essentially communal virtues. Daoist perfection, on the other hand, is more transcendent and deeply steeped in myth. It, too, begins with the individual and encourages ethical conduct and social responsibility, but in its higher stages focuses on venerating revealed scriptures, connecting to divine entities, ecstatically traveling to otherworldly realms, and ultimately going completely beyond the limitations of human life and world. Both traditions are eager to contribute to a greater sense of wholeness of the person, to peace and harmony in the world, and to a sense of cosmic integration and oneness. They start from a positive, life-affirming outlook and encourage being in the world, making a contribution to society, and finding happiness in this life. Yet they also retain a sense of a greater reality beyond, of a connection to higher cosmic realities, and express the strong urge to reach for the ultimate, for a life in oneness with Heaven and Earth.

6. God of Moses versus the "One and All" of Egypt

From Magic of Hypostatized Spirituality to Discriminating Paradigm of Non-Idolatry

Alex S. Kohav[1]

Abstract

The essay evaluates the significance and import of such otherwise loaded terms as "magic" and "idolatry." It offers an examination of respective uses of language in ancient Egypt and Israel (pictorial hieroglyphs versus alphabet-based); juxtaposition of deified human rulers and hypostasized spiritual entities against exclusive worship of a single, ineffable, and highest-scalar God; and notions such as cosmotheism (either "one-nature"-based polytheism or "one-nature"-based monotheism) versus monotheism of a "beyond-nature" sole deity; and assesses the distinction between "I am all that is" and "I am who I am." Both religions are seen as assuming positions along a selfsame mystical-transformational axis but at the axis's opposite ends. The extreme polarity between Egypt's and Israel's key religious stances is then noted semiotically: if Egypt's sensibility is iconic and symbolic pointing to strategies of ritualized imbuing of objects and ideas as symbols with supernatural significance, the Pentateuch's esoteric "second channel" (posited by the author) is allegorical and indexical pointing to direct, experiential knowledge of "God." The God of Israel represents an unprecedented third kind of linguistic transitivity—neither external nor internal intrinsically but one that is simultaneously external and internal vis-à-vis human subjectivity—altering humanity's "semantic organization of experience" (Halliday). In a radical departure from the realm of the imaginary, the symbolic, and the fantastic—the realm of "images," that is, symbols, archetypes, and psychic powers whose potency, however, was not in dispute—Israel's novel religion insisted that consciousness such as that of Egypt entailed divinization of that which is not divine, or God, thus amounting to idolatry and magic. The essay in

---

[1] This is a significantly revised and expanded version of an extended excerpt from my book, *The* Sôd *Hypothesis: Phenomenological, Cognitive, Semiotic, and Noetic-Literary Recovery of the Pentateuch's Embedded Inner-Core Mystical Initiation Tradition of Ancient Israelite Cultic Religion* (Boulder, CO: MaKoM Publications, 2013). Published with permission.

effect offers qualitative, value-weighted assessment of vital dissimilarities between two distinct, ancient traditions, both of which evidenced significant mystical alterations of consciousness.

> The encounter—or shock—between civilizations is always, in the last resort, an encounter between spiritualities—between religions.
> —Mircea Eliade, *The Two and the One*

> Religions . . . have come, through the centuries, to set different priorities, different techniques, different goals, different values for the enterprise and worth of being human. Thus the exegeses, which issue eventually in different religious systems, are profoundly different.
> —John Bowker, *The Sense of God*

> Religious people used to take for granted that other religions were simply wrong. Then it became fashionable to suppose that all the great religions agree on essentials. This claim, like other dogmas, was not examined closely in the light of facts. . . . One refuses to see the major religions as alternatives that challenge us to make a choice.
> —Walter Kaufmann, *Religions in Four Dimensions*

I. Introduction: Qādôš versus Sacer[2]

Given that all religions partake of the "sacred" or even may fully consist of it and represent it, and given that we now know—thanks to recent advances in neurobiology, consciousness studies, and cognitive science, among other fields—that practically all religious manifestations and experiences, including bona fide mystical ones, entail alterations of consciousness of one sort or another, is there therefore any reason to critique some of them but commend others? Is there or could there be any substantive or qualitative, value-weighted difference among them? Given the profound doctrinal confrontations between ancient Israel and Egypt, everything that hangs in the balance of their dichotomous beliefs and praxes will be resolved based on the answer to that question, and none more important than our ability to grasp their beliefs' respective meanings and significance.

The anthropologist Roy Rappaport has perhaps most sophisticatedly unpacked the complex conception, capturing, in a general sense, what we might call the "holy":

[2] I want to acknowledge Naomi S. S. Jacobs for helpful critique and comments on an earlier draft of this essay.

> The term [religion] denotes the domain of the Holy, the constituents of which include the sacred, the numinous, the occult and the divine, and also ritual, the form of action in which those constituents are generated. . . . The term "sacred" signifies the discursive aspect of religion, that which is or can be expressed in language, whereas "numinous" denotes religion's non-discursive, affective, ineffable qualities. The term "occult" refers to religion's peculiar efficacious capabilities . . . and "divine" . . . signif[ies] its spiritual referents. The term "holy" . . . is distinguished here from "sacred" and will be reserved for the total religious phenomenon, the integration of its four elements which, I will argue, is achieved in ritual.[3]

Are all religions, all spiritualities, and all mysticisms the same—or even just similar—as is still frequently claimed? In the ancient world, the answer certainly seemed to be yes:

> The growing political and commercial interconnectedness of the ancient world and the practice of cross-cultural translation of everything including divine names gradually led to the concept of common religion. The argument runs as follows: Peoples, Cultures, and political systems may be different. But as long as they have a religion and worship some definite and identifiable gods, they are comparable and contactable because these gods must necessarily be the same as those worshipped by other nations but under different names. The names, iconographies, and rites—in short, the cultures—differ, but the gods are the same. This concept of religion as the common background of cultural diversity and the principle of cultural translatability eventually led to the late Hellenistic mentality for which the names of the gods mattered little in view of the overwhelming natural evidence of their existence, and it was this mentality of Late Antiquity that the Deism of the seventeenth and eighteenth centuries returned to.[4]

Yet as Rappaport's composite concept of the holy entails, things can be extremely divergent depending on which aspect is emphasized in any specific religion or spiritual endeavor, what is devalued or omitted entirely, or what is left "unguided":

---

[3] Roy Rappaport, *Ritual and Religion in the Making of Humanity* (Cambridge: Cambridge University Press, 1999), 23-24.

[4] Jan Assmann, *Moses the Egyptian: The Memory of Egypt in Western Monotheism* (Cambridge, MA: Harvard University Press, 1997), 46-47, emphasis added. It is the same mentality that governs the New Ageism of our own times; cf. Wouter J. Hanegraaff, *New Age Religion and Western Culture: Esotericism in the Mirror of Secular Thought* (Albany: State University of New York Press, 1998). It is also a source of anthropology's current overreaction that makes practically all cross-cultural comparisons suspect.

> In the absence of the numinous the sacred is cut off from human feeling, and is not only devoid of vitality but alienated from human need. In the absence of the sacred the numinous is inchoate and may even become demonic. The unguided numinous, numinousness unfocused upon Ultimate Sacred Postulates, in glorifying experience, sensation and exultation themselves, not only does not sustain communitas, it encourages excess, narcissism, disengagement and hedonism. But even the conjunction of numinous experience and Ultimate Sacred Postulates is no guarantee of beneficence. The numinousness of the [Nazi] Nuremberg rallies should never be forgotten . . . the sacred may be degraded, the numinous deluded, the Holy broken.[5]

Indeed, even Nazism can be seen as being spiritual, albeit as "spiritual pathology."[6] The elusive issue here is the following fundamental idiosyncrasy: While the word for holy in Hebrew, qādôš, stands for "separate," or "set apart," and therefore, it would seem, is quite similar to or even identical with the corresponding Latin term *sacer*, it is nonetheless profoundly dissimilar from the latter.[7] The *sacer* is a notion that embraces all kinds of spiritualities and religious-mystical systems and traditions, requiring only that the *sacer* item in question not belong to the profanus. The Hebrew kadosh, in contrast, refers only to the *sacer* that is not idolatrous—a requirement that is easy enough to declare but exceedingly difficult to grasp. Anything is idolatrous if it is worshipped, divinized, deified, or venerated, yet is something other than "God."

The question of origins and the enduring enigma of ancient Israelite civilization, despite millennia of scrutiny of its written record—generally known as the Hebrew Bible or the Old Testament[8]—and its attendant disproportionate influence on humanity at large is still mired in controversy and opacity. This atypical civilization introduced, circa 1000 BCE,[9] several wholly original no-

---

[5] Rappaport, *Ritual and Religion*, 404, emphasis added.

[6] See, e. g., Harry Hunt, "'Triumph of the Will': Heidegger's Nazism as Spiritual Pathology," *Journal of Mind and Behavior* 19, no. 4 (1998): 379-414. See also my "Adam's Choice: Spirituality as either Self-Divinization Metapathology or Encounter with the Absolute Other," paper presented at "Consciousness and Spirit," Annual Meeting of the Society for Anthropology of Consciousness, School of Divinity, Yale University, March 19-23, 2008.

[7] The *sacer*—distinguished and delimited by its contrary, the *profanus*—necessarily encompasses, within itself, differing and even conflicting multiple aspects. If *profanus* marks our ordinary, indeed profane, or "consensus" reality and/or its constituents, then *sacer* is that which signifies the nonordinary and the not-mundane. It is that which exalts the human spirit in a way that *profanus* never can. It can manifest itself as a place, a thing, an idea, or a state of being—or as a being, including certain "marked" human beings.

[8] Technically, the Old Testament is not exactly the same as the Hebrew Bible; among other things, the former contains material such as Judith and Tobit, that is absent in the latter.

[9] For a dating that is sensitive to a broad context, see Frank Moore Cross, *From Epic to Canon: History and Literature in Ancient Israel* (Baltimore: Johns Hopkins University Press, 1998).

tions, such as the existence of only one god,[10] who is the creator of all reality[11] and is neither transcendent nor immanent (the latter, for example, indicating a manifestation in or as nature).[12] Instead of the binary opposition "transcendent/immanent"—which came into usage in medieval times—the ancient Israelite religion conceives a generally overlooked yet crucial and unprecedented feature.

Cross speaks of "evidence, preserved in epic, of Israelite connections with the peoples of the south who moved between Se'ir, Midian, and Egypt at the end of the Late Bronze Age [i.e., prior to 1,200 BCE] and the beginning of the Iron Age [post-1,200 BCE]" (51). I have used above the word *introduced* yet do not mean by it the date when the Pentateuch might have been committed to writing; most biblical scholars consider the latter to have taken place between 722 BCE and 587 BCE. It stands to reason that the mystical-experiential impetus for the birth of ancient Israelite religion likely originated centuries prior to the actual composing of the Pentateuch.

[10] Several earlier and later instances of a notion of oneness of the supreme deity might be mentioned here: one in Egypt, the other possibly in Babylon, while a Greek variation, almost half a millennium subsequent to Israel's First Temple's demise, involves the pre-Socratic philosopher Parmenides and, almost a millennium after Parmenides, Plotinus. Only the Egyptian precedent preceding the full-fledged Israelite paradigm shift will be briefly noted here, since it helps to highlight the distinctions involved when such occurrences are sometimes mistakenly conflated. The so-called Amarna texts reference the rule of Akhenaten, Pharaoh Amenophis IV in the 14th century BCE, indicating a brief period of Akhenaten's rule. Akhenaten abolished the traditional Egyptian beliefs and instituted a cult of Amun-Re, "the hidden god, whose symbols, images, and names are the many gods," Assmann, *Moses the Egyptian*, 194. "It is this last aspect of Amun's Oneness," comments Assmann, "that is of particular interest . . . because it is so closely related to the idea of esoteric monotheism and the 'god of the mysteries'" (ibid.). However, the reason for the very appearance of and the need for the "Mosaic distinction"—the latter a term that Assmann introduced himself—is the Mosaic rejection of the notion of an all-pervading, permeating presence of the "one" deity *in the manifested world* (of which the sun is a prime example, and "sun-god" is a key designation of Amun-Re). Equally if not more important is the extreme brevity of Akhenaten's rule, after which the cult of Amun-Re was removed as violently as it had been installed earlier. The Amarna experiment represented a marked aberration in the millennia-long Egyptian history and its traditional religious sensibilities and therefore cannot be seen as an *Egyptian* innovation, much less as a part of Egyptian tradition per se.

[11] The uncompromising Israelite monotheism sometimes causes difficulty for those who see unmistakable indications of monolatry—that is, worship of God without necessarily excluding the reality of other gods—in the Hebrew Bible itself and even in its key commandment, "No other gods before me"; why command this if "other gods" do not exist? Yet the Hebrew Bible's denial of other gods and its insistence on their spuriousness can be seen simply as recognition that even false or nonexistent gods can influence their adherents' minds.

[12] I use the term *transcendent* here in its customary sense in religious-theological and philosophical literature, to be distinguished from a very different usage of *transcendental* in philosophy following Kant (who incidentally strongly disparaged that which the designation *transcendent* stands for). In contrast to the novel Hebraic stance, the traditional Egyptian religion has emphasized the divine *in nature*, and especially *divine as nature* or reality, as we shall see.

This feature—which I am judging to be the foremost mark of Israel's God—is rare in its paradigmatic originality, since it denotes a sharp distinction between Israel's God and possibly all other conceptions of deities. This singular divergence from the more typical models of the divine goes further than the likewise unparalleled stance related to monotheism, namely, Israel's other paradigmatic originality, apropos monotheism on a universal—as opposed to the national or individual—scale. The even more significant characteristic I have in mind is related to what is called "transitivity" in linguistics.[13] Linguistic transitivity's most prominent advocate has been the founder of functional linguistics, M. A. K. Halliday, who categorizes it as "the cornerstone of the semantic organization of experience":

> Transitivity is the set of options whereby the speaker encodes his experience of the processes of the external world, and of the internal world of his consciousness, together with the participants in these and their attendant circumstances; and it embodies a very basic distinction of processes into two types, those that are regarded as due to an external cause, an agency other than the person or object involved, and those that are not.[14]

The "external cause" of the first transitive type specified by Halliday reflects the archaic humanity that was steeped in a worldview of objects and forces external to and acting on the human being. The second transitive type is the gradual emergence of human agency and self-sufficiency (it reaches its apogee in the rationalistic viewpoint of modern sciences eschewing any supranatural constitution of reality). In a sometimes desperate search for explanations of life's and the world's mysteries, people early on challenged this gradually emerging second transitive type by powerfully strengthening the first-type transitivity, which was in effect a relapse but on a somewhat higher level of the evolutionary spiral, as it were. It took place by way of endowing the world with magical properties and by populating it with mysterious forces and ghostlike beings including, at the upper end of the paranormal hierarchy, a great variety of gods.

The essential point I wish to convey here is that these gods, as a rule, were seen as fully belonging to the world, notwithstanding their deific status; that is, the gods were seen as being external to human interiority, yet there was no conception of "transcendence" in play that could, at least in some cases,

---

[13] Linguistic transitivity is distinct from the notion of transitivity in philosophy (logic) and mathematics.

[14] M. A. K. Halliday, "Linguistic Function and Literary Style: An Inquiry into the Language of William Golding's *The Inheritors*," in *The Stylistics Reader: From Roman Jakobson to the Present*, ed. Jean Jacques Weber (1971; London: Hodder Education Publishers, 1996), 56-86, here 81.

place the gods outside the immanent reality that human beings inhabit. Whether it is the case of Greek gods living atop Mount Olympus and looking and acting much like human beings do, sometimes quite hilariously so, or the Egyptian deities, some of whom, such as Osiris and Isis, likewise mimicked humans, while others were symbolized either by natural celestial bodies such as the sun or by certain animals, among them the crocodile.[15] It was simply unimaginable that any entity whatsoever could have its being outside "reality" as it was conceived by human beings, and not even gods could escape this worldly reality that human beings were born into. Such a sensibility of vivifying, animating the world would become a permanent feature of human psychology, a feature caused by the insatiable craving of humans to supply reasons and causes, and thus meaning, to an otherwise often inscrutable reality.[16]

We must examine the remarkable Israelite difference with this context in mind. The Pentateuch's overarching transitivity frame, in contrast to the two transitivity paradigms (one exterior, the other interior) discussed above, entails a third transitive type, one in which a supreme or ultimate agency—depicted as the God of Israel and the God of the whole of creation—that is simultaneously external and internal vis-à-vis human being's subjectivity. This god—differentiated as God—is emphatically unrelated to what James Paxson calls "metamorphic translations among ontological categories,"[17] such as reification or magical ensoulment of objects and entities belonging to the natural world.

---

[15] The specific examples of crocodile and serpent with the hawk's head will be detailed later, including the significance of such symbolization of deities.

[16] As a recent *New York Times* article by a well-known psychologist asserted, "We can't overcome magical thinking. It is part of our evolved psychology," Nathan C. DeWall, "Magic May Lurk inside Us All," *New York Times*, October 28, 2014, D5. Spinoza indulges in sarcasm in the appendix to the first part of his *Ethics*, when he extends human craving to imagining "that the gods direct all things for the use of men in order to bind men to them and be held by men in the highest honor," Benedict de Spinoza, *Ethics*, trl. Edwin Curley (1677; London: Penguin, 1996), 27.

[17] Paxson differentiates among the following: "substantialization, materialization, hypostasization, or the figural translation of any non-corporeal quantity into a physical, corporeal one; anthropomorphism, or the figural translation of any non-human quantity into a character that has human form; personification (prosopopeia), or the translation of any non-human quantity into a sentient human capable of thought and language, possessing voice and face. These definitions themselves break down into subsets that can operate separately or combine as figural hybrids: animification, or the figural translation of (1) a human agent into an animal, or of (2) an abstraction or inanimate object into an animal. . . . [R]eification (pragmapeia), or, if you will, 'dispersonification'—the translation of a human agent into an inanimate thing. . . . Thematically, these two tropes are related to: ideation, or the translation of a thing or human agent into an abstract idea, essence, spirit, or rarefied form. ('Rarefication,' in fact, often fits as a good synonym.) [T]opification, or the translation of an abstraction into a geographical locus." *The Poetics of Personification* (Cambridge: Cambridge University Press, 1994), 42-43.

The Mosaic religion of ancient Israel forcefully rejects the first transitive type's tendency to inflame its imaginative faculties in the direction of a magical outlook. It also severely tests, and at the same time contests, the second transitive type—one that tends to become inflamed by the dream of human self-sufficiency and power.

This Hebraic God is concealed, inaccessible, unimaginable, incomparable. Even so, God is closely involved with the world of human beings, both externally in the world per se and internally within human consciousness, freely reading (and sometimes implanting!) human thoughts, desires, and intentions. The third transitivity claimed here for Israel's God is bound to mean—if one thinks this through—that God "is" entirely outside our reality, or immanent reality, yet has free access to it. Seen this way, to keep insistently asking, "Does God exist?" is patently senseless, since God "is" outside existence as we know it. This God is without form and must not be depicted as any shape or object, living or inanimate. Crucially, the foundational Hebraic or ancient Israelite religion designated any attempt to the contrary as "idolatry." Moreover, it branded the prevalent popular perceptions of divinity-infused nature—then as now, often seen as the natural habitat and domain of gods or God or, in today's parlance, the dominion of "spirituality"—as pantheism. It also pressed curious, confusing, wholly original notions such as its conception of the "holy" and its utter abhorrence of magic.

Such an uncompromising stance—a determined, total rejection of magic—would have been quite deplorable in the minds of both ordinary Israelites of that time and all neighboring peoples: the ancient mind often relied on magic in its search for meaning.[18] It must surely be surprising that such a totalizing antimagical stance is likewise objectionable to our modern humanity today: magic is everywhere experiencing a massive resurgence, whether in the popular movies or even directly within the postbiblical religions.[19]

A magical mind-set, as noted above, is, if not a default position of human consciousness complementing human aspiration for autonomy, that is, self-sufficiency, independence, then one always already lying in wait just beneath the conventional consciousness of our daily exertions in the business of living. It is against this mind-set that the Mosaic religion of ancient Israel enunciated an implacable struggle. This struggle has apparently been lost, at least so far. The

---

[18] See, especially, Ori Z. Soltes, *Magic and Religion in the Greco-Roman World: The Beginnings of Judaism and Christianity* (Boulder, CO: Academia-West Press, 2017).

[19] Victoria Nelson speaks of the ever-present yearning for a magical worldview—as well as for "the divinization of the human," *The Secret Life of Puppets* (Cambridge, MA: Harvard University Press, 2001), ix. This is precisely what the "Mosaic distinction," discussed throughout this essay, revolted against. In her book, Nelson traces the by-now-widespread phenomenon, one that can only be labeled, in terms of the concerns of the present essay, as "the return of magical consciousness."

signs of magic's resurgence and its infiltration of Judaism itself are already unmistakable by the time of emergence of rabbinical Judaism (post-Second Temple era), perhaps even as early as the Second Jerusalem Temple period (516 BCE-70 CE).

Rabbinical Judaism's reintroduction of magical notions, however, including in its particular theology and praxis—as for example in Hassidism and among the ultra-Orthodox today—is outside the scope of the present essay.[20] The focus here, instead, is on the unrelenting struggle of the newly born Hebraic-Israelite religion, with what may be termed magical consciousness, which Egypt vigorously represented:

> The Biblical image of Egypt means "idolatry." It symbolizes what "the Mosaic distinction" excluded as the opposite of truth in religion. By drawing this distinction, "Moses" cut the umbilical cord which connected his people and his religious ideas to their cultural and natural context. The Egypt of the Bible symbolizes what is rejected, discarded, and abandoned. Egypt is not just a historical context: it is inscribed in the fundamental semantics of monotheism. It appears explicitly in the first commandment and implicitly in the second. . . . Egypt's role in the Exodus is not historical but mythical: it helps define the very identity of those who tell the story. Egypt is the womb from which the chosen people emerged, but the umbilical cord was cut once and for all by the Mosaic distinction.[21]

Assmann here captures the fact of the fundamental dichotomy of polar opposites, Egypt and Israel. However, beyond noting this polarity, he does not venture to pass judgment regarding value ascription. If one religion sees another as entailing "the opposite of truth," it would be indispensable to know why or whether it might be correct in its view or perspective.

The question of what constitutes idolatry, it bears pointing out, is not merely a "loaded term," a rhetorical fallacy calculated to win one's argument before it even starts. The idolatrous is that which is made so precious in one's eyes that it blinds the human being, blinds in a manner, which the medieval Kabbalists expressed by the evocative name of qĕlipôt, or "spiritual blinders" (sing. qĕlipāh). As will be demonstrated in the following discussion, much of the ancient Egyptian spiritual-religious worldview, mystical praxes, and unsur-

---

[20] Examples of this include rabbinical notions such as the Messiah, shared with Christianity; features such as endowing *mezuzot* (doorpost amulets) and other talismans and ritual objects, including the Torah itself—as published books and handwritten scrolls, as well as the letters of the Hebrew alphabet—with supernatural attributes; and beliefs such as that the future Third Temple will be built by God himself and it will descend, fully constructed, directly from the heavens (as fervently believed today by the Lubavitch Hassids, among others).

[21] Assmann, *Moses the Egyptian*, 208-9.

passed majesty of its monuments, temples, and what we would today call "art" may have been based on just such "blinders."

I suggest that any sort of magical consciousness and the Mosaic, mysterium tremendum-kind of mystical experience involve significant alterations of consciousness—thus making it imperative to differentiate among the different systems, traditions, and schools of mysticism. Magical consciousness does entail a mystical sensibility yet of a kind recoiled from by the new Mosaic "counter-religion," which is based on experiencing the greatest mystery of all, the mysterium tremendum.[22]

* * * * *

To explore these and related issues at some depth, we must, first, engage as the main lenses for our endeavor those originating in the period in which the Mosaic religion emerged: we wish to ascertain the reasons behind their thinking, motivations, and actions. We will also exploit some findings by Egyptologist Jan Assmann, who recognized how closely the above-noted Hebraic innovations fit a systematic pattern of opposition to, and strenuous rejection of, the foremost Egyptian tenets and beliefs; Assmann posits the helpful notion of Israel's foundational religion being a "counter religion" vis-à-vis that of Egypt. Beyond this seminal conceptualization, Assmann in addition attempts an analysis of the specific meaning of Israel's "Mosaic distinction," as he memorably characterized it.[23]

Second, however, we must note that with regard to ascertaining the meaning of the Mosaic distinction in terms of its true significance, Assmann is markedly less successful. His difficulty—similar to that of most other investigators—is tied to the following circumstance. The existence of an Israelite priestly, Temple-based, mystical-initiatory system—outlines of which were embedded as a "second-channel," esoteric narrative in the Pentateuch and the book of

---

[22] As detailed by Rappaport, in his *Ritual and Religion*, 377-79: "The numinous object is a *mysterium tremendum* in Otto's famous formulation [Rudolf Otto, *The Idea of the Holy*, 2nd ed., trl. J. Harvey (1923; Oxford: Oxford University Press, 1950), chap. 4]. It is *mysterium* because it is beyond creature comprehension. It is incommensurable with us; as Otto puts it, it is 'wholly other' (ibid., 25ff.). It is *tremendum* because, first, it is awful in both senses of the word: inspiring awe on the one hand, dread on the other. It is *tremendum*, second, because it has *majestas*, absolutely overpowering and perhaps all-absorbing (ibid., 20ff.). It is *tremendum*, third, because of its 'energy' or, as Otto's translator called it, 'urgency.' 'It everywhere clothes itself in . . . vitality, passion, emotional temper, will, force, movement, excitement, activity, impetus' (ibid., 23). It is experienced as alive in some sense. It is not merely an abstraction but a being, or, if it is not a being, it is something that possesses being, or is actively 'be-ing' itself."

[23] Assmann, *Moses the Egyptian*, 1 *et passim*.

Joshua—was posited only recently.[24] Thus, such attempts as Assmann's—which lack the primary raison-d'être of the Israelite religion, not to mention the insights into the "mechanics" of the authentic relationship that took place between the priestly initiates and God, to whose service the priests have dedicated themselves—necessarily go only so far. Additionally, they are seriously hampered due to a disregard of crucial differences between symbols and allegories; as we shall see, polarities such as these are indispensable for comprehending the profound difference wrought by the Mosaic distinction.

Third, the question of whether an individual depicted in the Pentateuch as Moses ever existed, specifically and literally, need not concern us here. Nor should we attend to fracases in biblical studies apropos the question of whether the biblical account of the exodus from Egypt ever took place. These issues are important, certainly, but they carry only peripheral import apropos the far more vital and urgent matter, namely, the meaning of the Mosaic religion precisely in its countering the religion of Egypt. Indeed, it is the intense focus of the ancient Israelite religion on and its sustained forceful opposition to the most central doctrinal positions of Egyptian religious and esoteric sensibility that serve as an unambiguous and decisive proof—if not necessarily of a massive and dramatic exodus of a whole people from Egypt—of a direct connection between the two religions under discussion. A charismatic initiate such as the one depicted as Moses—a disenchanted Egyptian dissident-adept who recognized the problems inherent in the religion of his old country and moved to a new land where he succeeded in establishing a religion that would forcefully counterpoise the old religion—is within a realm of distinct possibility. It is also the most plausible explanation for the remarkable parallels between the respective religious-cultic armatures of Egypt and Israel, even if these correspondences point to diametrically inverse, antithetical theological and contrary esoteric positions.

Finally, we will consider that the three so-called Abrahamic religions, namely, rabbinical Judaism of the last two millennia, Christianity, and Islam, in light of the above, in turn must also be seen as counter-religions—or, rather, as counter-counter-religions—for all three are counter to, albeit in very different and specific ways, the original counter-religion of the ancient Israelite religion (pace Egypt).

II. Hieroglyphic Images as the Target of the Second Commandment

The puzzle presented by the Second Commandment, "Thou shalt not make unto thee any graven image"—has tended to confound scholars no less than

[24] Foregrounding the fact of an existence of a "second-channel," esoteric content within the Pentateuch was the principal task of my earlier research presented in *The Sôd Hypothesis*.

average readers. The traditional tendency has been to associate it with idolatry and thus understand it as a prohibition of worshipping anything or anybody other than God.[25] The problem with this interpretation, one that typically is not fully recognized, is the notion of "worshipping": on the one hand, this commandment does not actually talk of worshipping; on the other hand, the preceding commandment, "Thou shalt have no other gods before me," already proscribes worshipping anything or anybody other than God. Thus a careful reader is faced with a pivotal question, one that is the hallmark of the Mosaic distinction: What is idolatry?[26]

In attempting to shed light on ancient Egypt, Assmann engages a perspective that is far more familiar to us than the obscure Egyptian one, namely, the Judaic-biblical outlook, and views Egyptian practices from that more familiar angle. This approach may seem to be at odds with the current ethnographic praxis and principle of anthropologists—which normally insists on studying each culture within its own distinctive framework.[27] Moreover, given the present controversial status of comparative research within religious and cultural studies,[28] Assmann's example is, if anything, courageous, even if, as an Egyptologist, he was likely spared, despite his method, the more disparaging, antagonistic storms within broader religious studies. The Second Commandment is

---

[25] This interpretation in the Jewish tradition became practically unavoidable, once "Thou shalt have no other gods before me"—deemed earlier as the First Commandment by the Septuagint and Philo—was combined, in the Talmud, with "Thou shalt not make unto thee any graven image" as a conjoined Second Commandment, with "I am the Lord thy God" now becoming the First Commandment (the latter was previously seen as a run-up or preamble to the Ten Commandments). Most Christian traditions consider all three sentences as part of the First Commandment (except for Lutheranism, which considers "I am the Lord thy God" a preamble).

[26] Marion's groundbreaking philosophical conceptualization of idolatry as "consign[ing] the divine to the measure of a human gaze," while highly relevant, will not be entered into in the present essay; I explore this aspect in a forthcoming paper. See Jean-Luc Marion, *God without Being*, trl. Thomas A. Carlson (Chicago: University of Chicago Press, 1991), 14.

[27] For example, "[Edmund Leach] tells the biblical student to reject the useless endeavors of comparative ethnography and to forget the purportedly historical framework in which the Bible stories are set. Instead, we should embrace the structural analysis of the Bible as an undifferentiated collection of 'sacred tales.'" Bernhard Lang, "Introduction: Anthropology as a New Model for Biblical Studies," in *Anthropological Approaches to the Old Testament*, ed. Bernhard Lang (Philadelphia: Fortress Press, 1985), 1-20, here 13.

[28] As Sarah Coakley puts it, "The nervousness about ethnocentric imposition of Western categories on the 'other' in matters of culture and religion has currently become so intense in some quarters as to make any sort of comparisons across traditions inherently suspect," "Introduction: Religion and the Body," in *Religion and the Body*, ed. Sarah Coakley (Cambridge: Cambridge University Press, 1997), 1-12, here 1.

the commandment devoted to iconoclasm,[29] and the situation Assmann wishes to explore is framed as follows: "The debate between Egyptian iconists and anti-Egyptian or Biblical iconoclasts has many aspects. . . . I am choosing one of them for closer study, an aspect which as far as I can see has up to now received only very little attention: the grammatological aspect of iconoclasm."[30]

Ancient Egypt was a country and culture that has not merely manifested occasional examples of secrecy and concealment of information of one sort or another. Instead, secrecy and concealment were practiced to a degree almost unimaginable elsewhere, both in the contemporaneous era and thereafter. To begin with—and in a way only partially approximating similar phenomena concerning Hindu Sanskrit or the status of Hebrew among the medieval and later rabbinical circles (where the lingua franca was typically either Yiddish, Ladino, or the languages of the local population in the Jewish diaspora), with Hebrew reserved for sacred study and related commentaries—the Egyptians deliberately created two languages. Having invented "hieroglyphs as a system of picture writing or natural signification but . . . also . . . alphabetic writing as a system of conventional signification,"[31] the Egyptians earmarked one language for sacred purposes ("Hieratic" or "Hieroglyphic"), the other for ordinary communication ("Demotic" or "Epistolic"). The assertion regarding their invention of the two writing systems, however, is strongly disputed.[32] Assmann distinguishes two

---

29 "The practice of destroying images, especially those created for religious veneration," freedictionary.com.

30 Jan Assmann, "Pictures versus Letters: William Warburton's Theory of Grammatological Iconoclasm," in *Representation in Religion: Studies in Honor of Moshe Barasch*, ed. Jan Assmann and Albert I. Baumgarten (Leiden: Brill, 2001), 297-311, here 297, emphasis added.

31 "There were two principally different writing systems, presumably in use side by side in ancient Egypt, one referring to things and concepts 'by nature,' that is iconically, and the other one referring to concepts and sounds 'by convention,' that is by arbitrary signs. . . . The Hieratic or Hieroglyphic script was interpreted as sacred (hieros = sacred), inscriptional (glyph = 'carved' sign) and iconic, the Demotic or Epistolic script was interpreted as profane (demos = common people), used for everyday communication (epistole = correspondence) and aniconic, that is, alphabetic. All this corresponds closely to historical reality as far as Modern Egyptology is able to reconstruct it except one detail: the equation of aniconic and alphabetic signs," Assmann, "Pictures versus Letters," 297-98.

32 Peter Daniels, "Introduction to Part II: Ancient Near Eastern Writing Systems," in *The World's Writing Systems*, ed. Peter T. Daniels and William Bright (New York: Oxford University Press, 1996), 19-20, here 19; Jean Bottéro, "Religion and Reasoning in Mesopotamia," in Jean Bottéro, Clarisse Herrenschmidt, and Jean-Pierre Vernant, *Ancestor of the West: Writing, Reasoning, and Religion in Mesopotamia, Elam, and Greece*, trl. Teresa Lavender Fagan (Chicago: University of Chicago Press, 2000), 3-66, here 19. Peter Daniels states that "it is universally recognized that the [Mesopotamian] cuneiform . . . and [Egyptian] hieroglyphic . . . writing systems are sufficiently dissimilar (one logosyllabic, the other logoconsonantal) that one could not have been adapted directly from the other. But the similarities of earliest attestation (ca. 3200 B.C.E.) and the combination of logography, phonography, and determinatives

ancient Egyptian languages written in three different scripts:[33] the Demotic, or vernacular, language and the "classical" language, which has "a cursive form called 'Hieratic' and an inscriptional and iconic form called 'Hieroglyphic.'"[34]

> [The hieroglyphic] picture writing or immediate signification was a matter of esotericism, mystery and the tradition of sacred knowledge whereas alphabetic writing was a matter of general and profane communication. In this image of ancient Egyptian grammatology, there was thus a close connection between iconicity and sacredness. Religion, priesthood, and mystery used icons, while the alphabet dominated the state, administration, and the public domain. . . . The sacredness of hieroglyphs was identified with the principle of immediate signification. Immediacy is a key word in this context: the signs conveyed their meaning without mediation either by language or by a conventional code.[35]

Let us note Assmann's point about the immediacy of signification in hieroglyphs. It entails a situation diametrically opposite the notions of delayed categorization, as articulated by Reuven Tsur:

> A [rapid] category with a verbal label constitutes a relatively small load on one's cognitive system and is easily manipulable; on the other hand, it entails the loss of important sensory information that might be crucial for the process of accurate adaptation. Delayed categorization, by contrast, may put too much sensory load on the human memory system; this overload may be available for adaptive purposes and afford great flexibility, but it may also be time-and-energy consuming and occupy too much mental processing space. Furthermore, delayed categorization may involve a period of uncertainty that may be quite unpleasant, or even intolerable for some individuals. Rapid categorization, by contrast, may involve the loss of vital information and lead to maladaptive strategies in life.[36]

---

are sufficient to convince Egyptologists . . . or suggest to them . . . that the idea of writing came from the Sumerians to the Egyptians," "The First Civilizations," in *World's Writing Systems*, 21-32, here 24.

[33] Robert Ritner adds a fourth Egyptian script: "The Egyptian script tradition is one of the world's longest, extending from the end of the fourth millennium BCE to at least the 10th century CE. During these four thousand years, four distinct but interrelated scripts were developed, often in complementary usage: Hieroglyphic, Hieratic, Demotic, and Coptic. . . . Hieroglyphs represent the fundamental Egyptian writing system, from which Hieratic, Demotic, and (to a lesser extent) Coptic are cursive derivatives," "Egyptian Writing," in *World's Writing Systems*, 73-87, here 73.

[34] Assmann, "Pictures versus Letters," 298.

[35] Ibid., 299, emphasis added.

[36] Reuven Tsur, "Issues in Literary Synaesthesia." *Style* 41, no. 1 (2007), 30-52, here 39. Tsur is the cofounder of the new discipline of cognitive poetics.

Immediate signification offered through the use of hieroglyphs is precisely what rapid categorization stands for: quick certainty—due to "a relatively small load on one's cognitive system"—as to the immediate answers to enormous, onerous questions of life's meaning, for example, but at a cost entailing "loss of vital information" (which means that one's certainty is misplaced).

Assmann offers an additional point, which he derives from William Warburton and Moses Mendelsohn.[37] Their line of reasoning implicates a "confusion of sign and signified," which ostensibly results in idolatry:

> In the beginning, people think, speak and write in images; only later do they turn to thinking in arguments, speaking in prose and writing with letters. The danger of picture writing lies in the confusion of sign and signified. Thus, an innocent thing such as a mode of writing can degenerate and turn into idolatry. But, Mendelsohn adds, we must always be careful not to see everything through our home-made glasses and to call idolatry what fundamentally might be only writing. In order to avoid the pitfalls of idolatry, God had Moses write down his laws in alphabetic letters, not in pictorial hieroglyphs.[38]

The argument here, however, is not carried to its meaning-bearing conclusion. Alleging merely a confusion of sign and signified is not enough for the appearance or explanation of idolatry since the two can be fused into one as a symbol.[39] The symbol, precisely for this reason, is often hailed as a superior

---

[37] William Warburton, *The Divine Legation of Moses Demonstrated on the Principles of a Religious Deist, from the Omission of the Doctrine of a Future State of Reward and Punishment in the Jewish Dispensation* (1738-41). Mendelsohn, states Assmann, "half a century after the first publication of Warburton's Divine Legation of Moses . . . brought grammatology and theology in an even closer connection in his booklet *Jerusalem*," "Pictures versus Letters," 308. See Moses Mendelsohn, *Jerusalem; or On Religious Power and Judaism*, trl. Allan Arkush (Waltham, MA: University Press of New England, 1983).

[38] Assmann, "Pictures versus Letters," 309.

[39] As Assmann himself points out in an earlier piece, "hieroglyphs are symbols which represent meaning; in other words, they are visible signs that stand for something invisible," "Semiosis and Interpretation in Ancient Egyptian Ritual," in *Interpretation in Religion*, ed. Shlomo Biderman and Ben-Ami Scharfstein (Leiden: Brill, 1992), 87-109, here 87. Such a definition, however, is not fully satisfactory either, since the symbol's role is to stand for something that cannot be otherwise represented—and not necessarily for what is merely invisible (see Paul de Man, "The Rhetoric of Temporality," in *Interpretation: Theory and Practice*, ed. Charles S. Singleton (Baltimore: Johns Hopkins University Press, 1969), 173-209; Murray Krieger, "'A Waking Dream': The Symbolic Alternative to Allegory," in *Allegory, Myth, and Symbol*, ed. Morton W. Bloomfield (Cambridge, MA: Harvard University Press, 1981), 1-22; Tzvetan Todorov, *Theories of the Symbol*, trl. Catherine Porter (Ithaca, NY: Cornell University Press, 1982).

expression[40] by thinkers from Goethe and Coleridge down to our present-day postmodernists.[41] It is also not quite enough to sustain the claim of the necessarily and expressly visual distinction attached to idolatry merely by noting the presentational character of hieroglyphic writing (as opposed to a representational one)[42] and the associated problematic rapid categorization (Tsur) or immediate signification (Assmann)—as is the case with the hieroglyphs. Visual communication, it is true, is very different from verbal communication, yet what exactly turns it into idolatry, and whether a nonvisual entity such as an alphabet-based depiction or an idea can also be idolatrous, has not been established in Assmann's analysis. It is to this task I turn next.

III. Hieroglyphs as Symbols, Visuality, Symbolism, and Idolatry

Richard Janney and Horst Arndt offer a helpful analysis of the differences between pictorial communication and a verbal, language-based one. Their essay compares "holistic" visual/pictorial messages with "sequential," or alphabet-based, language containing "translations" of the pictorial into verbal ones:

> Metaphorically speaking, the sequential symbolic [sic] mode possesses a powerful cognitive syntax, but lacks an adequate semantics in the realm of emotions and affective relationships. The holistic pictorial mode, on the other hand, seems to possess the emotional semantics, but lacks the necessary cognitive syntax for unambiguously defining the nature of the affective relationships it represents.[43]

One only need think of the great works of world literature, however—all

---

[40]There is also an opposite claim, one alleging the superiority of allegory; see, e. g., Walter Benjamin, *The Origin of German Tragic Drama*, trl. John Osborne (1963; London: Verso, 1998), and de Man, "Rhetoric of Temporality."

[41] See, e. g., Matei Calinescu, *Five Faces of Modernity: Modernism, Avant-Garde, Decadence, Kitsch, Postmodernism* (Durham, NC: Duke University Press, 1987).

[42] The presentational versus the representational was theorized by Benny Shanon, *The Representational and the Presentational: An Essay on Cognition and the Study of Mind*, 2nd ed. (1992; Exeter, UK: Imprint Academic, 2008) and, independently, Harry T. Hunt, *On the Nature of Consciousness: Cognitive, Phenomenological, and Transpersonal Perspectives* (New Haven, CT: Yale University Press, 1995)—both following Suzanne Langer's earlier conceptualizations.

[43] Richard W. Janney and Horst Arndt, "Can a Picture Tell a Thousand Words? Interpreting Sequential vs. Holistic Graphic Messages," in *Origins of Semiosis: Sign Evolution in Nature and Culture*, ed. Winfried Nöth (Berlin: Mouton de Gruyter, 1994), 439-53, here 449. This conclusion, however, is at least in part erroneous since the examples given in their essay of "translations" from visual messages into verbal ones are all done in a "telegraphic" manner that is bound to confirm the authors' assertion of the poverty of emotional semantics in the verbal form.

adhering to "the sequential symbolic mode"—to realize that the sequential presentation possesses far more than just powerful cognitive syntax; many, though certainly not all works of literature, clearly exhibit a presence of powerful emotional semantics. The reverse, however, is not true, and Janney and Arndt's essay does establish the "ideational ambiguity" of the pictorial-graphic messages.[44] What is specifically mentioned by these authors as lacking in the pictorial communication is such key deictic, or indexical, information as "what literally was done by whom, where, when, and why." Such critical specifying and orienting information "is perhaps not fully possible in a holistic picture."[45] Herein, then, lies a crucial, and in all probability fatal, quandary pertaining to any hieroglyphic, image-based language.

"Warburton explains idolatry as a sickness of writing, in the same way as more than 100 years later Friedrich Max Mueller explains myth as a sickness of language. Both idolatry and mythology result from a literalistic misunderstanding of metaphor."[46] Assmann concludes as follows:

> Eric Havelock coined the term "alphabetic revolution" which he interpreted as a Greek achievement leading to abstract thinking, logical reasonment [sic], scientific research, technology and everything else which shaped Western culture. . . . Yet . . . the invention of the alphabet (in the sense of non-pictorial signs relating exclusively to sounds) was not a Greek but a Semitic achievement and . . . it was in fact ultimately derived from Egyptian hieroglyphs.[47] The idea to correlate this grammatological revolution with an iconoclastic rejection of images, with monotheism and what Freud called a progress in intel-

---

[44] Ibid., 450.

[45] Ibid.

[46] Assmann, "Pictures versus Letters," 308. Such a claim loses a significant part of its force if one realizes that practically all the other *logoi* literalize their metaphors, too. Allegorical *interpretation*, called allegoresis (see below), is subject to such a tendency; vis-à-vis the philosophical *logos*, the unconscious conceptual metaphors of our childhood category formation are found seamlessly embedded in it, see, e. g., George Lakoff and Mark Johnson. *Philosophy in the Flesh: The Embodied Mind and Its Challenge to Western Thought* (New York: Basic Books, 1999), whose analysis posits that even the greatest philosophers were unconsciously dependent on such metaphors. The distinction between allegory and allegoresis entails the difference between two types of allegorization, one originating with the author, the other a tool of the interpreters: the former has been helpfully designated by Jon Whitman as "compositional allegory," whereas allegoresis is "interpretive allegory," "Preface," in *Interpretation and Allegory: Antiquity to the Modern Period*, ed. J. Whitman (Boston: Brill, 2003), xi-xv, here xi.

[47] Whether "the Semitic achievement" of inventing the alphabet derives from Egyptian hieroglyphs or originates in Mesopotamia has not been fully settled, see, e. g., Daniels, "First Civilizations," 25 and n. 113 above. In contrast, the link between Egyptian hieroglyphs and the Latin alphabet is more certain: "Egyptian writing had a dominant influence on both the Meroitic and Proto-Sinaitic scripts, and through the latter, Egyptian may serve as the direct ancestor of the contemporary Latin alphabet," Ritner, "Egyptian Writing," 82.

> lectuality . . . is at least as interesting a phantasy as its modern correlation with logical thinking, democracy and other allegedly Western achievements.[48]

The connection between visuality and idolatry, in the end, remains unclear in Assmann's inquiry, beyond the above-noted important effect of "immediate signification" that comes with the use of hieroglyphs (but without an assessment of its significance). The standard claim that with images there is the danger of people confusing them with the signified gods is likewise ambiguous, in this instance, since there is no indication that the Egyptians worshipped their hieroglyphic writings. In addition, the axis linking the "grammatological revolution" and the "iconoclastic rejection of images," while potentially and fascinatingly promising, is not developed beyond marking the simple fact of such a link's promise.

In an earlier work, Assmann takes a closer look at the hieroglyphic signification. Seeing the hieroglyphs as "symbols,"[49] he elaborates as follows:

> The Egyptian approach to reality . . . is marked by a strong belief in the power of symbols. And the power of a symbol resides precisely in the fact that it is not what it represents. This is what imbues symbols with meaning. For, in itself, as a "fetish," a symbol is nothing—a piece of stone, or wood, or gold. It is as an element in a bipolar relationship linking it to an entity in the other dimension that it becomes powerful. Its power is, therefore, relational, contextual and conditional.[50]

Here too a common but decisive error is committed, by failing to distinguish between symbol and allegory: it is allegory—rather than symbol—that "is not what it represents." By contrast, as specified by Coleridge, the symbol "always partakes of the reality which it renders intelligible; and while it enunciates the whole, abides itself as a living part in that unity, of which it is the representative."[51] Murray Krieger adds that "it is, of course, the participatory power of the symbol, partaking fully rather than pointing emptily, that allows it to overcome otherness, thereby distinguishing it from allegory."[52] Thus Egyptian

---

[48] Assmann, "Pictures versus Letters," 310-11.

[49] Assmann, "Semiosis and Interpretation," 87.

[50] Ibid., 88.

[51] Samuel Taylor Coleridge, "The Statesman's Manual, The Collected Works of Coleridge, Lay Sermons," ed. R. J. White (London: Routledge and Kegan Paul, 1972), 30, cited in Krieger, "Waking Dream," 5.

[52] Krieger, "Waking Dream," 5. Coleridge's misplaced venom against allegory, however, would be pertinent vis-à-vis allegoresis: "An allegory is but a translation of abstract notions into a picture-language which is itself nothing but an abstraction from objects of the senses; the principal being more worthless even than its phantom proxy, both alike unsubstantial, and the former shapeless to boot," Coleridge, "Statesman's Manual," 30, cited in Krieger,

"sacred symbols—cult images, cosmic phenomena, royal appearances"[53] are not merely allegories that stand for some other; they themselves are partaking of that other and thus are a "monistic"[54] blend or union with the "other," in this case the relevant gods. Assmann further speaks of a "sacred semiosis—or the process through which something comes to acquire a specific meaning," which, in the case of Egypt, enables the symbols to "have a distinctive visible form":

> They [the sacred symbols] are not gods themselves, but "stand for" and "point to" the divine, serving as vessels for a divine presence which is never substantial but always relational and contextual. But they are not mere images of the bodies of the gods, with the same outward appearance; they are in fact the bodies of the gods. The gods are conceived as powers that are free to assume or inhabit a body of their choice, and the cult images may serve—for the time of sacred communication—as their body, as might also, e. g., a cosmic phenomenon such as the sun-disk, the inundation of the Nile, a tree, an animal or the king.[55]

In light of what has been noted with regard to the distinction between symbol and allegory, such designates as "stand for" and "point to" vis-à-vis the symbol are in this context not only confusing and superfluous but also incorrect, since Assmann himself stresses in this passage that these are actual "bodies" "inhabited" by "the powers."

Furthermore, what Assmann does not notice is the following: We may have here the reasons for both the Second Commandment and its aniconism, along with a likely reasoning behind the objection to hieroglyphic script. The hieroglyphs, as a sacred script that utilizes images, can be easily seen as symbols vested with sacred powers. This would be very different from merely literalizing the metaphors that Assmann indicated earlier. Instead, the problem that the early Hebrew tradition might have had with this would be related not to the visual form of the symbol per se but rather to the notion of a symbolic letter—the hieroglyph—being the "body" that is "inhabited" by that which it represents.

Put another way, such a symbol is offensive to the new, revisionary Hebrew religious sensibility due to the symbol's "monistic" fusion, or even just symbiosis, with what one may call "the transcendent." One can see here a key, decisive distinction between the Egyptian magico-religious worldview, which

---

"Waking Dream," 5. Walter Benjamin, Paul de Man, and many others beg to disagree; the present essay endeavors to show the same.

[53] Assmann, "Semiosis and Interpretation," 89.

[54] Krieger, "Waking Dream," 4, et passim.

[55] Assmann, "Semiosis and Interpretation," 89.

infuses certain objects with supernatural significance and power, on the one hand, and, on the other hand, the Hebrew innovation—a counter-religion—that would deny acceptability to such a pantheistic worldview through a doctrinal abhorrence of it.[56]

The Hebrew God seems to be insisting on being seen as the Ultimate Other who cannot be parceled out to various objects, this side of the transcendence-immanence divide. YHWH, some fictional dramatic-anthropomorphic appearances notwithstanding, is the God whose effect may be traced only through history and events, as well as by way of morality, both of peoples and of individuals, elevating some, destroying others. The Hebrew God is also the numinous Other of mystical experiences, which, because they occur within the consciousness of the mystic, are immanent (rather than transcendent), some effects of which can be registered both psychometrically and empirically.[57]

IV. Magical Consciousness and Cosmotheism

It assuredly comes as a surprise to hear of rabbis harking back to Egyptian notions of magic. When one speaks of the "magic nature" of Egyptian knowledge, which involved a "traditional world picture . . . based on the idea that the world required the assistance of ritual in order to keep functioning,"[58] students of medieval Kabbalah, especially in its Lurianic variety, as well as of Hasidism and of modern Judaism's tiqûn ôlām ("mending the world") will readily recognize the same notion of "assistance to heaven."[59] Not only is there

---

[56] That it is pantheism, albeit under such terms as "cosmotheism" and even "nature monotheism," will be argued below.

[57] For examples of empirically measurable effects, via sensing the alteration of some aspect of consciousness that are detectable via EEG and/or fMRI, see, e. g., Alexander A. Fingelkurts, Andrew A. Fingelkurts, Sakari Kallio, and Antti Revonsuo, "Hypnosis Induces a Changed Composition of Brain Oscillations in EEG: A Case Study," *Contemporary Hypnosis* 24, no. 1 (2007): 3-18.

[58] Jan Assmann, "*Officium Memoriae*: Ritual as the Medium of Thought," in *Religion and Cultural Memory: Ten Studies*, trl. R. Livingstone (Stanford, CA: Stanford University Press, 2006), 139-54, here 149, 141, emphasis added.

[59] See, e. g., Brian L. Lancaster, *The Essence of Kabbalah*. (Edison, NJ: Chartwell Books, 2005), 100; Levi Cooper, "The Assimilation of Tikkun Olam," *Jewish Political Studies Review* 25, no. 3-4 (Fall 2014). The idea that actively promoting "repairing the world" may have something wrong with it, let alone be tied to Egyptian magic, is so counterintuitive that it might easily seem preposterous. Another way of framing this ancient human hubris (albeit seeing it only as a modern phenomenon): "Modern culture, whose metaphysics claims that as humans we create all meaning and value, is programmatically idolatrous, for value in a producer/consumer culture is only measured by what we make," Sheldon Isenberg, "Ideals, Pseudo-Ideals and the Evolution of Consciousness," in *The Ideal in the World's Religions: Essays on*

nothing of the sort exhibited in the Hebrew Bible itself, but also the "Mosaic distinction" was distinguished precisely by the acute struggle, for the first time in history,[60] against just such a self-assured consciousness proffering its patronizing assistance to "heaven" or even just to the world presumably in need of repairs.[61] Three Egyptian examples of such magical consciousness, each a major epistemic concern within the framework of the Egyptian way of thinking, can be given: (1) the sustaining of the life-giving energy of the sun; (2) the "cultic geography of the Late Period temples"; and (3) "Egyptian ideas about the flooding of the Nile," this last being of great annual benefit for the Egyptian agricultural economy.[62]

In his 1997 book, Assmann uses extensively the term "cosmotheism" referring both to polytheism in general and to the specifically Egyptian type of religiosity.[63] With Spinoza's pantheism the Europe of the Enlightenment rediscovered Egypt as a land peopled with "Spinozists and cosmotheists."[64] Were the Egyptians Spinozists and cosmotheists? At the same time, were they also indulging in esoteric, mystical, or magical arts?

---

the Person, Family, Society and Environment, ed. R. Carter and S. R. Isenberg, (St. Paul, MN: Paragon House, 1997), 93-120, here 97.

60 It was also the last time—as it has not been replicated since—but not because that effort resulted in a complete or final victory. Quite to the contrary, magical consciousness has thrived throughout known history and continues to do so in our own day, see, e. g., Hanegraaff, *New Age Religion.* Cf. Gregory Bateson's observation: "My view of magic is the converse of that which has been orthodox in anthropology since the days of Sir James Frazer. It is orthodox to believe that religion is an evolutionary development of magic. Magic is regarded as more primitive and religion as its flowering. In contrast, I view sympathetic or contagious magic as *a product of decadence from religion*; I regard religion on the whole as the earlier condition," Gregory Bateson and Mary Catherine Bateson, *Angels Fear: Toward an Epistemology of the Sacred* (New York: Macmillan, 1987), 56, emphasis added.

61 Cf. a recent article on Henry Kissinger by Walter Isaacson, "The Lion in Winter," *Time* magazine, September 22, 2014, 36-38, here 36. Isaacson notes the following: "The most fundamental problem of politics," wrote [Kissinger] in his dissertation, "is not the control of wickedness but the limitation of righteousness."

62 See Assmann, *Officium Memoriae*, 150.

63 In *Moses the Egyptian*: "The term 'cosmotheism' had been coined by Lamoignon de Malesherbes with reference to the antique, especially Stoic worship of the *cosmos* or *mundus* as Supreme Being. . . . Malesherbes could not have found a better term for what seems to be the common denominator of Egyptian religion, Alexandrian (Neoplatonic, Stoic, Hermetic) philosophy, and Spinozism, including the medieval traditions such as alchemy and the [Christian] cabala that might have served as intermediaries," 142.

64 "Spinoza's (in)famous formula *deus sive natura* amounted to an abolition not only of the Mosaic distinction but of the most fundamental of all distinctions, the distinction between God and the world. This deconstruction was as revolutionary as Moses' construction. It immediately led to a new appraisal of Egypt. The Egyptians were Spinozists and 'cosmotheists,'" ibid., 8.

> The object of the [purported] esoteric monotheism or the "mysteries" of the ancient Egyptians came to be identified [in the 18th century] as "Nature." In the idea of Nature as the deity of an original, nonrevealed monotheism, which survived in Egyptian religion under the almost impenetrable cover of symbols and mysteries, the Hermetic, hieroglyphic, and Biblical discourses on Egypt merge.[65]

This nature-based "monotheism" is not to be thought of as devoid of a deity or deities; on the contrary, it was in effect a return to polytheism, albeit united under the singular "Nature," thus enabling the imaginary "monotheism."[66]

"Cosmotheism," traced back to Egypt, is a crucial notion, because it sheds light both on the Egyptian religious theology and the "Mosaic distinction" that revolted against it. Also, to this very day it is an extremely widespread conception; it is, for example, a key tenet of New Ageism.[67] Assmann frames cosmotheism's essence as follows: "The [Mosaic] counter-religious antagonism was always constructed in terms of unity [versus] plurality. Moses and the One

---

[65] Ibid., 20-21.

[66] "Spinozism, pantheism, and all other religious movements of the time look to Egypt for their origins. Egypt appears to be the homeland of cosmotheism. *Hen kai pan* is the motto of a new 'cosmotheism' which appeared to provide a way to escape the Mosaic distinction and its confrontations and implications—such as revealed or 'positive' religion, error and truth, original sin and redemption, doubt and faith—and to arrive at a realm of evidence and innocence. The 'cosmotheism' of early German Romanticism is a return of repressed paganism, the worship of the divinely animated cosmos. In a way, it is a return to Ancient Egypt," ibid., 142-43. "*Hen kai pan*, One and All," is "the concept [Ralph] Cudworth was trying to substantiate with a vast collection of quotations from Greek and Latin authors[, viz.] the idea of primitive monotheism, common to all religions and philosophies including atheism itself. What is common to all must be true and vice versa; this was the basic assumption of 17th-century epistemology and was also implicit in the idea of 'nature' and in the concept of 'natural religion,'" ibid., 81. However, as Assmann takes pains to note, *Hen kai pan*'s provenance is Egyptian, not Greek: "[The formula] never appears [in Egyptian sources] exactly as *Hen kai pan*, but only occurs in more or less close approximations, such as *Hen to Pan*, *To ben kai to Pan*, and so on. . . . Thus as a result of his investigations, Cudworth had demonstrated the formula to be the quintessential expression of Egyptian 'arcane theology,'" ibid., 140. Either way, the concept is far from its seemingly innocent nature worship: "The *kai* in the Greek formula has the same meaning as Spinoza's *sive*. It amounts not to addition, but to an equation. In its most common form, the formula occurs as *Hen to pan*, 'All *Is* One,' the world *is* God. This is what cosmotheism means," ibid., 142. Assmann adds that "Egyptology was not the only discipline that forgot about the alleged Egyptian origins of *Hen kai pan*. With the 'Aryan turn' of Classical studies in later Romanticism, so convincingly described by Martin Bernal and Maurice Olender, the Egyptian source of *Hen kai pan* was forgotten by both classicists and philosophers. Hegel, Schelling, Schopenhauer, Coleridge, and whoever else quoted this formula in the 19th century used it to refer to the Eleatic school and not to ancient Egypt," ibid., 143.

[67] Cf. Hanegraaff, *New Age Religion*.

against Egypt and the Many. The discourse on Moses the Egyptian aimed at dismantling this barrier. It traced the idea of unity back to Egypt."[68] One of the key personalities cited by Assmann who did much to "dismantle the barrier" between "Moses and the One against Egypt and the Many" is the German philosopher Karl Leonhard Reinhold (1757-1825), aka Brother Decius as a Mason, in the Order of the Illuminates. It seems that both Mozart and Haydn "frequented th[e same masonic] lodge" as did Reinhold .[69]

> Reinhold's personal and most important contribution to [Moses/Egypt] discourse is his explanation of the Tetragrammaton. This passage is based on Voltaire's account of the "rites égyptiens." But whereas Voltaire maintains that the Egyptians called the Supreme Being by a similar or even the same name as did the Jews, namely, "I-ha-ho" or "Iao," Reinhold bases his equation not on the sound, but on the meaning. He accepts the Hebrew etymology from hayah and translates the name quite traditionally as "I am who I am," but equates this formula with the inscription on the veiled statue [of Isis] at Sais: "I am all that is."[70]

In fact, however, the difference between "I am who I am" and "I am all that is," says Assmann appropriately, "could not be more pronounced."[71] According to biblical theology, "God" creates existence itself, remaining outside or beyond existence itself. The Hen kai pan, or "All-in-One" formula, and the "I am all that is" description, by contrast, reference existence. Moreover,

> Plutarch's treatise De Iside and Osiride, . . . repeatedly states that the Egyptians['] . . . Supreme God [was] symbolized . . . by a crocodile. Horapollo "tells us, that the Egyptians acknowledging a pantokrator and kosmokrator,

---

68 Assmann, *Moses the Egyptian*, 168, emphasis added.

69 Ibid., 116.

70 Ibid., 118. "Plutarch tells the story of the veiled image in Sais in the ninth chapter of his treatise *On Isis and Osiris*. He wants to show that the Egyptians were acting upon the principle that the truth can only be indirectly transmitted by means of riddles and symbols and illustrates this point with three examples. The first is the custom of putting sphinxes at the doorways of the temples in order to insinuate that Egyptian theology contained enigmatic wisdom. The second is the veiled statue at Sais. The third example is the name of Amun, the Egyptians' highest god, meaning 'the hidden one,'" ibid.

71 Ibid. As Assmann notes, "Reinhold does not even mention the obvious difference between the two propositions 'I am *all that is*' and 'I am *who I am*.' In the first case, the deity points to the visible world or 'nature' in a gesture of identification; in the second case God points to nothing outside himself and thus withdraws the foundation of all cosmic identification or 'cosmotheism.' The Hebrew formula *æhyæh asher æhyæh* is the negation and refusal of every cosmic referentiality. It draws the distinction between immanence and transcendence, or, to use the terms of the time, of 'nature' and 'Scripture,'" ibid., 119-20.

an Omnipotent Being that was the Governor of the whole World, did Symbolically represent him by a Serpent." This "first and most divine Being," according to Eusebius, "is Symbolically represented by a Serpent having the head of an Hawk."[72]

While Assmann advises that "we have to understand [such symbols] on two levels," and that what they refer to "is[, at] the level of transcendence, the ineffable and hidden universal god, whom, of course, no image can represent,"[73] this once again betrays an inadequate grasp of either symbols or allegories. For if the crocodile or the serpent with the hawk's head are indeed symbols of the otherwise ineffable deity, such a symbol would be as good as useless unless it does what any symbol is supposed to do: "always partak[ing] of the reality which it renders intelligible; and while it enunciates the whole, abides itself as a living part in that unity, of which it is the representative."[74] "The participatory power of the symbol, partaking fully rather than pointing emptily, [is] that [which] allows it to overcome otherness,"[75] in this case the otherness of the Egyptian deity, the "ineffable and hidden universal god, whom, of course, no image can represent."[76]

The Egyptian symbols of deities do just that—namely, they do represent, that is to say, stand for, the Egyptian deities. In contrast, Elohim is described as the Hebrew deity's designation, and while, as a designation, it also represents that which it names, the only symbols involved are the Hebrew letters of this name. As individual letters, however, they do not point to anything and reference nothing in the terrestrial or cosmic realities; as letters, their symbolism is confined to representing certain associated sounds that in aggregate make up a word. It is true, however, that the Tetragrammaton, the name of the Hebrew deity revealed to Moses at the burning bush, is called the Ineffable Name due to its proscribed, or in any event unknown, pronounceability. Its letters do not make a recognizable word (except perhaps a composite of several transmutations of the verb "to be"),[77] and the medieval Kabbalah treats each of its four letters as symbolizing a different existential realm or "domain of being."[78]

---

[72] Ibid., 85-86.
[73] Ibid., 202.
[74] Coleridge, "Statesman's Manual," 30, cited in Krieger, "Waking Dream," 5.
[75] Krieger, "Waking Dream," 5.
[76] Assmann, *Moses the Egyptian*, 202.
[77] Thorleif Boman, *Hebrew Thought Compared with Greek*, trl. Jules L. Moreau (1954; New York: W. W. Norton, 1970).
[78] Lancaster, *Essence of Kabbalah*, 120; see also Chayyim Vital, *The Tree of Life: The Palace of Adam Kadmon*, trl. Donald Wilder Menzi and Zwe Padeh (16th c.; Northvale, NJ: Jason Aronson, 1999).

Can a crocodile or a serpent with a hawk's head be considered allegories rather than symbols? As Coleridge would have it, "an allegory is but a translation of abstract notions into a picture-language which is itself nothing but an abstraction from objects of the senses; the principal being more worthless even than its phantom proxy, both alike unsubstantial, and the former shapeless to boot."[79] Allegory is "a translation of abstract notions into a picture-language," without, as does a symbol, "partaking of the reality which it renders intelligible."

Yet allegory is not nothing and is meant to convey through its particular features something of the nature of that which it allegorizes. The crocodile and the serpent are both "lying low" in potentially menacing wait, while the hawk's head implies wide vistas and perhaps courage. Does one need, at this point, to stress the radically different conceptualization of the Hebrew deity, whose referential designations—Elohim and YHWH—are more akin to names rather than either a visible symbol or allegory, such as a crocodile or a serpent with the head of a hawk?[80]

V. Egypt's Structural Secrecy and the Notion of Split Religion: From Divine Symbolization Experience (Egypt) to Direct Experience of the Divine (Israel)

Turning to the issue of secrecy and concealment as it manifests itself in ancient Egypt, several trends can be distinguished. The first one is familiar to us from Greece and from other traditions, the split between the knowledge available to the initiated and to those who remain outsiders:

[79] Coleridge, "Statesman's Manual," 30, cited in Krieger, "Waking Dream," 5.

[80] Assmann further speaks of "visualization of the different forms in which the cosmogonic of the supreme and transcendent God is present in the world. The Egyptian pantheon is a composite form of this divine immanence. The seven *ba*s, the nine shapes or the million beings are variant expressions of the same idea that God is one *and* many, one *and* all, *Hen kai pan*, as the Greek formula runs," *Moses the Egyptian*, 203. The relevant formula cited by Assmann from a Ramesside magical papyrus is "the One who makes himself into millions," ibid., 205: "in other texts, 'million' is said to be his body, his limbs, his transformation and even his name: 'million of millions is his name.' By transforming himself into the millionfold reality, God has not ceased to be one. He *is* the many in that mysterious way, hidden and present at the same time, which this theology is trying to grasp by means of the *ba* concept," ibid., 206. While the medieval Kabbalah has adopted the Ten Sefirot of the *Sefer Yetzirah* (see *Sefer Yetzirah: The Book of Creation in Theory and Practice*, trl., with comm., Aryeh Kaplan [York Beach, ME: Samuel Weiser, 1990]) as ten immanent divine potencies, the Hebrew Bible itself has only one, but crucial, clue vis-à-vis this issue, viz., the divine name Elohim.

> The concept of split religion occurs in a nonantagonistic, a moderately antagonistic, and a radically antagonistic form. The nonantagonistic form is represented by most of the classical theories about Egyptian religion, such as those of Philo, Plutarch, Clement of Alexandria, and Iamblichus. It corresponds to the Stoic and Neoplatonic sociology of knowledge and can be subsumed under the notion of accommodation. Since human beings are differently equipped for grasping the truth, the distribution of knowledge within a society has to accommodate itself to these differences. There is one truth which fits Tamimo and another one that fits Papageno. Virtually all Classical sources agree that the famous wisdom which the Egyptian priests kept secret in the adyta of the temples was of this sort.[81]

Yet Egypt would easily showcase its exceptionalism in the sphere of secrecy as well. Its esoteric secrecy extended to such aspects as the ontological status of its gods, especially vis-à-vis its foremost god, Amun-Re. However, to call a conception such as described in Assmann's passage "monotheism," however "basic,"[82] is to needlessly obfuscate the issue. Instead, what unmistakably

---

[81] Assmann, *Moses the Egyptian*, 213. The concept of a split religion in a "moderately antagonistic and a radically antagonistic form" need not be discussed in detail here since, as Assmann indicates, they both entailed "extremely improbable theor[ies] about ancient Egyptian religion" that involved, in the case of the former, "protect[ing] the truth from vulgarization and spar[ing] the uninitiated the shock of disillusionment," and "the crudest distortion of Egyptian polytheism" that implied imposture on the part of the priests, who worked "the miracles as very human, behind-the-scenes machinations and manipulations," in the latter case (ibid., 214). See, however, Theodor Reik, *Mystery on the Mountain: The Drama of the Sinai Revelation* (New York: Harper and Brothers, 1959), for a sympathetic account of initiatory schemes that involve deliberate staging of the required induction settings. Also, cf. Clement of Alexandria: "The Egyptians do not reveal their Religious Mysteries promiscuously to all, nor communicate the knowledge of divine things to the Profane, but only to those who are to succeed in the kingdom, and to such of the Priests as are judged most fitly qualified for the same, upon account both of their birth and Education" (Clement of Alexandria, *Stromata*, book 5 [= Ralph Cudworth, *The True Intellectual System of the Universe: The First Part, Wherein All the Reason and Philosophy of Atheism Is Confuted and Its Impossibility Demonstrated*, 2nd ed. (1678; London, 1743), 314], in Assmann, *Moses the Egyptian*, 83).

[82] Assmann, *Moses the Egyptian*, 193-94. Assmann further summarizes his reasons for "the oneness of Amun": Amun "is, 1. the primeval god, who existed before the entire world; 2. the creator, who transformed the world from the primeval condition into the cosmos; 3. the life god, who gives life and spirit to the world in the form of the three life-giving elements; 4. the sun god, who completes his journey alone and illuminates and guards the world with his eyes; 5. the ruler god, who exercises rule over his creation and is represented by the king on earth; 6. the ethical authority, who watches over right and wrong, the 'vizier of the poor,' the judge and savior, the lord of time, 'favor,' and fate; 7. the hidden god, whose symbols, images, and names are the many gods," ibid., 194. "It is this last aspect of Amun's Oneness," comments Assmann, "that is of particular interest here because it is so closely related to the idea of esoteric monotheism and the 'god of the mysteries,'" ibid. Again, the reason for the

emerges from the description of cosmotheism is classical pantheism, even if the Egyptian version may have additionally provided for a transcendent aspect of its multipronged, multifaceted "one" deity.[83] Accordingly, Assmann adds that he "think[s] that there are strong connections between the Egyptian and Platonic concepts of a cosmic 'soul.'"[84] While Plato seems to import pantheistic notions from Egypt, the heart of the Mosaic distinction vis-à-vis ancient Egyptian religion consists precisely in rejecting them.

Assmann does not mention the curious parallels between the Egyptian manner of conceptualizing the hidden deity and what is, once again, the very nucleus of the ancient Israelite theology. These offer a content-based, additional indication of the new Israelite religion's Egyptian connection; as we shall see next, the Hebrew "counter-religion" revolts against the key tenets of the Egyptian religion—yet keeps a similar structural framework and approach.

The question of direct accessibility of and proximity to the Hebrew God is one example of a reverse parallelism between the ancient Israelite religion and corresponding ancient Egyptian notions. Methods of accessing the God of Israel are in fact the single most secretive aspect of the ancient Hebrew cultic religion and constitute the contents of the allegorized Sôd channel in the Pentateuch.[85] An ability to access the national deity—depicted most noticeably in

---

very appearance of the "Mosaic distinction"—which Assmann himself so forcefully articulates—is precisely because of the Mosaic rejection of the notion of an all-pervading, permeating presence of the "one" deity *in the manifested* world (of which the sun is an example).

[83] The latter aspect can be characterized as the "ontological Beyond": "The temporal relationship between preexistence and existence was transformed into an ontological one. In the paradigm of manifestation, the Hidden One inhabits an ontological Beyond, but not a temporal Beyond," Assmann, ibid., 195-96. Further, Amun "is absolutely hidden. No statement about him is possible. He is still beyond heaven and the underworld, the holy and the otherworldly regions of the world. He is hidden from the gods, who reflect his unfathomable nature in this remote sphere. He is even more hidden from humans. The scriptures give no information about him. He cannot be explained by any theory. . . . The god is called *ba* because there is no name for him. His hidden all-embracing abundance of essence cannot be apprehended. 'Amun' is merely a pseudonym used to refer to the god in the cosmic sphere of manifestation. Basically, every divine name is a name of the hidden one, but the term *ba* is used when the hidden one behind the multitude of manifestations is meant. *Ba* is the key concept of the 'paradigm of manifestation' as opposed to the 'paradigm of creation.' We translate the Egyptian term *ba* conventionally as 'soul.' This yields the idea that for the Egyptians the visible world has a 'soul' that animates and moves it, just as it did for the Neoplatonists, who believed in the *anima mundi*," ibid, 197.

[84] Ibid.

[85] Ziony Zevit, a prominent biblical studies scholar, observes that "God was accessible to all through prayer, even outside of the temple and sacred precincts" (personal communication, 2009). Yet my study, *The Sôd Hypothesis*, shows that accessibility to God in the ancient Israelite cultic religion of the First Temple, at least as far as the temple priesthood is concerned, was based on a radically and qualitatively different notion of "access to God," one that in-

several momentous passages in the Pentateuch, such as Jacob's all-night struggle, which resulted in his becoming Israel, a renaming that signified his psycho-spiritual transformation; Moses at the burning bush; or Abraham entertaining three visitors, one of whom is God—is paramount in and for the early Israelite cultic religion. In a sign of a significant disconnection from the temple-based religious sensibility, the rabbinical period has practically no accounts of direct encounters with the Divine (excluding the Merkabah mysticism and the marginalized medieval Kabbalah, which occasionally, i.e., unsystematically and unrelated to the prevailing overall rabbinical theology and praxis, did offer instances of divine proximity and intimacy).

The Egyptian "cultic communication is based on the principle that there is no direct confrontation between god and man. Everything in such communication must be symbolic."[86] The Hebrew Scripture, reflecting the "Mosaic distinction," strongly diverges from such a merely symbolic contact: instead of symbolic communication, it features case after case of just the kind of interrelating between human and God that cannot be described other than as direct. By dramatic contrast, the Egyptian theology conceives of the "more [than] human partner, who is the king . . . [who] is the sole terrestrial being qualified to communicate with the gods because," says Assmann, "according to Egyptian belief, sacred communication cannot take place between a god and a merely human being, but only between god and god."[87] It must be forcefully reiterated that the Mosaic distinction involves a rejection of such an exclusive and highly politicized access to a deity limited only to a king (as well as priests who approach the deity on behalf of a king).[88] Regarding human divinization, the Hebrew myth takes a strongly disapproving view, judging from import of the garden of Eden narrative. The full extent of the specific refusal to grant special powers principally only to kings becomes apparent, however, only when one is confronted with the presence of the concealed "second channel" in the Pentateuch. This esoteric stratum is devoted to "storing," in a figurative-esoteric manner, precisely the zealously guarded methods of achieving a communication with and access to God, an access that is in principle open to anyone who is capable of accessing this Sôd channel first.

The "completely symbolic character of the Egyptian cult," which Assmann sees as reserving a key role for "the connection between semiosis and

---

volved mystical alteration of consciousness. Furthermore, an initiatory system entailing mystical induction procedures is precisely what *The Sôd Hypothesis* proposes as the subject of the conjectured *Sôd* stratum in the Pentateuch. Such an access to God entails what Otto calls "*mysterium tremendum*"—a conception wholly inapplicable to mere verbal prayer; see his *Idea of the Holy*.

[86] Assmann, "Semiosis and Interpretation," 92, emphasis added.

[87] Ibid., emphasis added.

[88] See ibid., 93-94.

interpretation,"[89] can be recapitulated differently through the following remarkable statement: "Nothing in the Egyptian cult is just what it appears to be."[90] The Mosaic distinction sweeps aside this all-symbolic view of the sacred realm, which always requires interpretation. The obscure symbols requiring mediation of interpretation are replaced with the exposure to a living God's presence, as in the direct encounters mentioned above: the sacrifices in the Temple that are brought in and eaten together with priests in the presence of God are not symbolic, and neither is the experience of such a sacramental shared meal with the Deity; the experience of the Sabbath, too, is not about interpreting anything but about experiencing.[91]

> If the whole system of symbolization is discarded, the statues lose their power of reference and turn into mere "matter." They are blind and deaf, completely dead, even when compared to the "living God," who is not to be represented by statues and not to be approached by means of sacramental magic or mythological impersonation. The ideas of a living God and of unmediated communication bridge the semiotic distance between the signifier and the signified.[92]

---

[89] Ibid., 101-02.

[90] Ibid., 102. Here is the full quote: "Nothing in the Egyptian cult is just what it appears to be. The priest is not a priest; the statue is not a statue; the sacrificial substances and requisites are not what they are usually. In the context of the ritual performance all acquire a special 'mythical' meaning that points to something else in 'yonder world.' Thus, the priest assumes the role of a god and the statue the role of something other than its literal self. Everything in this sacred game becomes a kind of hieroglyph. . . . The worship of images—'idolatry' in the terminology of its adversaries—and the interpretive character of the Egyptian cult in general as well as of the role of language within the cult in particular, seem closely linked and interdependent. Idols function within a system of semiosis and interpretation; they are not holy in themselves, any more than words have meaning outside the language to which they belong or letters outside their own script."

[91] Here is another example of why, as asserted earlier, the rabbinical system, with its interpretive midrashic exegesis and limited experiencing, is a throwback to the Egyptian ways: "In Egypt ritual interpretation is transformative interpretation. It is part of the ritual itself. Transformation, as well as interpretation, are based on analogy. If *A* is to be transformed into/interpreted as *B*, an analogy between *A* and *B* has to be established. Most frequently and typically (but by no means exclusively), this analogy is found on the level of language and in the form of assonance: between *mrt* 'chest' and *t3-mrj* 'Egypt,' between *qnj* 'stomacher' and *qnj* 'to embrace,' etc. Language provides a network of connections and correspondences where everything coheres and which the priest and the magician use for the purposes of sacramental interpretation," Assmann, "Semiosis and Interpretation," 105-6. The similarity with rabbinical midrashic approach is unmistakable; see Michael Fishbane, *The Garments of Torah: Essays in Biblical Hermeneutics* (Bloomington: Indiana University Press, 1989).

[92] Assmann, "Semiosis and Interpretation," 102. "Idolatry and magic seem to be closely interrelated. The connection between magic and interpretation may not, however, be immediately self-evident. It has to be seen in the transformative power of interpretation. This

Assmann concludes his survey of the Egyptian religion over its long history by foregrounding its ever-increasing tendency toward "sacramental interpretation" that results in ever-deepening esotericism.[93] But the story of Egyptian religion would not be complete without the account of the "symbolic walls and protective zones" it erected as "a response to the experiences of the Persian and Ptolemaic periods" of foreign rule.[94] As Assmann notes, "An exact parallel is found in Judaea, where Jewish culture surrounded itself with the symbolic wall of the law against the Persian and Hellenistic threat to its cultural identity."[95] There is also another parallel, one with the history of the Jewish "textual community":[96]

---

power, for which the Egyptian language has a special word, *3hw*, turns a piece of meat into the eye of Horus, the offering of a stomacher into the performance of a life-restoring embrace and the consecration of four chests into a confirmation of political rule. The object or the action becomes what it *means*. It is precisely this transformative power which requires that the words be spoken as divine utterance, [when the king or a priest assumes] the role of a god. Interpretation means transformation," ibid., 105, emphasis added.

[93] "Over the course of time, sacramental interpretation developed into an art of considerable complexity. Above and beyond the surface structure of religion, actions and representations developed an immense universe of significations. At the end of this process, which was reached in the Greco-Roman period, cultic life turned into a mysteriously enigmatic game and the Sphinx became, very justly, the symbol of ancient Egyptian religion. *The more there was to interpret, the more mysterious the rites became.* The dialectics of interpretation and arcanization led to a cultural split between a surface structure of religious practices of sometimes appalling absurdity (e. g., the burial cult of sacred animals) and a deep structure of religious philosophy, which finally developed into hermeticism, where the sacerdotal science of Egyptian paganism and the philosophical religion of neo-Platonism met to form the last stage of Egyptian religion," ibid., 106, emphasis added.

[94] Jan Assmann, *The Mind of Egypt: History and Meaning in the Time of the Pharaohs*, trl. Andrew Jenkins (Cambridge, Mass.: Henry Holt, 2003), 393.

[95] "Mary Douglas [*In the Wilderness: The Doctrine of Defilement in the Book of Numbers* (Sheffield: Sheffield Academic Press, 1993)] has interpreted this stance as typical of an 'enclave culture,' which immures itself within a wall of ritual purity taboos. . . . In Egypt, the symbolic fortifications are 'abhorrence, taboo' (purity/impurity) and 'secrecy' (knowledge/betrayal of knowledge). These boundaries provide a context for the fantastic but probably not totally inaccurate statements made by Herodotus about the purity commandments observed by the Egyptians in their contact with the Greeks and probably with all foreigners. *No Egyptian would touch a knife or cooking utensil that had previously been used by a Greek, nor eat the meat of an animal slaughtered with a Greek knife. Nor could any Egyptian ever bring himself to kiss a Greek on the mouth.* Though both categories of distinction and self-segregation (abhorrence and secrecy, impurity and betrayal) had a long history in Egypt, their traditional function had been to divide sacred from profane, not indigenous from alien. Taboos were valid for the priests, not for Egyptians in general. . . . In the Late Period, the concept 'profane' underwent a change, as did the meaning of taboos and secrecy. The sacred objects and rites were protected not so much from the impure and the uninitiated but from the foreigner. Foreigners symbolized the ultimate in impurity and noninitiation," Assmann, *Mind of Egypt*, 394-95, emphasis added.

[96] Assmann (*Mind of Egypt*, 313) credits the term to Brian Stock.

> The [Egyptian] priests saw their most important function not as the cultivation of written traditions or the interpretation of sacred texts but the performance of religious rites. The texts were nothing other than the indispensable source for the correct performance of the rites.[97]

This Egyptian parallel with the Israelite temple priests, in contrast with the much later rabbinical "textual community," is striking. While for the priests the Torah was likely a useful, perhaps indispensable religious and mystical manual, both for the cultic rites and for personal mystical experiences and learning about access to the Divine, for the rabbis this text became Scripture, a holy object vested with almost magical powers and significance quite apart from whatever content it contained. The rabbis remained largely unaware of the concealed information meant only for the initiated temple priests.[98]

VI. The Semiotic Perspective

Finally, a semiotic perspective on what divides ancient Egypt and ancient Israel, at least as it pertains to writing. Assmann approaches such a perspective in terms that are highly pertinent—yet the conclusion he derives from it is, in the end, erroneous:

> The fundamental principle that informs all enigmatic modes of writing is deconventionalization.[99] Either conventional signs are invested with an unconventional meaning, or new signs are invented to replace the conventional ones. These potentialities reside in the fundamental openness of the hieroglyphic system, an openness that is itself a function of the iconic nature of hieroglyphic signs. Accordingly, cryptography was possible only with hieroglyphic script, not with the cursive script that was derived from it. . . .
>
> Hieroglyphs had a dual function: they stood for linguistic units on the phonemic or the semantic plane, and at the same time, like pictorial art, they iconically represented existing things. The process of conventionalization entails the discontinuing of representation on this second (iconic) plane. The sign comes to stand for a specific referent, regardless of whether the "origi-

---

97 Ibid., 414.

98 See Kohav, *Sôd Hypothesis*.

99 Assmann refers to Viktor Shklovsky (*Theory of Prose*, trl. Benjamin Sher [Normal: Illinois State University, 1991], 14), an important member of the Russian formalist movement in literary theory, to discuss the concept of alienation, "the goal of which is to heighten awareness and to prevent staleness of perception. Habit, says Shklovsky, makes 'life drift on into nothingness. Automatization devours everything, clothes, furniture, women, fear of war.' The function of art is to 'alienate' the objects of everyday reality so that they resist automatic perception. The gaze is arrested, orientation is difficult, automatic perception is replaced by conscious, laborious, complicated decipherment," ibid.

> nal" referent is still iconically recognizable as such. The sign must now only stand out distinctively and discretely from the other signs in the system.
>
> Almost all originally iconic scripts have shed their iconicity in the course of their development. To recognize an "a" (as a grapheme or phoneme) it is not necessary to recognize in it the bull's head it once signified. The development of hieroglyphs was very different. They retained their function as images even after they had become script characters. Their graphic quality, forfeited in the course of conventionalization, could be reanimated at any time.[100]

As my *Sôd Hypothesis* endeavors to illustrate, such a position—namely, that "cryptography was possible only with hieroglyphic script"—is wholly erroneous. It is here that my earlier investigation yielded the crucial insight (one that was quite unintended by Assmann): If the hieroglyphs iconically represented existing things while they simultaneously, in "a dual function," "stood for linguistic units on the phonemic or the semantic plane,"[101] one may question this latter function. In a "normal" alphabetical script this linguistic function "on the phonemic or the semantic plane" may seem to be all there is, as far as language is concerned; yet, crucially, there is also much more than meets the eye. As Paul Hernadi argues,

> Literary works, just like other verbal constructs, are capable of conveying information from one mind to another. Some critics prefer to approach texts as instruments of mimesis (words representing worlds), others as instruments of communication (messages from authors to readers). Yet literary works communicate and represent at the same time, and criticism as a whole should account for them both as utterances with potential appeal and as verbal signs representing worlds.[102]

I have noted elsewhere that "the mimetic axis of representation supplies the ostensible historical or other narrative background of its material, which is then presentationally interpreted to be the content of the other major axis, that of communication."[103] The issue I wish to draw attention to concerns the mimetic axis of representation: anything that represents something else would be considered, semiotically, a sign. According to Peircean taxonomy, there are three

---

[100] Assmann, *Mind of Egypt*, 415-16, emphasis added.
[101] Ibid.
[102] Paul Hernadi, "Literary Theory: A Compass for Critics," *Critical Inquiry* 3 (1976): 369-86, here 369, emphasis added.
[103] Kohav, *Sôd Hypothesis*, 47.

types of signs: the icon, the index, and the symbol,[104] to which, for cases involving literary works (including here also the Pentateuch), I would add the allegory.[105] Thus we can see that, apart from the iconic function of the hieroglyphs as pictures—their representational mimetic function—there could additionally be, in accordance with the Peircean taxonomy of a sign, two additional functions of the hieroglyphs, conceivably also coopting the indexical and the symbolic, or also the allegorical (if one takes into consideration just how different the allegorical is from the other three types of signs). Is hieroglyphic communication solely iconic, or could it also be indexical, or symbolic, or allegorical, or some combination of them?

It would seem that the contents or referential structure of any communication can consist of any of the following types of representations of communicated concepts and/or information, either singly or in some combination: (1) allegorization; (2) iconicity; (3) indexicality; (4) symbolization; (5) literal, or "surface," narrative. These types of mimetic representations, along with corresponding semiotic communicative intent, must each contribute—to the extent of their actual presence in the text and in addition to their respective mimetic content—to the content of the axis of communication, as and if intended by an author. It is then up to the reader to appropriately read the text so "encrypted" or endowed.[106]

---

[104] Charles S. Peirce, "Logic as Semiotic: The Theory of Signs," in *Philosophical Writings of Peirce*, ed. Justus Buchler (1940; New York: Dover, 1955). I wish to distinguish between iconic *as visual* and iconic as the Peircean, or semiotic, sign category, the icon. The Peircean "icon" as a sign of something is, of course, related to what it represents, typically by being its visual image—but not necessarily so; the icon need not be exclusively visual.

[105] As proposed in *The Sôd Hypothesis*, chap. 3, allegory is quite distinct from the other signs and must not be subsumed—at least with regard to literary works—under the symbol. See also, e. g., Reuven Tsur, "Aspects of Cognitive Poetics," in *Cognitive Stylistics: Language and Cognition in Text Analysis*, ed. Elena Semino and Jonathan Culpeper (Amsterdam: John Benjamins, 2002), 279-318, here 300-301. Hodge and Kress draw attention to the fact that "Peirce's treatment of modality [a kind of truth value attached to a proposition] is fairly rudimentary. Three forms of modality, and three kinds of sign, are not adequate to account for the full range of strategies . . . , and semioticians tend to overuse Peirce's terms for want of anything better," Robert Hodge and Gunther Kress, *Social Semiotics* (Ithaca, NY: Cornell University Press, 1988), 27.

[106] These paths were explored further, in terms of their applicability to the conjectured esoteric narrative within the Pentateuch, in several sections of *The Sôd Hypothesis*; see especially chap. 5.

Conclusion

This essay has demonstrated that while ancient Israel's founding religious principles were the polar opposites of the ancient Egyptian ones, in point of fact they are positioned along the selfsame axes, albeit at their opposite ends. This realization is both startling and very fruitful in its import. Thus, for example, Egypt's paradigmatic pattern of palpable iconicity and symbolism, but not of allegorization or indexicality, ought to lead one to probe whether these and/or the other two semiotic modes of signs—indexicality and allegoricity—may have been involved within the edifice of Israel's esoteric Torah, or Teaching, that is, within the Pentateuchal structure itself. It turns out that the extreme polarity between Egypt's and Israel's key stances is indeed fully reflected in the semiotic domain as well—as should have been expected. If Egypt's sensibility is essentially iconic and symbolic, the Pentateuch's esoteric "second channel," the veiled Sôd, is allegorical and indexical, pointing to direct, experiential knowledge of the Divine.[107]

[107] See Kohav, *Sôd Hypothesis.*

7. Toward an Existential Understanding of Christianity

Phenomenologies of Mystical States as Mediating between Kierkegaard's Christian Dogmantics and Early Gospel Accounts

Harry T. Hunt[1]

Abstract

The existential-phenomenological approach of the early Heidegger and Max Scheler to religion as an amplified empirical phenomenology of the human condition is connected with Heidegger's specific derivation of his Daseins analysis from the Christianity of Eckhart, Paul, and Kierkegaard. Resulting perspective is shown to be broadly congruent with the contemporary transpersonal psychology of higher states of consciousness—the latter largely based on Eastern meditative traditions. This descriptive transpersonal psychology of a mystical core to all religions—based on the direct experience of presence or Being, as developed by Rudolf Otto and elaborated by Laski, Almaas, and others—is then applied to selective Gospel narratives as a further step, past its beginnings in the early Heidegger and Rudolf Bultmann, toward a reconstruction of specific numinous states in early Christianity. This derivation of facets of the numinous from their presumed doctrinal schematizations and/or amplifications places Christianity closer to the goals of the meditative traditions and allows a more directly experiential understanding of doctrines of Christian redemption, loving compassion, and eternal life—as amplifications of the phenomenology of the inner forms of ordinary here-and-now consciousness, within which they are already foreshadowed.

> My name is written on David's line.
> I go to Heaven on the wheel of time
> — "Turtle Dove," traditional folk song

[1] Previously published in the *Journal of Mind and Behavior* 33 (2012): 1-26. Reprinted with permission. The author thanks David Goigoechea, Leo Stan, and Kathy Belicki for helpful suggestions, and Linda Pidduck for editorial assistance.

Existential and Transpersonal Understandings of the Sacred

As themselves aspects of the modern secularization of Christianity, there have been two complementary strands of inquiry into the essence of the sacred in terms of a spontaneous and cross-cultural felt core that would be differentially schematized into the world religions.

The first is existential-phenomenological: It begins with Friedrich Schleiermacher and his spontaneous sense of "dependence" on an all-inclusive totality beneath and within the unfolding moment.[2] It receives a major influence from Søren Kierkegaard's early phenomenology of Christianity in terms of dread, despair, faith, and a felt sense of eternity in the ongoing moment.[3] In his later works, however, based on his sense of an infinite distance between humanity and the absolute alterity of God, Kierkegaard turns back from this necessarily "indirect" phenomenology of the transcendent to what he regards as the "direct communication" of a Christian dogmatics opposed to all first-person mysticism.[4]

By contrast, the very early Martin Heidegger of the 1920s in lectures only recently translated, continues a reinscription of Christianity as the source for a phenomenology of the underlying forms of all human existence, based on "demythologized" readings of Eckhart, Augustine, Luther, Paul, and the early Kierkegaard.[5] It is surprising to see how much the secular, naturalistic *Daseins analysis* of *Being and Time* depended on an initial phenomenology derived entirely from Christianity.[6] Where Kierkegaard begins such a phenomenology and then turns back to orthodoxy, the later Heidegger proceeded on through Christianity

---

[2] Friedrich Schleiermacher, *On Religion: Speeches to Its Cultural Despisers*, trans. Richard Crouter (1799; Cambridge: Cambridge University Press, 1988); Jacqueline Marina, "Schleiermacher on the Outpourings of the Inner Fire: Experiential Expressionism and Religious Pluralism," *Religious Studies* 40 (2004): 130–33, 141.

[3] Søren Kierkegaard, *The Concept of Dread*, trans. Walter Lowrie (1844; Princeton, NJ: Princeton University Press, 1957); Kierkegaard, *Fear and Trembling*, trans. Walter Lowrie (1843; Garden City, NY: Doubleday, 1954); Kierkegaard, *Training in Christianity*, trans. Walter Lowrie (1850; New York: Vintage Books, 2004).

[4] L. Stan, Either Nothingness or Love: On Alterity in Sören Kierkegaard's Writings (Saarbrucken: VDM Müller Verlag, 2009); Søren Kierkegaard, Training in Christianity (1850; New York: Vintage Books, 2004); Kierkegaard, For Self-Examination and Judge for Yourselves (1851; Princeton, NJ: Princeton University Press, 1944).

[5] Martin Heidegger, *The Phenomenology of Religious Life*, trans. Matthias Fritsch and Jennifer Gosetti-Ferencei (1919; Bloomington: Indiana University Press, 2004); Heidegger, *Towards the Definition of Philosophy*, trans. Ted Sadler (1919; London: Continuum, 2008).

[6] Martin Heidegger, *Being and Time*, trans. John Macquarrie and Edward Robinson (1927; New York: Harper and Row, 1962); John Van Buren, *The Young Heidegger: Rumor of the Hidden King* (Bloomington: Indiana University Press, 1994); Benjamin Crowe, *Heidegger's Religious Origins* (Bloomington: Indiana University Press, 2006).

and eventually through his analysis of Dasein in *Being and Time*, into a more abstract mysticism of the felt sense of Being, which many have compared to Buddhism and Taoism.[7]

The early Heidegger, similarly to the later Max Scheler, had initially pursued his mentor Husserl's project for a "transcendental" phenomenology of the everyday human life world.[8] For Heidegger such a descriptive phenomenology of the "factical life" of *Dasein* can only be indirect and metaphorical, based on "formal indications" as his version of Kierkegaard's "indirect communication," since we already *are* that very being we seek to describe and there is no "outside" our human existence from which to describe it. Both Heidegger and Scheler independently concluded that such a phenomenology already existed. It *is* religion, as the maximum of human self expression, one that "fills out" or "inflates" Dasein so as to allow the fullest possible view of our deepest, necessarily implicit, formal dimensions.[9] So the reinscription of religion *becomes* phenomenology, and especially so for Heidegger with the "incarnation" of a Christianity that links Eckhart's abstract all-inclusive Godhead with the differentiated singularities of personal lives.

In the notes for his first lecture course, Heidegger derives the inner dimensions of everyday human existence from the enhancement of that experi-

---

[7] Martin Heidegger, *On Time and Being*, trans. Joan Stambaugh (1962; New York: Harper & Row, 1972); Heidegger, *Country Path Conversations*, trans. Bret Davis (1944–45; Bloomington: Indiana University Press, 2010); Harry T. Hunt, *On the Nature of Consciousness* (New Haven, CT: Yale University Press, 1995a); Graham Parkes, "Thoughts on the Way: *Being and Time* via Lao-Chuang," in *Heidegger and Asian Thought*, ed. Graham Parkes (Honolulu: University of Hawaii Press, 1987), 105–44; Reinhard May, ed., *Heidegger's Hidden Sources* (London: Routledge, 1996).

[8] Max Scheler, *On the Eternal in Man*, trans. Bernard Noble (1923; London: SCM Press, 1960).

[9] Note that Heidegger's and Scheler's insight of religion as the expanded self-expression of the fundamentals of human existence is *not* in itself any reductive or "projective" *explanation* of spirituality but rather its reinterpretation as the *descriptive* phenomenology of being human sought by Husserl. At the same time we can see the bases of the kind of self validation—fictive or not—that comes from projective explanations of religion in terms of early parental imagos (Sigmund Freud, *Civilization and Its Discontents* [1930; New York: W. W. Norton, 1962]; Ana-Maria Rizzuto, *The Birth of the Living God* [Chicago: University of Chicago Press, 1979]), an oceanic experience before birth (R. D. Laing, *The Facts of Life: An Essay in Feelings, Facts, and Fantasy*, [New York: Pantheon, 1976]), life energy (Henri Bergson, *Creative Evolution* [1907; New York: Modern Library, 1944]; Wilhelm Reich, *Character Analysis* [New York: Noonday Press, 1949]), and the collective bond of society (Emile Durkheim, *The Elementary Forms of the Religious Life*, trans. Joseph Swain [1912; New York: Collier Books, 1961]). These all describe fundamental contexts of human experience that will of necessity surface within the "expansions" of Dasein that are religion, and which can seem to approximate these successively inclusive totalities. These models "work" not necessarily in their own right, whether as explanations or metaphors, but because religion and mystical experience, whatever else they might be, are necessarily revelatory of *us*.

ence described in Meister Eckhart's medieval mysticism.[10] Thus we find in Eckhart the direct precursor to this insight:

> The eye by which I see God is the same as the eye by which God sees me. My eye and God's eye are one and the same. . . . You haven't got to borrow from God, for he is your own and therefore, whatever you get, you get from yourself. . . . God and I: we are one.[11]

Heidegger, after quoting Eckhart, adds, "You can only know what you are . . . Religion is transcendent life. . . . The point is to get down into . . . the grasp of a living moment. . . . The stream of consciousness is already a religious one.[12]

While Heidegger will reverse Eckhart's direction, seeking to know man via God, this derivation of Daseins analysis is certainly consistent with the emphasis in contemporary Christian theology on the sacred as something immanent and *within* the secular.[13]

The second strand of inquiry converging on the implications of a felt core for human spirituality culminates in the contemporary transpersonal psychology of "higher states of consciousness." It is often linked to various forms of New Age spirituality and focuses especially on the Eastern meditative traditions, understood as the maximum developments of the mystical core of all religion and so often seen as least encrusted with a potentially obfuscating dogma and myth. We could say that this perspective has its beginning with Friedrich Nietzsche's naturalistic understanding of ecstasy.[14] It comes into its own in William James on mysticism and Carl Jung on a cross-cultural archetypal imagination, with the function of conferring a sense of meaning and purpose in human existence, and in its most recent developments in Ken Wilber and A. H. Almaas.[15]

---

[10] Martin Heidegger, *The Phenomenology of Religious Life*, trans. Matthias Fritsch and Jennifer Gosetti-Ferencei (1919; Bloomington: Indiana University Press, 2004).

[11] *Meister Eckhart* [fourteenth century], trans. Raymond Blakney (New York: Harper & Row, 1941), 182, 206, 244.

[12] Heidegger, *Phenomenology of Religious Life*, 239, 240, 243, 254. Heidegger also quotes Windelband here ("religion is transcendent life"), who along with Dilthey, Natorp, and Bergson (Van Buren, *Young Heidegger*) was part of the matrix out of which Heidegger's early thought emerged.

[13] Harvey Cox, *The Future of Faith* (New York: Harper Collins, 2009).

[14] Friedrich Nietzsche, *The Will to Power*, trans. Walter Kaufmann (1888; New York: Random House, 1967); Harry T. Hunt, *Lives in Spirit* (Albany: State University of New York Press, 2003).

[15] William James, *The Varieties of Religious Experience* (1902; Garden City, NJ: Dolphin Books, 1961); C. G. Jung, *Two Essays on Analytical Psychology*, vol. 7 of *Collected Works of C. G. Jung*, trans. R. F. C. Hull (1928; Princeton, NJ: Princeton University Press, 1960); Ken Wilber,

A major bridge between these two strands already exists in the form of Rudolf Otto's phenomenology of a numinous felt core to all religious experience as set out in his influential *Idea of the Holy*, itself a major influence on both Jung and Heidegger.[16] The multiple dimensions of numinous feeling include a radical sense of dependency and finitude (Otto's "creature feeling") in the face of something "wholly other," with a fascination, ineffable wonder, and sense of absolute newness and bliss ("mysterium"), and a sense of awe, extraordinary energy and power, and a potential strangeness and uncanny dread ("tremendum").

These dimensions will vary in their degrees of separate development and mutual balance. A key point in Otto's analysis for what follows is that these felt dimensions will be variously embedded and "schematized" within the doctrines and dogma of the world religions. These latter are understood to have been inspired in the first place from such visionary states, while a fully absorbed contemplation in their doctrinal schematizations always retains the potential of re-evoking the original facets of numinous feeling.[17]

Integral Psychology (Boston: Shambhala, 2000); A. H. Almaas, *The Pearl beyond Price: Integration of Personality into Being, an Object Relations Approach* (Berkeley, CA: Diamond Books, 1988).

[16] Rudolf Otto, *The Idea of the Holy*, trans. John Harvey (1917; New York: Oxford University Press, 1958); C. G. Jung, *Psychology and Religion*, vol. 11 of *Collected Works of C. G. Jung*, trans. R. F. C. Hull (1938; Princeton, NJ: Princeton University Press, 1958); Heidegger, *Phenomenology of Religious Life*; Heidegger, *Basic Questions of Philosophy*, trans. Richard Rojcewicz and Andre Schuwer (1938; Bloomington: Indiana University Press, 1994).

[17] As Otto was a neo-Kantian, interested in the numinous as its own a priori intelligence, we can place his phenomenology with more recent attempts to understand spirituality as one form of our multiple symbolic intelligences—logical, artistic, scientific-mechanical, economic, and political (Robert Emmons, "Is Spirituality an Intelligence? Motivation, Cognition, and the Psychology of Ultimate Concern," *International Journal for the Psychology of Religion* 10 [2000]: 3–26; Harry T. Hunt, "Some Developmental Issues in Transpersonal Experience," *Journal of Mind and Behavior* 16 [1995b]: 115–34; Hunt, "A Collective Unconscious Reconsidered: Jung's Archetypal Imagination in the Light of Contemporary Psychology and Social Science," *Journal of Analytical Psychology* 57 [2012]: 76–98)—here as an abstract personal intelligence of the maximal expressive synthesis of human self-understanding. Consider in this regard Husserl's original terminology (Edmund Husserl, *Ideas: General Introduction to Pure Phenomenology* [1913; New York: Collier Books, 1962]; Dan Zahavi, *Husserl's Phenomenology* [Stanford, CA: Stanford University Press, 2003]) for the phases of consciousness—as in noesis, or cognitive-affective act; noema, as its patterned intentional meaning or content; and hyle, as the immediately sensed "stuff" or imagistic-sensory vehicles of expression. We could say that whereas these typically interface seamlessly in the more specific intelligences, the situation is radically different with spirituality. Here, the "expansion" and "inflation" from within Heidegger's Dasein, as his understanding of what happens in religious experience, intuits all-inclusive outer boundaries that can never be represented in full, since we are within them, and thereby drives apart, and so exposes, characteristic gaps among Husserl's phases. Thus the characteristic lack of direct connection between the noetic acts of meditation, prayer, fasting, dream quest, and social isolation, on the one hand, and the schematized noematic

A further illustration of the incipient overlap of the existential and transpersonal traditions comes with the surprisingly similar preoccupation with Meister Eckhart by both Heidegger and Jung in the early 1920s.[18] Both independently derive from Eckhart the identity of God with Being-as-such, the experience of Being as the core of the numinous, and in marked contrast to Kierkegaard's absolute alterity, the inner identity of God and humanity. Jung's own paraphrase of Eckhart directly echoes Heidegger above: "God is dependent on the soul. . . . The soul is the birthplace of God...giving rise to a feeling of intense vitality. . . . God [is] life at its most intense."[19]

Here we see why Jung could name his maximally integrative archetype of the sacred as the "Self," with the historical figures of Jesus and Buddha as exemplars of its most complete personal realization.[20] What Jung called this "relativity" of God to man also meant that both Jung and Heidegger risked and at key points succumbed to the personal inflation of a Gnostic mystical element of "becoming God", which Kierkegaard's more traditional Christian humility rejected as ontologically impossible.[21]

A final example of early and striking overlap between these two strands of analysis comes with the Russian spiritual teacher Gurdjieff, a major precursor to the later transpersonal movement.[22] As early as 1912 he was teaching an extraverted meditation to be practiced in the midst of everyday social life, which he termed "self remembering." In an intriguing anticipation of Heidegger,

---

content of the representations of mythology and dogma, on the other. The latter are in turn quite distinct from the more "bottom-up" hyletic states of mystical and visionary experience, which in contrast to the "top-down" narratives of a God of creation are more minimally schematized as a directly expressive emanation from a sensed ineffable source most developed in Plotinus and the Eastern meditative traditions. Thus we find the perennial tensions between mystics and their respective "religions of the book." These inevitable historical "distentions" between technique, doctrine, and numinous state, based on an intuitive inclusivity that can only be approximated in each cultural era, makes spirituality, as also attested by the very rigidities of dogma, our most fragile and easily disrupted form of symbolic intelligence, and this in ways so often destructive and distortive to both individual and group. The inherent pull toward an expressive understanding of all Being asks what is simultaneously open to our intuition yet closed to any final completion and consistency.

[18] Heidegger, *Phenomenology of Religious Life*; C. G. Jung, *Psychological Types*, vol. 6 of *The Collected Works of C. G. Jung* (1921; Princeton, NJ: Princeton University Press, 1971); Jung, *The Red Book* (New York: W. W. Norton, 2009).

[19] Jung, *Psychological Types*, 248, 251.

[20] C. G. Jung, *Aion*, vol. 9 of *Collected Works* (Princeton, NJ: Princeton University Press, 1959).

[21] See Hunt, *Lives in Spirit*.

[22] G. I. Gurdjieff, Views from the Real World: Early Talks of Gurdjieff as Recollected by his Pupils, ed. Jeanne De Salzmann (New York: E. P. Dutton, 1973); P. D. Ouspensky, In Search of the Miraculous: Fragments of an Unknown Teaching (New York: Harcourt Brace, 1949).

Gurdjieff pictured modern humanity as asleep and mechanical, having lost our natural access to essence or Being. Self-remembering is the cultivation of a here-and-now sense of Being, which, similar to Heidegger on authenticity, will gradually enable us to develop "permanent I" and "objective conscience." In contrast to our usual everyday involvements in which we lose ourselves and forget our Being,

> to remember one's self means the same thing as to be aware of oneself, I am. Sometimes it comes by itself. It is a very strange feeling . . . a different state of consciousness. By itself it only comes for very short moments, . . and one says to oneself "how strange, I am actually here." This is self remembering.[23]

The resulting experience of presence carries a sense of joy, clarity, and freedom reminiscent of Abraham Maslow on peak experiences, as "I am" states in which one experiences one's very identity as Being.[24]

Significantly for what follows, in various places Gurdjieff refers to his "fourth way" movement as "esoteric Christianity." He argues that it is impossible to sustain the Christian mandate for loving kindness and compassion toward others in the absence of our lost capacity for the experience of Being, still present/inferable in early Christianity: "Such as we are, we cannot be Christians. . . . Christ says 'love your enemies,' but . . . we cannot even love our friends. . . . In order to be a good Christian one must *be*. . . . If a man is not his own master . . . he is simply a machine, an automaton. A machine cannot be a Christian."[25]

> First one must be able [to be], only then can one love. Unfortunately, with time, modern Christians have adopted the second half, to love, and lost view of the first, the religion which should have preceded it.[26]

Gurdjieff's analysis here is congruent with both Kierkegaard's rejection of modern Christendom and his painful personal isolation, angry hypersensitivity to all social "humiliation," and deathbed regrets.[27] If Gurdjieff is right, we can then ask how early Christianity and its later "reformations" may have actually evoked this sustaining sense of Being.

---

[23] P. D. Ouspensky, *The Fourth Way* (New York: Alfred A. Knopf, 1959), 8.

[24] Abraham Maslow, *Toward a Psychology of Being* (Princeton, NJ: Van Nostrand, 1962).

[25] Gurdjieff quoted in P. D. Ouspensky, *In Search of the Miraculous: Fragments of an Unknown Teaching* (New York: Harcourt Brace, 1949), 102.

[26] Gurdjieff, Views from the Real World, 153.

[27] Bruce H. Kirmmse, *Encounters with Kierkegaard: A Life as Seen by His Contemporaries* (Princeton, NJ: Princeton University Press, 1996).

Existential and Transpersonal Approaches to the Experience of Being in Early Christianity

What light can Heidegger on the experience of Being and the transpersonal psychology of higher states of consciousness throw on the sense of presence in Christianity—turning them back on the Christianity that both traditions, along with so many, left behind? In contrast to Kierkegaard's own reversion from just such a phenomenology back to Lutheran orthodoxy, how would Heidegger—from within—and the transpersonal perspective—from without—*reinscribe* the inner life-world of Christianity?

From Within: Heidegger and Bultmann

For a time in the early 1920s, Heidegger and the Protestant theologian Rudolf Bultmann worked in tandem, but to very different effect, on a reconstitution of Being as the felt core of a "primitive Christianity" lived by the first apostles. Heidegger's early lectures show him "naturalizing" the Christianity of Eckhart, Paul, Luther, and Kierkegaard as a means toward his later analyses of Dasein,[28] whereas Bultmann would continue to use that existential analysis to reinterpret and demythologize the lived essence of Christianity.[29] For Bultmann Heidegger's openness of time ahead toward the mystery of death, which Heidegger adapts directly from Kierkegaard's phenomenology of dread, illuminates the core existential insight of Christianity as the freedom for a future within which all encounters are potential tokens of God's grace.[30] Later a more mystical Heidegger would turn back from Daseins analysis toward his initial fascination with Eckhart's continual "releasement" of the moment-by-moment gift of Being and time.[31]

---

[28] For early lectures, see Martin Heidegger, *Phenomenology of Religious Life;* Heidegger, *The Phenomenology of Intuition and Expression* (1920; London: Continuum, 2010); Heidegger, *Phenomenological Interpretations of Aristotle* (1921; Bloomington: Indiana University Press, 2001); Heidegger, *Introduction to Phenomenological Research* (1923; Bloomington: Indiana University Press, 2005). For later analyses of Dasein, see Heidegger, *The Concept of Time* (1924; London: Continuum, 2011); Heidegger, *Being and Time.*

[29] Rudolf Bultmann, *Primitive Christianity in Its Contemporary Setting*, trans. R. H. Fuller (London: Thames & Hudson, 1956); Bultmann, *Kerygma and Myth* (New York: Harper & Row, 1961).

[30] Rudolf Bultmann, The Presence of Eternity: History and Eschatology (New York: Harper & Row, 1957)

[31] Heidegger, *Country Path Conversations*; Heidegger, *The Question of Being* (1956; New York: Twayne, 1958); Heidegger, *On Time and Being.* While Peter Sajda ("Meister Eckhart," in *Kierkegaard and the Patristic and Medieval Traditions*, ed. Jon Stewart [New York: Ashgate, 2008], 237–54) stresses Kierkegaard's more obvious rejection of all mysticism as merely "aesthetic" and separated from revealed religion, David J. Kangas (*Kierkegaard's Instant: On Beginnings* [Bloomington: Indiana University Press, 2007]) shows an indirect influence of Eckhart

This earlier Heidegger had begun by analogizing the structure of our ordinary ongoing experience to a joining of Eckhart's bottomless sense of Being as Godhead with its expression as the differentiated personal soul of Paul and Luther.[32] Thus everyday experience is seen as springing forth in the immediate moment from an ineffable background "something" (Schleiermacher's *Etwa*, already anticipating Heidegger's Being) and then "temporalizing" into specific life events. Both source and personal emanation are equally unknowable in any final or certain sense and so are existentially "transcendent"—each human life its own double infinity. Christian love is reinscribed into the existential structure of care, and faith in eternal life into the authenticity of being ahead of oneself toward the unknown of death. Heidegger transforms "original sin" into the "formal indication" of a sense of inherent flaw or "falleness" in human existence, such that ordinary living "inclines away," "eludes," or "disperses" from its "as such."[33] It is a "ruinance" that is yet pervaded by the sense of the indeterminate "something" behind it—the God of Christianity reinscribed as a primordial experience of Being.

Religious experience is our potential for a more direct awareness of this expansiveness, outflow, or "effulgence" of life itself—the "relucance" or "reflectence" of our self-aware existence. God is the abstract form of all sensitive life, and our capacity to sense that means in Christian terms that the "kingdom" has already arrived as a "leftover" echo of and within each life event. The early Heidegger thus comes very close to an incipient version of the transpersonal psychology of mystical states as natural human phenomena begun by Maslow on "peak experience."[34] Numinous experience for Heidegger is latent within all human experience as the intensification into our self awareness of its underlying form – a bringing forward of its pre-worldly "something" and its "not yet" of time-ahead directly into experience as "moments of especially intensive life."[35] These show the "essence of life in and for itself."[36]

(through Tauler, Boehme, and Schelling) on Kierkegaard's own understanding of the fullness of the moment and its eternally outward movement as the openness of time ahead in *The Concept of Dread*. Thus Heidegger's reading of the early Kierkegaard could have helped support his own joining of Eckhart's Godhead and its "releasement" as the existential anxiety of personal being in time.

32 Heidegger, Phenomenology of Religious Life.

33 Heidegger, Towards the Definition of Philosophy; Heidegger, Phenomenological Interpretations of Aristotle.

34 Maslow, Toward a Psychology of Being.

35 Heidegger, Towards the Definition of Philosophy, 88.

36 Heidegger, *Towards the Definition of Philosophy*, 88. Heidegger, both early and late, ultimately leaves open whether such mystical states would merely be projections of our being alive, as they certainly are phenomenologically, or veridical ontological perceptions of a transcendent source and intentionality. How we view such a question, aside from decisions of faith, may also depend on what science does or does not learn about the place and potential inevitabil-

Now if Otto, Jung, and Heidegger are right about the numinous and its core in the experience of Being, as an inherent human response, then it will not simply disappear in a predominantly secular era. Indeed Otto's original phenomenology shows it to be broader than our modern, perhaps already secularized, understanding of "spirituality" or "religion." Facets of the numinous may arise as a sense of wonder, fascination, and mystery in the face of the immensities of the modern universe of physics. Meanwhile, its more uncanny, grotesque, and dreadful aspects appear in our subjective response to the atrocities of war and torture, or to the imagery of monstrous beings, blood, and dismemberment in the myths of tribal religions, contemporary video games, and psychedelic drug accounts.[37]

So what has happened more generally to this inherent category of experience in what may well be our historically unique era of secularization and materialization—aside, that is, from the obvious exceptions of renewed fundamentalism, New Age spiritualities, and the finite and more "polytheistic" sources of awe and fascination in nature, sports, and celebrities recently discussed by Hubert Dreyfus and Sean Kelly?[38] Pierre Hadot and Martin Buber, both citing Heidegger, have suggested that for the general population in our radically secularized civilization the sense of the numinous tends to manifest itself in its most primitive form—as the sense of the uncanny.[39] Buber finds a nightmarish "dread of the universe and dread of life," while Hadot suggests that as a culture we increasingly find existence itself to be uncanny, strange, and unreal, as somehow grotesque and bizarre, and in marked contrast to the fuller sense of wonder, mystery, and gratitude in the great axial religions.[40] Hadot is struck by the influence here of Sartre's novel *Nausea* as a primary response to the sheer facticity and increasing strangeness of Being.[41] Indeed for both Sigmund Freud

ity of life, and its self-aware development, in the universe of modern physics (Harry T. Hunt, "The Truth Value of Mystical Experience," *Journal of Consciousness Studies* 13, no. 12 [2006]: 5–43). The later Heidegger (*Schelling's Treatise on the Essence of Human Freedom* [1936; Athens: Ohio University Press, 1985]) does caution that before we dismiss intuitions of Being as mere anthropomorphizing, we should be more clear on whether we—inside our own being and without access to an outside—do or can finally know who and what we are. We may not be able to know in any final way what is metaphor of what—the universe of us or us of the universe.

[37] Stanislav Grof, *LSD Psychotherapy* (Pomona, CA: Hunter House, 1980).

[38] Hubert Dreyfus and Sean Kelly, *All Things Shining* (New York: Free Press, 2011)

[39] Pierre Hadot, *The Present Alone Is Our Happiness*, trans. Marc Djaballah and Michael Chase (Stanford, CA: Stanford University Press, 2011); Martin Buber, *Between Man and Man*, trans. Ronald Gregor-Smith (London: Routledge, 1947).

[40] Buber, *Between Man and Man*, 237; Hadot, *Present Alone Is Our Happiness.*

[41] Jean-Paul Sartre, *Nausea*, trans. Lloyd Alexander (1938; Norfolk, CT: New Directions, 1959).

and Andras Angyal, disgust and nausea are common accompaniments of the sense of the uncanny.[42]

For the early Heidegger modern culture has lost the sense of Being, so that in everyday life we flee from the "threat of existence itself," and certainly from anything to do with death as its final outcome, into a self-concealing denial and "tranquilization."[43] No longer "at home" in the world, Being itself becomes "uncanny" (*unheimlich*, un-homelike). No wonder Kierkegaard begins his attempt at the renewal of Christianity with *The Concept of Dread.* The "flight" from Being as something uncanny and strange would thus become an unwitting and self-reinforcing avoidance conditioning away from the incipient core of all spirituality and its sense of meaning in human existence. As Gurdjieff points out, spiritual practice thereby becomes relatively unsustainable, and doctrines of traditional Christian belief and ethic of loving compassion will lack crucial support in an ongoing sense of presence. Yet Heidegger's early analysis of Dasein and its "fallenness" was directly derived from a Christian spirituality that by definition then remains implicit within his understanding of ordinary experience and itself implies the underlying sense of Being and ongoing presence that would be its core. The possibility thereby emerges of some degree of reciprocal illumination and dialogue between the existentials of Gospel narratives and their hypothetical numinous core and/or realization.

From Without: The Application of Transpersonal Psychology to Early Christianity

The phenomenologist Max Scheler suggested some important limitations in Otto's analysis of a numinous core for all spirituality, which will in turn suggest some corresponding concerns for any attempted transpersonal psychology of Christianity.[44] In regard to the relation between the immediacy of the numinous and its selective schematization as religious doctrine, the usual view has been that of James, Jung, and contemporary transpersonalists that the former is primary, as reflected in overlapping mystical traditions. Thereby the conceptual and theological schematization of the numinous is seen as secondary, even potentially static and stultifying in the face of social-economic change and thus in need of periodic charismatic renewal.[45] Otto, as a Lutheran theologian, saw a more complex and reciprocal relation, and indeed in the second half of *Idea of the Holy* he pictures Protestantism as the fullest historical development and

[42] Sigmund Freud, "The Uncanny," in *Collected Papers of Sigmund Freud*, vol. 4, trans. Joan Riviere (1919; New York: Basic Books, 1959), 368–77; Andras Angyal, "Disgust and Related Aversions," *Journal of Abnormal and Social Psychology* 36 (1941): 393–412.

[43] Heidegger, *Concept of Time*, 221.

[44] Scheler, On the Eternal in Man.

[45] See Hunt, *Lives in Spirit.*

schematization of all facets of the numinous. Separate critiques by Scheler and later by Buber, while agreeing on a cross-cultural numinous core, actually prioritize doctrinal and ethical schematizations over their numinous mediations.[46] While on his extreme constructivist grounds Steven Katz would seem to have gone too far in rejecting any such shared numinous core, on the side of Scheler recent empirical research by Ralph Hood and his colleagues found that while the introvertive (dissolution of self) dimension of his mysticism questionnaire could be associated with measures of emotional disturbance, that effect was mitigated by higher scores on his "interpretation" dimension, as centered more on the broadly theological significance of such experiences.[47] Clearly "schematization" is not only or merely the "expression" of the numinous but also potentially its further developmental articulation and broader contextualization.

For Scheler numinous experience is *always* at least incipiently denominational, and religion is its channeling and semantic completion.[48] Religious acts are more than their mediating states, however central these must also be. The numinous is the inner process or means, in Husserlian terms the hyletic vehicle or sensory-affective by-product, of its noetic meaning, which like all intentionality points beyond itself—here as the intuition of an encompassing "world transcending" reality.[49] For Scheler and Heidegger it is this "outward" look away from explicit life events and toward an intuited sense of totality that allows religion to be the maximum expressive phenomenology of the human condition.[50] Scheler actually says that such transcendental intuitions cast the numinous back "like a shadow."[51] Both Scheler and Buber agree with Almaas more recently that valuing numinous states over their intentional significance in meaning and ethical action risks an unwitting "self-worship" or narcissism.[52] Thus their potential for psychiatric-like "metapathologies."[53] Numinous experiences are not ends but means.

Accordingly, in seeking the numinous facets of the experience of Being inspiring/inspired by early Christianity, it is important not to see these as something merely frozen and lost within Gospel accounts considered as static dog-

---

[46] Scheler, *On the Eternal in Man*; Buber, *I and Thou*, trans. Walter Kaufmann (1957; New York: Charles Scribner's Sons, 1970).

[47] Steven Katz, ed., *Mysticism and Philosophical Analysis* (New York: Oxford University Press, 1978); Ralph Hood et al., "Dimensions of the Mysticism Scale: Confirming the Three-Factor Structure in the United States and Iran," *Journal for the Scientific Study of Religion* 40, no. 4, (2001): 691–705.

[48] Scheler, *On the Eternal in Man.*

[49] Ibid., 250.

[50] Heidegger, *Towards the Definition of Philosophy*; Heidegger, *Country Path Conversations.*

[51] Scheler, *On the Eternal in Man*, 286.

[52] Buber, *I and Thou*; Almaas, *Pearl beyond Price.*

[53] Hunt, *Lives in Spirit.*

ma. Instead, these accounts can also be the maximum expressive articulation and realization of mediating numinous states fully implied, evoked, and embedded as the narratives of Jesus and the apostles. Thus transpersonal psychology becomes a contemporary means of reinscribing and de-embedding lived realizations of numinous experience that mediated many Gospel accounts and remain latent within them.[54]

Cartographies of Transpersonal Experience and Their Relation to Christianity and its Early Competitors

Marghanita Laski outlines multiple dimensions of ecstatic experience.[55] Like Otto's "creature feeling," there is the initiating sense of an existential lack or loss, as a stage of purgation, suffering, and desolation—also reflected in its schematization as a sense of "original sin" or inherent flaw. This is followed by experiences of "gain" and felt rebirth—in Pentecostal Christianity the sense of being "born again" and "saved." The path taken by this sense of "existential gain" can move toward mysticisms of love, as in Christianity, Knowledge, as in Plotinus, or will, strength, and power, as in early Stoicism.

Experiences of gain, as the equivalent of Otto's mysterium-tremendum, are mediated and evoked by what Laski terms the "quasi physical sensations" of ecstasy. These are metaphoric and/or directly imagistic expressive meanings based variously on experiences of height and depth, light, darkness, insideness, enlargement, and liquidity/flow. These facets of what she calls "intensity ecstasy" tend to develop in either of two directions in terms of fundamental shifts in one's sense of personal identity: either toward a dissolution of self, as in Eastern mysticism and Eckhart's Godhead, or toward a felt transformation/enhancement of self, which she also describes as "Adamic ecstasy," as in a sensed return to the condition of Adam and Eve before the fall.

Almaas has more recently divided this category of self transformation between "personal essence" or realization of the "pearl," as the spontaneous

---

54 By not so distant analogy, since the uncanny is a primitive and less articulated form of the numinous, we can model this reciprocity between numinous state and interpretive schematization by contrasting two imaginary situations, within which each phase will predominate and in turn bring forth the other as a developing reciprocal dialogue. In the first, sitting alone, late at night, one starts to feel a sense of eeriness and invisible presence, one that soon elaborates into a specific ghost narrative further directing and intensifying those feelings. In the second, one is reading a well-written ghost story by M. R. James and finds oneself increasingly suffused with specific facets of uncanniness and eeriness not actually mentioned at all in the story but which express its very essence. By analogy, then, New Age mysticism does the former with the fuller numinous, while a transpersonal psychology of the Gospels would do the latter.

55 Marghanita Laski, *Ecstasy* (Bloomington: Indiana University Press, 1961).

synthesis of genuine autonomy and empathic contactfulness, and "essential identity" or realization of the "point," in which one senses the identity of one's true self as Being itself.[56] Maslow's earlier discussion of self-actualization variously emphasized both components, but the former has more the connotations of personal "soul" and the latter of "spirit."[57] Almaas suggests that Jesus considered as "son of man" emphasizes more the loving humanity of "personal essence," while Jesus as "son of God" evokes more of the pure divinity of Christ as guiding Logos and power of all creation.[58]

Almaas, like Heidegger, sees the varieties of the numinous in terms of experiences of Being or presence that can manifest in different aspects, each with its own expressive physiognomy or quasi-physical sensory quality, also related to classical yogic chakras, and each evoking and being supported by a primary sense of Being. Presence, or in his terms, "essence,"

> is the direct experience of existence. Of course essence can be experienced as other things, such as love, trust, peace, and the like. But the sense of existence is its most basic characteristic . . . that sets it apart from other categories of experience.[59]

These aspects of Being can appear in genuinely ineffable and metaphoric expressions or in more inauthentic forms as the mere intensification of ordinary emotions. They include the qualities joy or bliss, will, strength, power or peace, noetic brilliancy or knowledge, and two aspects of love—merging essence, as the felt union or oneness of Platonic Eros, and compassion, as the loving kindness of Christian Agape.

To begin to contextualize Christianity within these frameworks, we can compare it to some of its early competitors within the Hellenized Roman era. The spiritual wisdom schools of the Stoics, the Epicureans, and Neoplatonism are understood by Hadot as distinct approaches to cultivating the experience of presence as originally inspired by the example of Socrates, and with each supported by different aspects of essence, here using the framework of Almaas.[60] The Epicureans were most explicit in cultivating a direct sense of existence, understood as the most subtle pleasure or joy open to the individual, while for the Stoics one's essential identity as Being was based on a radical autonomy of essential strength and will. Where early Christianity cultivated compassion/Agape as its essential aspect, the Stoics sought not to be "saved" but to

---

56 Almaas, *Pearl beyond Price.*

57 Abraham Maslow, *Toward a Psychology of Being.*

58 Almaas, *Pearl beyond Price.*

59 A. H. Almaas, *Essence* (New York: Samuel Weiser, 1986), 11.

60 Pierre Hadot, *What Is Ancient Philosophy?* (Cambridge, Mass.: Belknap Press, 2002); Hadot, *Present Alone Is Our Happiness.*

subordinate personal will to the universal will of God as revealed by ongoing events.[61] Despite their similar emphasis on a this-worldly spiritual realization, the personal and humanizing love of Christianity seems totally absent from the Stoics and the Epicureans. Meanwhile, a more abstract love in the sense of Platonic Eros was central to the dissolving of Self in the mystical school of Plotinus, although it in turn lacked all interest in the singularities of personal life and intimate contact with others central to Christianity. The gradual predominance of Christian love over systems based exclusively on joy, strength and will, and transcendent knowledge may have been inevitable as a deeply needed compensation for the harsh and competitive conditions of life suffered by the average person under Roman rule. The closest parallel to the Christian ethics of personal essence would have been a thoroughly secularized Aristotelian ethics of friendship and emotional balance, which, however, by definition would lack the numinous inspiration necessary for a charismatic movement.

The Phenomenology and Psychology of Numinous Experience in Early Christianity

Numinous qualities in the New Testament must be derived and evoked from the more "top-down" schematization of narrative and belief in Gospel accounts, in contrast to the more "bottom-up" emanationism of Eckhart and Plotinus. What was it like in transpersonal terms for the earliest followers of Christianity? By way of initial summary, we could say that the deeply felt acceptance of forgiveness of one's sins and assurance of eternal life would have the conjoined effect of removing guilt over the past and anxiety about the future, thus leaving the believers released into the state of ongoing presence and endlessly renewed "now" that Gurdjieff, Almaas, and Heidegger describe as the experience of Being. In turn, and in keeping with Gurdjieff's view of presence as the necessary support for Christian compassion, the gift and grace of that assurance of one's eternal Being will inspire a gratitude and grace in God's love that will spontaneously overflow toward all others.

If John Crossan and, earlier, Johannes Weiss are correct that the nature miracles of Jesus, tomb, and resurrection are later additions, then the earliest Christians were most likely to have been charismatically inspired by these more direct experiences of presence and compassion.[62]

---

[61] Epictetus [first century], *The Discourses* (Cambridge, MA: Harvard University Press, 1925).
[62] John Crossan, *Jesus: A Revolutionary Biography* (New York: Harper Collins, 1995); Johannes Weiss, *Earliest Christianity*, vol. 2 (New York: Harper Torchbooks, 1959).

Experiences of Implied Presence

If we ask what stops the felt experience of presence for Almaas, it is self-image. Self-image is based on fixed memories, more or less frozen in place by past anxiety, guilt, and shame. So if you fully believe that all sins are already forgiven ("Your sins are forgiven. . . . Your faith has saved you; go in peace," Luke 7:48, 50 [NEB]), then the resulting release of self-image from the past lands you in the present here and now. This differs from the later Kierkegaard's retreat to Lutheran orthodoxy in *Training in Christianity*, where as part of God's infinite distance, forgiveness is postponed into eternity. By contrast, as Weiss points out, the early apostles experienced themselves as already saved, with the immediate effect of a joyous release.[63]

In terms of our orientation to the future, while Heidegger's existential anxiety of being-toward-death can open toward the experience of Being, more often it buffers and "tranquillizes" that awareness. However, if for the early believers death had been annihilated and eternal life already begun within that futural openness, then once again one was released into the on-flow of here and now Being:

> Anyone who . . . puts his trust in him who sent me has hold of eternal life, and does not come up for judgement, but has already passed from death to life. . . . He shall never know what it is to die. . . . No one who is alive and has faith shall ever die.[64]

This can be taken as a top-down schematization of the spontaneous sense of timelessness and eternity within intense experiences of numinous ecstasy occurring outside any traditional religious context, as in the following account from James, where it is part of the noetic amplification of the quasi-physical metaphor of a fiery energy:

> I found myself wrapped in a flame-colored cloud. For an instant I thought of fire. . . . The next, I knew the fire was in myself. Directly afterward there came upon me a sense of exultation . . . immediately followed by an intellectual illumination impossible to describe. . . . I saw that the universe is a living Presence; I became conscious in myself of eternal life. It was not a conviction that I would have eternal life, but a consciousness that I possessed eternal life then; I saw that all men are immortal; . . . that the foundation principle of the world is what we call love, and that the happiness of each and all is in the long run absolutely certain.[65]

---

[63] Weiss, Earliest Christianity, vol. 2.
[64] John 5:24; 8:51; 11:26 (NEB).
[65] James, Varieties of Religious Experience, 360–61.

To fully sense Jesus's statement on "eternal life" already in the here and now would be to evoke this more immediate felt state of timelessness. Indeed, in several places Jesus announces, in contrast to possibly later doctrines of apocalypse,[66] that the eternal kingdom of God is already here—"on earth as it is in heaven." Jesus says: "You cannot tell by observation when the kingdom of God comes . . . for in fact the kingdom of God is among you."[67]

Even the more frequent statements that believers are to await a future second coming ("at the time you least expect him," Matt 24:44 [NEB]) encourages a "permanent wakefulness" and so Paul's perpetual sense of "newness," which creates a top-down schematization for Gurdjieff's "self-remembering" of ongoing presence. In the Gospel of John the story of Jesus and the Samaritan woman drawing water at the well makes use of a metaphor central to the phenomenology of presence in Almaas and Gurdjieff. After asking this woman, both alien as a Samaritan and also isolated from her own community, for water, Jesus says: "If only you knew what God gives . . . you would have asked him and he would have given you *living* water. . . . The water I shall give . . . will be an inner spring always welling up for eternal life."[68]

Later at a public festival Jesus says: "If any man is thirsty let him come to me and drink. He who believes in me . . .a stream of *living water* shall flow out from within him."[69] More than just a metaphor, flowing water is one of Laski's quasi-physical sensations of ecstasy.[70] Almaas stresses that its felt embodiment is a major form of the experience of numinous presence:

> Essence when experienced directly is seen to be some kind of substance, like water or gold . . . but it is not a physical substance. . . . Imagine that the water is self aware . . . of its own energy and excitation. Imagine now that you are this aware substance, this water. This is close to an experience of essential substance.[71]

Along these lines a Gurdjieff student describes her own experience of awakening to presence:

> A fleeting sensation of no longer being alone, separate, but reconnected to an immense presence. . . . Like a rain of gold showering down over my head,

[66] Weiss, Earliest Christianity, vol. 2.
[67] Luke 17:20–21 (NEB).
[68] John 4:10, 14 (NEB), italics added.
[69] John 7:38 (NEB), italics added.
[70] Laski, *Ecstasy*.
[71] Almaas, *Essence*, 54, 80.

shoulders, and back, I was completely aglow, inundated by a grace, both luminous and solid, which I received with surprise and wonder.[72]

Such experiences can be understood as the self-aware embodiment of William James's metaphor for ongoing consciousness as flowing stream.[73] In terms of the early Heidegger on the experience of Being as enhancing and revealing the inner dimensions of all experience, this may help to make some sense of his cryptic "the stream of consciousness is already a religious one."[74]

Experiences of Compassion/Agape

Loving compassion or Agape is the central aspect of the numinous supporting and supported by the experience of presence in Christianity. Indeed, for Rudolf Otto the original element in Christianity is the experience of God as loving Father. The gift of God's love, in the form of forgiveness and eternal life, confers an assurance and loving gratitude that can spontaneously overflow toward others. This sense of spontaneous overflow may be illustrated in the recent newscast of the audio recording of the utterly authentic voice of a young man hiding with several others in the dark and frightened silence of a restaurant food refrigeration room during a recent Mississippi tornado: "I love everyone." This image of the felt sense of God's absolute love spontaneously overflowing toward others was central to Luther's emphasis on faith over works and therein may reflect the influence of Eckhart and the German mystics on his theology.[75] The spontaneous experience of one's love for neighbor as "overplus" of what has been received fits well with the incident where Jesus says of the woman sobbing while cleaning his feet: "Her great love proves her many sins have been forgiven; when little has been forgiven, little love is shown."[76]

This experiential interpretation is also consistent with Bultmann's view that those who become loving toward others show that they have really experienced God's love.[77] It differs from the more conditional ethical interpretation, also supported by Gospel passages, where the love one will receive from God depends first on the effort made to love others. This works-predominant approach is reflected in Matthew 6:14 (NEB): "If you forgive others the wrong they have done, your heavenly father will forgive you," and in the later Kierkegaard's "like for like" in the appropriately titled *Works of Love*, where what one

---

[72]Ann-Marie de Vilaine-Cambessedes, "No Conscious Effort Is Ever Lost," in *Gurdjieff*, ed. Jacob Needleman and George Baker (New York: Continuum, 1997), 845.
[73] William James, *The Principles of Psychology* (1890; New York: Dover, 1950).
[74] Heidegger, *Phenomenology of Religious Life*, 254.
[75] Bengt Hoffman, *Luther and the Mystics* (Minneapolis: Augsburg, 1976).
[76] Luke 7:47 (NEB).
[77] Bultmann, *Primitive Christianity*.

does to others God "repeats" back to the doer "with the intensification of infinity."[78]

Certainly in the context of New Age spiritual groups,[79] loving compassion can have this more spontaneous first-person mystical element, central also to Eckhart's identification of Godhead and person that so fascinated the early Heidegger. It is sometimes described as the sense of an infinite and absolute love experienced as a light shining from "above" and "behind" and through the individual's heart, directed through one's own self as vehicle or medium, toward others who have evoked in one a sense of loving compassion. Such experiences may also be implied where Jesus states that he heals by the power of God, as later the apostles will heal through Jesus. Paul similarly states: "The life I live now is not my life, but the life Christ lives in me."[80] As phenomenological states these accounts make sense if we recall that numinous aspects feel transcendent and "wholly other," and that, with William James, they carry the felt sense that they "have" one, that is, happen to the person as if from an outside source, rather than the more everyday sense of one "having" experience. So a spontaneous response to the fully embodied experience of Christian Agape, in which the person feels transparent to something passing through him or her, can be a stunned: "Whose love *is* this?"

There is a similar first-person mystical element of "it has you" in Luther's own experience of faith, not as belief in a set of doctrines, but in terms of a state of "assurance" and "nearness" of God in the midst of everyday events that Otto and Hoffman suggest show the influence of the school of Eckhart, where Godhead permeates even the most painful and challenging experiences.[81] Here faith is not effortful but a gift of grace that allows one to look through and beyond each event for the grace hidden within it. "Everything takes its flavour from God and becomes divine; everything that happens betrays God when a man's mind works that way; things all have this one taste."[82] This is very far from the infinite alterity between God and humanity in Kierkegaard's later retreat to a more effortful orthodoxy of doctrine and belief, perhaps sadly bypassing his earlier capacity for its felt inward animation.

---

78 Søren Kierkegaard, *Works of Love* (1847; New York: Harper Vintage Books, 2009), 252.

79 Almaas, *Essence.*

80 Gal. 2:20 (NEB).

81 Otto, *Idea of the Holy*; Hoffman, *Luther and the Mystics.*

82 *Meister Eckhart*, 17.

Conclusions: Transpersonal and Phenomenological Understandings of Christian Faith

Mysticism, Dogma, and Faith

To the extent that the Christian believer comes to fully embody and live from the assurance of forgiveness of sins and an eternal life already begun, we would have a kind of top-down approximation to Gurdjieff's self-remembering of ongoing Being within the everyday social and personal world. This, if fully realized, would constitute a version of the inner- or this-worldly mysticism that is also the ultimate fruition of some Eastern meditative traditions,[83] as in the ox-herding pictures of Zen Buddhism where the realized meditator returns to a daily life now inwardly animated by enlightenment but outwardly indistinguishable from everyone else, or realized Taoist and Sufi sages ending up living anonymously in their communities as ordinary householders.[84]

Almaas similarly suggests that the Christian doctrine of a resurrection as already begun and continuously renewed moment by moment constitutes a potential integration of spiritual realization and the here-and-now secular order that is very different from the more preliminary radical rejection of world in most Gnostic and Eastern teachings.[85] To the extent that certain Gospel narrative schematizations are fully realized in terms of their numinous significance, there is a potential sanctification of life in this world—a phenomenologically realized "kingdom of heaven on earth" reminiscent of these not often attained "return" phases of some Eastern meditative paths. In terms of comparative religion, it is as if the access levels of Eastern meditative practice were skipped in favor of a direct schematization of their fullest possible realization within everyday life.

However, this setting out in narrative schematization of the ideal image of a spiritual enlightenment fully integrating sacred and secular will create a comparative dilemma for practicing Christians largely absent for those engaged in the more gradual step-by-step practices of the meditative traditions. Christians from the beginning of their adult lives are thus asked to act in terms of an image of full spiritual realization for which they cannot possibly be ready. They are implicitly invited to at best "role-play" a place of integral realization that few human beings will ever attain in any spiritual tradition, and without the difficult but step-by-step techniques of meditation, often helpfully separated from daily social life, that would gradually create the states of consciousness that could foreshadow this fuller realization.

---

83 Hunt, "Truth Value of Mystical Experience."

84 Toshihiko Izutsu, *Sufism and Taoism: A Comparative Study of Key Philosophical Concepts* (Berkeley: University of California Press, 1984).

85 A. H. Almaas, *Inexhaustible Mystery* (Boston: Shambhala, 2011).

The effect for those most seriously inspired by gospel teachings can be a deep frustration, impossibly harsh self-condemnation, and a decades long in-the-world equivalent of Laski's puration/suffering stage of mystical development, with little or no sign of transcending experiences of "gain" or existential fulfillment. While Edwin Starbuck located potential experiences of mid- and later life "sanctification" that do sound very much like Christian equivalents of Maslow's Being values of self-actualization, the serious Christian seems especially prone to two forms of a more fixating counterreaction.[86]

The first danger is what Harvey Cox has termed a clinging to "mandatory belief systems [that] nearly eclipse faith and hope."[87] This is the subtle violence of conceptual exclusivity and premature certainty. The early Kierkegaard was right that "indirect communication" is necessary if we are to evoke an authentic human inwardness. His later retreat to "dogmatics" as somehow the "direct communication" of a biblical God of absolute alterity came at the price of his earlier subtlety, poetry, and paradox needed to evoke the sense of the numinous. Whatever their faults, the later Heidegger, Jung, and Almaas understood there could be no "direct communication" of the sacred in an era of cultural secularization and so went forward with the search for a more radical renewal.

The second danger is that these frustrations of the Christian ideal of compassion or love, without its potential sustenance through realizations of a supporting sense of presence, have sometimes led to an unconscious and defensive inversion of value. There we have a fascination with imageries of violence, hatred, and destruction. This can be reflected in a kind of exclusive reveling in the agonies of the crucifixion, the Book of Revelation with its violent and near-psychotic imagery,[88] the endless elaborations of the tortures of eternal damnation, and the outwardly enacted barbarities and murderous cruelties of the inquisition and the early Puritans. It may be no accident that Gnosticism, as the major competition of a newly emerged Christianity, offered an elitist arrogance in contrast to a more difficult humility and often pictured creation itself as a malign and evil mistake,[89] a view of an "infinite distance" between God and humanity more recently reflected in some fundamentalist dismissals of the social world as entirely under the rule of Satan.[90]

Gurdjieff saw that his in-the-world practice of self-remembering could constitute a kind of esoteric Christianity in the sense of offering the sense of presence in here-and-now social reality needed to support and sustain Agape as

---

86 Edwin Starbuck, *The Psychology of Religion: An Empirical Study of the Growth of Religious Consciousness* (London: Walter Scott, 1899).

87 Cox, *Future of Faith*, 74.

88 Anton T. Boisen, *The Exploration of the Inner World* (1936; New York: Harper, 1962).

89 Karen L. King, *What Is Gnosticism?* (Cambridge, MA: Belknap Press, 2003).

90 Harold Bloom, *The American Religion* (New York: Simon & Schuster, 1992).

an authentic ethic of relationship. It is like digging a tunnel simultaneously from both ends, between the meditative practices so developed in Eastern traditions, here already in their most extraverted form in Gurdjieff and Almaas, and the narrative schematizations in the New Testament of a way of being-in-the-world that fully embodied would be indistinguishable from traditional notions of enlightenment in Buddhism, Taoism, and Sufism, and the closely related stories of the Hasidic Jewish tradition.[91] Here we can see the value of New Age transpersonalism both in its focus on the empirics and cognitive processes of meditation and in its providing a phenomenology of the core facets of the numinous de-embedded from their Gospel schematizations, themselves articulations of an ethic of enlightenment that goes far beyond what most could obtain from meditation alone.

Love as Fundamental Form of the Experience of Being

Something like Christian love or Agape would seem to tap into the deepest root of the numinous, considered as the fullest symbolic self-expression of both humanity and, with the early Heidegger, life in general. With respect to the former, the psychoanalyst D. W. Winnicott, now supported by copious research on mirror neurons and neonatal behavior, sees the core of humanness as manifesting from birth in the "mirroring" relation between infant and "mothering one."[92] The infant's fascination with facial (and vocal) expression involves the infant seeing itself reflected back in the interactive gaze and intonations of the parents. The parents' expressions in response to spontaneous manifestations of the infant's states are empathic and compassionate reflections back of these states, and this is the means by which young children begin to form a distinctly human sense of self.

What the infant experiences in the responsive face of the "mothering one" is a loving response to *itself*. The internalization of these elaborate mirroring reflections sets up the human self as an inner dialogic process, increasingly with the capacity to do that back to others.[93] Accordingly, Christianity's understanding of the reciprocal love and forgiveness between believer and God amplifies the heart of the human development of self. This, if the infant is to survive both physically and psychically, is the first and deepest pattern of our relating. Of necessity it lies beneath all later more-differentiated and even potentially

---

[91] Martin Buber, *Tales of the Hasidim: The Later Masters* (New York: Schocken Books, 1948).
[92] D. W. Winnicott, *Playing and Reality* (New York: Basic Books, 1971). Regarding research on mirror neurons and neonatal behavior, see Andrew Meltzoff and Michael Moore, "Early Imitation within a Functional Framework: The Importance of Person Identity, Movement, and Development," *Infant Behavior and Development* 15 (1992): 479–505.
[93] Winnicott, *Playing and Reality*.

contrary motives, as reflected in what he thought could be his last statement in this life by the young man facing the Mississippi tornado: "I love everyone."

This core of compassionate love goes to a "living truth" still deeper than Winnicott. James J. Gibson's psychology of perception itself is based on an inseparable and primary attunement between any organism and its environmental surround, such that as a condition of its potential existence the organism is "held" by its environment in a way that "gives" or "affords" the potential behaviors unique to each species.[94] Going further, Gibson shows how the sensitive feedback or "echo" created by organismic movement generates an "ambient ecological array" or "envelope of flow" back from its life-world that mirrors the exact size, shape, and speed of the specific creature thereby evoking it. If we amplify or anthropomorphize this relationship in human metaphoric terms, as part of what spirituality already does as human phenomenology,[95] we have an "allowing," "letting," "holding," and "giving" that is the existential core of all organismic life, again prior to all more more-specific behavior patterns, and perpetually foundational even if that creature is annihilated within seconds of its birth.

Amplified on the interpersonal level of human existence, this "holding" and "affording" pattern is reflected in Winnicott's empathic mirroring relation.[96] Amplified or in some sense "sublimated" as human spirituality, it is the

---

[94] James J. Gibson, *The Ecological Approach to Visual Perception* (Boston: Houghton Mifflin, 1979).

[95] To understand the core of religion as an anthropomorphizing of a given culture's understanding of the physical universe (Stewart E. Guthrie, *Faces in the Clouds: A New Theory of Religion* [New York: Oxford University Press, 1993]) carries no logical necessity of making that "illusion," especially given the necessity of metaphor in all human thought, artistic and scientific (George Lakoff and Mark Johnson, *Philosophy in the Flesh* [New York: Basic Books, 1999]). Given the lawfulness of life in this universe and its incipient "anthropic" possibility within the original physical constants after the "big bang" of cosmological creation, and given the lawfulness of our own human evolution based on the progressive interconnections of the separate senses, themselves attuned to the physical world (Hunt, 1995a), there seems to be no reason why we should not "put things in our own terms," since we must anyway, even in mathematics (George Lakoff and Rafael Núñez, *Where Mathematics Comes From: How the Embodied Mind Brings Mathematics into Being* [New York: Basic Books, 2000]). If part of this be religion, then so be it. It may be that our "anthropomorphizing" of the universe that generated us will capture aspects of the system complexity principles that in fact did lead in our direction.

[96] In contrast to Ana-Maria Rizzuto (*The Birth of the Living God* [Chicago: University of Chicago Press, 1979]) and other recent attachment theorists of early childhood (Lee Kirkpatrick and Philip Shaver, "Attachment Theory and Religion," *Journal for the Scientific Study of Religion* 29, no. 3 [1990]: 315–34), this approach does not so much see God as an adult projection of the primal parents, all-seeing and powerful from the infant's perspective. Rather it would be that early "mirroring" and "supportive" relationship which is the most basic human form of the still more primordial "holding" of all life. It is *that* which is amplified as the core of spir-

most fundamental form of mystical experience, in which love is felt to be the foundation of Being. Indeed just such an amplification of Gibson's mirroring of organism and surround and its relation to here-and-now presence is reflected in this often-cited statement of Jesus: "Look at the birds of the air; they do not sow and reap and store in barns, yet your heavenly Father feeds them. . . . So do not be anxious about tomorrow; tomorrow will look after itself."[97]

The "living truths" of the numinous reflected in Christian Agape rest on an amplified and objective perception of the existential foundations of all life. The early Heidegger was right: "Religion is transcendent life."[98] Spirituality is the full self-awareness of the basic facts of human life and all life in general, and as such these remain the perpetually elusive and forgotten deepest context and open ground of all that we do and feel.

Intentionality and Eternity

There may also be a more direct transpersonal psychology embedded in Jesus's assurance that he who has faith "shall never know what it is to die. . . . No one who is alive and has faith shall ever die." [99] We already have a research literature on the near-death experiences of revived persons, often approaching but not reaching the classical "white light" experiences of mysticism,[100] and yet with more occasional reports of hellish and psychotic-like disorientations.[101]

Both kinds of state, as we know from research on psychedelic drugs, suspend ordinary third-person objective time and can feel timeless and eternal.[102] Meanwhile, since Franz Brentano there has been speculation within the phenomenological movement that the principle of intentionality—that each moment of consciousness points beyond itself—might provide a felt basis for more-specific religious doctrines of "eternal life" or "immortality."[103] The very essence of intentionality as the organizing principle of all consciousness is that it always unfolds ahead of itself, endlessly "carrying forward" toward the next and the next.[104] Alternatively with the early Heidegger, each moment of our

---

ituality. The role of the parents in early life is its closest "factical" approximation. It is the *form* that is amplified, and only incidentally its multiple contents.

[97] Matt. 6:26, 34 (NEB).

[98] Heidegger, *Phenomenology of Religious Life*, 239.

[99] John 8:51; 11:26 (NEB).

[100] Michael Sabom, *Recollections of Death: A Medical Investigation* (New York: Harper & Row, 1982); Hunt, Nature of Consciousness.

[101] Bruce Greyson and Nancy Bush, "Distressing Near-Death Experiences," *Psychiatry* 55, no. 1 (1992): 95–110.

[102] For psychedelic drug research, see Grof, *LSD Psychotherapy*.

[103] Franz Brentano, *Psychology from an Empirical Standpoint* (1874; London: Routledge & Kegan Paul, 1973).

[104] Eugene Gendlin, "The New Phenomenology of Carrying Forward," *Continental Philosophy Review* 37 (2004): 127–51.

humanly self-aware consciousness contains both origin and goal in its perpetually felt sense of "not yet." As long as this not yet, carrying forward, *is* at all, it can have no directly felt termination. Even were such a termination actually pending, our experience of it would be this self-constituting eternity of always unfolding ahead into openness.

What this would mean is that from a first-person point of view, which is all we would have in this terminal situation, we indeed cannot die. Here first- and third-person criteria have gone their separate ways, and "third-person" issues of truth versus illusion have become irrelevant phenomenologically. The doctor's hypothetical watch indicating brain death would be irrelevant to a consciousness as long as it is consciousness unfolding into and as its most basic pattern. Meanwhile, extrapolating from the near-death literature, experience would become more and more fundamental as physiological arousal attenuates, with a concomitant phenomenal sense of timeless eternity, and the potential, after whatever else unfolds, to increasingly approximate some version of love, grace, and blessing, as above. If Heidegger and Scheler are right, the most basic principles of all religions, since based on consciousness itself, are latent within everyone and will emerge in situations of extreme personal crisis, mystical experience, and dying.

It is interesting to note that the growing irrelevance and separation of the third-person perspective from the inevitable primacy at that point of the first need not entirely eliminate, for the intimate survivors of the (third-person) deceased, a second-person perspective—especially since all three perspectival tenses have developed and are normally defined in terms of one another. It would be worth remembering that if all the dying, from their own point of view, are held within a pure unfolding present, which, again from their experience, lasts forever, and at least has the potential of approximating, in conscious self-awareness, the deepest "holding" and indeed "loving" structure of all life, then that can hardly be irrelevant for all those who still survive in this life and had a genuine I-thou relation with the deceased. The latter, in their own fullest experience, are "still" eternally present, here and now, and in their very essence. All of us already, from our first-person view, commune empathically with our living intimates in the various states in which we have known or indeed can imagine them, whether they are present or not. So whatever the projections and over-schematizations so often involved in doctrines of an afterlife, our intuitive sense of a "final state" or "fulfilled essence" of the deceased will invite some sense of an inner continuing dialogue on the part of those surviving and at a deep and essential level. Certainly cross-culturally, and especially interesting given all the intuitive religious schematizations of a first-person afterlife, there seems to be the human inevitability of a felt second-person relation as well, as also reflected upon by Jung .[105] Its imagined continuum has ranged from the primitive propitiation of "ghosts," to the further evolution of our memories in greater understanding, to the sense of receiving a guidance and blessing, often in dreams.

If in the above sense faith in eternal life is always justified, since it is implicit for everyone already in the onrushing flow-ahead of experience, does this make the explicit "belief" and "choice" of a spiritual path irrelevant? Have we come out to a sort of "democratic Gnosticism" in which there *is* a sort of secret knowledge, furnished here by existential-phenomenology and transpersonal psychology, that guarantees everyone immortal life, and not just some Gnostic elite, and this regardless of ethical conduct or conscious concern—a sort of phenomenological antinomianism? On the one hand, this could be a logical and humane extension of that universality of message asserted by the New Testament, yet narrowed even there to "believers" and later to specific church and sect. On the other hand, what remains unknowable is that while compassion may be the humanly amplified deepest structure of all life, whether any one of us arrives at *that* eternity directly, with our personal self-awareness—or only after quasi-eternal, psychotic-like hells, perhaps richly deserved, and finally stripped of all specifically human personhood, is not so clear. The empirical near-death literature implies both as open possibilities.

Accordingly "belief," and corresponding "ethical commitment" to a chosen preparatory spiritual path, may be very important for the lives of many persons. They will want to live a life most fully appropriate to the highest potential of being human and thus consistent with its deepest and phenomenologically eternal structures. It would seem most likely that given the above phenomenology of "mirroring" and "holding," and given that physiological death must at the end necessitate a profound relaxation of all physical tension, that the very final experience would be "positive," whatever the route by which we arrive there. If it should turn out, and none of us would potentially ever know this, that the "holy" arrive at this same place no quicker or better than the "lost," then surely, in that state of deepest acceptance and love, no one at either extreme could possibly have anything or anyone of which to complain. If, with the Christian message, the God of all Being incarnates as human and then promises "forgiveness" and "eternal life" and announces an eternal "kingdom of heaven," it is most difficult, and especially if this is itself an amplification of the phenomenology of the deepest patterns of all human existence, to see how any of it could really be "members only."

---

[105] C. G. Jung, *Memories, Dreams, Reflections* (New York: Pantheon Books, 1961).

Part II

Philosophy and Mysticism

Conjoined at Source?

8. Convergent Paths along the Via Spinoza

Philosophy and Mysticism from Socrates to Ibn 'Arabi and the Ba'al Shem Tov

Ori Z. Soltes

Abstract

Socrates and Plato mark a beginning point of philosophy in the West. One of the assertions that they make—and for my purposes, I do not functionally distinguish between the two of them—is that one must engage the myriad questions of existence by means of a rationalist methodology. At the same time, it is clear, both from the important role that mythos plays alongside logos in the dialogues and from certain ideas—such as that of the Ideas (Forms) themselves—that emerge as critical to Socratic/Platonic thinking, that their thought has a good deal more in common with mysticism than one might suppose or than they might wish to admit.

This essay's initial discussion of mysticism's fundamental features and focus demonstrates, surprisingly perhaps, that in important ways it is not at all antithetical to the concerns and focus of Socrates and Plato. From this foundation I turn to Spinoza, who stands at the beginning of "modern" Western philosophy. Like Plato—and unlike Descartes—Spinoza appears at first glance to present himself as hostile to mystical (and general religious) thought. But like Plato's thought, and in part in close if unconscious alignment with an important thread of mystical thought extending from Ibn' Arabi to the Baal Shem Tov, Spinoza's thinking has significantly more in common with panhenotheistic mysticism, in spite of his intense rationalism—and, paradoxically, in spite of how antithetical to "religion" in its traditional shape his thinking is—than he or we might suppose.

From Philosophy to Mysticism in Socrates and Plato

Socrates (469-399 BCE) and Plato (428-348 BCE) mark a beginning point for philosophy in the West. Among the elements that Socrates adds to the corpus of Greek thought preceding him is the matter of ethics. Prior to Socrates, the Greek term arête—virtue—had referred to the skilled ability to do something. The virtue of a shoemaker is to make good shoes and that of a politician to be a good politician. Socrates introduces the notion that ethics are part of what being "good" at anything should mean; arête acquires a moral component.

Plato furthers this development in exploring the various subjects that Socrates may or may not have directly himself addressed in a series of dialogues that invariably pit the master against various other thinkers. These opponents are often sophists, those claiming to be wise (sophos) and able to define certain abstract ideas such as piety (Euthyphro) or to teach others how to win an argument in a court of law even if one's argument is false; the latter subject causes Plato's Socrates to raise the definitional question of what constitutes justice (Gorgias).[1]

What we observe for the most part within the Platonic dialogues as a method, first of all, is a systematic process of analysis that highlights logic and reason, as Socrates's states his point of view and questions—often dismantling—the arguments of others. This style is operative even under conditions where the issue under consideration deals with a reality beyond that of the everyday. Thus in the Phaedo, for example, Socrates, waiting on death row in his jail cell and surrounded by his students, provides a succession of well-reasoned arguments for the legitimacy of belief in the immortality of the soul.

The problem with each of these arguments, as the questions of his disciples note in every case, is that rational arguments necessarily fall short when confronted with issues that transcend everyday human experience. Since nobody alive can know in the concrete, 2+2=4 sense what happens after death, every such argument necessarily offers no more than analogies from living human experience and must therefore fall short; no absolute conclusions are feasible. In the end, no amount of reasoning can really convince someone who does not believe, because no amount of reasoning can yield certain knowledge of the everyday sort with respect to a realm beyond everyday experience.

Conceding this, Socrates turns from reason—logos, an account of indeterminate length characterized by rational argumentation—to mythos. Mythos provides a narrative that answers a question or solves a problem based on be-

---

[1] A central question that has been asked for centuries regarding Socrates and Plato is where the thought of the first ends and that of the other begins. We can be fairly certain that Socrates, at least, wrote nothing down, and that, in addition to a handful of other Greek writers of Plato's generation and later, such as Xenophon, Plato has left us with by far the most comprehensive representation of Socratic and Platonic thinking. The answer to the question of where the two diverge has been variously suggested by a kind of chronological quantification of Plato's writings into early, middle, and later works, in which quantification it is argued that the earlier dialogues offer more pure Socrates and by the end we have shifted to more purely Platonic thought. For our purposes this issue is not essential, and I therefore simplify with the phrase "Plato's Socrates" to mean "the Socrates to whose thought we have access through Plato/Plato's writing" without attempting to parse the degree to which I am discussing Socrates's actual thought or Plato's actual thought.

lief, not reason. Socrates offers an account of the journey of the soul through the other world as a supplement to his reasoned arguments. He is quick to acknowledge that the journey he describes may or may not be factual, since he only knows about it, as it were, by hearsay, but affirms how he himself thinks that it is an accurate account of reality (Phaedo 114D).

In the end, Socrates supplements both logos and mythos with ergon: the action of quaffing the poisonous hemlock that he is handed by his jailer as if it were fine wine, demonstrating to his students at least that he truly believes in the immortality of the soul; that both logos and mythos as kinds of arguments are mere verbal supplements to a conviction that ultimately must transcend words.

For the purposes of our own discussion, what is important is that both the father of philosophical reasoning and his premier disciple and posthumous scribe repeatedly recognize the limits of reason and the need to think in transcendental ways if one is ultimately to arrive at Truth. One might look to Plato's Republic as the consummate codifier of this perspective in its discussion of the Forms (Ideas).[2] For there (and in other dialogues) Plato's Socrates notes that every concrete and abstract entity in our reality—whether a table or a bed or a just or pious act—takes shape and is defined by us as a table, a chair, an act of justice or piety because it emulates and imitates the ultimate transcendental Form (Idea) of "tableness," "chairness," "justice," or "piety."

These Forms exist in a reality beyond our own and inaccessible to us. They are eternal and immutable; objects and actions that we refer to by their various names (chair, table, just act, pious act) are more or less fully and perfectly what we call them depending on how successfully they offer emulation or imitation—the Greek word is mimesis—of the Forms, that is, by how successfully they partake of the Forms. The goal of Plato's Socrates in the dialogues is to arrive at an absolute definition of justice or piety or friendship or chairness or tableness by engaging in a discussion in which he and his interlocutors try to isolate what it is that, say, every act we term "just" has in common with every other act so labeled: if we could isolate what exactly it is that connects them to each other, we would have located their essence, their innermost core, their immutable, eternal what-it-is and thus located and grasped the Form of which and in which all such acts partake.

Where tables and chairs and beds are concerned, the implications of this process are relatively unimportant—when all is said and done, I can bang my hand on a chair or a table or a bed, and you can agree or not that what I have concretely indicated is what I claim it to be—and if we disagree, the earth will not disintegrate. But acts of piety and justice are abstract—I cannot touch them—and in a litigious, divinity-conscious society such as that of Athens in

---

[2] Plato, *The Republic*, trl. Desmond Lee and Melissa Lane (London: Penguin Books, 2007).

the time of Socrates and Plato, the consequences of not knowing what piety and justice are can be dire. For Socrates this is an issue of great importance in general terms. For Plato it is one with a very specific, concrete implication: failure to have clarity with regard to justice and piety led directly to Socrates's discussion of the soul and to his death.

There are, meanwhile, at least two consequences relevant to this discussion of the use of mythos and the method of exploring the Forms by (Socrates and) Plato. The first, to repeat, is that we are pushed to recognize that the fathers of Western logos—of accessing, exploring, and understanding the world through reason—themselves recognize the limits of reason for arriving at Truth, particularly the sort of moral truth contained in concepts like "piety" and "justice," all of which ultimately are subsumable within the greatest of Forms, the Good. The second is that the very assumptions that Plato's Socrates makes regarding the existence and definition of the Forms carry him beyond the limits of rational thought and thus place him, regardless of the terminology that he is represented as using, on ground distinctly reminiscent of that on which mystics, and not rationalists, have stood for centuries.

Mysticism is an intensified subset of religion. Religion supposes the existence of a realm other than and beyond our own, a realm believed to have created our own and therefore to have the power to destroy it. Every religious tradition directs itself toward that realm, through prayer and narrative (mythos) in order to assure a positive relationship with that other realm. That realm—in Latin it is called the "sacer," and its sibling that refers to our own realm is called the "profanus"—is multivalent and complex. It encompasses not only divinity but other aspects of the unknown and/or unknowable—or at least unintelligible: dreams, death, the wilderness. It is inherently neutral in its disposition toward the profanus but potentially positive or negative: when we go to sleep, we may have sweet dreams or nightmares or no dreams; when we die we may go to heaven or to hell or nowhere at all; when we venture into the deep woods nothing may happen, or we may be devoured by wolves or vampires or our fairy godmother may tap us on the shoulder and give us three wishes that wonderfully transform our lives.

Religion addresses the *sacer* in its divine aspect because, having created us, it has the power to destroy us: it can harm or help, further or hinder, bless or curse us. The process is fraught with complications from the outset. How do we address it? How do we converse with it, understand it, know what it wants from us so that it responds and so that we are blessed and not cursed by it? Every religious tradition shares the same answer as its starting point: the *sacer* reveals itself somehow to certain individuals at certain times and places, communicating that information in some form. Those individuals—sacerdotes: prophets, priests (and also heroes, poets, artists, pharaohs, and others who are believed to have a direct divine connection of one sort or another)—in turn reveal to their constituents the information necessary for their survival. A time comes in the life cycle of every religious tradition, however, when such individuals are no longer available, and others, lacking that direct connection to the sacer, do their utmost to interpret the words left behind by the *sacerdotes* in order to guide us.

The mystic believes that such individuals—interpreters, exegetes, commentators—access only the outer edges of the divine *sacer*. She believes that it is possible through some means or method to access a hiddenmost, innermost recess of the *sacer*—a *mysterion*—that can potentially offer a richer, fuller sense of how and why the *sacer* engendered the *profanus*, of what its intentions are for us, and how it would have us be. The mystic believes that it is possible to access information that will guide the community more effectively than is possible through the interpretations and instructions of a priesthood that is, in the end, secondary in its relationship to divinity.[3] The mystic wishes to and believes that it is possible to achieve a condition analogous to that of the prophets: to gain direct contact at a most intense level with the *sacer* at its most intense.

There are, of course, dangers. The mystical goal, as grand as it is, cannot be achieved without utter humility. The mystic must empty himself of self in order to accomplish this—otherwise it becomes an exercise in ego and will be inherently failure-bound, for if one is too filled with self there is no room for God within one. The mystic must transcend reason—the instrument most essential to engaging and understanding the *profanus*—and in so doing, empties his mind of reason as he empties his mind of self. But the question is whether the mystic can then regain his reason and ego: can he return from the *mysterion* intact—and can he communicate with others what the experience was in order to fulfill the purpose of benefiting the community?

For this discussion, our primary concern is limited to the question of the sense of the *sacer*, its *mysterion*, and the desire for contact with it. Reason and mysticism would at first glance appear to be simply and absolutely opposed to each other as methods of being in the world and thinking about it. To begin with, however, although they are defined as opposites, they may and in fact do coexist in the methodology of Socrates and Plato, rather than being ineluctably separate and unusable as cognates with regard to either method or goal. We may observe this in several ways. The very conviction that there is an ultimate *sacer*—the Forms—from which in essence all the elements of our *profanus* reality are derived bespeaks a mode of thinking that transcends the realm of reason.

One might suppose, however, that the Socratic-Platonic methodology remains rooted firmly in the conviction that the exercise of reason will yield

---

3 This recalls Plato's description of the arts in books 3 and 10 of the *Republic*: that art is twice removed from truth in that it imitates objects or acts that are already limited in being mere imitations/emulations/*mimeseis* of the Forms in which Truth resides.

access to the Forms. Where Euthyphro, Gorgias, and others are concerned, their limitations seem at first to be limitations of their willingness to continue the discussion with Socrates or of their ability to step beyond their pat preconceptions of what piety and justice are, rather than a limitation that is inherent within the human/profanus engagement of reality.

But there is more. The primary instrument of Plato's Socrates is language—Socrates is, after all, engaged in dialogues with Euthyphro, Gorgias, and others—an extraordinary instrument that separates humans from other species. It is an instrument that Socrates is shown to employ with unparalleled skill. It is, however, a limited instrument. Part of what we see in Socrates's discussions with sophists like Euthyphro and Gorgias is not just their limits and Socrates's greater dexterity but the limits of language itself. This truth is central to Plato's *Cratylus*, a dialogue that is all about language and its limitations.[4]

The mystic recognizes the limits of reason and its primary instrument, language, to her enterprise. But so does Plato in the *Cratylus*. For if we cannot be certain whether there is an inherent relationship between an entity and the word that refers to it (that "chairness" is inherently conveyed by the phonemic configuration resulting in the word "chair" and that "justice" is inherently conveyed by the phonemic configuration resulting in the word justice) and if, because we cannot, we cannot be certain when we are discussing "justice" and "chairness" that we are, as it were, on the same page—then how can we have an effective dialogue about anything?

If there must inevitably be a kind of tentativeness to every Socratic/Platonic discussion, and every conclusion of every discussion is necessarily aporetic, where are the absolutes that make the enterprise worth the effort? They are in the realm of the Forms—a realm in which Plato believes not because he is a rationalist, since he can rationally deduce the existence of the Forms only up to a point, but because in fact he is also a mystic. To whatever extent he (and/or Socrates) is a religious traditionalist—believing in, praying to, relating accounts about, and bringing offerings to the Olympian gods and recognizing their role in shaping and maintaining our reality in its diverse aspects—he believes in something more. The Forms transcend the gods themselves; they represent a deeper, more profound aspect of the *sacer*—a kind of *mysterion*—the engagement of which is the ultimate key to human survival.

[4] This dialogue was long ignored and treated as an extended sort of joke on Plato's part. Among the first works to see it as serious and indeed central to Plato's thinking and his recognition of the problematic of language is the original PhD dissertation that led to my *Problem of Plato's* Cratylus*: The Relation of Language to Truth in the History of Philosophy* (Lewiston, NY: Edwin Mellen Press, 2007). It carries this point into an extended discussion (and follows it into the 20th century to thinkers from Wittgenstein to Levinas).

That survival is not merely about physical life; it is about moral and ethical life. It is about the kind of life worth living—defined by Plato's Socrates as a life of constant examination and exploration of the sort in which we see Socrates engaged. It is about seeking the Forms by a particular dialogic method and within the hierarchy of Forms, ultimately being able to recognize what the Good truly is. The danger of that enterprise is how to do it, how to return from doing it—and how to communicate the results of one's enterprise. The purpose is to benefit the community, but the further danger is that the community and its leaders feel threatened by the one who offers an entirely different plane of engaging the *sacer* and/or that the one making the offer cannot express the wisdom she has gained in terms intelligible enough to the community so that it embraces rather than destroys her. This is spelled out all too clearly by Plato in the Allegory of the Cave, which occupies a prominent place in his *Republic* (514a-520a). It is one of the dangers that confronts the mystic.

The Problem of Language and Mystical Thought

The Sufi Muhammad al-Hallaj (d. 922) famously failed to communicate the consequence of his ecstatic experience in terms intelligible to his community; he kept babbling "*Anna al-Haqq, anna al-Haqq*" (I am the Truth, I am the Truth [i.e., Reality—i.e., God]), having become so filled with God that he could not disentangle himself from God and regain his self. As a consequence, he was misunderstood, labeled a heretic, and executed. Socrates was accused of heresy—of "bringing false gods into the city" of Athens that he so loved (and of "corrupting the youth")—and in the court could not communicate what he was about in a manner satisfactory to his jurors, so they condemned him to death. It is his failure to communicate to them—he, the supreme manipulator of language—that leads him to the jail cell and the discussion of the immortality of the soul in the *Phaedo* with which our own discussion began.

From the *Phaedo* we come to understand that in the courtroom, Socrates's failure to communicate was not a matter of his linguistic or psychological limitations, but rather because he chose not to offer the jury the words it wanted: having tasted the *sacer*, and believing unequivocally both in the immortality of the soul and in the idea that it is the best part of us, and also that its opportunities for gaining a deeper understanding of the *sacer*'s innermost essence—in brief, of the Forms—are exponentially greater in the *sacer* realm of death, he looked forward to his own demise, rather than fearing it. Al-Hallaj, according to the Sufi tradition, welcomed his own death, for having experienced the *mysterion*, he longed to return to it. Neither Socrates nor al-Hallaj would approve of suicide as a means of entering the *sacer*, because taking one's own life would be to demean the divine *sacer* that has embodied every soul for a purpose.[5] But if other circumstances lead to a quicker-than-natural return to a better, purer condition, ah, then, why not?

We have begun the transition in this discussion from a focus on Plato's Socrates to one on the Abrahamic world, and not only because of the brief comparison between Socrates and al-Hallaj. More broadly, the pairing between rational and mystical methods and goals is not at all limited to the pagan side of Western thought. An examination of the first series of Jewish and Christian mystics and, later, of key Muslim mystics shows that a condition parallel in a particular way to that of Plato's Socrates often manifests itself. Outstanding legalists often turn out to be central figures in the mystical thought of their respective traditions. These are rationalists whose commentaries, with their careful and precise parsing of words and their implications, define everyday parameters of thought and behavior for everyday practitioners of Judaism, Christianity, or Islam; their words are directed toward instructing those practitioners about living proper everyday lives. These rationalist commentators also contribute other-than-everyday ideas that the mainstream leadership would at least try to keep out of the hands and minds of those everyday practitioners and would at most consider heretical.

Thus, for instance, the early 2nd-century Rabbi Akiva is, on the one hand, associated with insightful comments in the shaping of the legalistic Jewish tradition. But he is also the one about whom that tradition offers a brief allegory of engaging the mysterion: four august rabbinic figures were involved in that engagement, and Akiva alone came back unscathed and whole ("one looked and died; one looked and went mad; one looked and cut the shoots, [i.e., apostasized]").[6] More than that, Akiva is traditionally viewed as the author (or at least the conveyer in writing of an oral document passed from God to Abraham and then down through two millennia of sacerdotal transmitters until Akiva) of what is arguably the earliest systematic text of Jewish mysticism, the *Sepher Yetzirah* (Book of Formation).[7]

Analogously, Augustine (354-428) is the patristic philosopher at the time when Christianity was assuming its definitive initial shape (the Christian Bible was canonized, for example, in ca 395) most distinctly responsible for and associated with the articulation of its most central truths—the triune nature of God, Original Sin, and the Virgin Birth—and the writer of a range of important

---

[5] The Greek word for "purpose" is *telos*, which will have significance to this discussion when we arrive at Spinoza.

[6] This passage is found in the Talmud, in Tosefta, *Hagiga* 14b.

[7] For details, see Ori Z. Soltes, *Mysticism in Judaism, Christianity and Islam: Searching for Oneness* (Lanham, MD: Rowan & Littlefield, 2008), chap. 3, section 2. See also Akiva Ben Joseph, *The Book of Formation or Sepher Yetzirah*, trl. Knut Stenring (Berwick, ME: Nicolas-Hays, 2004).

commentaries on the Bible and how to lead an ideal life of faith, hope, and love of God and one's fellow humans.[8] But Augustine is also associated with the early development of Christian mysticism; his commentary on the Song of Songs, for example, treats it as an allegory of the relationship between the mystical soul and the *mysterion*; and there are at least three passages in books 7 and 8 of his *Confessions* that can be characterized as mystical—as experiences of connection to the *sacer* that are ecstatic and in the last of these (with his mother as they leave Ostia to return to Hippo) a wordless experience of the Word.

It may be argued that mainstream Christianity is inherently mystical: that embracing the paradox of a God that is both singular and threefold or associated with a unique act of parthenogenesis that involves a woman who herself is miraculously conceived immaculately—that is, without the taint of Original Sin—requires a suspension of reason analogous to the suspension required of a mystic if he is to gain access to the innermost recesses of the divine *sacer*. Nonetheless, it develops, in large part under Augustine's tutelage, as a series of legalistic strictures that run parallel to those being developed for nascent Judaism by Akiva and his colleagues. Most importantly, both religions emphasize the advisability for practitioners to pray together as a community, following traditions that, building and even evolving upon themselves, are nonetheless all rooted in the biblical texts—the words of God to important *sacerdotes*—rather than as individuals in isolation, each following his own path and sense and method of how to engage the *sacer*, to say nothing of a *mysterion* within the *sacer*.

Akiva and Augustine should not be mistaken for identical figures but rather be recognized as offering parallels to each other, most particularly in their double place within the legalistic mainstream and within mysticism. The same may be said of Persian-born Abu Hamid Muhammad ibn Muhammad al-Ghazali (1056/8-1111): parallel but not identical to either Akiva or Augustine. Al-Ghazali was renowned as a jurist who, like his Jewish and Christian counterparts, was an essential figure in the ongoing shaping of that side of Islam early in the fifth century of its existence. But in 1095, at the age of thirty-six or thirty-seven, he underwent a profound spiritual crisis and stopped teaching altogether for a time and also writing, for the most part, about legalistic matters; he instead devoted most of the rest of his life to exploring and codifying the tenets of Sufism. He was in fact essential to establishing a positive relationship between Sufism and the Sunni Ashari Muslim mainstream because of the respect that he commanded as a jurist and his ability to apply the same rational and systematic legalistic methods of engaging God through the text of the Qur'an and its prior commentaries to the principles of mysticism and its goals.

---

[8] Augustine, *The Enchiridion on Faith, Hope and Love*, trl. J. F. Shaw, 4th ed. (Chicago: Henry Regnery, 1966)

Other examples might be cited of important thinkers who in one way or another crossed boundaries between mainstream religious thinking, which they approached by means of a tightly focused rationalism, and mystical thought, which, as an intensified version of religious thinking, should by definition eschew the rationalism that it transcends. For the purposes of this discussion, however, further instances are not necessary. Suffice it to say that the underlying conviction of religious thought is paradoxical: that there is a *sacer* that is wholly Other and yet, in having engendered the *profanus*, must by definition embed some of itself within the *profanus*; thus, while wholly Other, the *sacer* shares some sort of distinct sameness with the *profanus* and vice versa. How can God be both utterly Other and yet in some sense like us, who must in some sense be like God due to that embedment? Mysticism offers an even more intensified engagement of that paradox, in which God and the mystic can become one, indistinguishable from each other—yet remain distinct, both because human and divine are by definition distinct from each other (with the exception, and then only for Christians, of Jesus) and because to eliminate, or even to hope or try to eliminate, that distinction is either hopelessly egocentric or dangerous or both: it leads to madness, apostasy, or death.

Both philosophy as Plato's Socrates introduces us to it and Abrahamic religion, however the one might be rooted in reason and the other not, ultimately end up at a place that transcends reason. The story of Socrates and Plato has a mystical component to it. As a further paradox, where religion is concerned—of which in ordinary parlance, mysticism is a subset—the reference point of Plato's Socrates is the very same gods to which everyone else prays and sacrifices in the world of which he is part. His "mysticism" is part of philosophy—the larger "love (*philia*) of wisdom (*sophia*)"—rather than of religion, which "ties (Latin: *l-g*)" us "back/again (Lat.: *re-*)" to that which we believe has made us.

We are in part wrestling with vocabulary that we use in order to grasp the ideas we hope to grasp—and again and again find ourselves asking how the components of vocabulary fit those ideas, like so many squares or circles that may or may not be stuffed into boxes that are, rather, circular or square. The issue of words is unrelenting. *Mythos* as Socrates's predecessors understood it—gods'-truth accounts of events that no human can have actually witnessed with physical eyes and ears (which is why Hesiod's *mythos* regarding the beginning of our reality and the birth of the gods—the *Theogony*—spends the first 116 lines of its poem begging for divinely engineered inspiration: in-spiritation)—has become by Socrates's time an account whose fact level and reason level are viewed as doubtful.

It finds itself compared, in the Platonic dialogues, as we have seen, to *logos*, which is a purely reason-based account, and elsewhere (most obviously in Thucydides's *History of the Peloponnesian Wars*) is compared with *historia* as a presumably fact-based account of events as they truly happened. But not only does a careful read of Thucydides make it clear that most of what he describes and refers to as historia cannot be understood as absolutely fact-based (for reasons beyond this discussion), but—to return to the starting point of this narrative—reason and its primary communication instrument, language, prove themselves again and again inadequate to the task of learning absolute truth.

"Modernity" and the Reshaping of God's Role in the World

But what if there is no God? Or at least not a God of the sort in which Jews, Christians, and Muslims alike believe, from before Akiva to beyond al-Ghazali: an all-powerful, all-knowing, all-good Being that not only engendered us but is continuously interested in and involved with us, is indeed interventionist in human affairs on notable occasions? This sort of God would be very different from Plato's Forms, which are simply there. Human chairs and acts of justice may draw from, emulate, imitate, partake of the Forms, but the Forms neither are powers that have consciously created our world nor are they wedded to it by a conscious interest in it.

The God of the Abrahamic traditions and their mystical practitioners is a God of *telos*. That God made us and everything around us for a purpose—so we speak of a teleological understanding of reality, and one might say that the ultimate purpose of religion (and its subset, mysticism) is to understand what the divine *telos* for us truly is. A different view of reality that began to emerge in Western thought in the seventeenth and eighteenth centuries is often termed mechanistic, by which we mean a view of reality as having been begun—either by some accident or because some Superior Being began it, but if the latter, by a Superior Being that has no ongoing interest in or involvement with the world in general and humans and human affairs in particular. Things just keep going like a well-crafted Swiss watch—like a perfectly made machine—and there is no metaphysically imposed purpose to it. Humans must shape their own purpose for they are alone in continuing to shape the world that began before their existence and without their input.

The development of this perspective—a secular, rather than religious perspective—was gradual. Certainly an age devoted in the West to wars of religion helped facilitate this. After centuries spent slaughtering those outside the faith, from pagans to Muslims; tearing itself apart in schisms and persecutions within the faith, from the Catholic-Orthodox Schism of 1054 to the burning of the last known heretical Cathar leader in 1321; and slaughtering, force-converting, or exiling Jews and Jewish communities from the Rhineland to Portugal—after centuries of bloodletting in these and other contexts, the hegemonic Western Christian Church was torn apart further by the Protestant Reformation, which was followed by the Counter-Reformation and then more than 150 years of further slaughter of Catholics by Protestants and Protestants by Catholics, in the name of the God of love.

Add to this a century of exploring the planet and its breadth and diversity—which completely redirected the European sense of the physical world in tandem with the redirection of its sense of the psychological and spiritual world—followed by an era of industrial, scientific, and political revolutions. The concatenation of such events over the course of time might and apparently did lead at least certain individuals to questions regarding a Supreme Being defined not only by its power and knowledge but by its love and compassion for the creation in general and for humankind in particular.

The first series of individuals who overtly asked questions regarding God did so from a perspective of still unequivocally believing in the existence of such a Being. Thus, for example, the French Catholic mathematician and philosopher Rene Descartes (1596-1650), renowned for beginning his inquiry into truth by theoretically doubting the reality of everything and reigniting a sense of conviction regarding at least some parts of reality, initially reduces certainty, in both his *Discourse on Method* (1637) and his *Meditations* (1641), to the certainty of his own existence.[9] The underlying principle of his oft-quoted "*Cogito ergo sum*" ("I am thinking therefore I exist") is that, regardless of the range of ways in which I could be deceived and deluded, if there is a "me" who is in the process of thinking on whatever level, even that of being deceived and deluded with regard to virtually everything, then that "me" must exist. Even deception and delusion require a "me" to experience the profound error of believing in things that don't exist.

Descartes uses that process of moving from radical doubt to absolute indubitability to develop a range of ideas, beginning with his own certain existence, and arriving at, arguably, the most important of these ideas: God's existence. Approaching this within his Third Meditation, he talks about different ideas, one of them being God, which he defines as "an infinite substance, eternal, immutable, independent, omniscient, omnipotent, and by which I and all the other things that exist (if it be true that any such exist) have been created and produced. . . . I must conclude from all that I have said hitherto, that God exists; for, although the idea of substance is in me, for the very reason that I am a substance, I would not, nevertheless, have the idea of an infinite substance, since I am a finite being, unless the idea had been put into me by some substance that was truly infinite."[10]

There are two key issues that require note in this statement and its larger Cartesian context. The first is that the method he introduces to the process of

---

[9] Rene Descartes, *Discourse on Method and the Meditations*, trl. F. E. Sutcliffe (London: Penguin Books, 1968).
[10] Ibid., 124, emphasis added.

achieving certainty in both the *Discourse* and the *Meditations* begins by stripping away every conceivable certainty and is thus emphatically rational—or perhaps we might label it logical, in the Platonic sense of purely *logos*-bound. He applies that method, ultimately, to the deduction that God exists. The second issue, however, is that in the end the application of this method to the God question cannot avoid a certain circularity that, try as it might, cannot completely disconnect it from the ontological argument as it was pressed into service by medieval thinkers like Anselm of Canterbury and Thomas Aquinas. For the argument is predicated on a definition of God that Descartes and others embrace simply because they embrace it, and without this, his proof falls apart.

Put otherwise, God is defined as Descartes defines God because Descartes believes in God as God is thusly defined. Once that definition has been embraced, the logical and reasonable conclusion that God exists becomes inevitable for the very reason that he states—as well, perhaps for other reasons on which he and others have elaborated. For example, if I define God as perfect and believe that the "mere" idea of something is less perfect than that something actualized, extant, then a nonexistent God would be less than perfect (less perfect than one that exists) and that would contradict the essence of God as a perfect Being. But Descartes's arrival at certainty regarding God's existence is, paradoxically, a beginning point of "modern" philosophy because it raises the very question of circular reasoning for thinkers a few generations down the road.

In the end, then, one of the starting points of "modern" philosophy, the thought of Descartes, is considerably more connected to traditional beliefs than one might at first suppose, even as it begins to push open doors through which others will walk. Descartes spent more than twenty years living in different parts of the Netherlands, including three stretches of more than a year each in Amsterdam. Among the individuals he influenced was a former Jesuit freethinker, Franciscus Van den Enden, who would later become the teacher of Latin and mentor to the young Jewish thinker Baruch (Benedict) Spinoza (1632-77). Spinoza—a promising rabbinical student in the Sephardic community that traced its origins to Portugal and Spain and found refuge in a city that was both the capital of a republic that had gained its political independence from Spain in the late 16th century and also remained largely open to diverse religious beliefs—would transform the vocabulary of philosophy with regard to the relationship between *profanus* and *sacer* and so complete the process of bringing philosophy into a new era.

Certainly Spinoza presents his thought as antithetical to—even hostile to—traditional religious thinking, if we understand such thinking as based on narrow considerations of "chosenness." Thus the two religious communities with which he was most intimately familiar, the Jewish and the Christian, each thought of itself as uniquely chosen by God with regard to a covenantal relationship, and as such, spiritually superior to the other (as well as to all others). The main thrust of Spinoza's *Theologico-Political Treatise* is to undercut this sort of sensibility. His statement that the biblical text itself offers a God who proclaims, "My Name shall be great among the Gentiles; and in every place incense shall be offered in My Name, and a pure offering; for My Name is great among the heathen, saith the Lord of Hosts," words that "abundantly testify that the Jews of that time were not more beloved by God than other nations"[11] is part of a lengthy argument that asserts, among other things, that supercessionist ideas of any sort miss the point of true religion.

Spinoza may be understood to be the beginning point of a modernist approach to analyzing and understanding the Bible. The *Theologico-Political Treatise* is precisely that: the first work that exhaustively and in detail considers the text of the Bible in a manner that may be considered both rational and very little affected by particularist prejudices. Indeed, consistent with this nonparticularist viewpoint, although Spinoza's primary focus is the Hebrew Bible, he makes no distinction between it and the New Testament as "Bible." Trained as a Jewish biblical scholar, he demonstrates a viewpoint that is both Christian and Jewish—or rather, neither of these, per se.

Five particular issues relevant to our discussion emerge in the course of the Treatise—a number of times, but one may find all five within closely placed paragraphs in the first two chapters ("Of Prophecy" and "Of Prophets") of this work. The first is that he defines prophecy as a means by which certain individuals, like Moses and the apostles, are able "to have possessed the mind of God."[12] The second is that he distinguishes between the intellect and what it can understand, on the one hand, and the capacity for possessing the mind of God, on the other: "the prophets only perceived God's revelation by the aid of imagination, that is, by words and figures either real or imaginary."[13] Whether what they perceive as divine messages are real or not, they do so by a different capacity from that of the straightforward intellect. But the reality of what they perceive is always validated "by some sign to certify them of their prophetic imaginings."[14]

The third element is that he asserts that everyone has the potential to have that capacity, "this being the same for all men," although (and this is part of his critique of sectarianism) that fact "is less taken into account, especially by the Hebrews, who claimed pre-eminence, and despised other men and other

---

[11] Benedict Spinoza, *Theologico-Political Treatise*, trl. R. H. M. Elwes (reprint, New York: Dover Press, 1955), chap. 3, p. 48. This edition is a reprint of the Bohn Library Edition containing the R. H. M. Elwes translation of the Latin original published by George Bell & Sons in 1883, so the page numbers cited here and subsequently refer to the Bohn edition.

[12] Ibid., 24.

[13] Ibid., 24-25.

[14] Ibid., 28.

men's knowledge."[15] In a world where most readers would consider "Hebrew" and "Jew" to be synonymous terms, one can understand how leaders within his community would have been distressed by this last pair of clauses, since those leaders would be concerned that the larger Christian community would be offended at the Jewish sense of superiority toward Christians that it suggests.

They would also have been distressed at his statement that "the Bible clearly implies that God has a form, and that Moses when he heard God speaking was permitted to behold it, or at least its hinder part,"[16] which reflects a remarkably literalist reading for someone trained in the Jewish tradition that considers any reference to physicality with respect to God allegorical. It is certainly true that to hold a view of God as having a physical aspect would be considered heretical from a Jewish viewpoint—half a step from outright apostasy. But Spinoza never abandoned his Judaism for Christianity, although he was forced (or chose) to leave the Jewish community, for trading one particularist creed for another would not have been an appropriate path for a seeker of universalist truth.

The fourth particularly noteworthy element within the same few paragraphs is the beginning of an idea for which Spinoza will perhaps become best known and most commonly misunderstood: a kind of equation of God with Nature: "Nature herself is the power of God under another name, and our ignorance of God is co-extensive with our ignorance of Nature."[17] Later on, in the *Ethics* (to which I shall shortly turn more fully), he will use the phrase *Deus sive Natura*—"God or Nature" (part 1, proposition 4, Proof)—to summarize that equation.[18] But in the sentence that immediately precedes the one that I have just quoted in the *Treatise*, he observes that "everything takes place by the power of God," which statement, as we shall see, is part of his articulation of God's omnipresence and engagement in the world—hardly the perspective of an atheist or of one who views God as the power that engendered our reality and then turned away from it, leaving us on our own to find *telos* in our existence by ourselves.

The fifth aspect of his discussion that is particularly relevant is that it is circular—on two levels. It is circular because it validates its points by reference to the Scriptures, which it takes to be the unquestionable word of God and because, as with Descartes, it presupposes not only God's existence but God as commonly defined: all-knowing, all-powerful, all-good, and interested and in-

[15] Ibid. 24 (both quotations).

[16] Ibid., 17.

[17] Ibid., 25.

[18] Where the *Ethics* are concerned, I do not refer to page numbers since the sections, in vol. 2 of *Ethics Selected Letters: On the Improvement of Human Understanding*, trl. R. H. M. Elwes (reprint, New York: Dover Press, 1955), are discreet enough for easy location.

volved in our world. In commenting, for example, on the issue of false revelations, he notes that "God never deceives the good, nor His chosen, but (according to the ancient proverb, and as appears in the history of Abigail and her speech), God uses the good as instruments of goodness and the wicked as means to execute his wrath. This may be seen from the case of [the prophet] Micah above quoted."[19] Indeed, to repeat, far from being heretical, much less atheist, Spinoza's sense of God is perfectly consistent with the traditions he has inherited; where he diverges from those traditions is in his unequivocal nonsectarian viewpoint (that God is not drawn more to one group than to another) and in the introduction of terminology that has been too often misconstrued—first by his own contemporaries and then by subsequent commentators.

That circularity is most concisely—and perhaps unconsciously—expressed in the *Ethics* (part 2, prop. 11, Proof) when Spinoza writes, regarding the nature of the human mind, that "an idea is the first element constituting the human mind . . . [but] the idea itself cannot be said to exist; it must therefore be the idea of something actually existing. But not an infinite thing [i.e., God, for there is no other infinite thing]. For an infinite thing . . . must always necessarily exist. . . . Therefore the first element, which constitutes the actual being of the human mind, is the idea of something actually existing. Q.E.D." Put otherwise: my mind cannot conceive of God if God does not exist, so God must exist or I could not imagine that there is a God.

The *Theologico-Political Treatise* was published in 1670—anonymously, and in Latin, rather than in the vernacular—and raised a storm of controversy. Surely what distressed some of its readers, at least, was not what it said regarding Scripture or God—it does not really question the validity of either—but the fact that it does undercut the supercessionist sensibilities of Christians and the superior sensibilities of Jews vis-à-vis each other (and vis-à-vis all others). Blinded by the offense taken at Spinoza's universalism, his critics railed against him as a heretic or worse.

Philosophy, Mysticism, and Human Harmony

His masterwork—bringing our discussion back to its beginning point: the shaping of moral virtue—would come later: The *Ethics* was in fact published posthumously, but it furthers what are, for the purposes of our discussion, the most salient issues already raised in the *Treatise*. First of all, not only is the entire work an exercise in rationalist thinking, but Spinoza specifically understands reason as offering humans the most effective instrument for functioning in the world, as, for instance, in part 4, prop. 35: "In so far as men live in obedience to reason, do they always necessarily agree in nature"—which he then expli-

[19] Spinoza, *Theologico-Political Treatise*, 28.

cates in the accompanying Proof, concluding that "men, in so far as they live in obedience to reason, necessarily do only such things as are necessarily good for human nature, and consequently for each individual man . . . in harmony with each man's nature . . . [and thus] in harmony with each other."

We might recognize two interwoven principles in this statement that carry back all the way to Plato's Socrates but also resonate with a range of other thinkers throughout history. The goal—the *telos*—of humans is ultimately to live in harmony with one another, and the most complete human being is the philosopher who is constantly cross-examining himself and others to arrive at an understanding of the Good; the goal of the philosopher is to seek out the Good, the understanding of which is the key to that harmony. The primary instrument of achieving this for Spinoza, as for Plato's Socrates, is reason, which is contrasted with being "assailed by emotions that are passions." In fact, "emotion . . . is a confused idea" (part 3, prop. 48, "General Definition of the Emotions").

We might also ask what it is that Spinoza means by "nature" (natura) in this passage, and it turns out that this is a term he often uses. He means God, for he equates God and Nature, in a literal sense; he refers, as we have previously noted, to *Deus sive Natura* specifically in part 4, Preface, also equating them there with "eternal and infinite Being."

We might understand this equation in at least three possible ways. One might be to suppose that his intention is to replace a personified understanding of God with something that, in lacking a personified condition, lacks a personalized relationship with humans (or with creation in general). He would be thinking as Buddhism does, when it speaks (as for example in the *Dhammapada*) of all of us as derived from and having as a goal to return to being a part of pure Being—like drops of water ultimately and ideally to be resubsumed into the ocean. Being, like the ocean, is simply there; it didn't create us, just as the ocean didn't create the drops of water that are within and outside it; and when we achieve release (*moksha*) into a condition of *Nirvana*, our individual selves are swallowed up by Being. As such, "God" would certainly appear to be other than God as that term is traditionally used by Christians and Jews, for such a God might be construed as an entity that created the world but, having done so, retains no particular interest in its progress through time.

But everything that Spinoza says about God, whether he uses the term *Deus* or the term *Natura*, militates against that understanding: the very terminological relationship between *Natura naturans* and *Natura naturata*—"nature naturing" and "nature natured"—at the very least suggests a more intimate relationship between God and creation, since by definition, given this pair of phrases, God is embedded within us, within the natural world—within everything. Of course, one could still suppose that the mind of God becomes disconnected from creation once that mind has finished creating: a father can deposit part of himself (sperm) into what eventuates as his offspring and, having done so, disappear without ever having a relationship with that offspring.

Those who saw or see Spinoza as disconnecting a personified God from creation because of his choice of terms no doubt imagine his intention as something of this sort. They would be missing both the third way of understanding the *Deus sive Natura* equation and Spinoza's own discussion of God that peppers the *Ethics*. In the first place, that third way is by means of the rabbinic notion of God's Name as ineffable. Whatever term one uses falls short, and every term is ultimately a circumlocution for God's true Name, particularly if, like Spinoza, we understand what a name is in traditional terms: that it conveys the essence of its bearer. How can humans convey absolute Being in words developed in a world of predication, where everything that exists, exists as something?

Spinoza recognizes this and alludes to the stunning conversation between Moses and God in Exodus 3:14—in which the latter responds to Moses's query about who God is with the words "I am/will be that am/will be"—in writing of Moses's understanding of God as "a Being Who has always existed, does exist, and will always exist, and for this cause he calls Him by the name J-H-V-H."[20] This important moment of biblical exegesis becomes the basis for Spinoza's equation of God's essence with God's existence: "the existence of God and His essence are one and the same" (part 1, prop. 20). God is the only Being of which this may be stated: that God is, is what God is, and what God is, is that God is. God and God's mind, like God and God's Name, are one and the same and not only eternal but the same as eternity.

Embedded within this—and embellished by other, related issues that fall outside the range of this brief essay—are three issues to which I would draw particular attention. One is that everything Spinoza writes about God, no matter how rational the arguments, is both predicated on his belief, when all is said and done, that such a God—a God of pure Being, of all-encompassing infinity and eternity, all-everything—exists, and to whatever extent he might wish to prove God's existence, say, by reference to Scripture, he is caught up in the circularity that is inevitable and inherent in dealing with the realm of the *sacer* in its divine aspect.

Moreover, his entire discussion of God and our relationship to God draws not from a *logos*-bound, philosophical vocabulary but from that most intense branch of religion, mysticism. He writes, for example, in part 4, prop. 28 that "the mind's highest good is the knowledge of God and the mind's highest virtue is to know God," explaining in his accompanying proof that "the mind is not capable of understanding anything higher than God, that is, than a Being absolutely infinite [referencing his own definition 6 in part 1—

[20] Ibid., chap. 2, 36.

"Concerning God"—of the *Ethics*]. . . . The mind's highest utility or good is the knowledge of God." This sort of statement reflects the very sensibility of the mystic who seeks that knowledge and believes it achievable without sacerdotal intermediation.

This is further clarified when Spinoza specifies that this sort of knowledge—he calls it *conatus*—is of a particular sort. It is beyond everyday knowledge of everyday things—of which the first sort of knowledge is called opinion or imagination, and the second sort called reason (part 2, prop. 40, Note 2)—and is called by him intuition, "a third kind of knowledge . . . [that] proceeds from an adequate idea of the absolute essence of certain attributes of God to the adequate knowledge of the essence of things" (ibid.). From this third kind of knowledge "arises the intellectual love of God . . . [from which] arises pleasure accompanied by the idea of God as cause" (part 5, prop. 22, Corollary).

"The intellectual love of God . . . is eternal" (part 5, prop. 33 and Proof). That sort of love, like the knowledge with which it is synonymous, is both accessible to anybody and hidden from easy access. Such hidden, esoteric knowledge—knowledge of the *mysterion*—is what the mystic seeks and believes he can attain, against all reasonable and logical odds. Such knowledge is a subsidence into the *mysterion*. It is what, for example, the early 13th-century Sufi Ibn 'Arabi (1165-1240) asserts when he observes that "he who knows himself understands that his existence is not his own existence, but his existence is the Existence of God."[21] That individual becomes the Complete, Perfect Man (*al-Insan al-kamil*).[22]

Again and again, the mystical process of seeking that knowledge is associated with a transcendental love, which is precisely where Spinoza takes the discussion: "He who loves God cannot endeavor that God should love him in return" (part 5, prop. 19), for to do so, "he would desire that God, whom he loves, should not be God" (Proof), yet "this love towards God is the highest good which we can seek for under the guidance of reason" (prop. 20, Proof). And further, it turns out, since "God loves Himself with an infinite intellectual love" (part 5, prop. 35) and "the intellectual love of the mind towards God is that very love of God whereby God loves Himself" (prop. 36), "it follows that God, in so far as he loves Himself, loves man, and consequently, that the love

---

21 Ibn Al'Arabi, *The Treatise on Being (Risale t-ul-Wujudiyyah)*, trl. T. H. Wier (Cheltenham, UK: Beshara, 2007).

22 Given that Muhammad, seal of the prophets, is the one understood to be *al-Insan al-kamil*, then we understand the implications of Ibn 'Arabi's comment: every mystic has the potential to become like a prophet—a *sacerdos* through whom God communicates to the *profanus*. This is, of course, consistent with what every mystical tradition asserts as its aspiration: for the practitioner to become a sacerdotal conduit analogous to the prophets.

of God towards men, and the intellectual love of the minds towards God are identical" (Corollary).

The mystic, subsumed into and swallowed up by love for God, does not expect God's love back—that would be too egocentric, and the mystic must be emptied of ego—but at the same time that he seeks God, he believes that God is seeking him, so God, paradoxically, does love the mystic as the mystic loves God. The successful mystic can no longer distinguish himself from God and God from himself: lover, love, and beloved become three elements that can no longer be distinguished from one another. This notion is conveyed in kabbalah by the term *Shekhinah*—the "presence" or "indwelling" of God, conceived as a loving, female aspect of the God that is beyond gender, with which the mystic (a male above the age of thirty-six or forty) merges. It is expressed in Sufism by a range of thinkers, from Rabi'a to Rumi, whose imagery is filled with the vocabulary of love.[23] It extends in Christian mysticism to the passionate imagery of women mystics from Hildegard of Bingen to—most famously—Teresa of Avila, whose articulation of the ecstatic sense of loving mergence with God is in part facilitated by the idea that God assumes human form on one unique historical occasion as a male, so that she can, as a female, merge spiritually with Him.

It is against the background of this very mystical—*mythos*-bound—turn of discussion that Spinoza's universalism may be understood (which is the second issue to which I wish to draw particular attention). His philosophy of universal tolerance—of more than that, of universal embrace—is based on his conviction that God equally embraces us all, that prophecy is not found only in one group or that God choses one group over another to love. As each prophet envisions God differently, because God impresses Itself upon each in accordance with that individual's particular capacities,[24] so God relates to all peoples with equal fervor, however different the particular words of divine revelation may be from one people and its texts to the next.

Divine and Human Love Along the Via Spinoza

Like the mystic, the traveler on the Via Spinoza not only loves God but loves his or her neighbor, for just as God (*Natura naturans*) expresses Itself in the world around us (*Natura naturata*) and just as all of creation (*Natura naturata*) exists in the mind of the Creator (*Natura naturans*), then if one loves God one must love human beings, and as we love human beings we more fully love God.

---

[23] See Coleman Barks and John Moyne, trl., *The Essential Rumi* (San Francisco: HarperCollins, 1995).

[24] Spinoza, *Theologico-Political Treatise*, chap. 2, 30-42.

This is the Augustinian concept of *caritas* rearticulated. One may also see it more definitively expressed (for Augustine is not clear whether *caritas* applies to non-Christians) centuries before its time (our species as a whole has not yet fully arrived at that time) quite eloquently by Ibn 'Arabi—for instance in these words:

> My heart can take on any form:
> A meadow for gazelles,
> A cloister for monks,
> For the idols, sacred ground,
> Ka'ba for the circling pilgrim,
> The tablets of the Torah,
> The scrolls of the Qur'an.
>
> My creed is love;
> Wherever its caravan turns along the way,
> That is my belief,
> My faith.

Aspirants of diverse spiritual traditions can become one with God. The heart to which he refers is both his heart, assuming an omnimorphic condition—and the heart of God. This sort of sensibility is echoed a generation later by another Sufi, Jalaladdin Rumi (1207-73), in a number of places. Thus:

> I go into the Muslim mosque
> and the Jewish synagogue
> and the Christian church
> and I see one altar.

And again, even more broadly:

> Not Christian or Jew or Muslim, not Hindu,
> Buddhist, Sufi, or Zen. Not any religion
>
> or cultural system. I am not from the East
> or the West, not out of the ocean or up
>
> from the ground, not natural or ethereal, not
> composed of elements at all . . .
>
> My place is placeless, a trace
> of the traceless. Neither body nor soul.

I belong to the beloved, have seen the two
worlds as one and that one call to and know,

first, last, outer, inner, only that
breath breathing human being.[25]

Moreover, anyone and everyone can gain access to the *mysterion*. It is part of the mystic's conviction that, with proper training and proper focus, concentration, and sincerity, anybody can be a mystic—which means achieving the sort of intimacy with God attested for prophets and apostles in the Bible—and nobody requires sacerdotal intermediation and guidance in order to relate to God. This sensibility is echoed by Spinoza in his *Treatise* when he asserts that "in Psalm 33:15, it is clearly stated that God has granted to all men the same intellect in these words, 'He fashioneth their hearts alike.'"[26] More directly to this issue, he notes a number of times in the *Ethics* that "that, which gives knowledge of the eternal and infinite essence of God is common to all" (part 2I, prop. 46, Proof); that "the infinite essences and the eternity of God are known to all" (prop. 47, Note).

He again and again observes that "this love of God . . . is common to all men" (part 5, prop. 20, Proof), which is "wherein our salvation, or blessedness, or freedom, consists: in God's love towards men" (prop. 26, Note). The mystic loves all humankind because, emptied of self, he is emptied of the ego-bound particularistic thinking that defines most of us most of the time—but any of us can empty ourselves of this. And the mystic is bound to try to improve the world as part of the mystical experience—which is, after all, the *telos* of the *Ethics* in the first place.

Nor is Spinoza's sense of God and God's relationship limited to God and humans. His shaping of that double revolution in particularized terminology, referring to *Deus sive Natura* and to the pair, *Natura naturans* and *Natura naturata*, also echoes Ibn 'Arabi as it anticipates the thinking of the Ba'al Shem Tov—"Master of the Good Name"—the founder of the Hassidic phase of Jewish mystical thought in the mid-18th century. The Ba'al Shem Tov—a *tzadik* (righteous one)—taught his followers, the *hasidim* (pious ones), that God could be found not only in the revealed words of the Torah, through endless study, but out in the woods, which are filled with the results of God's creative activity. Love of God can be expressed through enthusiastic passion (*heetlahavoot*) for the

---

[25] Both this poem and the preceding fragment have long been ascribed to Rumi—and this is validated, among other reasons, by the large number of unequivocally attributed passages that convey the same sort of sentiments—although they are not found in the *Mesnevi* or in the *Divani Tabrizi Shams*.

[26] Spinoza, *Theologico-Political Treatise*, 49.

human and natural world, conveyed through wordless music and dance that embodies intense, unwavering focus (*kavanah*)—and not only through minute, intellectual dissections of legalist commentaries.

All four thinkers—Ibn 'Arabi, Rumi, Spinoza, and the Ba'al Shem Tov—express a panhenotheistic view of reality: the one (*heno*) God (*theos*) is found in everything (*pan*). Far from being disconnected from creation, Spinoza's God is intimately embedded in, involved with, and evidenced throughout creation—all creation. The challenge is to recognize this.

Such a view is easily mistaken by some for pantheism—sensing gods everywhere, in every tree and stream—but it is not the same thing. It is about sensing the one God everywhere—even if one does not refer to God by the term "God" ("*deus*" in Spinoza's Latin-language terms), and instead refers to God as, say, *Natura naturans*. One might suppose that Spinoza's critics, in lambasting him as a heretical thinker, did so not only for his choice of terminology, which seems to those who don't look closely enough to reduce God to a depersonalized Nature, as well as for his nonsectarian perspective, but also for what they mistook to be a pantheistic, rather than panhenotheistic, view of reality.[27] The odd thing, of course, is that he had not written any of this yet when he was first hauled before the Sephardic rabbinical court in Amsterdam, and he seems not to have spoken in his own defense at all at that time.

That he could have—like Socrates—is clear from his first encounter with a court of law, in 1654, when he won a decision against his half-sister, Rebecca, regarding their father's inheritance (which he promptly turned over to her, having made his point but also making the further point that justice, and not material possessions, was what mattered to him). He apparently continued to annoy enough small-minded but politically connected people to be accused of heretical views—he was even attacked on the synagogue steps by a knife-wielding antagonist who yelled, "Heretic!" When he appeared before the local Sephardic rabbinical court in 1656, he apparently chose not to mount the defense that he surely could have, preferring the estrangement from his community during which he began to write the things that, had he written them before 1656, would have more legitimately opened the door to exile.

Like Socrates, it was not Spinoza's inability to express himself but rather his decision not to do so that allowed his accusers to have their day with regard to views mistakenly represented as heretical and impious. Unlike Socrates he embraced exile, whereas Socrates, older and with an appropriate moral legacy for his sons as a concern, embraced death rather than exile. But it is clear from Spinoza's writings that he would have been as calm as Socrates was had he

---

[27] Subsequent commentators on Spinoza seem to have sometimes made the same error, but pantheism and panhenotheism are very different concepts, and it is the latter that Spinoza articulates.

faced death at that point, since, like Socrates, he believed in the immortality of the soul and believed that it offers the most distinct connection to God for us humans.[28]

Over 135 years ago, M. Ernest Renan asserted that "nobody has come nearer to the ideal life of the philosopher than Spinoza."[29] Perhaps nobody, anyway, since Socrates, who is, after all, represented by Plato as exemplifying what he claimed was the consummate human life: to be a philosopher—a lover of wisdom—who spends his years examining issues and seeking Truth and embraces death with equanimity. If Spinoza believed that Truth could ultimately be found through the judicious exercise of reason—*logos*—then it must also be noted of him that, like Socrates, he married reason to a pattern of *mythos* that is distinctly mystical. For Truth is hidden deep within the recesses of the mind of God, to which anyone may gain access if he or she can accede to the third form of knowledge and, transcending physical needs, passions, and ordinary knowledge, merge through love both universal and very particular with that Being that is ultimate, unalloyed Existence.

---

[28] For Spinoza's articulation of the idea of the immortality of the soul through its knowledge of God, see *Ethics*, part 5, prop. 20, and also prop. 42, *Note*, second paragraph.
[29] M. Stuart Phelps, trl., "Spinoza: Oration by M. Ernest Renan," delivered at the Hague, February 21, 1877, *New Englander and Yale Review* 37, no. 147 (November 1878): 763-76.

9. Not How the World Is, But That It Exists

Wittgenstein on the Mystical and the Meaningful

Jacob Rump

Abstract

This essay deals with the relationship between the mystical and meaning in Ludwig Wittgenstein's early philosophical work, especially the *Tractatus Logico-Philosophicus*.[1] The interpretation offered here is intended not primarily for professional scholars of Wittgenstein or historians of the early 20th century philosophy, but for those broadly interested in connections between mysticism and meaning and in what contributions Wittgenstein's early work might make to the subject. My goal is to explain his conception of the relationship between the mystical and meaning to the interdisciplinary reader not well versed in Wittgenstein's early philosophy or the vast body of scholarship that has grown up around it, without entirely ignoring the insights into other areas of philosophy that have made the *Tractatus* highly respected even by those philosophers who most vigorously and completely disagree with his idiosyncratic views.

Mysticism and Meaning in Early 20th-Century Western Philosophy

In Western philosophy, understandings of the relationship between meaning and mysticism in the early 20th century can be roughly but usefully divided into two broad camps: on the one hand, some philosophers, aware of the long and varied tradition of religious and secular mysticism and wary of the rise of scientism and the consequent crisis of meaning and value in the first part of the 20th century, turned to some version or another of mysticism as a way of preserving the threatened notion that there are means of insight into the human condition not explainable in purely natural-scientific terms. In the other camp, philoso-

[1] Scholars often divide Wittgenstein's work into "early" and "late" (if not into even more specific periods) to mark important shifts in his thought. Since his remarks concerning the mystical occur primarily in works written before 1920, this essay is limited to that early period.

phers impressed with the power of the new logic of Gottlob Frege and Bertrand Russell or the recent scientific advances in now-independent fields like psychology and sociology operated with an implicit and at times even explicit rejection of the mystical as a genuine field of inquiry, at least as concerned "serious" philosophical questions related to epistemology, the theory of meaning, and logic. On this view, mysticism was fine as an object of study for scholars of religion or those still interested in the broadly speculative or "metaphysical" preoccupations of the 19th century, but it was no serious topic for the emerging program of philosophy-as-analysis. This division concerning mysticism was in reality not so finely drawn, of course, but it reflects an important reality of two opposed ways of thinking about the topic around the turn of the 20th century.

Representative of the first of the camps sketched above is Aldous Huxley's *The Perennial Philosophy*. Huxley's book, an amalgam of mystical and religious citations from a great variety of world religious and philosophical texts, including many Eastern ones, sought to show that "the ethic that places man's final end in the knowledge of the immanent and transcendent Ground of all being—the thing is immemorial and universal."[2] On Huxley's view (again, very broadly characterized), the relation between meaning and the mystical is to be conceived in terms of *knowledge*. The mystical functions as a source of secret knowledge, timeless teachings, or eternal truth, which in each case is understood to involve a sort of *meaning*, even if that meaning is conceived in an apophatic context in which it cannot be adequately captured or uttered.

As Huxley notes in the book, the perennial philosophy consists of a sort of knowledge that has rarely been available to professional philosophers: for the most part, it is a knowledge reserved for mystics and other figures of religious and spiritual—and not primarily academic-philosophical—persuasion:

> In regard to few professional philosophers and men of letters is there any evidence that they did very much in the way of fulfilling the necessary conditions of direct spiritual knowledge. When poets and metaphysicians talk about the subject matter of the Perennial Philosophy, it is generally at second hand. But in every age there have been some men and women who chose to fulfill the conditions upon which alone, as a matter brute empirical fact, such immediate knowledge can be had; and these few have left accounts of the reality they were thus enabled to apprehend and have tried to relate, in one comprehensive system of thought, the given facts of this experience with the given facts of their other experiences.[3]

---

[2] Aldous Huxley, *The Perennial Philosophy* (New York: Harper & Row, 1944), vii.
[3] Ibid., ix.

For Huxley, as a matter of *empirical necessity*, the comfortable life of the philosopher and the poet does not provide the conditions for mystical knowledge, which demands experiences of a sort different not only in intensity but in kind from those of ordinary social and professional life. Only this different type of experience can provide the "direct spiritual knowledge," complete with its own facts, which is said to be different in kind from that of the poet and the philosopher and to constitute the perennial philosophy. Huxley's vision of mysticism as perennial philosophy thus consists of *hidden knowledge* of a set of *facts* of a special sort.

Some more-academic philosophers were also drawn to such accounts of mystical experience and knowledge, foremost among them William James. James's *The Varieties of Religious Experience*, in its discussion of Christian mystics, for example, sees mystical experiences as revealing a realm of "metaphysical" truth and knowledge distinct from that of the everyday world: "The kinds of truth communicable in mystical ways, whether these be sensible or supersensible, are various. Some of them relate to this world,—visions of the future, the reading of hearts, the sudden understanding of texts, the knowledge of distant events, for example; but the most important revelations are theological and metaphysical." [4]

In the other camp, the spirit of exact scientific inquiry that marked early programs of logical, conceptual, and linguistic analysis led many philosophers in the early 20th century to approach the question of the relation of the mystical to meaning, if at all, through the analysis of mystical *language* and the examination of claims concerning the ineffability of religious doctrines. Bertrand Russell notes the distinction at the very outset of his essay "Mysticism and Logic," where he distinguishes "two very different impulses, the one urging men towards mysticism, the other urging them towards science"[5] and questions the common tendency to see the investigation into meaning and the investigation of the mystical as radically distinct. If there is such a thing as "mystical meaning," it is surely a far cry from meaning in the "exact" sense, as a phenomenon of words, sentences, and propositions.

At the same time, however, Russell maintains that the radical separation of science and mystical thought cannot be maintained. He reserves a place for the mystical, albeit one secondary in status to the more exacting processes of science, through which all inquiry into truth must ultimately pass:

> Of the reality or unreality of the mystic's world I know nothing. I have no wish to deny it, nor even to declare that the insight which reveals it is not a

---

[4] William James, *The Varieties of Religious Experience* (Oxford: World's Classics, 2012), 313.

[5] Bertrand Russell, "Mysticism and Logic" (in *Mysticism and Logic and Other Essays*. London: George Allen and Unwinn Ltd., 1959 (1917), 1-32), 1.

> genuine insight. What I do wish to maintain—and it is here that the scientific attitude becomes imperative—is that insight, untested and unsupported, is an insufficient guarantee of truth, in spite of the fact that much of the most important truth is first suggested by its means.[6]

While mysticism as a form of *intuition* may be useful to the philosopher as a starting point for inquiry, that inquiry, insofar as it is truly philosophical, must then proceed according to the more exacting procedures of science and logic. This primary role in the progress of knowledge is one that cannot be ascribed to something as inexact and nonscientific as mystical insight. Thus for Russell, while a place is reserved for mysticism in the broader spectrum of human wisdom, it "is to be commended as an attitude toward life, not as a creed about the world";[7] whereas "scientific philosophy comes nearer to objectivity than any other human pursuit, and gives us, therefore, the closest constant and the most intimate relation with the outer world that it is possible to achieve."[8]

The Importance and Uniqueness of Wittgenstein's Account

Wittgenstein's own philosophical conception of the relationship between meaning and the mystical is highly important in this early 20th-century context for several reasons. (In enumerating these, I will also sketch the basic claims and structure of the rest of this essay.) First, his position is unique in its rejection of both sides of the above-noted dichotomy. On my reading, while Wittgenstein did conceive of the mystical as a realm of ethical or axiological values "whereof we cannot speak," he did not, like the many versions of the mysticism-friendly camp described above, subscribe to the view that the mystical contains discrete hidden truths or deep meanings (irrespective of the question of their effability). As I will argue later, Wittgenstein's conception of the role of the mystical in meaning is *formal*, and not directly concerned with any particular mystical *content*. At the same time, the status of the mystical is neither rejected outright nor conceived merely as a question of linguistic, conceptual, or logical analysis: the mystical is not something that can be understood simply by more closely examining mystical language or signs.

Indeed, the mystical is of central importance for Wittgenstein's overall theory of meaning in his early work precisely because it is *not* describable within the province of a system of representation: its role is not that of having specific, linguistically determinable *sense*. Properly speaking, for Wittgenstein, the mystical "itself" has no *meaning* at all. Its involvement in the structure of mean-

---

[6] Ibid., 12.

[7] Ibid.

[8] Ibid., 32.

ing—and thus Wittgenstein's conception of the relation of the mystical and meaning—is *indirect.* This can be expressed at this point in a preliminary way by saying that for Wittgenstein the mystical is the experience or recognition of the world as *meaningful.* The importance of this insight is supposed by him to be *both logical and ethico-religious.*

This dual concern for the ethical and the logical is a second reason for the importance of Wittgenstein's account of the mystical and meaning in the context of early 20th-century Western philosophy, for he stands perhaps uniquely with a foot in both of the camps described above. This position is on par with Wittgenstein's peculiar status as a figure in the history of Western philosophy more broadly: he is considered to be both a forefather of the philosophy of language and the "analytic" tradition, and yet is also regarded as a sort of quasi-religious mystic who, despite his great talents at logic and analysis, seems to have been at least as interested in writers like Kierkegaard, Tolstoy, and the Christian mystics as he was in the mathematical logic of Russell and Frege.[9] The *Tractatus*, like its author, seems to be driven by two almost incompatible purposes, at once a complex and painstakingly precise treatise on logic, language, and meaning, and a seemingly aphoristic work addressing foundational ethical and religious concerns through abstract gestures to the ineffable and the mystical. And while the character of Wittgenstein's philosophy was famously much changed in his later work (a topic outside my scope here), this dual concern for the logical and the ethical, and the conviction that they must be understood in relation to each other *both despite and because of their difference*, remained central to Wittgenstein's thought even in its later stages.

Finally, the convergence of these two points of significance marks yet another: Wittgenstein's early thought concerning meaning and the mystical embodies the more general philosophical and existential preoccupations of early 20th-century Continental intellectual life, concerns that linger in our collective consciousness even today. Wittgenstein's ideas concerning the mystical and meaning are an historical testament to the worries and ambitions of an age of anxiety, what philosopher and theologian Paul Tillich has called "the loss of an

---

[9] As Russell wrote in a 1919 letter after spending a week in daily meetings with Wittgenstein going over the propositions of the *Tractatus*: "I came to think even better of it than I had done; I feel sure it is really a great book, though I do not feel sure it is right. . . . I had felt in his book a flavour of mysticism, but was astonished when I found that he has become a complete mystic. He reads people like Kierkegaard and Angelus Silesius, and he seriously contemplates becoming a monk. It all started from William James's *Varieties of Religious Experience*, and grew (not unnaturally) during the winter he spent alone in Norway before the war, when he was nearly mad. . . . He has penetrated deep into mystical ways of thought and feeling, but I think (though he wouldn't agree) that what he likes best in mysticism is its power to make him stop thinking" (Wittgenstein, *Letters to Russell, Keynes, and Moore*, edited by G. H. von Wright (Ithaca, NY: Cornell University Press, 1974), 82).

ultimate concern, of a meaning which gives meaning to all meanings,"[10] a condition of perpetual war and spiritual meaninglessness still confronting "developed" Western societies almost a century later. The final section of this essay accordingly offers some brief remarks on what we might take away from the conception of the mystical in Wittgenstein's *Tractatus* beyond the world of technical philosophy, and what implications this quintessentially modernist text might have for a "postmodern" age.

Most approaches to the mystical in Wittgenstein's early work have emphasized the relationship of the mystical to the ethical. In what follows, I take a slightly different route—as befits an essay for a volume on mysticism and meaning—focusing instead on the mystical's relation to Wittgenstein's theory of meaning by way of his conception of logical form. Thus, though the professed ethical orientation of the *Tractatus* is not ignored, I will not assume from the outset that Wittgenstein's conception of the mystical is proffered in answer to inherently ethical concerns. Avoiding this presupposition and approaching the relationship between the mystical and meaning more directly will allow me to show how Wittgenstein's conception of the mystical and its ethical implications is not a complementary layer of insight "added to" an essentially logical work, but rather is an essential part of his overall concern, arising directly from a theory of logic and meaning crafted in response to the spiritual crisis of the early 20th century.

God, the Mystical, and the Meaning of Life

Wittgenstein's interest in what he calls "the mystical" can be traced back at least as far as his 1914-16 notebooks.[11] These notebooks, written largely during his time on the front during the First World War and organized only by date, contain many of the passages that would be reformulated into the numbered propositions of the *Tractatus* (along with much else that never made it into the book). Here, alongside the austere logical preoccupations already evident in his extant prewar writings, we see a newfound focus on questions about God, happiness, good and evil, and the meaning of life: "To believe in a God means to understand the question about the meaning of life. To believe in a God means to see that the facts of the world are not the end of the matter. To believe in God means to see that life has a meaning."[12] This connection between what lies beyond the facts and the meaning of life would become, in the *Tracta-*

[10] Paul Tillich, *The Courage to Be* (New Haven, CT: Yale University Press, 1952), 47.
[11] Cf. Thomas Baldwin, "Philosophy and the First World War," in *The Cambridge History of Philosophy 1870-1945*, ed. Thomas Baldwin (Cambridge: Cambridge Univ. Press, 2012), 375.
[12] Ludwig Wittgenstein, *Notebooks 1914-1916*, ed. G. H. von Wright and G. E. M. Anscombe, 2nd ed. (Chicago: University of Chicago Press, 1979), 74.

tus, one of the central notions underlying Wittgenstein's conception of the mystical.

This takes us to the heart of the seemingly opposed intentions manifest in Wittgenstein's early work. On the one hand, he wishes to continue the careful scientific work in philosophical and mathematical logic learned from predecessors like Frege and Russell. At the same time, in the notebooks stemming from the war years, we begin to see emerge a portrait of a young man deeply troubled by the crises and destruction of his time, and increasingly concerned with broader existential or "metaphysical" questions that seem to reach beyond the narrow parameters of the then-dominant strains of scientific philosophy. As Wittgenstein explains in the only passage in the notebooks to use the word "mystical," these concerns are not so much contemplated as *felt*: "The urge toward the mystical comes of the non-satisfaction of our wishes by science. We *feel* that even if all *possible* scientific questions are answered *our problem is still not touched at all*." The paradoxical conclusion to this remark is paradigmatic of the idiosyncratic flavor of his early thought: "of course in that case there are no questions any more; and that is the answer."[13] This notion of the inherent limits of scientific thought will be central to the overall project of the *Tractatus*.

Reflecting a conception common in his day, Wittgenstein in the notebooks diagnoses the condition of early 20th-century European life as one of crisis. The progress of scientific knowledge had continued seemingly unchecked, and yet among its results was a rapid industrialization that threatened many traditional ways of life and a new efficiency in warfare that made possible the previously unfathomable magnitude of killing in the fields and trenches of the Great War. He was one of a large number of writers—though not so many professional philosophers—sounding the alarm of a "crisis" of intellectual and moral foundations in early 20th-century Europe.[14] Wary of a culture increasingly oriented toward scientistic or positivistic conceptions of knowledge that limited truth claims to empirically verifiable phenomena observed by the value-neutral scientist and left no room for questions of value, Wittgenstein writes,

> At bottom the whole *Weltanschauung* of the moderns involves the illusion that the so-called laws of nature are explanations of natural phenomena. In this way they stop short at laws of nature as at something *impregnable* as men of former times did at God and fate. And both are right and wrong. The older ones are indeed clearer in the sense that they acknowledge a clear terminus, while with the new system it looks as if *everything* had a foundation.[15]

---

[13] Ibid., 51, emphasis in original.

[14] The complicated relationship of Western philosophy to the Great War, and the surprisingly rare treatment of this topic in English-language sources, is discussed in Baldwin, "Philosophy and the First World War."

[15] Wittgenstein, *Notebooks*, 72, emphasis in original.

The intellectual "crisis" of this modern worldview is thus a crisis of foundations—not of the foundations of scientific inquiry per se but of the broader cultural and intellectual system into which the facts and theorems of the scientist are to fit alongside the strivings and cultural institutions of modern life. These latter, Wittgenstein recognizes, cannot simply be grounded in the research results of the empirical sciences. There are aspects of life that matter—and indeed, as we shall see later, matter very much for Wittgenstein—that lie outside the domain of scientific fact and observation. Meaning, insofar as it involves not only the propositions of scientists but also the everyday significances and values of this wider life, cannot be explained by simple reference to empirical facts. And yet according to the modern scientific worldview of Wittgenstein's day (which is in many ways still ours today), nothing with the prestige and intellectual weight of science can be established outside that realm of facts in which "it looks as if everything had a foundation."

Thus the appeals to God, the mystical, and "the question of the meaning of life" in Wittgenstein's wartime notebooks seem to signal a recognition—a *felt*, spiritual recognition, not a precise scientific observation—of the need to account for the feeling that "the facts of the world are not the end of the matter." At the same time, Wittgenstein the logician, who held himself to the very highest standards of scientific scholarship and descriptive analysis, saw that it would be hopeless and unconvincing to accomplish such recognition by simply ignoring the questions of logic and meaning to which he had already begun to devote himself before the Great War. Besides, in the fields of philosophical logic and the theory of meaning, he still had much to say.

The Isomorphic Schema of Fact and Representation

Thus, to fully understand the importance and uniqueness of Wittgenstein's conception of the mystical, we would do well to begin with his conception of logic and theory of meaning, all the while keeping in mind that we cannot assume that this should be elevated to his "primary" concern or downplayed as secondary. Wittgenstein's systematic conception of meaning in the *Tractatus* can be schematically represented as a three-tiered structure.[16] Each level in the schema has both an ontological aspect (logical atomic *objects* at the most basic level, the arrangement of those objects into basic *states of affairs* at the interme-

[16] This interpretation of the basic meaning schema of the *Tractatus* owes much to interpretation of Leonard Goddard and Brenda Judge, in *The Metaphysics of Wittgenstein's Tractatus* (Melbourne: Australasian Journal of Philosophy Monograph Series, 1981). While I have drawn on a variety of commentaries throughout this exegesis, the schema presented here was developed on the basis of their text more than any other, although the interpretation is my own, and differs from theirs in several respects, most notably in its not explicitly emphasizing the metaphysical aspects of the work.

diate level, and the combinations of such basic states of affairs into more-complex *facts* at the highest level) and a representational aspect that refers to the correlated ontological entity (*names* that refer to *objects*, *elementary propositions* to basic *states of affairs*, and [nonelementary] *propositions to facts*). Represented in a diagram:

ction in the System	gical Aspect	somorphic "Mirroring"	Representational ect
re-complex nbinations basic states of affairs/ ementary propositions	ts *sachen*]		positions *ze*]
ic arrangements of ects/ names *showing* cal form	States of Affairs *achverhalte*]		mentary tomic") Proposi- s *lementarsätze*]
ndamental, "atomic" ples ose arrangement ermines logical form	ects *egenstände*]		nes *men*]

As the diagram indicates, according to Wittgenstein, the symmetry between the ontological and representational aspects of this system is perfect: as with names and objects, there is a direct, one-to-one correspondence between elementary propositions and states of affairs, such that each elementary proposition represents one and only one state of affairs, and each state of affairs is represented by exactly one elementary proposition.[17] Furthermore, Wittgenstein famously claims that states of affairs are logically independent of one another,[18] that "from the existence or non-existence of one state of affairs it is impossible to infer the existence or non-existence of another,"[19] and, thus, correlatively, that "one elementary proposition cannot be deduced from another,"[20] and no elementary proposition can be contradicted by another elemen-

---

17 Roger White, *Wittgenstein's Tractatus Logico-Philosophicus* (London: Continuum, 2006), 85.
18 Ludwig Wittgenstein, *Tractatus Logico-Philosophicus*, German text with translation by D. F. Pears and B. F. McGuinness (London: Routledge & Kegan Paul, 1961), 2.061. (All references to the *Tractatus* refer to remark number in lieu of page.)
19 Ibid., 2.062.
20 Ibid., 5.134.

tary proposition.[21] At the top level of the schema, the same perfect mirroring relationship is understood to hold between propositions and facts of the world to which they (uniquely) refer. According to Wittgenstein, the ontological makeup of reality is perfectly represented or "mirrored" at each level of analysis by a representational aspect. Most importantly, this mirroring relation means that any *possible* state of affairs—even one that does not in fact obtain—(for instance, that I *could have* had eggs for breakfast this morning, although I in fact had yogurt instead) is representable in language. If something could be the case, it must be representable in language.

This perfect symmetry is guaranteed by the atomistic structure of the schema, grounded in the objects at the most basic level. These *logical* objects are not to be confused with everyday material entities. They are not physical but theoretical, and they mark the necessary endpoint of logical analysis, the basic building blocks of the system whose combinations *just are* the basic logical states of affairs in the same way that the combinations of the latter *just are* the facts of the world. Because the schema is *logical* in character, these are determinations not of actuality—of what actually is the case—but of possibility, of what could be the case. Thus the total possible combinations of objects determine the totality of possible states of affairs in the world, which in turn determine the totality of possible facts in the world (remember, again, that these terms are to be taken in a purely logical and not in an empirical sense). Because of the perfect mirroring relationship between these logical entities and the representational entities referring to them, we can access the former by means of an analysis of the latter: We analyze propositions into elementary propositions and analyze these latter into names, which names will correspond one-to-one with objects. A logical analysis of the formal possibilities of meaning is thus reached through an analysis of language.

One more element of this schema is of the utmost importance for understanding the relationship between meaning and the mystical: Wittgenstein makes clear from the outset that the *world* to which the propositions of the *Tractatus* refer is very distinctly conceived in logical (not physical or material) terms: The very first proposition of the book states that "the world is the totality of facts, not of things." Wittgenstein's project is thus an analysis of the logical structure of reality, not an explanation of its physical makeup or an inventory of the everyday objects or things that exist within the world. In terms of my example above, Wittgenstein is interested not in the eggs or the yogurt but in *the fact* that I indeed had the latter for breakfast and the fact that I could have had the former. It is thus stipulated at the outset that the *Tractatus* will be concerned with an *extremely impoverished* conception of the world, one concerned exclusively with the logical relations between (possible) facts and their repre-

---

[21] Ibid., 4.211.

sentation, an analysis of the totality of "facts, not things."[22] The tractarian world is devoid of any sort of nonfact (physical things, emotions, values, etc.) that we might wish to include in an account of the contents of everyday human experience.

One of the greatest interpretive difficulties the *Tractatus* presents lies in the question of the intention underlying this impoverished conception of world: Is it Wittgenstein's goal to illustrate the questionability or even absurdity of limiting proper philosophical inquiry to this strictly formal, logical domain, or does he genuinely believe that only "the totality of facts" and the structures reached by logical analysis matter in our interpretation of the world? The question is whether for Wittgenstein what lies "beyond" the facts (if anything does) really matters, or if only the facts and the propositions referring to them (and their constituents) do. In terms of the book's famous closing remark, "what we cannot speak about, we must pass over in silence,"[23] is that which we cannot speak about meaningful, even if it cannot be put into words, or is it rather the case that "the limits of my language" are also the limits of the meaningful or even of thought itself?

The Picture Theory and Logical Form

In additional to this complex and multilevel schema, Wittgenstein's early theory of meaning relies on his famous "picture theory" and an associated conception of logical form. A brief thought experiment can help to illustrate this theory: take a table, on which is set a flower vase to the left and a teacup to the right, and which takes up the whole of my field of vision, to be the complete field of entities, the *facts* concerning which make up my *world* (all terms in italics to be taken in the tractarian technical sense described above). I now wish to represent this *world* in a painting. In one sense, I will do this by simply depicting a table, a vase, and a teacup. But in another important sense, this is not all that I do. For in representing the objects, I also necessarily display something else, namely, the spatial relationship *between* the table, the vase, and the teacup. While this does not consist in painting another *thing* in addition to the three entities, it is nonetheless necessary for the depiction of this *world* as a world of *facts*. If I paint the same three objects, but with the vase to the right and the teacup to the left, even if I have represented all three *things* quite clearly, I have not properly represented the basic *fact* or *state of affairs* that is the case in this *world*.[24]

---

[22] Ibid., 1.
[23] Ibid., 7.
[24] For the purposes of this thought experiment, we are concerned only with this one fact in this world. I therefore ignore the issue of other potentially obtaining facts that might be related to it and thus involved in its depiction.

Nevertheless, in the terms of the *Tractatus*, this incorrect painting is not entirely without sense: it has represented a *state of affairs* different from the actual one (the *fact* of how the three objects actually are arranged in reality) and has thus shown a possibility that does not obtain. But this possibility nonetheless appears as meaningful; it has a *sense* or *meaning* independently of whether the *state of affairs* it "proposes" is found to be true or false. This is a very different scenario than if I were to paint a state of affairs that did not even make sense (say, where the represented spatial relations between the entities somehow defied the physics of three-dimensional space, as in an M. C. Escher drawing). In *that* case, one could judge such a picture to be nonsensical "a priori," *without* needing to appeal to any experience of the facts supposedly depicted: it is not as if I would need to first observe the picture, then check it against potential matches in my field of vision, and only then decide that it is nonsensical: in Wittgenstein's terminology, I can know that it is nonsensical from its *logical form alone*.

This is the case, Wittgenstein thinks, because the possibility of the picture making sense is ultimately tied to *logical form*; only on this basis is it possible to recognize the picture as a possible depiction of reality. In line with the emphasis on "facts, not things," what is important in determining whether the proposed depiction of reality is justified a priori is thus not the specific entities depicted (for human beings are always inventing new and unexpected things with little resemblance to previous familiar objects)[25] but rather the way in which the relation between the entities in my picture, whatever they may be, corresponds or could potentially correspond to the *relation* between the entities in reality, because of shared pictorial (and logical) form: "What a picture must have in common with reality, in order to depict it—correctly or incorrectly—in the way it does, is its pictorial form."[26] Wittgenstein thus distinguishes between the content of the picture, which is *depicted* [*abgebildet*], and the pictorial form, which is displayed [*aufgewiesen*]: "A picture cannot, however, depict its pictorial form: it displays it."[27]

This account of picturing is then extended, making it clear that Wittgenstein intends the notion to apply to more than mere spatial examples, and that he takes it to show something essential about the very logical form of the *world*:

---

[25] For example, in an earlier age, the object that we now know as a cell phone would perhaps have been unimaginable as an object on the table, although the fact that this is now a familiar object shows that it was not *impossible*. But the impossibility of the teacup and the cell phone occupying exactly the *same spot* on the table is deducible independently of cell phones and of teacups, since it is a matter of spatial *form*, independent of the specifics of content. Wittgenstein conceives of logical form (as distinguished from content) as operating in an analogous way.

[26] Wittgenstein, *Tractatus*, 2.17.

[27] Ibid., 2.172.

"What *any* picture, of *whatever* form, must have in common with reality, in order to be able to depict it—correctly or incorrectly—in *any way at all*, is logical form, i.e., the form of reality."[28] The notion of logical form is then used to explicate the propositional connection between language and reality: "a proposition is a picture of reality: for if I understand a proposition, I know the situation that it represents,"[29] and "a proposition *shows* its sense. A proposition *shows* how things stand *if* it is true. And it says that they do so stand."[30]

This explains Wittgenstein's insistence that if something can be the case (as a fact or state of affairs), it *must* be representable in language, since logical form contains the laws according to which the specific content expressed in a given proposition—either one that corresponds to a fact in the world or one that is meaningful but actually false (such as my having had eggs for breakfast)—corresponds to a (possible) state of affairs. And, importantly, the necessity of this "mirroring" is attributed to the *form* of representation alone, not the specific *content* (eggs or teacups or vases) it expresses.[31] According to Wittgenstein, the proposition thus *shows* (but does not express, does not *say*) its form, while it *says* (linguistically expresses) its specific content.

The full technical details of Wittgenstein's account of these issues is extremely complex and widely debated in the literature and is beyond the scope of this essay. But a bit of additional explication of the relationship between showing, saying, and logical form will be helpful before I return to the question of the mystical and the meaningful in the following section. To borrow an example from David Keyt,[32] in the proposition "Seattle is west of Spokane," which can be expressed in the logical notation used by Wittgenstein in the *Tractatus* by "sWk," it is not strictly correct according to Wittgenstein to say that "W" "stands for" the relation "being west of" in the way that "s" stands for "Seattle" and "k" for "Spokane." The relational term in the proposition, like the directional arrow in the margin of a map, "does not enter into a triadic relation" with the terms in the proposition and thus cannot be named. Asking for the thing that the relational predicate ("W" in our example) represents would

---

28 Ibid., 2.18, emphasis in original.

29 Ibid., 4.021.

30 Ibid., 4.022, emphasis in original.

31 As Wittgenstein puts it, the proposition is a picture that "reaches right out to" reality, and the relation between its elements is not another *thing* that mediates the relation. (See Wittgenstein, *Tractatus*, 2.1511).

32 David Keyt, "Wittgenstein's Picture Theory of Language," *Philosophical Review* 73, no. 4 [1964]: 493-511. Though I begin with Keyt's example, the development and interpretation given here is my own. Keyt's article is largely a response to specific interpretations of Copi and Anscombe and makes no mention of the relation of the theory of the proposition to the claim that "logic is transcendental," which is central to my treatment in the following discussion.

be like asking for the element on the map that illustrates that Seattle is west of Spokane. The "element" on the map that demonstrates this relation is not another *element* on the map at all; it is not a road, or another town, or the representation of a specific piece of land, or some symbol standing for "being west of."[33] What shows that Seattle is west of Spokane is the state of affairs represented by the total situation depicted on the map, which is not some particular element of the map in the way that towns and roads are. In Wittgenstein's language, the proposition depicting this state of affairs (sWk) thus *shows* something that it does not and cannot *say*.

The form that is *shown* (or "pictured") by the relation between the names in the elementary proposition, like the relation of cardinal directions in the map example, is a necessary condition for representation and yet for that very reason not something directly representable in the proposition. For Wittgenstein, logical form must be independent of the accidental "happening and being-so" of the world, just as "being west of" is itself independent of Seattle, Spokane, and any other location represented on a map; *that* someplace can be west of someplace else is one of the prior conditions that makes a map a map, because of the isomorphism (the "mirroring") between geographical relations on the face of the earth and the directional and distance relations[34] on the two-dimensional map. The same applies in the *Tractatus* for the relation of a meaning (sense) to the proposition by means of logical form: though it is not something representable, not some *thing* in the world, logical form is nonetheless a necessary condition for there being meaning in the world, and it is *shown* in every proposition, though it cannot be *said* or expressed like the content of the proposition.

The Transcendental Role of the Mystical and the Ineffability of Value

With this discussion of logical form in place, we can now return to the topic at hand: Wittgenstein's account of the mystical. For the mystical and the logical are assigned the same basic status in the *Tractatus*: both are concerned with

---

[33] Although the directional arrow in the margin of the map might be said to be such an element, it is ultimately superfluous to the function of the map itself and only really plays a role in *re*orienting us if, for example, the top of the map is to be read as south and the bottom as north. The fact that this is really only necessary on maps with nonstandard orientation only reinforces the isomorphic relation between the map and the world that makes the representation possible. (Cf. Keyt's very different discussion of the arrow and the scale in "Wittgenstein's Picture Theory of Language," 510.)

[34] Given a proper "method of projection," another aspect of Wittgenstein's conception that exceeds our scope here (cf. *Tractatus* 3.11).

what Wittgenstein calls "the world as a limited whole" or "*sub specie aeterni*."[35] Insofar as logical form is not derived from specific propositions referring to specific facts (or elementary propositions referring to states of affairs) but is a *condition of possibility* that ontologically precedes them, it cannot be something represented in the "great mirror" that is logic. Rather, like the directionality of the map in our example above, logical form functions as the isomorphic mirroring relation *itself*. Consequently, Wittgenstein claims, "Logic is not a body of doctrine, but a mirror image of the world. Logic is transcendental."[36]

To understand the significance of this claim, think about our ability to understand propositions that refer to states of affairs that do not obtain. We can understand the meaning of statements about what is not the case (like my having eggs for breakfast). Wittgenstein takes this to imply that our conception of meaning cannot be derived from the facts alone; it goes, as he put it in the notebooks, "beyond the facts." And we can recognize this even though each of us has experienced only a small subset of the totality of actual facts obtaining in the world (since as spatiotemporally limited beings we cannot be everywhere and at all times). As the above examination of the picture theory showed (think of the discussion of the M. C. Escher drawing), we are able to determine what *makes sense* independently of the direct comparison of that sense with the facts of reality. We thus seem to be capable of recognizing a set of possible meanings wider than the set of meanings pertaining to the actually and presently obtaining facts. How is this possible?

Such recognition relies on our conception of the logical-representational system *as a whole*—in Wittgenstein's tractarian terms, a conception of the overall logical form wider than what can be provided through the content of the "totality of facts" alone. Otherwise our conception of logical form and thus our logic could not be understood to apply with certainty beyond the individual cases already known to us to be factual. And yet this wider application is precisely what logic is supposed to accomplish: logic is the fixed system of rules according to which we can differentiate between what is contingently not the case but could be (because it accords with logical form and thus is *logically possible*) and what is simply nonsense (contradicts logical form and is thus *logically impossible*). And logic must do this independently of experience; otherwise it is not logic at all but only a "best guess" on the basis of inductive reasoning about whatever facts we happen to know about the world.[37]

---

[35] Ibid., 6.45.

[36] Ibid., 6.13.

[37] Wittgenstein's insistence on the a priori (experience independent) status of logic stems from his concern, shared with other early 20th-century logicians such as Frege and Husserl, to avoid the fallacy of *psychologism*, a position represented in the work of contemporaries such as William James. According to a psychologistic conception of logic, there is no difference in principle between the propositions of logic and empirical generalizations on the basis of

But as soon as we accept this account of the "transcendental" character of logical form as the set of conditions of possibility "beyond" the world of facts, we see that a theory of meaning cannot be limited exclusively by "worldly" empirical constraints: the ultimately determinant conditions of the possibility of meaning cannot be derived from what happens to be the case in the world; the latter instead somehow presupposes the former. This issue is raised by Wittgenstein already in a 1914 notebook entry: "That shadow, which the picture as it were casts upon the world: How exactly should I grasp of it? Here is a deep mystery. It is the mystery of negation: This is not how things are, and yet we can say *how* things are *not*—for the proposition is only the *description* of a situation. (But this is all still only on the surface.)"[38] How is it possible for there to be a constraint on meanings logically prior to their actually obtaining (or not) "on the surface," in the world?

I believe that it is just this question that Wittgenstein attempts to address with his appeal to *the mystical*. He *addresses* the question: he does not answer it. For, on his conception, the mystical is not a matter of some ineffable truth, but rather that which stands at the limit of any attempt at explanation, and outside the world of facts:

> 6.4312 [...] The solution of the riddle of life in space and time lies *outside* of space and time. (It is certainly not the solution of any problems of natural science that is required.)
>
> 6.432 How the world is is a matter of complete indifference for what is higher. God does not reveal himself in the world.[39]
>
> 6.4321 The facts all contribute to the task, not to the solution.[40]
>
> 6.44 It is not *how* the world is that is mystical, but rather *that* it is.[41]
>
> 6.45 The viewing of the world *sub specie aeterni* is its viewing as a whole—a limited whole. The feeling of the world as a limited whole is the mystical.[42]

---

experience. Such a position, in the eyes of its many critics, fails to recognize and explain the fact that the propositions of logic are not merely likely or probable but *necessary*. For one clear account of the problem in historical context, cf. Richard R. Brockhaus, *Pulling Up the Ladder: The Metaphysical Roots of Wittgenstein's Tractatus Logico-Philosophicus* (La Salle, IL: Open Court: 1991), 65-106.

[38] Wittgenstein, *Notebooks*, 30, emphasis in the original.

[39] Translation modified: "Wie die Welt ist, ist für das Höhere vollkommen gleichgültig. Gott offenbart sich nicht in der Welt."

[40] Translation modified: "Die Tatsachen gehören alle nur zur Aufgabe, nicht zur Lösung."

[41] Translation modified: "Nicht wie die Welt ist, ist das Mystische, sondern daß sie ist."

[42] Translation modified: "Die Anschauung der Welt sub specie aeterni ist ihre Anschauung als—begrenztes Ganzes. Das Gefühl der Welt als begrenztes Ganzes ist das mystische."

The "mystery of negation" referred to in the notebooks passage is thus not the question of the particular laws or rules governing the a priori *structure* that allows for such a situation, "*how* things are in the world," which is something Wittgenstein believes himself to have demonstrated—to the degree any such demonstration is possible—in the logical propositions of the *Tractatus*, but *that* such a structure exists: that only this particular set of actualized possibilities, our world of facts, exists, despite the much broader set of possibilities. The fact that there is *this* contingency, and yet not total contingency, leads to the more general recognition—which Wittgenstein thinks should cause us great wonder and consternation, but which we tend to take as a mere matter of course—that there can be a world of facts that obtain at all only in the broader context of a set of possible meanings, all of which do not and cannot simultaneously obtain. In effect, a world in which every meaningful proposition, every proposition that *could* obtain, *did* obtain, would contain no value at all. And for Wittgenstein, *this itself* is not a fact in the world but something beyond the tractarian world because it is "beyond the facts." As Wittgenstein commentator and translator Brian McGuinness expresses this point,

> Wittgenstein seems to think that any origin or cause would in fact be inside the world and would hence form not a solution but rather part of the problem to be solved. To put it more in his own terms: he holds that if the value of the world resided in the fact that, say, it had been created for a purpose by God, then its creation for a purpose would be one of the facts which there were in the world. Moreover (he appears to think), if it were a mere matter of fact that God had created it, there would still be room for a question why this matter of fact was a matter of fact. It is clear that in this way we reach a demand for an explanation (in a certain sense) of the world that will derive the sense of the world, the reason why there is a world, from some necessary features of all possible worlds.[43]

In the *Tractatus*, the worry about "the question of the meaning of life" in the wartime notebooks—with which I began above—is transformed by way of Wittgenstein's complex account of logic and language into the very "explanation (in a certain sense)" of the sense of the world, an "explanation" that the *Tractatus* explicitly opposes to the mere contingency of the exclusively factual tractarian world. Because of its transcendental character, that which ultimately determines meaning cannot be on the level of the natural sciences, which are concerned only with the facts in the world and the corresponding "propositions of natural science—i.e., something that has nothing to do with philoso-

---

[43] Brian McGuinness, "Mysticism," in *Approaches to Wittgenstein: Collected Papers* (London: Routledge, 2001), 140-159, here 149.

phy."[44] The realm of meaning is not dependent upon the wider realm of natural science but rather the reverse. And this means that what ultimately makes our propositions *meaningful* (be they those of natural science, of religion, or simply of the happenings of everyday life)—that which gives them *sense*—is not some further set of facts in the world:

> 6.41 The sense of the world must lie outside the world. . . .
> If there is any value that has value, it must lie outside all happening and being-so [*So-Seins*]. For all happening and being-so is accidental. What makes it nonaccidental cannot lie *within* the world, since if it did it would itself be accidental. It must lie outside the world.[45]

This "explanation" is called by Wittgenstein "the mystical," a claim corroborated by Wittgenstein's friend Paul Engelmann's understanding of the *Tractatus*, which had the benefit of extended direct explanation from the author:

> As Engelmann understood the *Tractatus* and what Wittgenstein explained about it, Wittgenstein and the logical positivists shared a common endeavor in trying to draw "the line between what we can speak about and what we must be silent about." "The difference is only that they have nothing to be silent about. . . whereas Wittgenstein passionately believes that all that really matters in human life is precisely what, in his view, we must be silent about." Among Wittgenstein's "mystical conclusions," Engelmann thought, are, e. g. that the sense of the world must lie outside the world (*Tractatus* 6.41)—yet, he observed, "he [Wittgenstein] does not doubt that there is such a sense"; that no value exists in the world, yet "that which endows things with the value they have, which they show, is therefore simply not in the world . . . but that cannot be said"; that "There is indeed that which is unutterable. This makes itself manifest, it is the mystical" (cf. *Tractatus* 6.522)—"(but not a 'bluish haze surrounding things' and giving them an interesting appearance [as Wittgenstein once said in conversation])."[46]

While everything that is expressible must follow "the logic of our language,"[47] and this includes the totality of facts in the world, in my view Wittgenstein's appeal to the mystical amounts to an insistence that there are significant ele-

---

[44] Wittgenstein, *Tractatus*, 6.53.
[45] My translation: "Der Sinn der Welt muss ausserhalb ihrer liegen. Wenn es einen Wert gibt, der Wert hat, so muss er ausserhalb alles Geschehens und So-Seins liegen. Denn alles Geschehen und So-Sein ist zufällig. Was es nicht-zufällig macht, kann nicht *in der Welt* liegen, denn sonst wäre dies wieder zufällig. Es muss ausserhalb der Welt liegen."
[46] Peter Hacker, "Was He Trying to Whistle It?," in *The New Wittgenstein*, ed. Alice Crary and Rupert Read (New York: Routledge, 2000), 353-88, here 372-73.
[47] Wittgenstein, *Tractatus*, 4.003.

ments of human life that do not fit neatly into the predicable structures of our language and cannot be determined *even in principle* by the investigations of natural science. Such elements are not, properly speaking, *meanings*, and they are not *in the world* (are not facts); but they nonetheless are responsible for the *meaningfulness* or sense of the world as a whole, "that it exists," while themselves remaining outside it. McGuinness's gloss on this point, using the vocabulary of the *Tractatus*, is again exemplary:

> That something is means that there are objects [in the technical sense of the *Tractatus* as discussed above]; that there are objects means that there are possibilities each of which must either be realized or not; that there are such possibilities means that there is a world. Conversely what the mystic finds striking is not that there is the particular world there is—for he is not interested in how the world is—but that there is a world—namely, that some possibilities or other (no matter which) are realized—which is no more than to say there is a set of possibilities some of which (but no determinate set of which) must be realized, which is no more than to say that there are objects. The only difference between the ordinary man and the mystic is that the latter is not content to accept this existence and to operate within it; he is filled with wonder at the thought of it.[48]

We can now see why interpretive debates about the *Tractatus* have centered on the status of that which the book suggests is ineffable and outside the world conceived as consisting exclusively of facts. If Wittgenstein's real interest in the *Tractatus* is, as he wrote in a famous letter, "that which is not written,"[49] then his account of meaning ultimately rests on an element of the logical system as a whole that concerns not merely the a posteriori world of facts but the much broader and for Wittgenstein more primary question of "the meaning of life." The mystical is in this sense not subsidiary to the theory of logic and meaning presented in the *Tractatus* but that which lies at its very core.

The Mystical as Meaningful

If we fail to give adequate weight to Wittgenstein's conception of "the mystical" and focus only on the directly logical and linguistic schematic of the *Tractatus* (as many commentators have done, especially early in the history of scholarship on the book), we end up with a reading of the *Tractatus* in which the con-

---

48 McGuinness, "Mysticism," 147.

49 Cf. the letter to von Ficker in Ludwig Wittgenstein, *Prototractatus: An Early Version of the Tractatus Logico- Philosophicus*, German text and facsimile with English translation, ed. B. F. McGuinness, T. Nyberg, and G. H. von Wright, trl. B. F. McGuinness and D. F. Pears (Ithaca, NY: Cornell University Press, 1971), 15-16.

tours of propositional language and a correspondence theory of truth concerned only with the facts in the world determine everything that matters for the theory of meaning—a reading that ignores the broader spiritual concerns that I have insisted drove Wittgenstein's early thought around the time of the Great War: the insight according to which, as Wittgenstein wrote in his notebooks, "the facts of the world are not the end of the matter."[50]

With his account of the mystical in the *Tractatus*, I believe Wittgenstein is attempting to show that, in everyday life, there are myriad *meaningful* aspects of experience that are not and could not in principle be articulated in language, because they are not matters of *fact*. If we fail to recognize this, we may begin to mistake the impoverished tractarian "world" for the actual world of human experience and life, and to think that the *real* world in which we live and act can be reduced—at least insofar as it can be understood by human beings—to the meanings prescribed by the language in which we talk about it or the scientific propositions that attempt to explain it. As discussed above, this latter view is of a piece with the increasingly scientistic worldview that Wittgenstein and others felt had led to the "crisis" of humanity so turbulently affecting Western spiritual life around the time of the Great War.

Thus Wittgenstein's conception of the mystical functions as a necessary and fundamental component of his overall account of meaning, even though the mystical plays no role in contributing specific, linguistic *meanings*. As outside the tractarian world *qua* "totality of facts," the mystical is not a realm of "secret meanings" but the condition of *meaningfulness* or *significance* as such: a characteristic awe directed not at how the world is, but at the feeling of wonder *that* a meaningful world exists at all. What is most important for Wittgenstein is precisely that which, according to the *Tractatus*, cannot be represented in language though it may be shown; a condition of the possibility of the impoverished tractarian world and thus something that also exceeds its factual, representational limits.

Thus my insistence above that Wittgenstein's *Tractatus* does not advocate "mysticism" or contain any "ineffable" or secret doctrine (the first position characterized in the first section with reference to Huxley and James). Wittgenstein is not claiming that that which is outside the tractarian world is some set of ineffable *facts*, deep *truths*, or hidden *knowledge*. To say that the sense of the world lies outside the world cannot be to say that it exists as a separate and prior realm of facts, since the totality of facts must be *within*, or, more precisely, must *be* the tractarian world.[51] Nor is it to say that there are ineffable "truths," in any standard sense, since truth occurs only in the world, at the level of facts and propositions. Nor is it to say that the mystical is a fixed set of ineffable

---

[50] Wittgenstein, *Notebooks*, 74.
[51] Wittgenstein, *Tractatus*, 1.1.

meanings, since meanings for Wittgenstein are expressed in propositions and thus are always effable, even if not the case.

It is rather to say that that which is a condition of the very possibility of truth and propositional meaning is neither itself a truth nor interpretable as a discrete set of truths or of hidden "meanings." It is not a matter of a question to which there is some deeply hidden answer or of a sort of potential truth claim: as I put it above, the mystical functions as a way of *addressing* the question at the root of the theory of meaning, without constituting a fixed *answer* to it. The mystical thus ultimately functions as a sort of unexplained explainer: the root of what Wittgenstein understood to be the sense of wonder we feel when we contemplate the existence of the meaningful world as a whole: "not how the world is, but *that* it exists." The final simplicity of this claim with regard to everyday human life against the background of the complex logical theory in which it is developed is a testament to the insight and elegance of Wittgenstein's deeply human thought.

Wittgenstein's Lessons Learned

As I have argued at the outset of this interpretation, it is difficult to grasp the import of Wittgenstein's conception of the role of the mystical in meaning unless we keep in mind the broader sociocultural milieu in which he wrote, and especially the sense of "crisis" that pervaded European culture during and immediately after the First World War. With that broader context in view, however, the prima facie oddity of a book that claims at once, through its careful logical and linguistic analyses, to have "found, on all essential points, the final solution of the problems" and at the same time to have shown "how little is achieved when these problems are solved" becomes less puzzling.[52] In the Great War, Wittgenstein found himself confronted with a world being torn apart, a world in which the advancements made possible through scientific precision no longer complemented the values and conceptions of everyday human life; a world in which the orienting concepts and godheads of previous generations had been displaced, but nothing new had been allowed to take their place, too few had bothered to ask whether a replacement might be necessary, and too many had assumed the task undesirable or impossible. In such a world, what was perhaps most needed was a justification for finding value—any source of value at all—in life: a reason for the continuation of living by guaranteeing that it is "possible for one so to live that life stops being problematic."[53]

Of course, the Great War in the midst of which the *Tractatus* was forged was all too quickly eclipsed by another one, and the crisis of modernity so

---

[52] Ibid., p. 5 (these quotes are from the [in]famous last line of Wittgenstein's preface).
[53] Wittgenstein, *Notebooks*, 74.

pressing already in Wittgenstein's youth was once again neither solved by international conflict nor assuaged through scientific or technological advancement. As Paul Tillich would write in 1952, in his own diagnosis of the spiritual crisis of modern Western life, "The anxiety of meaninglessness is anxiety about the loss of an ultimate concern, of a meaning which gives meaning to all meanings. This anxiety is aroused by the loss of a spiritual center, of an answer, however symbolic and indirect, to the question of the meaning of existence."[54]

Wittgenstein's remarks concerning the mystical are, I have argued, an attempt to persuade us of the persistence—even if merely indirect or symbolic—of such ultimate value and meaning. And he recognized, like few others before or since, that such a guarantee could not be made in ignorance of logic, language, and the facts of the world, but only by looking first through and then *beyond* them to find what is greater. Whereas for Russell mystical intuition represented an important but ultimately secondary concern, a mere precursor to the exact analyses of science, for Wittgenstein the scientific world of facts must ultimately rest on the more primordial and meaning-giving aspects of a world whose value lies "beyond the facts." This is the ethical message of Wittgenstein's *Tractatus*, one that we would do well to heed today.

In a contemporary world in which it is too commonly believed that what matters is either already explained and decided or soon to be taken care of by cashing in the promissory notes of science, technology, and global affairs, we might do well to recognize the crises of Wittgenstein's age in our own, and to heed—or at least to consider—his unique response to those problems. For the "answer," the "explanation" of meaning offered by means of the mystical in the *Tractatus* functions in an unexpected manner. The solution we arrive at is neither a specific answer, nor a prescription, nor a fixed meaning. It is not something *said* but something *shown*, something we must recognize as already before our eyes, "in the vanishing of the problem. (Is not this the reason why those who have found after a long period that the sense of life became clear to them have then been unable to say what constituted that sense? There are indeed things that cannot be put into words. They *make themselves manifest*. They are the mystical.)."[55]

---

[54] Tillich, *Courage to Be*, 47.

[55] Wittgenstein, *Tractatus*, 6.521-6.522 (translation slightly modified).

Part III

Psychological, Linguistic, & Semiotic Turns

10. Mystical Maps and Psychological Models

States of Consciousness in Language Mysticism of the *Zohar*

Brian "Les" Lancaster

Abstract

Mapping, or modeling, mind processes and states of consciousness is identified as a key area of consonance between psychology and mysticism. Broadly similar goals are advanced by these two areas of human inquiry using complementary methods. In integrating the two, a critical role for hermeneutics is identified, which can enhance the neurophenomenological project to increase understanding of consciousness by opening complexly codified mystical texts to the scientific discourse in psychology. This claim is exemplified by study of the states of mystical consciousness depicted in the *Zohar*, the central text of kabbalah. Characteristics of three mystical states of consciousness portrayed in the *Zohar* are explored and possible neurocognitive correlates identified. The states are understood as relating to progressively earlier phases in processing systems that normally eventuate in mundane consciousness, exemplified here in terms of perception. The first state entails perceptual intensification and intuition of supernormal meaning. It may relate to hyperactivation of recurrent perceptual neural systems interacting with feedforward pathways and concomitant attenuation of systems generating the normal self-construct. The second state is characterized by an all-knowing sense, whereby the mystic is, as it were, in rapport with the pattern underlying all things. This state points to increased awareness of normally preconscious associative functions whereby current sensory input triggers diverse memory engrams. The final state is one in which there is no awareness of form, only "light." It is proposed that this state be understood in terms of phenomenality in the absence of intentionality.

Hermeneutic Neurophenomenology and Modeling

In this essay I explore some ways in which psychology and mysticism can be juxtaposed to mutual benefit. In the most general terms, these areas of endeavor share common ground inasmuch as they are both interested in understanding the nature of mind and in promoting ways to bring about individual transformation. In the case of mysticism, the core quest to experience oneness with the divine, or the ultimate in whatever form it may be construed, has given rise to a wealth of textual material that, directly or indirectly, imparts insights into mental processes and transformative practices. And it is, of course, axiomatic that psychology is directed toward understanding the mind and finding efficacious means for transforming the lives of those who may be suffering or more generally aspire to enriched ways of being. Given this commonality, we may reasonably seek to apply insights and data from the one area to the other, and to address the extent to which integration between them becomes possible.

In this section introducing the essay, I focus on methodology, in particular the need to incorporate a hermeneutic approach in relation to the textual sources available from mystical traditions. I situate my approach as an extension to that of *neurophenomenology*,[1] which has in recent years advanced the dialogue between spirituality and cognitive neuroscience.[2] Antoine Lutz and Evan Thompson define neurophenomenology as follows:

> Neurophenomenology stresses the importance of gathering first-person data from phenomenologically trained subjects as a heuristic strategy for describing and quantifying the physiological processes relevant to consciousness. The general approach, at a methodological level, is (i) to obtain richer first-person data through disciplined phenomenological explorations of experience, and (ii) to use these original first-person data to uncover new third-person data about the physiological processes crucial for consciousness.[3]

This approach has recruited those trained through spiritual disciplines and made use of their refined phenomenological insights into the nature of mind and consciousness. However, the traditions have generated a wealth of such insights additionally in their classic texts, and restricting our approach to "live" insights in the name of phenomenology means ignoring a vast resource of

---

[1] Francisco J. Varela, "Neurophenomenology: A Methodological Remedy for the Hard Problem," *Journal of. Consciousness Studies* 3, no. 4 (1996): 330-49.

[2] Jason N. Blum, "The Science of Consciousness and Mystical Experience: An Argument for Radical Empiricism," *Journal of the American Academy of Religion* 82, no. 1 (2014): 150-73, doi: 10.1093/jaarel/lft073; Antoine Lutz, John D. Dunne, and Richard J. Davidson, "Meditation and the Neuroscience of Consciousness," in *The Cambridge Handbook of Consciousness*," ed. Philip D. Zelazo, Morris Moscovitch, and Evan Thompson, 499-555 (Cambridge: Cambridge University Press, 2007); Antoine Lutz and Evan Thompson. "Neurophenomenology: Integrating Subjective Experience and Brain Dynamics in the Neuroscience of Consciousness," *Journal of Consciousness Studies* 10, no. 9-10 (2003): 31-52; Evan Thompson, "Neurophenomenology and Contemplative Experience," in *The Oxford Handbook of Science and Religion*, ed. Philip Clayton and Zachary Simpson, 226-35 (Oxford: Oxford University Press, 2007).

[3] Lutz and Thompson, "Neurophenomenology," 32.

enormous relevance to the psychological study of the mind. All the great traditions have accumulated teachings about consciousness and the nature of mind, many of which may be valuable to cognitive neuroscience in its quest to explore mental processes and conscious states. An instructive example derives from the Abhidhamma ("higher teaching") within the canon of Theravada Buddhism, which includes detailed analyses of the sequences of mental processes associated with thought and perception.[4] A number of authors, myself included, have examined the Abhidhamma material, suggesting ways in which its insights may be combined with data from cognitive neuroscience to arrive at new hypotheses and theoretical models.[5] Thus, drawing on textual, as well as phenomenological, sources is a critical dimension of the endeavor associated with neurophenomenology.

In any case, the distinction between these two sources of data—textual and experiential—cannot be sustained: not only do the classic texts that discuss the nature of the mind clearly depend on first-person investigation in the first place, but also contemplatives exploring their mental processes in the present are invariably doing so in a context that includes prior study of such texts. We should accordingly include textual material alongside phenomenological data in addressing the relevance of mysticism in the study of mind and consciousness.

Given that sacred texts may have a valuable role to play in the science-religion dialogue, the question of how exactly we read the texts becomes a central concern. To take an example in relation to the texts of the Abhidhamma, their transformational orientation means that the analysis of mental processes is given through the lens of soteriology. The question for the Abhidhamma is not simply how does a given mental activity unfold—as it is for cognitive neuroscience—but rather what do I need to know about mental processes in order to advance on a journey to escape the suffering associated with habitual respons-

---

[4] The dividing line between "spirituality" and "mysticism" is at best somewhat blurred. I include discussion of texts from the Abhidhamma within my consideration of mysticism since the analysis of features of mind found in these texts is predicated on the primacy of the transformational imperative, which I regard as a defining feature of mysticism. Similarly, on the grounds that Buddhism quintessentially entails inner meditation, Smart regards it as the "most mystical of religions." Ninian Smart, "Mysticism and Scripture in Theravāda Buddhism," in *Mysticism and Sacred Scripture*, ed. Steven T. Katz, 232-241 (Oxford: Oxford University Press, 2000, 232).

[5] Rahul Banerjee, "Buddha and the Bridging Relations," *Progress in Brain Research* 168 (2007): 255-62, doi: 10.1016/S0079-6123(07)68020-0; Georges Dreyfus and Evan Thompson, "Asian Perspectives: Indian Theories of Mind," in *The Cambridge Handbook of Consciousness*, ed. Philip D Zelazo, Morris Moscovitch, and Evan Thompson, 89-114 (Cambridge: Cambridge University Press, 2007); Brian L. Lancaster, "On the Stages of Perception: Towards a Synthesis of Cognitive Neuroscience and the Buddhist *Abhidhamma* Tradition," *Journal of Consciousness Studies* 4, no. 2 (1997): 122-42; idem, *Approaches to Consciousness: The Marriage of Science and Mysticism* (Basingstoke, UK: Palgrave Macmillan, 2004).

es. Or, in more technical language, the Abhidhamma authors were primarily interested in the *karmic* implications of mental processes.

For these reasons I propose incorporating a *hermeneutic* component to extend the integration of neuroscientific and phenomenological data that defines neurophenomenology. Aside from the above point that a textual component is invariably present within reports of experience, my approach is predicated on the important role that exegesis itself plays in the genesis of mystical experience. The seeming distinction between study and practice masks the role played by sacralized study in enabling the exegete to attain the profound experience that is presumed to have underpinned the ability of the author to write the text in the first place. Writing about the role of hermeneutics in Judaism, Daniel Boyarin states that "hermeneutics is a practice of the recovery of vision, [namely] . . . the unmediated vision of God's presence."[6]

A seminal text on which Boyarin and others have drawn in asserting this nexus between exegesis and experience concerns the 2nd-century teacher Ben Azzai:

> Ben-Azzai was sitting and interpreting, and fire was all around him. They went and told Rabbi Akiva, "Rabbi, Ben-Azzai is sitting and interpreting, and fire is burning all around him." He went to him and said to him, "I heard that you were interpreting, and the fire burning all around you." He said, "Indeed." He said, "Perhaps you were engaged in the inner-rooms of the Chariot [mystical speculation]." He said, "No. I was sitting and stringing the words of Torah [to each other], and the Torah to the Prophets and the Prophets to the Writings, and the words were as radiant / joyful as when they were given from Sinai, and they were as sweet as at their original giving. Were they not originally given in fire, as it is written, 'And the mountain was burning with fire' (Deut. 4:11)?"[7]

Clearly, the fire "burning all around him" is to be understood metaphorically as portraying the profound inner state achieved through the exegetical imagination ("stringing" the words of sacred texts). The selfsame experience of the divine as that vouchsafed to those present at the revelation on Mount Sinai is available to Ben Azzai through his hermeneutic practice.

Scholars of Jewish mystical texts have emphasized this "inspired" or "pneumatic" quality that exegetes bring to their task.[8] Indeed, Rabbi Akiva's

---

[6] Daniel Boyarin, "The Eye in the Torah: Ocular Desire in Midrashic Hermeneutic," *Critical Inquiry* 16 (1990): 532-50, here 549.

[7] *Midrash, Song of Songs Rabbah*, Vilna ed. (first published 1887), 42.

[8] Moshe Idel, *Kabbalah: New Perspectives* (New Haven, CT: Yale University Press, 1988); Elliot R. Wolfson, *Through a Speculum That Shines: Vision and Imagination in Medieval Jewish Mysticism* (Princeton, NJ: Princeton University Press, 1994).

assumption in the above extract is that the "fire" is indicative of Ben Azzai's involvement in mystical work. Kabbalistic texts such as those of the *Zohar*, the most important work of the kabbalah, are invitations to nonordinary states and can only be fully entered into from such states. As Moshe Idel writes, the Torah—which lies at the core of the *Zohar*'s hermeneutic intent—is "a text thought to have been written under divine inspiration, [and] can only be properly understood by re-creating an appropriate state of consciousness."[9] Accordingly, these kabbalistic sources can furnish rich data about mystical states of consciousness and the factors involved in attaining them.

In applying the approach of neurophenomenology to kabbalistic texts in particular, a further issue encountered is that of the codification embedded in the texts. A psychologist interested in drawing on the texts' meaning for purposes of their potential input into the scientific study of mind and consciousness must employ a further hermeneutical step in decoding their authors' intent.

Perhaps more fundamental to the challenge under consideration here is the extent to which textual material gives direct insight into processes of the mind and states of consciousness. The Abhidhamma texts explicitly address processes such as thought and perception, as well as states of consciousness. Kabbalistic texts, by comparison, even when decoded, are more directed to explicating the mind of God or the relations between intra divine potencies than to analysis of the finer points of the human mind. It should be borne in mind, however, that a central tenet of the kabbalah holds that human and divine realms are *isomorphic*, meaning that exploration of the "divine" mind implicitly conveys insights into the human psyche.[10] As Elliot Wolfson puts it, "In seeing God, one sees oneself, for in seeing oneself, one sees God."[11]

In summary, then, I am proposing an extension to the reach of neurophenomenology. There is no doubt that a religion such as Buddhism is exemplary for neurophenomenology since its practices train observation skills that enable detection of moment-to-moment processes of the mind.[12] Nevertheless, when key kabbalistic texts have been decoded and recognized as manuals explicating intricacies of altered conscious states, then they too feed an attuned phenomenology. Reading the texts in this way inescapably leads to introspection on the nature of mind and paths to altered states. I would argue that recogni-

---

[9] Moshe Idel, *Absorbing Perfections: Kabbalah and Interpretation* (New Haven, CT: Yale University Press, 2002), 187.

[10] Moshe Idel, *Enchanted Chains: Techniques and Rituals in Jewish Mysticism* (Los Angeles: Cherub Press, 2005); Shimon Shokek, *Kabbalah and the Art of Being* (London: Routledge, 2001).

[11] Elliot R. Wolfson, *Language, Eros, Being: Kabbalistic Hermeneutics and Poetic Imagination* (New York: Fordham University Press, 2005), 39.

[12] Thompson, "Neurophenomenology"; B. Alan Wallace, *Choosing Reality: A Buddhist View of Physics and the Mind* (New York: Snow Lion, 2003).

tion of this hermeneutic extension of neurophenomenology is essential if neurophenomenology is to find application in those traditions in which introspection plays second fiddle to exegesis.

In addition to the foregoing argument about the ways in which "data" from mysticism should be treated to bring them into the neurophenomenological project, I should like to introduce a second foundational point, namely, the central role that *modeling* plays in both mysticism and the sciences of the mind.[13] Building models of the mind is seminal for both mysticism and psychology and offers a critical area of intersection that I explore in the remainder of this essay. Theorizing in psychology invariably entails the construction of models that reflect the metaphors by which the mind is to be understood.[14] The model attempts to systematize the various component processes within an overall framework given by the metaphors current within the particular school of thought. While the level of explanatory structures that comprise the metaphorical framework varies—neural, cognitive, or psychodynamic, for example—the goal is always to advance understanding of the aspect of the mind being modeled.

Mystical systems similarly work with models, which are generally directed to understanding reality (necessarily including the mind) and the path by means of which mystical goals may be attained. In order to distinguish the two kinds of model, I shall refer to mystical models as "maps," reserving the term "model" for the psychological approach. This accords with usage in general, since more often than not the modeling function for mystics is directed toward understanding and communicating the "journey" to whichever goal is at the forefront in their tradition—gaining wisdom, liberation from the wheel of birth and death, union with God, and so on. Mandala images, temple plans, medicine wheels, and the kabbalistic tree of life, for example, are intricate, often beautiful expressions of this function. The mandala is "a map through which the ordinary mind can be transformed."[15] The relevance of these maps to psychology comes from their polyvalent meanings; whatever "outer" form may be referenced, they invariably speak powerfully to the "inner" landscape. The metaphysical connotation of the map assumes a degree of isomorphism across the

---

[13] Brian L. Lancaster, "On the Relationship between Cognitive Models and Spiritual Maps: Evidence from Hebrew Language Mysticism, *Journal of Consciousness Studies* 7 (2000): 231-50; idem, *Approaches to Consciousness*.

[14] Robert R. Hoffman, Edward L. Cochran, and James M. Nead, "Cognitive Metaphors in Experimental Psychology," in *Metaphors in the History of Psychology*, ed. David E. Leary, 173-229 (Cambridge: Cambridge University Press, 1990); George Lakoff and Mark Johnson. *Metaphors We Live By* (Chicago: University of Chicago Press, 1980).

[15] Susan M. Walcott, "Mapping from a Different Direction: Mandala as Sacred Spatial Visualization," *Journal of Cultural Geography* 23, no. 2 (2006): 71-88, here 73.

ontological landscape. The mandala, for example, as emphasized by Jung[16] and Tucci,[17] is as much a depiction of the relationship between conscious and unconscious realms of mind as it is a representation of a temple, city, or the entire cosmos. Similarly, the kabbalistic tree of life, which is said to depict stages in the emanation of the Godhead as well as the various realms of heavenly influence, is equally an exemplar of stages in the unfolding of thought from its deepest unconscious source through to the level of immediate, accessible consciousness. Thus, in the rather cryptic language of the *Zohar* we read that

> Thought is beginning of all, and being Thought, it is within, concealed and unknowable. As this Thought expands further, it approaches the place where spirit dwells, and when it reaches that place it is called *Binah*, Understanding, for it is not as concealed as at first, although it is concealed. This spirit expands and generates a voice blended of fire, water, and spirit—namely north, south, and east. This voice is totality of all others. This voice conducts speech, conveying a word.[18]

In this scheme, each *sefirah*,[19] or divine emanation, becomes a different development of thought in the movement from unconscious ("concealed") to conscious, as symbolized by key kabbalistic terms such as Understanding, voice, and the directions of space. Moreover, the same scheme provides the psychological framework for the mystic's quest to gain experience of the higher, divine realm: "The *sefirot* . . . are both the ontic realities that constitute the divine realm and the psychological paradigms by means of which the mystic visualizes these realities."[20] Again, the tree of the *sefirot* becomes a map of the divine realm, which is isomorphic to the terrain of the human psyche.

My interest has focused on the relationship between such mystical maps and psychological, especially cognitive, models. The epistemology of mysticism brings an additional degree of insight to that given by the scientific approach of psychology and neuroscience on its own. All models in psychology depend on the integration of research data with introspective insight into the processes being modeled, and as argued by neurophenomenologists, it is in the spiritual traditions that we find some of the most profound approaches to introspection.

---

[16] Carl Gustav Jung, "The Symbolism of the Mandala," in *Psychology and Alchemy*, vol. 12 of *Collected Works*, 2nd ed. (1944; London: Routledge & Kegan Paul, 1968).

[17] Giuseppe Tucci. *The Theory and Practice of the Mandala, with Special Reference to the Modern Psychology of the Unconscious*, trl. Alan H. Brodrick (1949: London: Rider, 1961).

[18] *Zohar* 1:246b, in *The Zohar: Pritzker Edition*, trl. and ed. Daniel C. Matt, 7 vols. (Stanford, CA: Stanford University Press, 2004-13), 3:511.

[19] The *sefirot* (plural) represent successive focuses through which the divine essence unfolds from the level of transcendence to that of immanence in relation to the human sphere.

[20] Wolfson, *Through a Speculum That Shines*, 72.

It is only the *trained* mind that can discern detail of mental processes to the level of detail commensurate with the scientific data of third-person observation.

Again, my work on the Abhidhamma serves well to illustrate this project to relate mystical maps and cognitive models. As I remarked earlier, the orientation of the Abhidhamma is soteriological, meaning that its analysis of mind processes is intended to guide the student on a journey: "Studying Abhidhamma can be compared with studying a map, but the map has to be used; one has to travel in order to reach the destination or, rather, to achieve one's goal."[21] My integration of the Abhidhamma's analysis of moments of perception and our grasp of the micro-stages of perceptual processing as detected through neurocognitive research generates what I might term a hybrid. The model generated through cognitive neuroscience becomes no longer a view of perception alone but is tinged with the quality of a map inasmuch as the effects of spiritual and mystical practice are incorporated. At the same time, the Abhidhamma's map is enriched by fleshing out detail of the stages of perception by reference to cognitive neuroscience's model of the processing stages that lead to the final percept.[22]

My focus in the following pages is the nexus of meaning between the kabbalistic quest to map the path to God and the scientific endeavor to model the processing strategies of the brain and the psyche. Mystics engaged in kabbalistic work place themselves in a context ruled by a map of the two-way dynamic between the divine and the human realms. The map determines all facets of meaning for the mystic, since everything encountered is viewed as being derived from the map. As my earlier discussion has suggested, entering into the hermeneutic world that provides the legend for the map is where we begin.

1. Modeling the Map of the *Zohar*

> "*O God, You are my God, I search for You* [*ashaḥareka*]" (Psalm 63:2). . . . I will enhance the light that shines at dawn [*be-shaḥaruta*], for the light that abides at dawn does not shine until enhanced below. And whoever enhances this dawn light, although it is black, attains a shining white light; and this is the light of the speculum that shines. Such a person attains the world that is coming.
>
> This is the mystery of the verse "and those who seek Me [*u-meshaḥarai*] will find Me" (Proverbs 8:17); *U-meshaḥarai* - those who enhance the black light (*meshaḥara*) of dawn.[23]

---

[21] Ven. Agganyani, "Abhidhamma, Southern," in *Encyclopedia of Sciences and Religions*, 1:1-12 (Dordrecht, Netherlands: Springer, 2013), 1:2.

[22] Lancaster, "On the Stages of Perception"; idem, *Approaches to Consciousness*.

[23] *Zohar*, ed. R. Margoliot, 6th ed., 3 vols. (Jerusalem: Mosad ha-Rav Kook), 2:140a; cf. translation in Matt, *Zohar*, 5:289-90.

The scriptural context for this extract is the distinctive feature of Psalm 63, namely, that it is the only psalm that provides a specific location in its heading ("A psalm of David when he was in the desert of Judah"). The *Zohar*'s implicit question concerns the mentioning of the location—why is it necessary? The text unfolds in a way predicated on the seemingly archetypal motif that the desert evokes spiritual and mystical experience.

The above extract is typical of the *Zohar*'s "concealing and revealing" of its map. Unless we can enter into its hermeneutic style and decode its symbolic language, the observation that this passage "outlines the nature and process of the mystical path"[24] would remain obscure. It is typical of the *Zohar* that teachings emerge through associative play with the scriptural text (i.e., diverse meanings stemming from the Hebrew root *Sh-ḥ-r* emphasized above). Also typical of the *Zohar*'s style is the concealed way in which mystical experience is portrayed in relation to the intradivine dynamic. Searching for God is here portrayed as stages in the experience of light, akin to the changes one might witness in the progression of light from dawn to morning. First is the experience of "black light," a light characterized by emptiness. Subsequently—assuming the mystic is capable of the requisite ability to "enhance the black light"—comes the experience of the shining white light. We find similar motifs in Sufism, where the black light "reveals the very secret of being, which can only 'be' as 'made to be.'"[25] The mystic is enjoined to enter the mystery of the black light and to become engaged in the process whereby it is made to shine.

Fully decoding this passage demands an understanding of the *Zohar*'s mystical symbolism. In brief, the black light symbolizes the *sefirah Malkhut*, otherwise known as the Shekhinah, the feminine intradivine potency, also symbolized by the moon. The shining white light is the *sefirah Tiferet*, symbolically the sun and in this context the male intradivine potency. Events of nature thus become saturated with intimations of the intradivine drama: "The natural phenomenon of sunrise is understood to reflect a supernal dynamic within the divine self, the process of the two inner-divine lovers uniting as one light."[26] Crucially, the passage concerns not only the relationship between these two divine potencies but also the role of the mystic in promoting the divine union and sharing in the experience of the union:

---

[24] Melilah Hellner-Eshed, *A River Flows from Eden: The Language of Mystical Experience in the Zohar*, trl. Nathan Wolski (Stanford, CA: Stanford University Press, 2009), 84.

[25] Henri Corbin, "The Visionary Dream in Islamic Spirituality," in *The Dream and Human Societies*, ed. G. E. von Grunebaum and Roger Cailloi, 381-408 (London: Cambridge University Press, 1966), 398.

[26] Eitan P. Fishbane, "The *Zohar*: Masterpiece of Jewish Mysticism," in *Jewish Mysticism and Kabbalah: New Insights and Scholarship*, ed. Frederick E. Greenspahn, 49-67 (New York: New York University Press, 2011), 62.

> The *maskil*, wise of heart, "arrays" [cf. "enhances"] the black light of dawn, and in so doing ascends to the state of consciousness known as the "speculum that does not shine"—the dimension of the sefirah *Malkhut*. Working within this dimension he attains and ascends to a higher level—the "speculum that shines," the symbol of the sefirah *Tiferet*.[27]

The thrust of the *Zohar* revolves around *journeying*, be it that of the Shekhinah in her quest to be reunited with the masculine intradivine potency or that of the mystic ascending to higher states of consciousness and traveling ever deeper into the mystery of the divine. A recurring motif for the *Zohar* is the "walking story,"[28] whereby teachings unfold following the text's description that two rabbis were journeying from A to B. The fact that two people were walking on a journey is clearly more than happenstance; it hints at the relationship between physical (geographical) and sacred (psychological and transcendent) space that typifies the *Zohar*'s central principle of correspondence. The wanderings of the companions who populate the *Zohar*'s narrative mirror those of the exiled Shekhinah, who wanders in search of her consort, the male divine. For Nathan Wolski, the paths the companions of the *Zohar* tread have a reciprocal twofold function: they facilitate entry into divine mysteries for those who walk them and they enable the divine to experience being in the world. Moreover,

> walking on the way . . . demands a special state of consciousness, and the Companions are able to both notice and then decipher seemingly innocuous signs and symbols. In this heightened mystical-poetic state everything is meaningful, with all of reality grasped as a semantic field where everything is a sign pointing beyond itself.[29]

Given its principle of correspondence across human and divine realms, at the same time that the *Zohar*'s map addresses the inner workings of the divine it also depicts the mystic's ascent into the states of mystical consciousness necessary for one who would engage with the intradivine dynamic and thereby facilitate rectification in the world. It is these states of mystical consciousness on which I shall focus, since I wish to explore their details as revealed through the hermeneutic and phenomenological approach identified above and examine how they may relate to research in cognitive neuroscience.

---

[27] Hellner-Eshed, *River Flows from Eden*, 84.
[28] David Greenstein, *Roads to Utopia: The Walking Stories of the Zohar* (Stanford, CA: Stanford University Press, 2014).
[29] Nathan Wolski, *A Journey into the* Zohar*: An Introduction to the* Book of Radiance (Albany: State University of New York Press, 2010), 195.

In her study of the *Zohar*, Melilah Hellner-Eshed[30] identifies three principal states of mystical consciousness, which she terms "Rose Consciousness," "Tree of Life Consciousness," and "White Light Consciousness." Naming the first state *Rose Consciousness* derives from the *Zohar*'s opening discourse on the "rose of the valley" depicted in the biblical Song of Songs. Just as the whole edifice of the *Zohar* opens with this metaphor, so Rose Consciousness is viewed by Hellner-Eshed as the initial mystical state through which the further states may be accessed. For the *Zohar*, the rose depicts the Shekhinah, the feminine potency of the divine and presence of the divine in the world. In the passage I have cited, this state of Rose Consciousness is that attained by the mystic who engages with the "black light of dawn." It is the state in which one becomes aware of the divine presence. Rose Consciousness is strongly imbued with a sense of *yearning*. At one and the same time, it is the yearning of the mystic for the divine and the yearning of the Shekhinah for her consort, the male divine potency.

Phenomenologically, the state seems to be characterized by intensification of emotion and of the senses through which one discerns, as it were, an extra quality in the world. The field of vision and of the other senses enlarges; one is drawn into the present, and the world of the senses is no longer merely a collection of images; it becomes rather a rich tapestry through which, for the author of the *Zohar*,[31] a normally unseen presence is glimpsed or at least intuited.

The *Tree of Life Consciousness* to which Rose Consciousness opens is named after the central glyph of the kabbalah. The tree of life is the master map depicting the entirety of creation from its ultimate source—the first stirrings to action in the recondite mind of God—to the final manifestation of the divine presence in the physical universe. For Hellner-Eshed, this state of consciousness is characterized by centeredness and an inner knowing of all things (i.e., spanning that entirety of creation); it conveys at one and the same time both the center of the tree of life and its totality. It entails an experience of radiance:

> This is the light of the sun, the light of Torah, the King seated on His throne, the truth, the light of day, the center, the heart, the center bar [of the Tabernacle] running from end to end, the firmament, and the radiant light like

---

[30] Hellner-Eshed, *River Flows from Eden.*

[31] The question of the authorship of the *Zohar* has not been definitively answered. As far as its date is concerned, most likely the work integrates material that had been transmitted through an oral tradition over prolonged periods of time prior to its being committed to writing in the 13th century. Whether the entire work is attributable to one author is similarly debatable. For simplicity I refer to the author of the *Zohar* in the singular, although it seems to me likely that a mystical fraternity lies behind the writing.

> which the enlightened wish to shine. Generally speaking, this light is associated with stability and majesty.[32]

In distinction to Rose Consciousness, awareness of time is transcended in the state of Tree of Life Consciousness. The former "is a dualistic, changing state of consciousness," whereas the latter "is stable, concentrated, and unchanging."[33] The tree of life is traditionally associated with the Torah (Proverbs 3:18), which is the unchanging center of Judaism. Of particular relevance is the characteristic of Torah study that sees the primary imperative as a striving for unity, the "stringing" of words with which Ben Azzai was occupied in the earlier quote from the Midrash.[34] Torah study involves pursuing diverse opinions, arguments, and interpretations, thus drawing on the associative potency of the mind, yet always seeking to unify divergences, for "these and these are the words of the living God."[35] These key features of Torah study become internalized in the mystic's attainment of Tree of Life Consciousness. The associative faculty is enhanced not only by means of additional hermeneutical and mystical ways of exploring texts but also by using intensive practices that magnify the tendency toward effervescent mental output. (The role of such practice will be explored in the final section of the essay.) From a phenomenological perspective, I suggest that this is a state in which one can become flooded with associations while being somehow attuned to the all-embracing, and unifying, meaning that seems to lie just beyond the fountain of associative activity. The all-knowing quality arises because the mystic is in touch with that spirit of unification characterizing the tree of life, and accordingly "the quality of the ego is experienced as more expansive or united with something larger than itself."[36]

White Light Consciousness brings integration with the oneness and unity at the heart of all being. The light is the light of the Holy Ancient One, a term used by the *Zohar* to convey the unknowable essence of divinity; it is "a white like which there is no whiteness in the world."[37] Hellner-Eshed identifies White Light Consciousness with the undifferentiated roots of thought; it amounts to the alignment of the human mind with the "amorphous dimension that precedes order and language."[38] Whereas Rose Consciousness is depicted as having a feminine quality and Tree of Life Consciousness as being masculine, White Light Consciousness transcends any duality associated with gender.

---

[32] Hellner-Eshed, *River Flows from Eden*, 269.
[33] Ibid., 345.
[34] *Midrash, Song of Songs Rabbah* 1:10.
[35] *Eruvin* 13b, in *Talmud Bavli*, standard ed., 18 vols. (Vilna: Re'em, 1908).
[36] Hellner-Eshed, *River Flows from Eden*, 348.
[37] *Zohar* (1978), 3:165b; 3:129b.
[38] Hellner-Eshed, *River Flows from Eden*, 349.

The *Zohar* portrays the process of creation as the unfolding of divine thought from its origin in concealment through to outer manifestation: "From within the concealed of the concealed, from the initial descent of *Ein Sof* [the limitless divine essence], radiates a tenuous radiance, unknown, concealed in tracing like the point of a needle, mystery of concealment of thought."[39] The radiance is termed "nothingness,"[40] and White Light Consciousness may be understood as the closest humans can come to that nothingness.

Parallels to these three states of mystical consciousness can be drawn with those identified in Evelyn Underhill's classic 1911 study,[41] which draws mainly on the testimony of Christian mystics. It is not my intention to make an extensive comparative examination of the stages of mystical consciousness as found in the world's religions—my task is more circumscribed, focusing as it does on the states we may discern in the *Zohar*'s narrative. Nevertheless, the case for proposing cognitive and neural correlates of mystical states will be strengthened to the extent that at least some of their parameters have cross-religious parallels. Underhill identifies five phases in the mystical path, two of which are essentially transitional stages between the first and third and the third and fifth phases. It is the first, third, and fifth that bear comparison with the three states identified from the *Zohar*. Although Underhill classes them as stages, it is evident from her descriptions that each is associated with a given state of mystical consciousness—a point that underpins my assertion of parallels with the states discussed here.

The first stage Underhill identifies as *awakening of self*, characterized by intensification of emotion and perception. Her remark that "the flowery garment of the world is for some mystics a medium of ineffable perception, a source of exalted joy, the veritable clothing of God"[42] would certainly apply to the Rose Consciousness that Hellner-Eshed claims as the first state of mystical consciousness portrayed in the *Zohar*. Following the purgatory second stage, Underhill identifies the *illumination of self*, in which the self has "pushed through to another order of reality."[43] Parallels with features of the Tree of Life Consciousness include the "deep, intuitional knowledge of the 'secret plan,'" the "Consciousness of the Absolute," and the sense that the soul is participating in the "great life of the All."[44] Finally, following a further purification in stage four—the dark night of the soul—the mystic attains to the *unitive life* in which

---

[39] *Zohar* 1:21a, in Matt, *Zohar*, 1:161.

[40] *Zohar* 1:65a, in Matt, Zohar, 1:380.

[41] Evelyn Underhill, *Mysticism: A Study in the Nature and Development of Man's Spiritual Consciousness*, 3rd rev. ed. (1911; New York: E. P. Dutton, 1912), 231, https://archive.org/details/mysticismstudyin00undeuoft.

[42] Ibid, 231.

[43] Ibid., 280.

[44] Ibid., 281, 290, 536.

"the deepest, richest levels of human personality have now attained to light and freedom. The self is remade, transformed, has at last unified itself."[45] Among many parallels, the "self-naughting"[46] that Underhill cites as central to attainment of the unitive life is equally characteristic of White Light Consciousness.

The critical proposal I make in examining mystical states in terms of cognitive and neural processes is that the mystical states arise when processes involved in the normal state of consciousness become inhibited. In other words, the mystical states are not so much adding onto the processes that sustain normal consciousness, but rather they arise due to attenuation of aspects of normal processing. More precisely, mystical states should be understood in relation to the *sequence* of processes that correlate with distinct *dimensions* of consciousness. Each of the three states identified above comes to the fore when the mystic identifies with progressively earlier stages in the sequence.[47] Instructive in this context is the formulation by Harry Hunt,[48] who understands the mystical experience of light as the result of a "turning around" of the normal process of perception. The mystic becomes aware of the more primitive aspects of cognitive processing, which would normally be obscured in a full perceptual or thought process.

How then can the stages eventuating in a normal state of consciousness be conceptualized? Figure 1 presents a simplified model of perception and memory that proposes a series of stages eventuating in the percept being incorporated into an "I-narrative" that is to be understood as the core of the normal state of consciousness. The narrative derives from a specific brain module, termed by Michael Gazzaniga[49] the *interpreter*: "The interpreter module . . . notes the cacophony of reactions of all of the [other brain] modules and constructs theories and beliefs as to why we act and feel the way we do. It is this system that gives each of us our own personal narrative—our story."[50]

The stages in the model have been identified from research in cognitive science (e.g., implicit processing, role of expectancy, etc.) and neuroscience (e. g., relationship between feedforward and recurrent neural systems). In brief, the model proposes that initial processing of the sensory input generates a distinctive array of activation in systems set to respond to specific features in the sen-

---

[45] Ibid., 498.

[46] Ibid., 508.

[47] Lancaster, *Approaches to Consciousness.*

[48] Harry T. Hunt, "A Cognitive Psychology of Mystical and Altered-State Experience," *Perceptual and Motor Skills* 58, no. 2, Monograph Supp. 1-V58 (1984): 467-513.

[49] Michael S. Gazzaniga, *The Social Brain: Discovering the Networks of the Mind* (New York: Basic Books, 1985).

[50] Michael S. Gazzaniga, "Shifting Gears: Seeking New Approaches for Mind/Brain Mechanisms," *Annual Review of Psychology* 64 (2013): 1-20, here 18, doi: 10.1146/annurev-psych-113011-143817.

sory world ("neuronal input model"); the neuronal input model activates structures in memory having features in common with the current input.

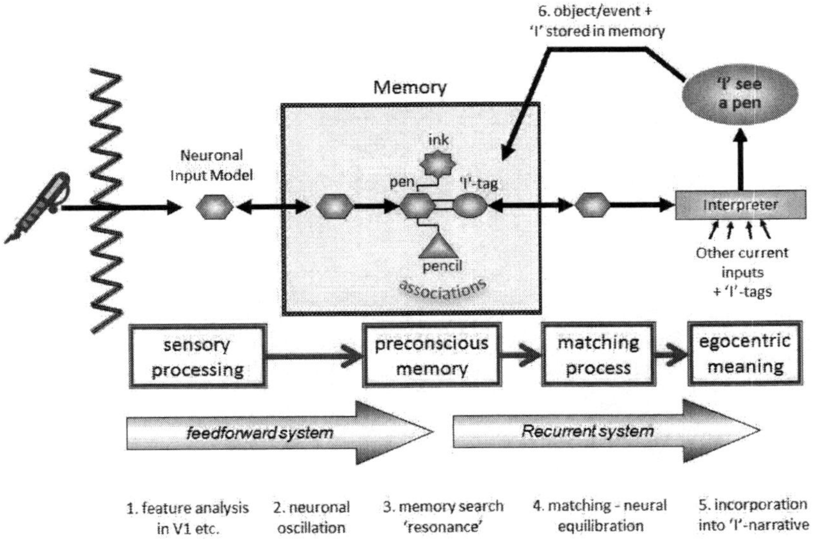

Figure 1. A model of the stages in perception (after Brian Lancaster, *Approaches to Consciousness: The Marriage of Science and Mysticism* [Basingstoke, UK: Palgrave Macmillan, 2004]), 133, 174.

In psychological terms, the activated structures are associations to the input model. It should be noted that this memory function is preconscious,[51] occurring rapidly following the input arriving at the senses. The sensory-memory activity entails the so-called cognits proposed by Joaquin Fuster and Steven Bressler to span more or less widespread neural networks of the areas of the cortex in which associations are formed. The richness of associations arises since "cognits profusely interconnect, overlap, and share nodes of common

---

[51] The term "preconscious" is problematic inasmuch as these early processes are deemed to be imbued with certain "dimensions" of consciousness (see continuation of text). They are pre-"conscious" to the extent that "consciousness" is understood in terms of the end stage of perceptual activity only (I-consciousness). Issues of terminology in the study of consciousness are fraught with inconsistency, and my approach to identifying the different dimensions of consciousness in terms of operationalized processes in perception is intended to overcome at least some of the inconsistencies.

association."[52] The cognits maintain their integrity by establishing a unique pattern of oscillation frequencies across the neural network. The recurrent neural system becomes involved in forming the cognits, effectively generating an iterative quest to match the activated memory structure with the input model. If it matches, then the object represented is selected for inclusion in the I-narrative. The term "I-narrative" is intended to convey the fact that ongoing perception is effectively a narrative construction in which the central feature is the ego, or "I." It should be noted that "I" is viewed not as a substantive preexisting entity but rather as a kind of hypothesis constructed by the interpretative systems to give retrospective coherence to the ongoing mental activity.[53]

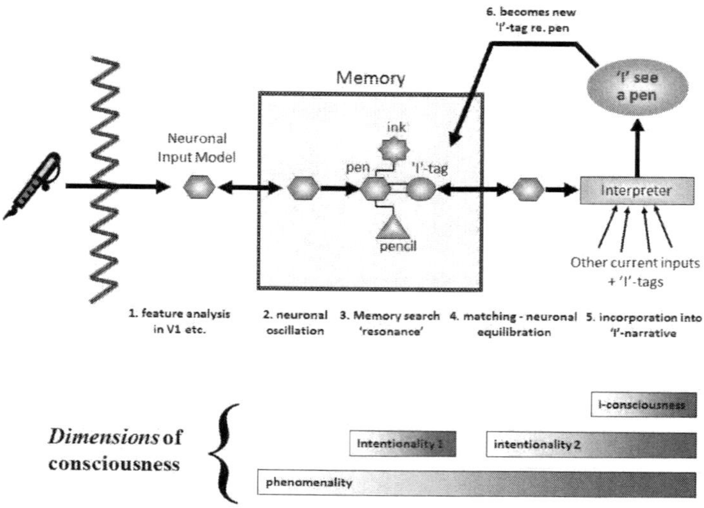

Figure 2. Dimensions of consciousness

As far as consciousness is concerned, it is only the output of the entire system that may be identified with normal, mundane consciousness. However, in line with other researchers[54] I identify different *dimensions* of consciousness, each of which is associated with a specific stage in the model, as illustrated in figure 2.

---

[52] Joaquín M. Fuster and Steven L. Bressler, "Cognit Activation: A Mechanism Enabling Temporal Integration in Working Memory," *Trends in Cognitive Sciences* 16, no. 4 (2012): 207-18, here 208.

[53] See Lancaster, *Approaches to Consciousness*, for detail.

[54] For example, Imants Barušs, "Metanalysis of Definitions of Consciousness," *Imagination, Cognition and Personality* 6 (1987): 321-29; idem, "What We Can Learn about Consciousness from Altered States of Consciousness," *Journal of Consciousness Exploration & Research* 3 (2012):

What I would call the essence of consciousness, its *phenomenality* (the fact that there is something it is like to have an experience, even if the experience is *without content*), is present from the time the input model is constituted. Phenomenality is the *hard* problem of consciousness,[55] and it remains unclear whether it can be attributed to the brain, and if so, how the relationship is effected, or whether it may be a fundamental property not limited to neural activity. In the absence of any definitive evidence to tie down the origination of phenomenality, each individual's view has as much to do with his or her general belief system as it does with the data available.[56] In any case, the proposal here is that, irrespective of its origination, phenomenality underpins all the other dimensions of consciousness.

The activation of preconscious associations entails a form of intentionality that I identify with Freud's notion of the *primary process*. Accordingly I term it *intentionality 1*. Intentionality 2, by contrast, is the dimension of consciousness relating to the match between the input model and one from the activated associations. It arises as the mind locks onto the central percept. We may view intentionality 2 as corresponding to Freud's secondary process; it is reality oriented and consistent with the goals of the ego. Finally, *I-consciousness* is the dimension that dominates the everyday state, centered as it is on the I-narrative. These dimensions are, as it were, cumulative in the sense that when I am conscious of some object (such as the pen in figure 1), intentionality 2 is present to I-consciousness, and the whole experience is imbued with phenomenality. In other words, *I* (I-consciousness) *see* (experience—i.e., phenomenality) *the pen* (intentionality 2). Under normal circumstances, intentionality 1 is not incorporated into I-consciousness. It may, however, gain entry into the I-narrative under conditions such as those associated with hypnagogic imagery, in which there is a relaxation of the inhibition on associations normally brought about by the matching process.

A crucial point to note is that recognizing these differing dimensions of consciousness overcomes the problematic distinction between "conscious" and "unconscious" realms of mind. The associations activated by the input model, for example, are not strictly "unconscious," but they are normally inaccessible from the I-narrative.

805-19, http://jcer.com/index.php/jcj/article/view/227/257; Ned Block, "On a Confusion about a Function of Consciousness," *Behavioral and Brain Sciences* 18 (1995): 227-47, doi: 10.1017/S0140525X00038188; idem, "Two Neural Correlates of Consciousness," *Trends in Cognitive Sciences* 9, no. 2 (2005): 46-52, doi: 10.1016/j.tics.2004.12.006.

[55] David Chalmers, "Facing Up to the Problem of Consciousness," *Journal of Consciousness Studies* 2 (1995): 200-219.

[56] Barušs, "What We Can Learn"; Imants Barušs and Robert J. Moore, "Measurement of Beliefs about Consciousness and Reality," *Psychological Reports* 71 (1992): 59-64, doi: 10.2466/pr0.1992.71.1.59.

I have argued that mystical states of consciousness arise when there is a shift in the way we identify with these dimensions of consciousness. Normally, we identify almost exclusively with the I-narrative. It seems to me that mystical states involve relative detachment from the I-narrative and a concomitant increase in awareness of the preceding stages. Given that there are three preceding stages—namely, the penultimate stage in which sensory input and memory structures become matched, the next preceding stage involving associative activity, and the earliest stage during which the neuronal input model is constructed—we may postulate three mystical states. As illustrated in figure 3, an attenuation of activity in the end stage and/or an augmentation of activity in the associative stage may be expected to correlate with the shifts entailed in the first two of these mystical states. In terms of classical spiritual and mystical practices, the former arises through apophatic meditation directed toward stilling the mind, and the latter entails katophatic practices such as visualizations in which disciplined exploration of associations is encouraged.

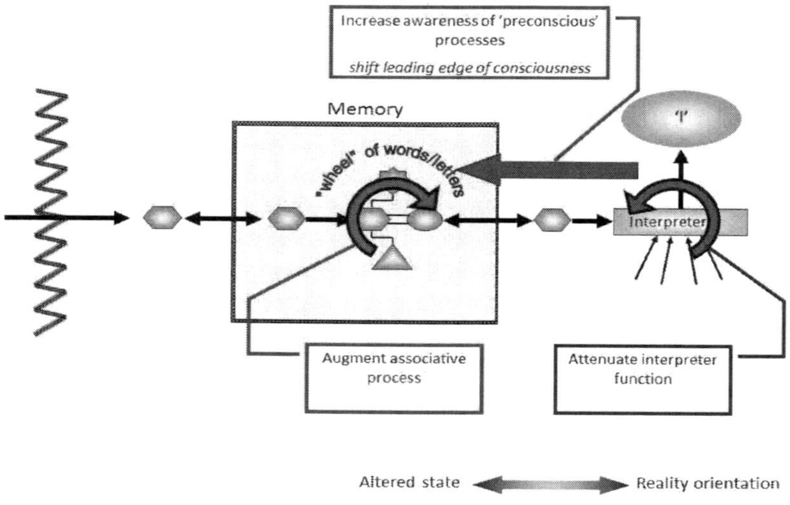

Figure 3. The effects of spiritual practice

Armed with the above model and my operationalization of the effects of spiritual practice, I can now return to the states of mystical consciousness found in the *Zohar*. An immediate set of parallels presents itself since I have identified three *dimensions* of consciousness additional to the normal I-consciousness, each dominating in one of the three stages preceding the normal state of consciousness in the processing model, and Hellner-Eshed[57] argues that the *Zohar* portrays three principal mystical states of consciousness. Beyond the simple concordance of number here, the real issue is whether the putative correspondences encompass the features of experience that, on the one hand, would accompany the dimensions of consciousness I identify and, on the other, characterize the *Zohar*'s mystical states. The objective here is not simply to explain mystical states in neuroscientific terms. Neurophenomenology encourages an integration of the two vantage points, meaning that the phenomenology of the mystical states will be used to guide conclusions about the cognitive and neural processes, just as the data from cognitive neuroscience may be expected to help understand the mystical states.

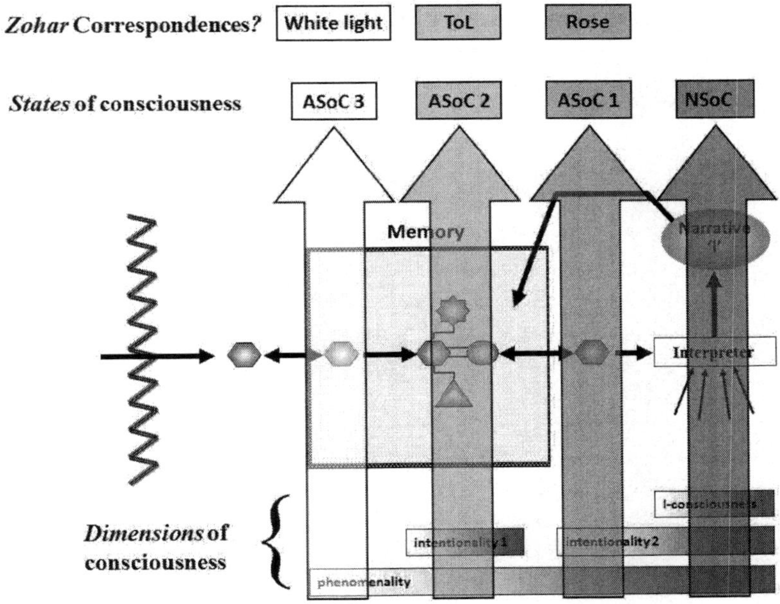

Figure 4. Dimensions of consciousness and corresponding altered states of consciousness

I am proposing that each of the dimensions of consciousness will dominate a specific state of consciousness (see figure 4). In the normal state, I-consciousness is dominant. It is implicit that in this normal state I access information according to my needs and desires. The figures above focusing on a single frozen moment and a single object in front of my eyes cannot do justice

[57] Hellner-Eshed, *River Flows from Eden*.

to the complex array of contents in my consciousness at any given time. The point I wish to emphasize here is that I-consciousness will always be distracted by whatever may be playing through those needs and desires. Thus, for example, seeing the pen may be associated with frustration inasmuch as I am uncertain of the way to proceed in my current writing, or with desire if I am about to write to someone from whom I have reason to expect something, and so on.

I have not yet explained a feature of the above figures that comes in at this point. I have proposed a "tagging" system whereby information present at any given moment of consciousness becomes stored in conjunction with the self-representation that has been constructed at that time. In effect, the constructed self-representation becomes a tag attached to the memory—an "*I-tag*" (see figures above). While this posited I-tagging system can be instructive in relation to spiritual notions of the intractability of egocentric states, I have advanced it in the first place[58] to account for extensive observations in cognitive neuroscience regarding *implicit memory*.[59] In short, research suggests that some apparent disorders of memory may arise from inconsistencies in the I-tagging system rather than failures of information storage per se.[60] Details of this possibility need not concern us here; I simply wish to stress the role of the I-tag system in effecting the ability of a current construction of I to access those schemata that can enhance consolidation of its own status.

If construction of the self-representation and concomitant I-narrative were attenuated, the center of consciousness would shift, moving from the normal state of consciousness (NSoC) to what I shall term for simplicity *altered state of consciousness 1* (ASoC 1). As portrayed in figure 4, in the terms of the model under discussion ASoC 1 would include intentionality 2 in the absence of the normal I-narrative, meaning that accessing egocentric information will be attenuated. In her analysis of *Zoharic* states Hellner-Eshed[61] specifies intensification of perception and emotion, and augmentation of associative processes as being among the key properties of Rose Consciousness. The model presented in the figures here is focused on memory and perception, but there is no reason to doubt that the release from I-consciousness would not similarly intensify

---

[58] Brian L. Lancaster, *Mind, Brain and Human Potential: The Quest for an Understanding of Self* (Shaftesbury, UK: Element Books, 1991).
[59] See, for example, Daniel L. Schacter, C.-Y. Peter Chiu, and Kevin N. Ochsner, "Implicit Memory: A Selective Review, *Annual Review of Neuroscience* 16, no. 1 (1993): 159-82, doi: 10.1146/annurev.ne.16.030193.001111.
[60] John F. Kihlstrom, "The Psychological Unconscious and the Self," in *Experimental and Theoretical Studies of Consciousness*, Ciba Foundation Symposium no. 174, 147-67 (Chichester, UK: John Wiley, 1993); idem, "Consciousness and Me-ness," in *Scientific Approaches to Consciousness*, ed. Jonathan D. Cohen and Jonathan W. Schooler, 451-68 (Mahwah, NJ: Lawrence Erlbaum, 1997); Lancaster, *Mind, Brain and Human Potential.*
[61] Hellner-Eshed, *River Flows from Eden.*

emotion. The release from I-consciousness might also bring about increased awareness of the normally preconscious associations to the neuronal input model. The main claim, however, is that an individual experiencing ASoC 1 has heightened focus on the perceptual objects—the matched schemata in the figures—with little distraction by the ruminations of the I-narrative that normally dominates I-consciousness. Perhaps this should be viewed as a *mindful* state of consciousness.[62] In terms of neural correlates, feedforward and recurrent systems[63] would be active, meaning that perceptual activity (and related emotions) would be pronounced, but the interpretive systems underlying the construction of self[64] would be attenuated.

A further shift toward earlier stages in the model leads to ASoC 2, in which intentionality 1 becomes dominant. The state would be similar to ASoC 1 inasmuch as egocentric thinking attaching to the I-narrative is attenuated, but differs from the first altered state to the extent that associational activity dominates. How might the phenomenology of the second *Zoharic* mystical state identified by Hellner-Eshed[65] aid our understanding of ASoC 2?

The key characteristic of the *Zoharic* state is a richer sense of knowing, a sense of somehow being in touch with the pattern that underlies all things, and of being an active participant in the dynamics of that pattern (which, in the *Zohar*'s distinctive narrative means promoting the union of female and male divine potencies). I believe that these characteristics may point to increased contact with the "unconscious"[66] when experiencing ASoC 2,[67] akin, for example, to the state accessed through *active imagination* in Jung's analytical psycholo-

---

[62] Bikkhu Bodhi, "What Does Mindfulness Really Mean? A Canonical Perspective," *Contemporary Buddhism* 12 (2011): 19-39, doi:10.1080/14639947.2011.564813; Peter Malinowski, "Mindfulness as Psychological Dimension: Concepts and Applications, *Irish Journal of Psychology* 29, no. 1-2 (2008): 155-66, doi: 10.1080/03033910.2008.10446281.

[63] Stanislas Dehaene, Jean-Pierre Changeux, Lionel Naccache, Jérôme Sackur, and Claire Sergent, "Conscious, Preconscious, and Subliminal Processing: A Testable Taxonomy," *Trends in Cognitive Sciences* 10, no. 5 (2006): 204-11, doi: 10.1016/j.tics.2006.03.007; Victor A. F. Lamme and Pieter R. Roelfsema, "The Distinct Modes of Vision Offered by Feedforward and Recurrent Processing," *Trends in Neurosciences* 23, no. 11 (2000): 571-79, doi: 10.1016/S0166-2236(00)01657-X; Simon van Gaal and Victor A. F. Lamme. "Unconscious High-Level Information Processing: Implication for Neurobiological Theories of Consciousness," *Neuroscientist* 18, no. 3 (2012): 287-301, doi: 10.1177/1073858411404079.

[64] Lancaster, *Mind, Brain and Human Potential*; Gazzaniga, "Shifting Gears."

[65] Hellner-Eshed, *River Flows from Eden.*

[66] Again, a reminder of terminological problems is required. I use the term "unconscious" since that is engrained in our culture. However, the "un" may be misleading since in the terms presented here, ASOC 2 is imbued with two dimensions of consciousness: phenomenality and intentionality 1. The "un" merely connotes that content is inaccessible from the mundane state of "I-consciousness."

[67] Lancaster, *Approaches to Consciousness.*

gy. Again, due to the limitations of a static representation, the above figures cannot capture the extensive ramifications of the associative process that must be ever unfolding, like ripples continually spreading and interacting from disturbance on the surface of water. The associations depicted in the figures are simply trivial connections to a mundane stimulus at a single moment. It would be more realistic to envisage the associations as comprising a veritable panoply of ever-changing images, most of which remain normally inaccessible from the NSoC. It is this process of accessing such normally unconscious imagery and, more especially, of effecting contact with the effervescent process that continually activates complex associations that, I suggest, brings the sense of a wider sphere of knowledge to the individual experiencing ASoC 2.

The final state predicted by the model is ASoC 3, in which we would find phenomenality in the absence of intentionality. The connection to the White Light Consciousness that Hellner-Eshed[68] discerns in the *Zohar*'s scheme should be readily apparent. "The white light becomes a throne for a concealed light—invisible, unknowable—settling upon the white light. Then the light is perfect."[69] The experience of light is probably the most universal feature of mysticism,[70] and on account of the absence of any form in the experience, it approximates a *contentless* state of consciousness.[71] Whether such states are contentless in an absolute sense need not concern us here. There is good evidence that phenomenality may be separable from intentionality regardless of whether such a state should be viewed as having positive value.[72] Of course, White Light Consciousness for the companions of the *Zohar* is of ultimate value, but here the link with cognitive neuroscience is broken since the meaning of the experience introduces ontological issues. Such awareness of preverbal and prereflective aspects of lived experience, which, as expressed by Lutz and Thompson,[73] normally "remain simply 'lived through,'" becomes for the mystical fraternity of the *Zohar* a gateway to a transcendent level of being. As noted by Alexander and Andrew Fingelkurts,[74] we have no scientific way to answer the

[68] Hellner-Eshed, *River Flows from Eden.*

[69] *Zohar* 1:83, in Matt, *Zohar*, 2:32.

[70] Hunt, "Cognitive Psychology"; Matthew T. Kapstein, ed., *The Presence of Light: Divine Radiance and Religious Experience* (Chicago: University of Chicago Press, 2004).

[71] Cf. Robert K. C. Forman, ed., *The Problem of Pure Consciousness* (Oxford: Oxford University Press, 1990); idem, ed., *The Innate Capacity: Mysticism, Psychology, and Philosophy* (Oxford: Oxford University Press, 1998).

[72] Philip R. Sullivan, "Contentless Consciousness and Information-Processing Theories of Mind," *Philosophy, Psychiatry and Psychology* 2 (1995): 51-59.

[73] Lutz and Thompson, "Neurophenomenology," 37.

[74] Alexander A. Fingelkurts and Andrew A. Fingelkurts, "Is Our Brain Hardwired to Produce God or Is Our Brain Hardwired to Perceive God? A Systematic Review on the Role of the Brain in Mediating Religious Experience," *Cognitive Processing* 10, no. 4 (2009): 293-326, doi: 10.1007/s10339-009-0261-3.

question of whether the brain state generates the mystical state of consciousness or is a necessary receiving condition for some "higher" level of mind.

Language Mysticism: Whirling the Wheel of Meaning

In a recent discussion of mysticism and the cognitive neuroscience of consciousness, Jason Blum[75] argues that the ineffability of mystical states accords with research into consciousness. Far from being a linguistic construction, the basis of consciousness is preverbal, having more of an emotional than a linguistic nature.[76] Hellner-Eshed similarly views the ultimate state of consciousness in the *Zohar*'s scheme, White Light Consciousness, as "beyond the horizons of language."[77] Nevertheless, for the most part it is the mysticism inherent in language itself that fascinates the author of the *Zohar*, as Wolfson reminds us:

> In the final analysis, according to the *Zohar*, language is a completely appropriate medium to attain gnosis of the divine and ultimately achieve communion therewith, for, from the kabbalistic perspective, the twenty-two foundational letters of the Hebrew alphabet constitute the very substance of God.[78]

Kabbalah is quintessentially a mysticism of language.[79] It is no exaggeration to state that all its major themes are either directly concerned with letters and words or are metaphorically described in relation to the processes involved in generating speech from thought. As Idel puts it, the kabbalists view language as "the spiritual underpinning of reality"[80] and the Hebrew letters as constituting "a mesocosmos that enables operations that can bridge the gap between the human—or the material—and the divine."[81] While the *Zohar* cultivates a mainly theosophical understanding of such language mysticism, other kabbalistic authors describe intensive practices that employ key elements of language to attain altered states. The extent to which these kinds of practices lay behind the

---

[75] Blum, "Science of Consciousness."
[76] Cf. Antonio R. Damasio, *The Feeling of What Happens: Body and Emotion in the Making of Consciousness* (New York: Houghton Mifflin Harcourt, 1999).
[77] Hellner-Eshed, *River Flows from Eden*, 348.
[78] Elliot R. Wolfson, "Letter Symbolism and Merkavah Imagery in the Zohar," in *Alei Shefer: Studies in the Literature of Jewish Thought Presented to Rabbi Dr. Alexandre Safran*, ed. Moshe Hallamish, 195-236 (Ramat-Gan, Israel: Bar-Ilan Press, 1990).
[79] Lancaster, "Cognitive Models and Spiritual Maps"; idem, *Approaches to Consciousness*; idem, *The Essence of Kabbalah* (London: Arcturus, 2005).
[80] Moshe Idel, *Hasidism: Between Ecstasy and Magic* (Albany: State University of New York Press, 1995), 219.
[81] Moshe Idel, "Reification of Language in Jewish Mysticism," in *Mysticism and Language*, ed. Steven T. Katz, 42-79 (Oxford: Oxford University Press, 1992), 43.

ability of the author of the *Zohar* to convey knowledge of higher states is largely unknown, but I suspect that a common core lies within the theosophical kabbalah of the *Zohar* and the so-called *ecstatic kabbalah*, which focuses on techniques for attaining higher states. As Wolfson notes, the view that polarizes these two strands "fails to take seriously the many shared doctrines that may be traced to a common wellspring of esoteric tradition with much older roots."[82]

One of the sources that conveys that "common wellspring" is the *Sefer Yetsirah*, a short work thought to date from the early centuries of the Common Era that focuses largely on the role that individual Hebrew letters play in the work of creation. God is portrayed as realizing the work of creation through permuting the letters:

> He placed them in a wheel. . . . The wheel revolves forwards and backwards. . . . How? He permuted them, weighed them, and transformed them. *Alef* [the first letter] with them all and all of them with *alef*; *bet* [second letter] with them all and all of them with *bet*.[83]

At the same time as it depicts the linguistic technique by means of which God is thought to create the world, the *Sefer Yetsirah* encourages the mystic to emulate the divine, giving rise to esoteric practices involving intensive ways of permuting and combining letters.

Traditions of mystical practice drawing on these words of the *Sefer Yetsirah* may be viewed as extending the emphasis on associations that is central to the rabbinic style of exegesis. The mind schooled in *midrashic* lore would be sensitized to the fluidity in language whereby one Hebrew word is substituted for another on the basis of phonic or etymological associations. As is brought out in an extract from an early kabbalistic work, *Sefer ha-Bahir*, all words are effectively access points, or nodes, to associations that are crucial for the constellation of meanings they convey: "What is a 'word'? As is written, '[Apples of gold in settings of silver is] A word fitly [Hebrew *of'nav*] spoken' (Proverbs 25:11). Do not read 'fitly' [*of'nav*] but 'its wheel' [*ofanav*]."[84] The mystic is enjoined not to be satisfied with a word's immediate meaning. The path to the "apples of gold" requires accessing the "wheel" of meanings to which any given word relates. In characteristic fashion, the instruction itself is conveyed via the very

---

[82] Elliot R. Wolfson, "Abraham ben Samuel Abulafia and the Prophetic Kabbalah," in *Jewish Mysticism and Kabbalah: New Insights and Scholarship*, ed. Frederick E. Greenspahn, 68-90 (New York: New York University Press, 2011), 85n7.

[83] *Sefer Yetsirah* 2:4-5. See Ithamar Gruenwald, "A Preliminary Critical Edition of Sefer Yezira" (in Hebrew), *Israel Oriental Studies* 1 (1971): 132-77. For the English translation, see also Aryeh Kaplan, *Sefer Yetzirah: The Book of Creation* (York Beach, ME: Samuel Weiser, 1990).

[84] *Sefer ha-Bahir*, in *The Book Bahir: An Edition Based on the Earliest Manuscripts*, ed. Daniel Abrams (Los Angeles: Cherub Press), 33.

technique it encourages. The vowel-less form of Hebrew scripture means that the word generally translated as "fitly" could be articulated differently, giving the word meaning "its wheel." The reading of a scriptural text becomes "fitting" to the extent that its words are elaborated in terms of their "wheels of associations" and subtleties of meaning.

This emphasis on wheel-related imagery, and the importance of associational practices that it implies, supports my arguments in the previous section. While I have focused there on mystical *states* of consciousness, the tradition of practice stemming from these words of the *Sefer Yetsirah* gives insight into the *processes* for attaining those states. One of the most influential of the kabbalistic mystics who taught practices stemming from the *Sefer Yetsirah*, Abulafia, reinforces this wheel-related imagery in his instructions for esoteric techniques of working with a name of God: "Examine all its combinations and move it and turn it about like a wheel returning around, front and back, like a scroll."[85] As Gershom Scholem points out, Abulafia's practice entailed developing associations in a controlled meditative state:

> In fact this is nothing else than a very remarkable method of using associations as a way of meditation. It is not wholly the "free play of association" as known to psychoanalysis; rather it is the way of passing from one association to another determined by certain rules which are, however, sufficiently lax.[86]

Abulafia equated the wheel of the letters with the *Active Intellect*,[87] a term introduced by the Aristotelian philosophy that informed much medieval Islamic and Jewish speculative thought. In the sequence of celestial intelligences emanated from God, the Active Intellect functioned as intermediary between the divine and the human spheres. Abulafia's system was directed toward achieving mystical union with the Active Intellect by imitating its mode of operation. The letter-working and hermeneutic activity that Abulafia taught was viewed as emulating the linguistic operations of the Active Intellect.

---

85 Cited in Moshe Idel, *The Mystical Experience in Abraham Abulafia*, trl. Jonathan Chipman (Albany: State University of New York Press, 1988), 21.

86 Gershom G. Scholem, *Major Trends in Jewish Mysticism* (1941; New York: Schocken Books, 1961), 135.

87 The identity of the wheel of the letters and the Active Intellect is "proved" through the cryptic logic known as *gematria*, whereby two or more phrases may be seen to display equivalence of meaning if their numerical values are equal. *Gematria* depends on the fact that each Hebrew letter is also a number, *alef* = 1, *bet* = 2, and so on. The *Sefer Yetsirah* describes the wheel of the letters as giving 231 gates, 231 being the number of two-letter combinations from the set of 22 letters of the Hebrew alphabet. In this case, then, Abulafia equates the Hebrew *Yesh ra'el* ("There are 231" or "Israel") with *sekhel ha-pu'al* ("Active Intellect") since both phrases have the same numerical total (541).

In mystical thought, emulation leads to conjunction, meaning that the linguistically based practices lead to a higher, or "prophetic," state of consciousness identified with the Active Intellect. Psychologically speaking, these changes no doubt derive from the role that language normally plays in structuring the self and shaping our capacities for categorical perception of the world. By working to counteract such normal functions of language, these mystical practices would no doubt lead to alterations in the self-sense and in the ways in which the world is experienced. As Idel has stressed, the practices that Abulafia taught can best be understood as "an attempt to transcend [language] by deconstructing language as a communicative instrument . . . , which . . . would lead the mystic beyond the normal state of consciousness."[88]

The model advanced earlier gives some basis for conjecturing what lies "beyond the normal state of consciousness." However, simply noting the upsurge in associational activity and the deconstruction of the normal narrative base of consciousness promoted by Hebrew language mysticism may seem somewhat prosaic when viewed in relation to the potent vistas opened up by the kabbalists. In part this raises ontological issues: the Active Intellect is an attractive goal for mystical work in view of its divine status, and any conjectured reorientation of the schematizing function of the mind may seem two-dimensional by comparison. Of course, exploring changes in brain function associated with mystical states need not imply that there is nothing beyond the brain in this context. For example, the brain state may be a necessary condition for accessing the divine,[89] or brain systems may be isomorphic with macrocosmic systems.[90] Leaving aside the ontological issues and taking a purely psychological perspective, however, let me bring this exploration to a close with some speculation about the potentially long-lasting reorganization of memory systems and personality that may ensue from the intensive language-based practices taught by Jewish mystics.

Language-based practices in the kabbalah invariably entail focusing on one or more divine name. I conjecture that by reconnecting deconstructed language elements with the various (and elaborate) permutations of the name(s), the mystic is effectively bringing a schema of the all-encompassing divine Being into the role normally played by "I"-tags. Normally—that is, in the mind not saturated with mystical states—the "I"-tags attaching to memories would play a superordinate role in indexing memories and giving rise to the key sense that

---

[88] Moshe Idel, *Language, Torah, and Hermeneutics in Abraham Abulafia*, trl. Menahem Kallus (Albany: State University of New York Press, 1989), xi.

[89] Fingelkurts and Fingelkurts, "Is Our Brain Hardwired?"

[90] Brian L. Lancaster, "The Hard Problem Revisited: From Cognitive Neuroscience to Kabbalah and Back Again," in *Neuroscience, Consciousness, and Spirituality*, ed. Harald Walach, Stefan Schmidt, and Wayne B. Jonas, 229-52 (Heidelberg: Springer, 2011).

any memory accessed is "owned"; the personality is infused with an egocentric orientation. I conjecture that prolonged and repeated working with the letters of the various divine names—visualizing and chanting them, permuting them and expanding them, and, crucially in this psychological context, linking them with other words having their own constellations in memory—would bring about a shift in memory indexing. A more *transpersonal* tagging system, giving a larger sense of scale than that inherent in the normative egocentric indexing, becomes consolidated. As I have suggested elsewhere,[91] the memory system would become, as it were, "reformatted" in relation to a higher-order indexing system, with "I"-tags being substituted by (for want of a better term) *God-tags*. Just as mundane "I"-tags are given currency by one's own name, so the mystic's intense contemplative working with the various divine names is hypothesized as eventuating in this shift in the operational scale of the intellect.

In this context, a suggestive motif is that of the juxtaposition of the human "I" and that of the divine in the zenith of Abulafia's language mysticism. Idel has drawn attention to Abulafia's notion of the "circle of prophecy" that incorporates "two I's—both human and Divine."[92] Abulafia views this circle of prophecy as the unification of divine and human power, a conception supported by two biblical verses in which the Hebrew for "I" is repeated with no other words between (Deuteronomy 32:39 and Isaiah 48:15). For Abulafia, this biblical phraseology juxtaposing the repetition of "I" is to be understood as depicting the human-divine union, which is identified with the prophetic state of consciousness and with the Active Intellect. Whatever the more cosmic significance of such a state, I am suggesting that the shift in scale to a transpersonal, theocentric memory indexing system would be the enduring psychological consequence of a mystic's achieving awareness of his or her union with the divine "I."

---

[91] Lancaster, *Approaches to Consciousness.*

[92] Idel, *Kabbalah*, 64.

11. Becoming a Buddha

A Semiotic Analysis of Visualizations in Tibetan Buddhism

Louis Hébert[1]

Abstract

This essay analyzes some elements of *Vajrayana* Buddhism using François Rastier's theory of anthropic zones. According to Rastier, the semiotic layer of social practices can be divided into three anthropic zones: identity, proximal, and distal. The identity zone corresponds chiefly to the individual. The proximal zone corresponds primarily to one's fellow creatures. The distal zone is populated with absent, imaginary, or unknown objects (a word to be taken in a broad sense). The zones coincide with two worlds: the obvious world (made up of the identity and proximal zones) and an absent world (consisting of the distal zone). An *empirical* boundary is formed between the identity zone and the proximal zone, and a *transcendent* boundary is formed between the first two zones and the distal zone. Rastier uses the term "fetish" for objects on the first boundary, and the term "idol" for objects on the second boundary (with no pejorative nuances).

Clearly, religions make extensive use of the distal zone and idols. The essay examines *sādhana* texts primarily (practice texts), in which complex visualizations are used to invite the practitioner to be progressively transformed into an enlightened being, or Buddha, in the course of the session. The practitioner travels in his mind—but with the intention of actually going there one day—from the identity zone to the distal zone, and this is done through the mediation of a Buddhist deity that functions as an idol. In principle, the practitioner is motivated by *bodhicitta*, which is the desire to reach enlightenment for the benefit of his fellows, of which Buddhism has an expanded inventory, including humans, animals, and others. Thus he ultimately comes to "love others more than himself," to value the proximal zone more than the identity zone.

[1] Translated from the French. Unless otherwise noted, translations are the author's.

A *sādhana* is a type of practice in *Vajrayāna*, or Indo-Tibetan tantric Buddhism, through which the yogi, or practitioner, attains the state of the *yidam*, which is his tutelary deity, or personal buddha:

> In other words, it is a comprehensive method for mastery of the ordinary accomplishments (Sk., *siddhi*) [the miraculous powers to be used in the service of compassion] and the supreme accomplishment [enlightenment, one's entry into dynamic *nirvāṇ a* through the elimination of negative emotions and erroneous thinking]. The *sādhanas* are both the central core and the structural framework of any tantric ritual [a ritual based on Buddhist texts known as "tantras"], performed by a group or in the solitude of a retreat. . . . The *sādhana* texts are structured as guides, which describe the visualizations, each step of the practice, the rituals acts to be performed, and so on.[2]

In the *sādhanas* consulted for this essay, complex visualizations are given through which the practitioner is invited to be progressively transformed into the enlightened being, or Buddha, that the *yidam* represents, such as Avalokiteśhvara, the enlightened being who symbolizes compassion, or Padmasambhava, the semilegendary founder of Buddhism in Tibet.

From the perspective of Rastier's theory of anthropic zones, the practitioner travels in his mind—but in view of actually going there, using his intention—from the identity zone to the distal zone, where transcendence resides, and this is done through the mediation of a Buddhist deity. Rastier uses the term "idol" (with no connotations) for these mediators between the distal zone and the two others, the identity and the proximal zones.

This analysis will deepen our understanding of the *sādhanas* of Buddhist tantrism generally, but also, since all religions strongly invoke the distal zone, we will deepen our understanding of religion as a phenomenon, particularly its mystical aspects. Finally, this analysis provides a way to introduce this particular theory of Rastier's to an English-speaking audience—perhaps for the first time—and an opportunity to consider how best to apply it and conceptualize it as well. The analysis is the latest milestone in a series of semiotic analyses of elements of Buddhism undertaken by the author.[3] The author is not a scholar

---

[2] Philippe Cornu, *Dictionnaire encyclopédique du bouddhisme* (Paris: Seuil, 2006), 491.

[3] Louis Hébert, "Sémiotique et bouddhisme: Carré sémiotique et tétralemme (catuskoti)," in *Performances et objets culturels*, ed. Louis Hébert and Lucie Guillemette, 103-28 (Québec: Presses de l'Université Laval, 2011); idem, ed., *Sémiotique et bouddhisme*, special issue of *Protée* 39, no. 2 (Autumn 2011); idem, "Sémiotique et bouddhisme: Quelques repères," *Sémiotique et bouddhisme*, special issue of *Protée* 39, no. 2 (Autumn 2011): 5-8; idem, "Opérations de transformation dans l'iconographie du bouddhisme tibétain," *Sémiotique et bouddhisme*, special issue of *Protée* 39, no. 2 (Autumn): 81-94; idem, "Les opérations de transformation" [expanded ver-

of Buddhism and therefore will exercise the utmost caution in proceeding with the analysis and presenting the results.

First, we will engage Rastier's theory of anthropic zones, with some clarifications and additions. Then we will examine a particular *sādhana* text to see what trajectory is taken through these zones and boundaries, and how the inventories of beings within them change as the text progresses.

According to Rastier, the semiotic layer ("domain" or "sphere" in older terminologies) of social practices can be subdivided into three zones, which he calls "anthropic" (relating to man, from the Greek *anthropos*, or "man").

Theory: The Three Layers or Domains of Practice

In Rastier's view, culture involves three *domains*, although we would add that the most characteristic of these three is undoubtedly the second, where culture comes to reflect upon itself. In an effort to remedy the inadequacies of the ontological dualities (e. g., physical world/cognitive world), Rastier proposes a tripartite scheme: physical domain / semiotic domain / mental processes, or cognitive domain.[4]

This hypothesis can be summarized as follows: "a *culture* could very well be defined as a multi-layered system of social practices."[5] Any *social practice* is a codified activity, involving specific relations between three domains,[6] or in current terminology, three *layers*: 1. A physical domain (or *phenomenal-physical layer*) formed by the material interactions occurring in it. 2. A semiotic domain (or *semiotic layer*) composed of the signs (symbols, icons and signals, etc.) that are exchanged or employed in it. 3. A mental process domain (or *[re]presentational layer*) unique to the agents and heavily socialized, in general.[7]

In this tripartite scheme, the semiotic domain mediates between the physical world and the world of mental processes: the plane of expression (of signifiers) has preferred correlates in the physical domain, and the plane of content (of signifieds) has them in the mental domain.[8] The physical correlates linked to the signifiers are stimuli (Klinkenberg) and the cognitive correlates of the signifieds are mental images (but not in an exclusively visual sense) or multimodal

---

sion of "Sémiotique et bouddhisme: Quelques repères"], *Signo* Web site, directed by Louis Hébert, http://www.signosemio.com/operations-de-transformation.asp.

[4] François Rastier, Marc Cavazza, and Anne Abeillé, *Sémantique pour l'analyse* (Paris: Masson, 1994), 4-5; François Rastier, *Sémantique et recherches cognitives* (Paris: Presses universitaires de France, 1991), 237-43.

[5] Rastier, Cavazza, and Abeillé, *Sémantique pour l'analyse*, 211, emphasis added.

[6] Ibid., 224.

[7] Mental processes are not purely physical (i.e., "natural"), as a rule; they are largely determined and structured by social (i.e., "cultural") factors.

[8] Rastier, Cavazza, and Abeillé, *Sémantique pour l'analyse*, 5.

simulacra (Rastier). Next, Rastier further clarified his tripartite scheme by considering it from the perspective of the opposition between *Umwelt*—the world unique to individuals—and *Welt*, as defined by Jacob von Uexküll:[9]

> The "internal states" of human subjects are *presentations*, not representations, because they appear in specific interfaces between the individual and his surroundings; however, they do not represent these surroundings or this interface. The substrate of the surroundings (primarily the physical substrate), the ***Welt*** in the background—we will call this the *background world*.[10] In this way, we want to rearticulate the oppositions between the phenomenon and the object, the event and the fact. The *surrounding world* [***Umwelt***] is composed of the presentational layer and the layer of the semiotics of practices. The physical layer does not appear as it is, but as it is perceived, i.e., to whatever degree it has an impact on the presentations (of "objects" or of signifiers [signifieds, too, possibly?]); we have borrowed the term "pheno-physical" from Thom.[11]

The tripartite scheme takes the form[12] of the three layers, the Umwelt and the Welt:

Surrounding world (*Umwelt*):	(re)presentational layer
	semiotic layer
Background world (*Welt*):	pheno-physical layer

The Three Anthropic Zones

The semiotic layer is characterized by four main *categorial divisions*; the homologies between the zones they articulate define three *anthropic zones*:

> The semiotic layer of the human *Umwelt* is characterized by four very broad discontinuities or divisions, which seem to be attested in various ways in all described languages, so they may be hypothetically considered as anthropologically significant. . . . The homologies between these divisions serve to dis-

[9] Jakob von Uexküll, *Mondes animaux et mondes humains* (1934; Paris: Denoël, 1956).

[10] Translator's note: Rastier's term, *arrière-monde*, literally means "back-world," but Nietzsche's term "*Hinterwelt*" is also translated as "back-world." I simply revert to the German "*Welt*," since it is commonly used in English. For Rastier's term "*entour*" (the "world around" or "surrounding world"), I use "*Umwelt*."

[11] François Rastier, "Anthropologie linguistique et sémiotique des cultures," in *Une introduction aux sciences de la culture*, ed. François Rastier and Simou Bouquet, 243-67 (Paris: Presses universitaires de France, 2002), 247.

[12] Diagram from Rastier, "Anthropologie linguistique et sémiotique des cultures," 247.

> tinguish three zones: a coincident one, the *identity zone*; an adjacent one, the *proximal zone*; and a foreign or extrinsic one, the *distal zone*. The principal division is the one separating the first two zones from the third. In other words, the opposition between the identity zone and the proximal zone is secondary to the opposition separating these two zones taken together from the distal zone. A distinction is thus created between an *obvious world* (made up of the identity and the proximal zones) and an *absent world* (made up of the distal zone). The three zones . . . are created, established, populated, and constantly rearranged by cultural practices. . . . The content of the zones is obviously different from one culture to the next, and a fortiori from one social practice to the next.[13]

To be more specific, the distal zone is "populated with absent, imaginary, or unknown objects."[14] The following table shows the four divisions and the three zones.[15]

	Identity zone	Proximal zone	Distal zone
1. Person	I, WE	YOU	(S)HE, ONE, THAT
2. Time	NOW	RECENTLY SOON	PAST FUTURE
3. Space	HERE	THERE	OVER THERE ELSEWHERE
4. Mode	CERTAIN	PROBABLE	POSSIBLE UNREAL

As for the division between persons, note that the third person "is defined by his or her absence from the interlocution (even if physically present)."[16] In the distal zones of the temporal (or local) and spatial divisions are the elements that have the "defining property of being absent from the *hic et nunc*,"[17] that is, from the here and now. The distal zone is the only one that is specific to humans, and in this sense, it is characteristic of human culture:

---

[13] François Rastier, "Objets culturels et performances sémiotiques: L'objectivation critique dans les sciences de la culture," in *Performances et objets culturels*, ed. Louis Hébert and Lucie Guillemette, 15-58 (Québec: Presses de l'Université Laval, 2010), 19-20.
[14] François Rastier, "Glossaire," 2012, manuscript in possession of author.
[15] Table from Rastier, "Anthropologie linguistique et sémiotique," 249.
[16] Rastier, "Objets culturels et performances sémiotiques," 19.
[17] Ibid.

> Compared with animal languages, the distinguishing feature of human language is no doubt the possibility of talking about what is not there: in other words, the distal zone. . . . The proximal zone, where one's fellows are recognized as such, is quite likely part of other mammals' *Umwelt*. But the distal zone remains unique to the human *Umwelt*, no doubt because it is founded in language.[18]
>
> In short, the distal zone is the source of presentations with no immediate perceptual substrate. In common philosophical parlance, the proximal zone is where the empirical is found, and the distal zone is where the transcendent[19] resides.[20]

The Two Boundaries

There are two boundaries or border areas between the three zones: "The *empirical* boundary resides between the identity zone and the proximal zone, and the *transcendent* boundary between the first two zones and the distal zone. We have proposed the following names, with no pejorative nuances: *fetishes* for objects at the empirical boundary, and *idols* for objects at the transcendent boundary."[21] Note that in anthropology, a fetish is an object to which magical power is attributed (in psychology, the term "fetishism" refers to a sexual perversion); an idol is the representation of a deity, which is worshipped as if it were the actual deity. The following diagram[22] on subjects and boundaries shows how the zone boundaries are structured and, correspondingly, the interfaces between zones:

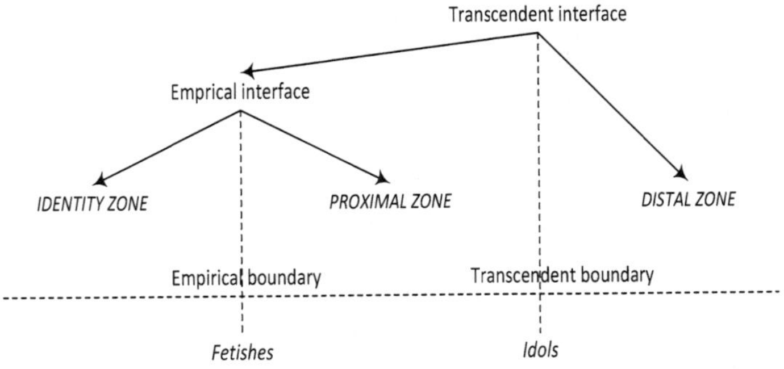

[18] Ibid., 19-20.
[19] By definition, transcendence is beyond the world. Languages, and more broadly, semiotic systems, are obviously within the world and thus immanent. However, they can "represent" either immanent or transcendent elements (God, for example).
[20] Rastier, "Objets culturels et performances sémiotiques," 22.
[21] Ibid. The opposition between *empirical* and *transcendent* is taken from François Rastier, "Réalisme sémantique et réalisme esthétique," *Théorie, littérature, enseignement* 10 (1992): 81-119.
[22] From Rastier, "Objets culturels et performances sémiotiques," 23.

The table[23] below gives some indicative examples of fetishes and idols, matched to the domains, or layers as mediators between anthropic boundaries.

Boundaries Layers	Empirical boundary	Transcendent boundary
	fetishes	idols
(Re)presentational layer	fantasies	beliefs
Semiotic layer	signs (words, jewels, currencies, etc.), tools transitional objects (e. g., dolls)	works (works of art, codes, laws, philosophical, scientific and religious theories, ritual objects) instruments (e. g., musical, scientific, rituals)

The table presents a typology of cultural objects, which is part of the typology of "things" developed by Rastier (loosely based on a typology by Krysztof Pomian):[24]

> *Let us first distinguish between natural bodies* [i.e., "any form of materiality, not just solids"], *cultural objects*, and the *waste* produced in the transformation of bodies into objects. The production trajectory goes from the bodies to the waste. *Artifacts* include the cultural objects and the waste: the cultural objects invite an interpretation that makes their production an act of generating meaning; the waste is consigned to meaninglessness. Cultural objects [i.e., "any product of an objectification process that can proceed as such from a social practice: a musical score, for instance"] are in turn divided into three categories: (a) *tools* and *instruments*, which are more complex (and also include instruments of communication, such as the media); (b) *signs* (linguistic and nonlinguistic: words, symbols, numbers, etc.); and (c) works, which are a result of elaborating on signs by means of tools. Between signs and works, a difference in complexity can be observed: it is the combined action of tools and signs that produces works. . . . They are the end point of the inherent movement of the human actions that produce them, by creating mediative structures between the proximal world and the distal world: the arts, religions, and sciences.[25]

23 Adapted from Rastier, "Objets culturels et performances sémiotiques," 22.

24 Krzysztof Pomian, "Histoire culturelle, histoire des sémiophores," in *Pour une histoire culturelle*, ed. Jean-Pierre Rioux and Jean-François Sirinelli, 73-100 (Paris: Seuil, 1996).

25 Rastier, "Objets culturels et performances sémiotiques," 17-19.

The following diagram[26] gives a general outline of the praxeological typology of things:

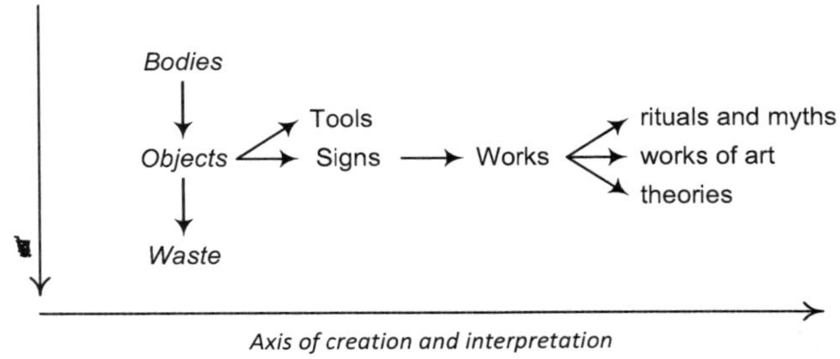

Fetishes and idols do not in themselves have any objective property that grants them this semiotic status. The "semiotic decision" (to borrow an expression from Klinkenberg) and the operations associated with it are what give them this status:

> Of course, the fetish, like the idol, has no "objective" physical property that warrants the fascination accorded to it: It simply reifies the fascination attached to it in such an exclusive way that it is decontextualized and becomes an object in itself, emanating an attraction of its own, with no determination. Now decontextualization is a defining feature of the absolute: that which determines without *being* determined. Thus a fetish seems to exert power, and exert it effectively, as it trumps all else with the aura that testifies to its mysterious symbolic power.[27]

The three characteristics of fetishism are abstraction, generalization, and amplification:

> Some time ago, Alfred Binet identified three distinctive features of fetishism as a "concentration" (1887, 107):[28] (1) a tendency to *abstraction*, or detachment of the fetish negates all context (the whole woman is in her eyes), and so the fetish object may suddenly become a part (just eyes, not the whole woman); (2) the tendency to *generalization* seems to be the price paid for this abstraction (not those particular eyes, but all eyes); (3) finally, a tendency to *amplification*

[26] From Rastier, "Objets culturels et performances sémiotiques," 20.
[27] Ibid., 47.
[28] Alfred Binet, *Le fétichisme dans l'amour* (1887; Paris: Payot, 2001).

leads a shoe fetishist, for example, to value very high heels. The tendency to amplification is rooted in the stylization peculiar to the world of fantasy. . . . As one can see, the reifying effects of fetishism closely resemble those of neopositivism: decontextualization, despecification, and an obsessional invasion of objects. Positivism has all the characteristics of a persistent anxiety dressed up as evidence. But while commodity fetishism promoted dollars to idols and stimulated the God market, conversely, the idolatry of Being causes idols to degenerate into fetishes—fascinating little decontextualized objects. Thus the terms and key words that seem to sum up everything, and fascinating objects of hypotyposis, from Achilles's shield to Charles Bovary's cap, that shine before our eyes by virtue of descriptive *enargeia*.[29]

Factors of Relativity

We would say that the semiotic status of the elements within the anthropic zones is affected primarily by the following variables: which zone they are classified in, where they are positioned in this zone (how close or distant), whether they have fetish and/or idol status, and to what degree they have fetish and/or idol status. For the zones and their boundaries are by no means categorial; they can be scalar, incremental, and have depth: for example, the unreal is undoubtedly more distal than the possible is. One element might be viewed as an idol of greater intensity than another element. Moreover, it is not out of the question, particularly in fictional works, that, all factors of relativity being otherwise constant, one element may belong to two zones simultaneously; or it may be classed as both a fetish and an idol; or it may be both a fetish and a non-fetish-non-idol, or what have you.

An element's status may vary over different cultures and practices, as Rastier noted. We should add that it may vary along with any of the factors of relativity, the observer, and the time of observation in particular.

These statuses and the factors of relativity can be "real" or else thematized in a semiotic product (such as a news article, a novel, a painting), that is, incorporated into its semantic content. For example, the real politicians mentioned in a news article and the characters of a novel are thematized observers, and the time in which they develop, the time of the story in which they act, is thematized as well. So we must distinguish between real and thematized fetishes and idols. Semiotic products themselves can be fetishes (everyday items, like recipes and news articles) or idols (mythical products, such as novels and essays); whether they are fetishes or idols, semiotic products can thematize (incorporate in their semantic content) both fetishes and/or idols equally well. For

---

[29] Rastier, "Objets culturels et performances sémiotiques," 47-48. [Enargeia stands for "vivid imagery"— Ed.]

example, a news article may talk about newspapers (a fetish thematizing a fetish) or a novel (a fetish thematizing an idol); a novel may talk about newspapers (an idol thematizing a fetish) or a novel (an idol thematizing an idol). Thus one anthropic element may incorporate multiple elements of a status identical to, or different from, its own. For example, Adam Smith's economic theory—an idol, therefore—contains an element that is a hyper-idol (being the superlative idol within this idol of a theory): "the invisible hand" that allegedly regulates the market. This can occur when a "real" element incorporates a thematized element as part of itself. For example, an artwork idol such as a literary text may talk about fetishes (such as currency and stuffed animals) and idols (such as other literary texts, fictional or not).

Some examples and details follow, to clarify fetish/idol status (real or thematized). This status is relative.

(1) The status can change depending on the observer: what is a fetish for one observer may be an idol for another, or neither one for someone else, provided that idols and fetishes are not conceived as an all-inclusive set.

(2) The status can change depending on the time of observation: For a single observer, yesterday's fetish may be promoted to today's idol or yesterday's idol can degenerate to today's fetish; an element that is neither a fetish nor an idol may attain idol status later, and so on. As a rule, a change over time is caused by a transformation in the observing subject and/or in the object, or in the knowledge that the observer has about the object (e. g., he believed the element was an idol because it had "magical powers," which turned out to be an illusion).

(3) Idol/fetish status can also vary along with a change in point of view (general/particular) with reference to the object being observed, the observing subject, and/or the time of observation. Three contrasts can be distinguished with respect to general/particular perspectives: they are whole/part, class/element, and type/token. For example, an object that is an idol *as a whole* may be a fetish (or neither one, just an ordinary element) in one or more of its *parts*; an object that is an idol as a *class* may have one or more *elements* that are merely fetishes or ordinary objects; an object that is an idol as a *type* may be viewed as a mere fetish in one or more of its *tokens*. The same principle applies to the observing subject, considered as a whole or divided into parts (e. g., the id, the ego, and the superego as parts of the psyche), taken as a class or an element (all Westerners versus a specific Westerner), seen as a type or a token (the average Westerner versus a particular Westerner). The same principle also applies to time, which can be conceived as a whole or in parts (a particular period versus its subdivisions), as a class or elements thereof (periods of war versus a specific period of war), or as a type or a token thereof (periods of war in general versus a particular period of war). Clearly, the status of a unit can change from one particularity to another: for instance, one unit might be a fetish in one

of its parts and an idol in another part. When the particular characteristics do not match, their content can be echoed on the general level in several different ways. Consider time and whole/part relations. The fact that an element was an idol yesterday, a fetish today, and tomorrow it becomes an idol again can be interpreted simply as a sequence of states each lasting a day (idol -> fetish -> idol), without situating it in an overall time period lasting three days. Or conversely, it can be carried to the general level, in three basic ways: (1) as an idol-fetish, if one is reporting the ambiguity without weighting it; (2) as more idol than fetish, if one is recognizing the predominance of the idol status; (3) as an idol (simply), if one "rounds" to the predominant value (idol, assigned twice) by discarding the differing value (fetish, assigned once).

(4) Finally, fetish/idol status can change depending on the inventory of interdefined elements, either in a single temporal position or with a shift in temporal position, and either for a single observer or for a change of observers. What is a fetish relative to a particular idol may be an idol relative to some other fetish. For example, relative to an airplane maintenance instruction sheet, a recipe may be viewed as a work, that is, an idol, while simultaneously it is viewed as a fetish relative to *In Search of Lost Time* by Proust. This interdefinitional relativity, which brings together at least three elements, can be converted to a scale that gives different weights to the fetish/idol parts within whole elements. Different scales can be used. For example, on a scale from maximum fetish-ness to maximum idol-ness, a recipe would be somewhere in the middle. On a scale from minimum idol-ness to maximum idol-ness, the instruction sheet would be at the low end (which might correspond to zero intensity).

Summary of Anthropic Zone Analysis

To perform an analysis with the anthropic zones, one takes an inventory of the elements (by name and kind) of one or more of the five positions (the three zones and two boundaries); one defines the position(s) of one or more elements; and one records the changes in the inventory and/or positions. Change occurs as a function of the usual factors of relativity: the observing subject (individuals, groups, societies, cultures, etc.), time, space, shifts between elements, transformations in one element, variations in which elements are present, and so on.[30] But one must remember that these factors can change without any change in inventory and/or position (for instance, two different observing subjects may agree on the position of a particular element). With regard to the tra-

[30] The same general principles—the inventory of positions, assignment of elements to positions, trajectories, factors of relativity—are valid for some other analytical tools, if not all: the actantial model, the canonical narrative schema, the semiotic square, the tensive model, and others.

jectories between positions, the possibilities are travel between zones, travel from one boundary to another, travel from a boundary to a zone or the reverse, and staying put (a preservation operation).

The following are some examples of the principal trajectories:

> 1. From zone to zone: from the identity to the proximal or distal zone, as in the famous line from Arthur Rimbaud's poem: "*I* is someone else" ["*Je* est un autre"].
>
> 2. From boundary to boundary: the fetish becomes an idol, which is what happens in the divinization of money or in the hyperbole of advertising.
>
> 3. From a boundary to a zone: In the title *God, Shakespeare and Me* (a play by Woody Allen), the idol assimilates the zone of his fellows (in one possible interpretation, where God becomes a fellow creature); another example is Jesus becoming a man, making him a fellow creature.
>
> 4. From a zone to a boundary: In another possible interpretation of the Woody Allen title, the identity element might become an idol (using irony, the "Me" is put on the same footing as God).[31]

These trajectories produce different effects, which can be serious or funny (which is obvious from the examples).

A *Sādhana* Text Summary and Analysis

No reference (title, author, etc.) will be given for the *sādhana* we will be studying here, because the Tibetan teacher from whom we learned about this text stated that he wanted no "publicity." We have analyzed the text in its French and English translations. Although this *sādhana* appears to contain more elements than the average *sādhana* of this type, it does not seem to contain any elements that are not commonly found in other *sādhanas* of the same type.

Sādhanas always comprise three parts: the preliminaries (or preparation), the main part, and the conclusion.[32] The text we are studying follows this pattern.[33]

[31] There is at least one other possible interpretation, in which none of the above (God, Shakespeare, me) is engaged in an anthropic trajectory. There is simply a collision between the first two, which are idols to different degrees, and the last, who is merely a being in the identity zone.

[32] Cornu, *Dictionnaire encyclopédique du bouddhisme*, 491-92.

[33] The page numbers for quotations from the English translation are given in parentheses.

Preparation

Preliminaries. The text advises as follows: "In a pleasant place, sit on a comfortable seat. Then check your motivation and . . . [generate an] extraordinary positive attitude [*Bodhicitta* mind or awakening mind]" (p. 7).

In the Mahayana tradition, which is the foundation of Buddhist tantrism, the right motivation in any spiritual practice is to reach enlightenment for the benefit of all sentient beings. The sentient beings, which are ultimately those that have the capacity to suffer, include humans, of course, but also animals, the gods, the demigods, the hungry ghosts, and the damned. We see that Mahayana Buddhism extends the proximal zone considerably (the zone containing one's fellows). Moreover, as we will see later, this zone comes to assimilate the identity zone and/or to become more valued than it.

Both here and at other places in the practice, the practitioner is explicitly invited (and implicitly, during the whole practice) to visualize himself with the infinity of beings, his fellow creatures in the proximal zone. This inclusion of all sentient beings, both as goals of the practice and as co-practitioners, serves to increase the intensity of the practice and decrease the possibility of egocentrism.

Recitation. The prayer of the awakening mind, or *bodhicitta* prayer, is recited three times, expressing the desire to attain enlightenment for the benefit of all sentient beings. Now the practitioner vows to take action "at all costs" so that "all sentient beings" may reach enlightenment (p. 7), that is, to do what is necessary to reach enlightenment himself. Indeed, once enlightenment is attained, one's power to help all beings is vastly expanded.

Visualization. The practitioner visualizes his teacher before him in the form of Avalokiteśhvara (the *bodhisattva* of compassion). The teacher-Avalokiteśhvara is "surrounded by a retinue of [his] present teachers and those of the lineage, / The *yidams* [the practitioner's tutelary Buddhas], Buddhas, *bodhisattvas* [*dhyanis bodhisattvas*, or emanations of Buddhas], *dākas* and *dākinis*, / And the guardian deities who possess the eye of wisdom [those who have attained enlightenment, as opposed to the Protectors of the World]" (p. 9).

Note that the teacher is surrounded by enlightened beings, either completely or at least primarily (if the *dākas* and *dākinis* present are not all enlightened), just as he himself, as Avalokiteśhvara, is enlightened. Thus the teacher has moved from the zone of his "fellow creatures" to the distal zone, that of transcendence. The beings in his personal proximal zone, at least the most immediate portion of it, like him, are transcendent beings, relative to the practitioner. This is where the relativity of points of view is quite obvious. The teacher is both in transcendence and the mediator thereof (and thus an idol) for the practitioner. This puts him at the boundary of transcendence and beyond it.

There are two ways to conceptualize the merging of the teacher and Avalokiteśhvara: the two have merged or, as the text seems to indicate, the teacher's being is the same, but his appearance (called "seeming" in Greimas semiotics) has transformed to reveal his true being, which is that of an all-compassionate enlightened one. In this case, it is not a merging of two beings but rather a merging of a new seeming with the same being.

Invitation. "To them [the teacher-Avalokiteśhvara and his entourage of deities] I and the six classes of beings [humans, animals, etc.] pray with devotion: . . . / Out of great compassion, with the infinite emanations of the body of form, / Come to [us in] this place of offerings made with faith" (p. 9).

While the teacher has grown more intense upon becoming Avalokiteśhvara, the practitioner has also grown more intense (although remaining himself) by uniting with the multitude, for whom he becomes the spokesperson. For the multitude of Buddhas, then, there is a corresponding multitude of supplicants. The multitude is also in Avalokiteśhvara himself, since in the form used in the *sādhana*, he has four arms, obviously to emphasize his desire to help all beings and his ability to do so, and on his head he carries Amitabha, the Buddha whose emanation he is. Thus there are two dual characters: the teacher-Avalokiteśhvara is parallel to Avalokiteśhvara-Amitabha. With respect to the practitioner, then, there are three "distances": the closest being is obviously the teacher, followed by Avalokiteśhvara and then Amitabha. The teacher functions as an idol, an intermediary between the practitioner and Avalokiteśhvara; and the latter functions as an idol between the practitioner and Amitabha. Moreover, Amitabha is a "messenger" himself, a manifestation, an aid, and a representation of the transcendence that the practitioner seeks, and therefore an idol.

Prayer to the Teacher. The practitioner generates "bodies as countless as the atoms of the universe" (p. 9) to invoke the teacher and proclaim and praise his qualities. Note that now the proliferation is internal; no longer are all other sentient beings uniting with the practitioner; instead, the practitioner himself is multiplying in order to increase the value and effects of his praise. The practitioner finds himself populating and saturating the proximal zone from the very center of the identity zone, which is himself. We see two types of reduplication: In the first, a form is reduplicated as a different form: the teacher is reduplicated as Avalokiteśhvara, and Avalokiteśhvara as his entourage (actually, since the entourage will merge with Avalokiteśhvara, as we see later, one could assume that the entourage is ultimately just an emanation of the latter). In the second type, a form is reduplicated as an identical form.

One of the qualities of the teacher is to consider "others more important than himself" (p. 11).

The spiritual contest plays out in the first two zones, whose relative value to the subject changes and is ultimately reversed. Swâmi Prajnânpad, a teacher of Advaita Vedanta (a tradition that is not Buddhist), outlined the path to true compassion in a striking way: "Only myself, myself and others, others and myself, others only."[34]

The zone of one's fellow creatures—the proximal zone—becomes more important than the identity zone, due to the incorporation of the distal zone. The Mahayana practice of *tonglen* (Tib., "exchanging self and others") works along these lines:

> The first stage is to see yourself and others as equally important—others want to be happy and want not to suffer, just as you do. So you should wish happiness for others in the same way that you wish it for yourself, and wish that they may avoid suffering, just as you do. The second stage is the exchange of yourself and others; you wish that others may have your happiness and that you may take their suffering. There is a third stage, which is to cherish others more than yourself, like the great *bodhisattvas*.[35]

Next, the practitioner offers the mandala (a ritual offering) and recites the "call for blessings," known as "the prayer to the lineage teachers" of the practice in question (p. 15).

First, he invokes Shakyamuni (known as the Buddha, founder of Buddhism), Manjushri, the *bodhisattva* of wisdom, the great Indian masters (Nagarjuna, Asanga) and the "long lineage of *bodhisattvas* of India and Tibet," and finally, the practitioner's teacher. At the end of each group of representatives of the lineage, he recites: "We pray [that we may] perfectly attain the benefit of others" (pp. 15-17) by becoming "like you, the buddha's heirs" (p. 19).

It is clear that the end point of the lineage is, or could be, the practitioner: the lineage thus culminates in the identity zone.

The practitioner asks for the blessings of the lineage; he prays for the gift of "renunciation born from fear of the sufferings of *samsāra*, [and] / Non-attachment and disgust for the experiences of both existence [*samsāra*] and peace [*nirvāna*]" (p. 17).

In this case, the *nirvāna* that is described as "disgusting" is what is known as static *nirvāna*. For in Mahayana Buddhism, there is a distinction between static *nirvāna* (liberation) and dynamic *nirvāna* (enlightenment); Mahayana teaches that one must go beyond the first to reach the second, where one remains simultaneously in *nirvāna* through wisdom and in *samsāra* (our conditioned world) through compassion for those who are suffering.

---

[34] Cited in Arnaud Desjardins, *Les formules de Swâmi Prajnânpad commentées par Arnaud Desjardins* (Paris: La Table Ronde, 2003), 121.

[35] Dilgo Khyentse Rinpoche, *The Heart of Compassion: The Thirty-Seven Verses on the Practice of a* Bodhisattva (Boston: Shambala, 2007).

With the exception of Manjushri, all the beings listed are historically attested humans who, by and large, attained enlightenment (in order to achieve the greatest benefits, they must be seen as enlightened, at any rate). These teachers are obviously fellow creatures, at least the ones that are historical figures, but they are distinguished from one another by their temporal remoteness or proximity, meaning their degree of integration in the zone of absence, that is, the distal zone. As we can see, participation in a zone can be incremental (different degrees of belonging to a zone can be distinguished) and inverse (the more presence in one zone, the less presence in another). These teachers are also idols who enable others to reach transcendence. In short, they inhabit transcendence and are the mediators thereof.

At this moment in the practice, the practitioner, no doubt enabled by the fervor and purity of the prayer, is instructed to visualize: "From the syllable *Hrīh* in the heart of the teacher, the Great Compassionate One [Avalokiteśhvara], [there are rays of light emanating onto] the surrounding retinue [Buddhas, teachers, etc., mentioned above], who melt into light and dissolve into the main deity. The main deity, the teacher, the Great Compassionate One, descends onto the crown of your head; visualize him there, clear and brilliant, smiling joyfully" (p. 19).

In other words, the proximal zone of the teacher-Avalokiteśhvara is brought into the identity zone by means of a fetish-light, and the teacher-Avalokiteśhvara draws close "physically" to the practitioner; this physical proximity resembles that of one's nearest and dearest fellows (parents, spouses, friends), who are ultimately participants in the identity zone. However, to clearly show the gap separating the two entities, the more "noble" part of the practitioner (according to Buddhism)—his head—is touching the deity's feet, which is the most "impure" part.

The practitioner imagines himself again with "all mother beings" (p. 19), and they pray to the teacher "with one voice" (p. 19). A prayer to Avalokiteśhvara follows, enumerating his spiritual qualities; each couplet ends with the verse: "Precious teacher, to you we pray."

Since the practitioner has passed through numerous incarnations since "time without beginning," all sentient beings have been his benevolent fathers and mothers at one time or another. Thus he cannot but want to repay their kindnesses. The fellow creatures, including strangers and enemies, are brought nearer in the proximal zone and even incorporated into the identity zone, inasmuch as they are seen as the parents of the practitioner.

Then the teacher-Avalokiteśhvara, still in the practitioner's visualization, produces a stream of five-color nectar flowing from the deity's body and filling the practitioner's body and mind, "purifying all the negative actions and obscurations [that the practitioner has] accumulated since beginless time" (p. 21).

In other words, the light is what allowed the merging of deities in the teacher-Avalokiteśhvara earlier, thereby incorporating his proximal zone into his identity zone, whereas now a luminous nectar is what plays this mediating role for the practitioner. Light thus serves to merge and concentrate spiritual energy and to purify. By incorporating the mediator into his body, the practitioner approaches the distal zone and is thus ready for the main practice.

Main Practice

Initiations. As a result of his preparation, the practitioner receives the usual initiations, which are self-initiations here, of body, speech, and mind, and the fourth initiation. He imagines merging with the deity, doing so through each of the "three doors," that is, body, speech, and mind: "May your body become one with mine, / May your speech imbue mine, / May your mind blend with my own" (p. 157).

The teacher-Avalokiteśhvara has merged into him: "The teacher dissolves into you; visualise yourself suddenly as the Great Compassionate One" (p. 157).

The practitioner has incorporated another being into his identity zone—one who has become him—and this is how he reaches the distal zone, already attained by this other being for the practitioner's benefit.

Emanating from the heart of the practitioner-Avalokiteśhvara are "rays of light beams" that "touch all beings." The practitioner visualizes himself "and all sentient beings in the form of the Exalted One [Avalokiteśhvara]" (p. 157).

Once again, we note that these are rays of light emerging from a central entity and shining onto peripheral entities, once again in order to transform them: one is transformed by merging, and the other by becoming identical. And once again, the practice is expanded many times over, and it is also de-individualized and extended to all fellow creatures in the broadest sense, meaning all sentient beings. The identity zone of each being and the associated proximal zone are effectively emptied into the distal zone; there is only transcendence. This can be seen as either an immanentization of transcendence or a transcendentalization of immanence. In any event, the mythical, apotheotic moment has now been attained—and it is clearly utopian and symbolic, since the number of sentient beings is no doubt infinite—in which all beings have left *samsāra*, having attained enlightenment. Meanwhile, in the words of Shāntideva, the practitioner utters the wish that "For as long as space remains, / For as long as sentient beings remain [in the *samsāra*], / Until then may I too remain / To dispel the miseries of the world."[36]

[36] Cited from Matthieu Ricard, *La citadelle des neiges* (Paris: Nil, 2005), 137.

In summary, the practitioner has visualized the teacher-Avalokiteśhvara in successive positions: before him, above his head; filling him with luminous nectar; and finally, merged with him. The first stage is, of course, the one in which the deity has not yet appeared before him.

In Catholicism, the deity is incorporated through food—bread and wine. Here, it is incorporated through a type of food as well: a nectar. However, unless we are mistaken, in the first case, the practitioner does not become Christ, according to theological tradition, whereas in the second case, he does become Avalokiteśhvara.

Mantra Recitation. Next, the practitioner recites Avalokiteśhvara's mantra as many times as possible: "*Om Mani Padme Hung*" (the Tibetan pronunciation is "*om mani paymay hung*"). At the end, he must "rest [remain] in a state free of all references" (p. 157), meaning outside dualistic, conditioned thinking.

Finale

Dedication of Merits. To finish, the practitioner proceeds with the dedication of merits, or the positive karma accumulated from the practice. He wishes that merit may allow him to attain enlightenment and that all beings without exception may do the same. In other words, he prays that his visualization may become reality. He also wishes that the merit he has accumulated might allow him in successive lives to obtain "a precious human body" (p. 159), and that he might then be guided by a spiritual teacher. All existence in *samsāra* is suffering and as such, is not desirable. Suicide is out of the question, since it does not put an end to suffering (because one is reincarnated); worse yet, suicide amplifies suffering (by gathering more negative karma). Of all possible kinds of existence (animals, gods, the damned, etc.), human life is said to provide the best opportunity for attaining liberation and enlightenment and thus finding one's way out of *samsāra* (and for then being in a position to help others find their way out). The practitioner thus prays to be reborn as a human, and since liberation and enlightenment are practically impossible to attain unaided, he asks for a situation in which he will be guided by an authentic teacher.

The practitioner next invokes the teachers, the *yidams*, the *dākas* and *dākinis*, the protectors and guardians of the dharma, so that they may gather in "massed clouds of compassion" (p. 159) and bring down "a rain of blessings" (p. 159).

We note that this closing prayer invokes more or less the same entities that were addressed at the beginning. But what a long road has been traveled since then! Through his visualization, the practitioner has become the transcendent equal of those he was invoking at the beginning, from the most remote depths of his immanence.

Virtuous Wishes. At the very end, the practitioner is asked to conclude "with virtuous wishes for temporary [temporal] and ultimate good" (p. 159), with ultimate well-being obtained through enlightenment, naturally. The teacher who introduced us to this *sādhana* suggests reciting a special text for this purpose, consisting of a short concluding prayer on the growth of the "enlightened mind" and a prayer for the longevity of all the teachers.

Concluding Remarks

The teacher is a fellow creature, at least in his *nirmanakāya*, as we shall see below. In taking the form of the practiced deity Avalokiteśhvara in the visualization, he becomes an idol who represents transcendence and makes its attainment possible. The teacher-deity approaches the practitioner "physically" in increments ("absent," then in front of him, above him, in contact through the nectar, in him, and even becoming him). The corollary of this "descent" is the "elevation" of the practitioner, who in the end becomes an idol by replication. In this transformation, the zone of his fellow creatures is incorporated: all sentient beings seek transcendence, all sentient beings receive it, and all sentient beings become transcendence in becoming the teacher-deity. The teacher-deity proliferates in order to "pervade" the practitioner's identity and proximal zones in their entirety; this is after he has resorbed his own proximal zone by integrating and condensing his own sublime entourage. The practitioner has also populated his identity zone with innumerable selves, which then spill over into his proximal zone, so to speak: they are selves, after all, but other selves. In short, among other things, we see that the visualization reduces the diversity of the beings in the proximal zone and at the transcendent boundary and increases the beings in the identity zone, which as a rule contains only one being.

A *sādhana* involves three types of performance. First, the *sādhana* is a text asking to be read. In this sense, the units that belong to the three zones and the two boundaries are thematized units, integrated into semantic or semiotic contents (as opposed to [re]presentational contents).

But the text is first and foremost a score, meaning that it serves as an aid to an "external" ritual performance other than just a straight reading, even aloud. This second performance engages the mind (with visualizations, mental attitudes, etc.), word (mantras and other texts to recite), and action (the mandala offering, which includes ordinary acts and *mudrās*, or symbolic acts). In this sense, the *sādhana* integrates all three layers of a practice: the phenomenal-physical, the semiotic, and the (re)presentational.

This complex choreography is repeated so that, by means of it and other practices and meritorious acts, the transformation that is sought, visualized, and felt really does come about, which is the third performance. When the transformation occurs and the practitioner attains enlightenment, he "generates" three "bodies", known as *kāyas*. Through his *dharmakāya* (or absolute body), he enters unfathomable and inexpressible transcendence; in other words, he is beyond the idol—in the distal zone, not on its boundary. But in his compassion, the "new" buddha "generates" two *rupakkāyas* (bodies of form), two idols, who will work for the good of those beings who "remain" in *samsāra*: the *sambogakāya* (body of enjoyment), which is perceptible only to the great bodhisattvas of the eighth to tenth lands,[37] and the *nirmanakāya* (appearance body), the everyday manifestation of an enlightened teacher to ordinary beings (the enlightened teacher appears in the form of a human being like us).

---

[37] The ten lands are the stages of spiritual development that precede enlightenment. In the first land, one attains liberation; after the tenth land, one attains enlightenment. From one land to the next, spiritual powers and wisdom become more developed (the cognitive veils are gradually lifted from one land to the next, and then at the moment of enlightenment they disappear entirely).

Coda

A New Age for the Mystical?

12. Mysticism in the New Age

Are Mysticism and Science Converging?

Richard H. Jones

Abstract

For the past forty years, "New Age" advocates have claimed that the old "dualistic" science of Newtonian physics was the fundamental source leading to the conflict of science and religion, and that today the "new science" (in particular, quantum physics) is converging in a general worldview and in specific theories with "Eastern mysticism." The essay explores this New Age claim of the convergence of scientific and mystical claims about reality. The focus is Buddhism, Advaita Vedanta, and quantum physics. The issues covered include the differences in mystical and scientific subjects (i.e., the "beingness" of things in the world or their ontological source versus understanding how things work); the different intents of mysticism and science (i.e., soteriological goals versus disinterested understanding); the differences between mystical awareness and scientific observations; the misuse of science and the misunderstanding of Asian mysticism leading to distortions in comparisons; and the overall insubstantiality of the alleged convergences. Examples include the different meanings of "emptiness" in mysticism and in science, the role of consciousness in quantum physics, and whether the Buddha can be classified as a "scientist." The authors to be noted include Fritjof Capra, Amit Goswami, Ken Wilber, Deepak Chopra, B. Alan Wallace, and Neo-Buddhists including the Dalai Lama.

The "New Age" movement as it has developed over the last few decades involves a spirituality that draws on Western and Eastern religious traditions, psychology, holistic health programs, and other sources. It seeks support for its holistic claims on mind, body, and spirit and on the unity of the world in consciousness research and science—in particular, quantum physics.[1] The claims of the relation of mysticism and science in New Age thought will be the focus here.

---

[1] For an overview, see James R. Lewis and J. Gordon Melton, eds., *Perspectives on the New Age* (Albany: State University of New York Press, 1992).

Buddhism was first portrayed as scientific by Western apologists in the mid-19th century. Soon Western-influenced Neo-Vedantists were doing the same for Hinduism. With a few exceptions, the issue of the relation of mysticism and science languished quietly until being revived in the 1960s and took off in the mid-1970s, when Fritjof Capra and Gary Zukav published books that are still popular today.[2] The former's *The Tao of Physics* is considered "one of the canonical books of the New Age movement" [3] and "the epitome of New Age science in the eyes of the public." [4] Books on how mystical thought may have influenced physics have also appeared.[5] However, the question of the relation of mysticism and science has remained confined basically to New Age writers. Some scientists have shown interest in mysticism, but probably more scientists today would agree with Stephen Hawking who, in responding to his colleague Brian Josephson's interest in Asian mysticism, said that the idea of mystical influence on science is "pure rubbish," adding: "The universe of Eastern mysticism is an illusion. A physicist who attempts to link it with his own work has abandoned physics."[6]

The New Age approach would offer a new way to integrate mysticism into our lives. In particular, it would remove one popular reason to reject mysticism: the notion that mysticism necessarily conflicts with science. The New Age claim is not merely that science and mysticism are compatible or that scientific findings support mystical claims. Rather, a staple of New Age thought is that today science and Asian mystical claims are actually *merging*. That is, after hundreds of years of strenuous work, modern scientists are finally discovering what mystics have known for thousands of years. It is as if scientists after struggling up the mountain of empirical knowledge found mystics meditating at the top.

The old "dualistic" and "reductive" science arising from Newtonian physics is being replaced, and today relativity, particle physics, and biology are becoming one with the theories of Buddhism or of an abstract "Eastern mysti-

---

[2] Fritjof Capra, *The Tao of Physics: An Exploration of the Parallels between Modern Physics and Eastern Mysticism*, 4th ed. (1975; Boston: Shambhala Press, 2000); Gary Zukav, *The Dancing Wu Li Masters: An Overview of the New Physics* (1977; New York: HarperCollins, 2001).

[3] John Brooke and Geoffrey Cantor, *Reconstructing Nature* (Edinburgh: T & T Clark, 1998), 80.

[4] Wouter J. Hanegraaff, *New Age Religion and Western Culture: Esotericism in the Mirror of Secular Thought* (Albany, NY: State University of New York Press, 1998), 74.

[5] E.g., Ken Wilber, ed., *Quantum Questions: Mystical Writings of the World's Great Physicists* (Boulder, CO: Shambhala New Science Library, 1984); David Kaiser, *How the Hippies Saved Physics: Science, Counterculture, and the Quantum Revival* (New York: W. W. Norton, 2011). See also Richard H. Jones, *Piercing the Veil: Comparing Science and Mysticism as Ways of Knowing Reality* (New York: Jackson Square Books/Createspace, 2009), chap. 4 on the possible influence of mysticism in the history of science.

[6] Quoted in John Boslough, *Stephen Hawking's Universe* (New York: Quill, 1985), 127.

cism." The popular alternative-medicine practitioner Deepak Chopra tells us that scientists have "wound up with nothing less than a mystic's universe."[7] Others tell us that the Buddha made claims about subatomic levels of structures that are only now finally being confirmed by scientists. Buddhists have "uncovered at least the basic principles of subatomic physics through their meditation practices,"[8] and modern physics "echoes" the investigations of Buddhism.[9] In the end, mystics and scientists are saying the same thing, just in "different languages."[10]

The Vagueness of the New Age Claims

The New Age enthusiasm for the convergence of science and mysticism is unfortunately not well supported. Mysticism could converge with science in two ways: mystical claims about the nature of the world could converge with scientific theories, and mystical experiences as a particular way of knowing reality could converge with the "scientific method" as a way of knowing reality.[11] But one persistent problem is that those who see parallels between mysticism and science—namely, "parallelists"—do not clarify what precisely they are claiming. They throw together an amalgam of different ideas: science and mysticism "share the same insight" or have "common ground"; they are "harmonious" or "consistent"; scientific claims "mirror" mystical claims; scientific claims are "implicit" in mystical insights; each endeavor has "implications" for the other; the two have a "synergy"; mysticism "anticipates" or "resonates with" scientific claims; one "validates" or "verifies" the other; a "fusion" or "integration" between the two is occurring; or a "confluence" of science and mysticism will produce something new. However, the alleged relations are advanced without precise definitions or the specification of how exactly, for example, science can verify a mystical metaphysical claim.

The most commonly used terms are "parallels," "converging," "complements," and "confirms." But parallelists use these terms without realizing that

---

7 Deepak Chopra, foreword to *The New Science and Spirituality Reader*, ed. Ervin Laszlo and Kingsley L. Dennis (Rochester, VT: Inner Traditions, 2012), ix.

8 Wes Nisker, *Buddha's Nature: Who We Really Are and Why This Matters* (London: Rider, 1998), 18.

9 Matthieu Ricard and Trinh Xuan Thuan, *The Quantum and the Lotus: A Journey to the Frontiers Where Science and Buddhism Meet* (New York: Crown, 2001), 10.

10 Capra, *Tao of Physics*, 8; Victor N. Mansfield, *Tibetan Buddhism and Modern Physics: Toward a Union of Love and Knowledge* (West Conshohocken, PA: Templeton Foundation Press, 2008), 88, 141, 162.

11 Mysticism and science can also interact through the general metaphysics of each mystical tradition less connected to mystical experiences. Such broader metaphysics will not be discussed here.

these concepts are very different: if mystical claims *parallel* scientific claims, then the claims are fulfilling analogous roles in different conceptual systems but their substantive content is different, so they cannot *converge*; if the claims are *converging*, they are not separate *complements*; if the claims are *complements*, they are not *confirming* each other; indeed, if science and mysticism are *complements*, they cannot directly *influence* or *affect* each other but are *separate* endeavors that give some knowledge that the other omits; one endeavor cannot both *complement* and *reveal* the other's truths at the same time. Nevertheless, parallelists throw these terms around haphazardly, sometimes in the same sentence.[12]

Parallelists make much of the problems that practitioners in the two different endeavors have with language when encountering phenomena outside the everyday realm of experience. Apparent paradoxes also appear in both endeavors. Nevertheless, parallelists cannot make any substantive convergence out of these problems. Merely because both scientists and mystics have problems expressing what they encounter does not mean that they must be encountering the *same thing*. Both mystics and scientists must use metaphors when encountering the unexpected outside the everyday realm, but this is not a very profound commonality, especially since philosophers and linguists now point out that *all* our thought is permeated with metaphors. All the use of metaphors means is that mystical and scientific thought is human thought encountering something new; it tells us nothing about whether scientists and mystics are talking about the same thing. So too, mysticism and science may share some abstract vocabulary, but the terms in the actual contexts of their systems of thought show that their referents diverge: simply because discussing God and the quantum realm presents problems does not mean that God *is* the quantum realm. More argument is needed to make that equation.

It will be argued here that all the New Age claims on the convergence of mysticism and science are in fact groundless because mysticism and science deal with different dimensions of reality: mysticism deals with experiencing the "beingness" of things in nature or the ontological source of the being of the self or all of the natural world in a reality transcending the natural realm, while science deals with discovering how nature works. (A broader definition of "mysticism" covering other types of experiences may produce other types of claims, but New Age advocates typically focus on the claims in Buddhism, Hinduism, and Daoism connected to these experiences. Thus, a narrow definition of mysticism is warranted here.) The epistemic differences between mysticism and science may not be as great as is usually supposed, but the difference

---

12 E.g., Ricard and Thuan, *Quantum and the Lotus*, 276.

in their subject matter and objectives forecloses any substantive convergences, even when their terminology seems to converge.[13]

Do Science and Mysticism Have the Same Subject Matter?

Parallelists usually go no further into the nature of science than noting that science involves empirical observations and claiming that Newtonian science is reductionistic.[14] Only one point about science must be emphasized here: basic science is about *how things in nature work*—that is, identifying the structures in nature responsible for the lawful changes in phenomena that we observe and offering both tentative explanations of phenomena in terms of these underlying causes and also theories of those structures' nature that ultimately depend on observations checkable by others. Realists and antirealists disagree on whether we can gain any genuine knowledge of those alleged causal structures that we cannot experience.

Mystics, on the other hand, in other states of consciousness focus on the "beingness" of the natural world or its source. Introvertive mystics focus on inward experiences of the source of being in the experiencer or in all the world. Extrovertive "mindfulness" mystics make claims about the impermanence and interconnectedness of the macro-objects we actually experience in the everyday world, not anything about features of the submicroscopic world that they have not experienced. These mystics apprehend something common to all reality—the sheer "is-ness" of things—by lessening the grip that our mental conceptions normally have on our perceptions. Nor do mystics make claims about any reality that cannot be directly experienced, unlike theoretical scientists, even if there is more to that reality than is experienced. Scientists, on the other hand, work through the mediation of our concepts to find structures underlying the changes we experience in the everyday world. Thus, extrovertive mystics and scientists look at different aspects of the natural realm: the beingness common to all things versus the causal structures operating in nature.

In this way, scientists focus precisely on the differentiations among phenomena that mystics bypass. Scientific experiences remain ordinary, everyday-type observations, even when scientists are studying extraordinary parts of nature through experimentation or technology-enhanced observation; mystics' experiences are extraordinary even when they are looking at the ordinary. To

---

13 For more on New Age distortions, see Jones, *Piercing the Veil.* For more on the general relation of mysticism and science, see Richard H. Jones, *Philosophy of Mysticism: Raids on the Ineffable*, forthcoming, chap. 8.

14 However, scientific analysis is not necessarily *reductionist.* See Richard H. Jones, *Analysis and the Fullness of Reality: An Introduction to Reductionism and Emergence* (New York: Jackson Square Books/Createspace, 2013), chap. 3.

determine how things work, scientists must distinguish objects and see how they interact with one another, and differentiations among phenomena are necessary for that. Physicists are interested only in what is measurable by the interaction of objects. This includes fields and the smaller and smaller bits of matter that are now being theorized. Even the *mass* of an object is measured only by the interaction of objects. And since beingness is common to all particulars, it cannot be studied scientifically: beingness is uniform for all phenomena, and thus it cannot be poked and prodded to see how it interacts with something else. Hence, no hypotheses about the nature of beingness can be scientifically tested in any way. Thus, beingness is not a different scientific level that scientists simply cannot reach externally; rather it is an aspect of reality that is free of differentiations.

In such circumstances, it is hard to argue that mystics are making claims about the underlying features of nature that scientists are revealing regarding the causes of things or that scientists are approaching the same aspect of reality as mystics are. Rather, mystics realize a dimension of reality that is missed in scientific knowledge and vice versa. Scientists and mystics each see something different about reality, and their subjects are irrelevant to each other. Thus their claims do not cross, let alone converge, at any point. Both endeavors are interested in what is "fundamentally real" but in different aspects of it—they are not merely reaching the same substantive claims through different routes. Mystical experiences do not give us any scientific knowledge of reality, and no science gives us any mystical knowledge.

But New Age parallelists only see that both mystics and scientists are approaching reality and are out to gain knowledge; thus they assume without argument that mystics and scientists are engaged in gaining the same type of knowledge through different techniques. Parallelists do not consider that there may be fundamentally different aspects of what is real that must be approached through different functions of the mind and that this would foreclose any substantive convergence of knowledge claims. This parallelist failure extends even to physicists making comparisons to Asian thought.[15]

The Tension between Mysticism and Science

To New Age advocates, the experiential nature of mysticism makes mystics more like scientists than practitioners of other forms of religiosity. However, they overlook how classical mystics' religious objectives affect their endeavor.

---

[15] E.g., Victor N. Mansfield, review of *The Tao of Physics* by Fritjof Capra, *Physics Today* 29 (August 1976): 56; idem, "Mādhyamika Buddhism and Quantum Mechanics: Beginning a Dialogue," *International Philosophical Quarterly* 29 (September 1989): 371-91, and idem, *Tibetan Buddhism and Modern Physics*.

For example, the point of the Buddha's teaching is to end the pervasive dissatisfaction, frustration, and suffering entailed by merely being alive (*duhkha*). Buddhism is not a "science of the mind" in any sense connected to natural science.[16] Buddhism's central objective is not to acquire disinterested knowledge about how something works; rather it is to transform the person to end suffering. To substitute a disinterested focus on how the parts of nature work—including even the mental states involved in ending suffering—in order to learn more about the universe distorts the fundamental soteriological nature of Buddhism entirely. Today "Neo-Buddhists," including the Dalai Lama, find scientific discoveries in physics, cosmology, and biology fascinating, but they must admit such discoveries in the final analysis are irrelevant to their central quest. As the respected Theravada Buddhist scholar Walpola Rahula has said, while some parallels and similarities between Buddhism and modern science may be intellectually interesting, they are "peripheral and do not touch the essential part, the center, the core, the heart of Buddhism."[17]

A scientific interest in nature's structures is not a way to any type of mystical enlightenment: identifying and explaining the structures of reality only increase attention to the differentiations in the world and will never lead to the calming of the mind by emptying it of differentiated content that leads to an experience of beingness. The Buddha condemned astronomy/astrology as a wrong means of livelihood because it was unrelated to the religious concern.[18] The Buddha even forbade monks a practice as valuable in our eyes as medicine since it interfered with their quest for selflessness.[19] To use the Buddhist analogy: if we are shot with a poison-tipped arrow, we does not ask who made the arrow or what the arrow is made of (or any other scientific question related to the arrow)—we just want a cure for the poison.[20] So too, what is vital here and now is finding a way to the deathless state, not wasting time on scientific questions about the construction of the universe. The means to doing so is to end a false sense of permanence in the world and in the mental life, with its accompanying ungrounded emotions, not to learn the scientific mechanisms at work causing this sense, let alone all the other mechanisms in the world. The Buddha would no doubt leave all scientific questions unanswered (including those involving the brain) since they are irrelevant to the soteriological problem of suf-

---

16 Contra José Ignacio Cabezón, "Buddhism and Science: On the Nature of the Dialogue," in *Buddhism and Science: Breaking New Ground*, ed. B. Alan Wallace (New York: Columbia University Press, 2003), 49-50.

17 Quoted in Martin J. Verhoeven, "Western Science, Eastern Spirit: Historical Reflections on the East/West Encounter," *Religion East and West* 3 (June 2003): 45.

18 *Digha Nikaya* I.12.

19 *Digha Nikaya* I.12, I.67-69.

20 *Majjhima Nikaya* I.63.

fering, just as he did with questions about the age and size of the universe.[21] Overall, Buddhism has been hostile to science throughout its history.[22]

All classical mystical traditions have such religious goals and no interests in natural causes. Daoism in classical China is a good example of the rejection of the discursive type of knowledge of which science is the paradigm: the Daoist interest in nature remained contemplative and did not lead to a scientific interest in how things in nature work.[23] We cannot simply equate any interest in nature with a scientific interest in understanding the hidden causal order behind things that explains how things work. Daoists were interested in flowing with patterns inherent in nature through nonassertive action (*wuwei*), not in any scientific findings or explanations of the efficient causes of those patterns. In the Daoist "forgetting" state of mind (*xu*), our mind is no longer guided by our own mentally conceived divisions of nature but responds spontaneously to what is presented without any preconceptions. Anything free of conceptions cannot guide scientific observations or theorizing since scientific observations and experiments involve predictions and theorizing based in our conceptions.

Overall, science increases the amount of conceptual differentiations in our mind by its analyzing, selecting, measuring, and theorizing. It utilizes the analytical function of the mind and increases attention to the differentiations within the phenomenal world and thus diverts attention from what mystics consider the only approach for aligning our lives with reality (calming the mind by freeing it of a sense of ego and conceptual differentiations). For mystical experiences to occur, one needs to empty the mind of the very stuff that is central to science. The aim is to achieve a knowledge inaccessible to the analytical mind.

Thus, science and mysticism pull in opposite directions, and most practitioners of either endeavor may very well dismiss the other as a waste of valuable time and energy. This picture is complicated by the fact that mysticism involves more than just cultivating mystical experiences; it also involves attempts to understand the significance of these experiences and to lay out the general nature of a person, the world, and transcendent realities for a way of life. However, the divergence of interests and subject matters in science and mysticism means that it is impossible to say that science and mysticism "converge" or that science "confirms" the specifically mystical claims of any tradition or vice versa.

---

21 *Digha Nikaya* I.13, III.137; *Majjhima Nikaya* I.427; *Anguttara Nikaya* II.80.

22 Donald S. Lopez Jr., *Buddhism and Science: A Guide for the Perplexed* (Chicago: University of Chicago, 2008), 216.

23 See Richard H. Jones, *Mysticism Examined: Philosophical Inquiries into Mysticism* (Albany: State University of New York Press, 1993), chap. 6.

The Difference in Content

In short, science and mysticism substantially diverge in their core subjects and interests. However, most New Age parallelists see the same or similar terms being used in mysticism and in discussions of science but miss the differences in context and thus believe that mystics and scientists are discussing the same thing. That scientists and mystics are discussing *different aspects* of what is fundamentally real is completely overlooked.

For example, parallelists misconstrue the "search for unity" by not distinguishing the unity of being in mysticism from the unity of structures in the sciences. Any scientific unity unifies apparently different structures (e. g., unifying magnetism and electricity), while the oneness of being has no parts to unite.[24] Mysticism is neutral on the question of whether physicists can reduce the apparent levels of structures to only one fundamental level of physical structure, or whether, as antireductionists assert, nonphysicists are also discovering equally fundamental levels of structuring. Nothing in any classical mystical tradition suggests any interest in attempting to unify the structures at work in the world. Mystics do not seek a more comprehensive unification than scientists or pursue a Grand Unified Theory.[25] Any Theory of Everything in physics would be simply irrelevant to the mystics' concerns since it would remain a matter of structures. Nothing on this subject is disclosed in mystical experiences. Perhaps if more scholars used "*identity* of being" when discussing such mystical systems as Advaita Vedanta and not "*unity*" (which suggests a unification of parts), fewer parallelists would be misled concerning "oneness."

The most important point concerning external phenomena is that extrovertive mysticism remains exclusively on the level that can be *directly experienced.* Buddhist theorists do categorize mental structures, but only in the context of how to end suffering, not out of a disinterested desire to discover all the structures of the mind. And nothing in the writings of the great Asian spiritual masters suggests that mystics become aware of the quantum realm or experience subatomic structures or anything other than the mind or the everyday level of phenomena in the external world.[26] Nothing in their writings remotely suggests

---

[24] Contra David Lorimer, "Introduction: From Experiment to Experience," in *The Spirit of Science: From Experiment to Experience*, ed. David Lorimer (New York: Continuum, 1999), 17-29.

[25] Contra Renée Weber, *Dialogues with Scientists and Sages: The Search for Unity* (New York: Routledge & Kegan Paul, 1986), 1-16.

[26] New Age writers commonly argue that the sense of connectedness that mystics have is caused by quantum-level interconnections and that mystics sense the cause. But a simpler explanation is that mystics have "knowledge by participation" in the beingness of the everyday level or the mind. There is no reason to believe that mystics experience the underlying

that they were "quite adept" at seeing into matter and space-time, or that through meditation mystics realize that energy comes in discrete packets ("quanta").[27] Contrary to what Fritjof Capra says, mystics in higher states of consciousness do not have "a strong intuition for the 'space-time' character of reality"[28] or any other scientific explanatory structure.

Indeed, the connection of space and time would be news to Buddhists—nothing in Buddhist teachings would predict that time is connected to space. In fact, Theravada Buddhists would be quite surprised by this: they exempt space, but not time, from being "conditioned" (*samskrita*).[29] This makes space as independent and absolute as is possible within their metaphysics and precludes any encompassing holism. Nor did Nagarjuna or any other Buddhist connect space with time in their analyses. Nor is Ervin Laszlo's physics-influenced idea of an "Akashic field" "rediscovering the true meaning of the ancient Vedas"; rather it is imposing a new doctrine on the Indic notion.[30] In classical Indic culture, space (*akasha*) is a substance pervading the world and thus is not "empty space," but it is not the source of anything else or in any sense *the* fundamental reality—it is not any type of "field" connecting everything with everything else nor out of which entities appear. Rather, space is one of the five elements of the world (the others being earth, water, fire, and air); it is not the ground or source of anything else but is independent of all other elements and uninfluenced by them. Nor is there any reason to believe that depth-mystical experiences are of "the four-dimensional space-time continuum" of relativity theory or the "ground manifold state" out of which quantum phenomena emerge and are reabsorbed: according to physicists, the "space-time manifold" is a structured aspect of reality, and thus it is no more "pure beingness" free of all structures than anything in the everyday world or any other phenomenon.

Like mysticism in general, Buddhism has no interest in the analysis of underlying structural layers of physical organization or in identifying the lowest structural level of physical realities. Buddhism has no scientific view of the nature of matter,[31] and there is no such thing as a "Buddhist physics."[32] Bud-

---

causes of everyday phenomena any more than we do when we experience solidity in the everyday world. Thus there is no reason to attribute a new paranormal power to mystics.

27 Contra Wes Nisker, "Introduction," in *Einstein and Buddha: The Parallel Sayings*, ed. Thomas J. McFarlane (Berkeley, CA: Seastone, 2002), viii, ix.

28 Capra, *Tao of Physics*, 171-72.

29 *Anguttara Nikaya* I.286.

30 Ervin Laszlo, *Science and the Akashic Field* (Rochester, VT: Inner Traditions, 2004).

31 Contra Arthur Zajonc, ed., *The New Physics and Cosmology: Dialogues with the Dalai Lama* (New York: Oxford University Press, 2004), 5.

32 Contra Fred Alan Wolf, *The Spiritual Universe: How Quantum Physics Proves the Existence of the Soul* (New York: Simon & Schuster, 1996), 169.

dhism has never given a *physical* analysis of matter.[33] The closest concept in Buddhism to "matter" is "form" (*rupa*), which is one of dozens and dozens of "factors of experience" (*dharmas*) in the Abhidharma analyses of experience. And even then "form" relates only to our experience and not to "matter in itself"—it is about the form of things that we directly *experience* and not any possible *substance* behind them. By naming things, we give what is actually real a form based on our perceptions—hence, the common phrase for the physical world: "name and form" (*nama-rupa*). Identifying a new subatomic level in an analysis of matter will not lead to discerning the *dharmas*, which are experiential in nature—if anything, the scientific analysis of matter only increases the danger of discriminations for the unenlightened by introducing a new layer of possible objects and creating new distinctions.

So too, mysticism and science may share a general ideal methodology—that is, careful observation, rational analysis, open-mindedness, and having background beliefs.[34] But this too is only on an abstract level: in actual practice, the differences in objectives between cultivating mystical experiences versus scientific observation and explanation cause very different *implementations* of any abstract general principles. In the end, the only commonality may be features that any enterprise would have that seeks knowledge of reality and encounters things we would not expect from our ordinary experience in the everyday world. Mystics and scientists value types of experiences (conception-free experiences versus concept-driven observations) and conceptualizations (becoming free of conceptualizations versus coming up with better conceptualizations of how nature works) very differently, and this precludes any deeper convergence in "method."

In sum, scientists and mystics are doing basically different things. The difference is not only that different states of consciousness are involved. Rather, mystics do not directly experience the same "truth" that scientists arrive at tentatively or approximately through the route of theory and experiment. Nor do mystics reach a new structural reality that scientists fail to reach. Each endeavor, if each is in fact cognitive, pursues the depth of a dimension of reality but not the same dimension. The *content* of science and mysticism will always remain distinct; thus their theories and ideas can never *converge* into one new set of theories replacing those in either science or mysticism. Nor, since their content will always remain distinct, can one endeavor to incorporate the other or be reducible to the other. So too, meditators may permit neuroscientists to scan their brains while they meditate in order to gather data on their brain activity, but no further "collaborative effort"[35]—let alone a "synthesis," "fusion," or

---

33 Contra Ricard and Thuan, *Quantum and the Lotus*, 107.

34 E.g., Wallace, *Buddhism and Science*, 1-29.

35 Contra Zajonc, *New Physics and Cosmology*, 7.

"conceptual unification" of the two endeavors—is possible. Nor can either endeavor discredit or confirm the other. Mystics' claims about the impermanence and interconnectedness of the experienced everyday realm in no way "validate" or "verify" scientific theories of any underlying structures, nor can scientific claims about structure verify mystical claims about beingness or its source.[36]

The "Emptiness" of Reality

As an example of the difference, consider the ideas of the emptiness in Buddhism and science. Much attention is being paid to the Madhyamaka tradition's concept of emptiness (*shunyata*). The Dalai Lama sees an "unmistakable resonance" between Nagarjuna's notion of emptiness and the new physics.[37] Physicists speak of the emptiness of phenomena on the subatomic level, and Buddhists speak of the emptiness of phenomena, so New Age parallelists conclude that physicists and Buddhists are actually discussing the same thing.

However, the Buddhist claim concerns the lack of any permanent entities in what we experience in the everyday realm—the emptiness of all phenomena of any "inherent self-existence" (*svabhava*) that would permanently separate one thing from another as distinct and self-existing realities. This lack of self-existence has nothing whatsoever to do with scientific notions of emptiness: it is the *metaphysical* absence of any power of self-existence, not anything about the absence of *material* in some space.[38] Nevertheless, parallelists see Buddhist emptiness as connected to the emptiness of solid matter on the quantum level.[39] The physicist Victor Mansfield thinks particle physics and Madhyamaka Buddhism have "many deep links" and "remarkable and detailed connections."[40] But they in fact do not converge on the substance of their claims. The

---

[36] Contra Nisker, "Introduction," vii-viii.

[37] His Holiness the XIVth Dalai Lama (Tenzin Gyatso), *The Universe in a Single Atom: The Convergence of Science and Spirituality* (New York: Morgan Road Books, 2005), 50.

[38] On the other end of the scale, the cosmologist Harry Lam makes a similar claim for the emptiness of space. See Harry Chi-sing Lam, *The Zen in Modern Cosmology* (Hackensack, NJ: World Scientific, 2008); but see Jones, *Piercing the Veil*, 101-2.

[39] E.g., Danah Zohar and Ian Marshall, *The Quantum Society: Mind, Physics and a New Social Vision* (London: Bloomsbury, 1993). These authors equate the quantum vacuum from physics not only with the Buddhist Void but with all other religious concepts of a source of the natural world: God, Meister Eckhart's Godhead, and Being—the quantum vacuum, and these are all names for the same thing since they are all names of the source of our being (240, 275). Leaving aside the issue of whether the different religious concepts are interchangeable, this is an instance of treating realities that are traditionally presented as transcending the entire natural universe (i.e., transcending the realm of reality open to sense experience and thus open to scientific investigation) as in fact parts of the natural realm.

[40] Mansfield, *Tibetan Buddhism and Modern Physics*, 6.

scientific notion of "emptiness" comes from the idea that there are no solid particles in a subatomic sea of energy, but the mystics' claim stands or falls on the complete impermanence and interconnectedness of what we actually experience in the everyday world. Buddhists did not have to wait twenty-five hundred years to have their claims related to nirvana to be confirmed or disconfirmed by physicists.

This lack of "self-existence" has nothing to do with any alleged interaction of space, time, and matter.[41] Nagarjuna says nothing about that scientific issue, so his ideas on the impermanence of the experienced realm cannot be considered "anticipations" of that issue. Nor did the Buddha twenty-five hundred years ago in any way set out the hypothesis that elementary particles are not solid or independent.[42] In fact, the early Abhidharma Buddhists posited discrete and undestroyable minute *particles of matter* (*paramanus*) not open to sense experience, and yet they affirmed the impermanence of the experienced realm—such particles simply do not affect the impermanence that Buddhists are interested in. Thus, if physicists find permanent bits of matter on the quantum level, it would not refute a mindfulness tradition like Buddhism because it does not affect the impermanence of the "constructed" things of the everyday world that we actually experience.[43]

Nor did Nagarjuna have any concept of a "Void." Nagarjuna's emptiness is not the "quantum vacuum" out of which things arise.[44] It is not a reality that is the *source* of anything. The term simply denotes the true state of everything in the phenomenal world—that is, the absence of anything that would make a phenomenon permanent, independent, and self-existent (*svabhava*). The state of emptiness itself is not a self-existent reality; it too is empty of any inherent self-existence. It is not an inherently existing continuum out of which we carve conventional entities; each phenomenon is empty, and the totality is also empty of self-existence. But parallelists routinely reify emptiness into a cosmic "Void" or "Absolute Reality" that is an underlying source of phenomena. However,

---

41 Contra David Ritz Finkelstein, "Emptiness and Relativity," in *Buddhism and Science: Breaking New Ground*, ed. B. Alan Wallace (New York: Columbia University Press, 2003), 383.

42 Contra Matthieu Ricard, "On the Relevance of a Contemplative Science," in *Buddhism and Science: Breaking New Ground*, ed. B. Alan Wallace (New York: Columbia University Press, 2003), 274.

43 Nature's laws and forces (e. g., gravity) may be eternal or permanent in some sense, but this permanence does not affect the Buddhist picture of reality any more than does the permanence of the law of karma—the Buddhist view concerns the *impermanence of things that we experience* in the world of interacting laws, not the nature of the laws. Whatever scientists discover about the permanence of laws, the world we actually experience still appears impermanent and constantly changing, and this is the focus of Buddhist mindfulness.

44 Contra Raja Ramanna, "Divergence and Convergence of Science and Spirituality," in *Science, Spirituality and the Future: A Vision for the Twenty-First Century*, ed. L. L. Mehrotra (New Delhi: Mudrit, 1999), 163.

according to Nagarjuna, anyone who reifies the mere *absence* of anything that could give self-existence into a *reality* of any kind is *incurable* (*asadhyan*).[45]

Consciousness and the Phenomenal Realm

Another recurring problem in New Age works involves comparisons of consciousness and Advaita's Brahman. For example, the physicist Amit Goswami gives consciousness a role in physics and also treats consciousness as the ground of being.[46] However, there is nothing in, for example, Advaita's Brahman doctrines about consciousness affecting, or interacting with, an object—in fact, all that is real is only Brahman, and thus there is nothing for Brahman to interact with.[47] Brahman does not even cause the entire material realm since what is conscious cannot cause what is unconscious.[48] In Advaita, Brahman is never portrayed as any type of causal agent in the phenomenal world; thus to make it the cause of the wave-function collapse in particle physics is to change its nature. Brahman is the same undifferentiated reality for all phenomena and thus cannot explain why one phenomenal state of affairs is the case rather than another; thus it cannot function as a scientific explanation. It is not that mystics go further than physicists on observation[49]—what mystics are claiming about what is experienced in depth-mystical experiences that are free of all differentiated content is fundamentally different from any alleged interaction of the observer and observed in particle physics.

In mindfulness mysticism too, there is nothing about a subject's consciousness affecting objects: we "create" objects by imposing artificial *conceptual boundaries* onto what is really there in the world—in Buddhism, creating the world of "name and form" out of what is really there (*yathabhutam*, *tattva*)—not by somehow *physically affecting* what is actually there. That is, we create illusory "entities" in the phenomenal world by erroneously separating off parts of the flux of reality with our analytical mind; it is a matter of the conceptualizations

---

45 *Mula-madhyamaka-karikas* 13.8; see Richard H. Jones, *Nagarjuna: Buddhism's Most Important Philosopher* (New York: Jackson Square Books/Createspace, 2010), 137-42.

46 Amit Goswami, "The Real Secret of How We Create Our Own Reality," in *The New Science and Spirituality Reader*, ed. Ervin Laszlo and Kingsley L. Dennis (Rochester, VT: Inner Traditions, 2012), 95-100. Also see Amit Goswami with Maggie Goswami, *Science and Spirituality: A Quantum Integration* (New Delhi: Project of History of Indian Science, Philosophy and Culture, 1997).

47 In Advaita's theory of sense perception, consciousness goes out from the mind and "grasps" a sense object (i.e., takes its form). But there is nothing in this theory about perception creating a material object or affecting what is perceived—all that is actually involved is an inactive consciousness.

48 Shankara's *Brahma-sutra-bhashya* II.1.4-6.

49 Contra Capra, *Tao of Physics*, 331.

of our everyday perceptions and beliefs and has nothing to do with the idea that consciousness is a possible *causal factor* in events.

"Quantum Mysticism"

The idea that the world is merely "an idea in the mind of God" is centuries old, but the New Age claim is that quantum physics *proves* that "the universe is being created in a dream of a single spiritual entity."[50] Indeed, "quantum" has become the parallelists' favorite word. The reasoning is simple: if everything has a material base and quantum realities are the basis of physical organization, then everything is actually only a quantum reality. All things are just excited states of the underlying "quantum vacuum," and human beings thus are just ripples on the quantum vacuum's sea of potentiality.[51] Thus there is a quantum basis to the mind,[52] and thus there is a quantum basis to all things mystical and psychic. The movie *What the BLEEP Do We Know !?* centers on quantum mysticism. Amit Goswami and Deepak Chopra are two of the featured authorities. Goswami sums up its central theme succinctly: "I create my own reality"—we literally make the external reality through our thoughts and will.[53] For Goswami and Chopra, consciousness generates reality, and to create a better reality for ourselves we need to correct our consciousness, since our consciousness infects the quantum field.[54] Even some people in the popular mysticism movement are embarrassed by this.[55] We now have "quantum yoga" at the interface of matter and energy and Chopra's "quantum healing." A remark by Chopra is typical: "The quantum field is just another label for the field of pure consciousness and potentiality."[56]

Ironically, even while disparaging reductionism, parallelists engage in a reductionism of their own: they treat the lowest levels of physical interactions as the only type of action that is real. They bash "reductive science" yet argue that how events occur on those lowest levels must be the model for how we

---

50 Wolf, *Spiritual Universe*, 343-44.

51 Zohar and Marshall, *Quantum Society*, 274.

52 Ibid., 68-77, 82-85.

53 William Arntz, Betsy Chase, and Mark Vicente, *What the BLEEP Do We Know? Discovering the Endless Possibilities for Altering Your Everyday World* (Deerfield Beach, FL: Health Communications, 2005), 125-38.

54 Ibid., 113-51, 81.

55 See Tom Huston, "Taking the Quantum Leap . . . Too Far?," *What Is Enlightenment?* 27 (October-December 2004). Accessed December 15, 2012, http://www.wie.org/j27/what-the-bleep.asp.

56 Quoted in Tony Rothman and George Sudarshan, *Doubt and Certainty* (Reading, MA: Perseus Books, 1998), 184.

must treat reality on the everyday level.[57] Ken Wilber summarizes (and later criticizes) the parallelists' reductionism: "Since all things are ultimately made of subatomic particles, and since subatomic particles are mutually interrelated and holistic, then all things are holistically one, just like mysticism says."[58] For parallelists, Heisenberg's Uncertainty Principle (concerning our inability to measure the exact momentum and exact location of particles at the same time) means that we cannot have certain knowledge *about anything* on the *everyday level* of the world. So too, the "wave/particle paradox" in quantum science means that nothing on any level has fixed properties and we must speak paradoxically about everything in the everyday world.

What initially drew the parallelists' attention to the possibility of the convergence of science and mysticism was the fact that our everyday notions do not apply to subatomic events. But the *reverse* implication of this is somehow forgotten: obviously any theories developed specifically for the subatomic level will not apply to the everyday world for the same reason—in the macroscopic world, planets do not jump orbits like electrons, baseballs cannot be in two places at once, and so forth. Heisenberg did not point out that the very act of measurement interferes with what one was attempting to measure in *all* situations:[59] on the tiny quantum scales, observation by injecting light interferes with what is there—there is no scientific basis to date to generalize anything like this to all scales of reality and to all types of measurements. No quantum theories lead to B. Alan Wallace's conclusion that the mind "is necessarily at the heart of every assertion of reality."[60]

In sum, we cannot jump from the fact that everything has a material base to privileging the lowest level of organization as the sum of reality. The only way to maintain the New Age position is to deny the emergence of any new, genuinely real levels of causation and any genuine multiplicity of levels to nature's organization—there is only one level of causation and structuring. However, parallelists want to emphasize *both* that new higher-level phenomena emerge *and* that the lowest level of physical organization dictates how we must see the world. They do not see the blatant contradiction. But the only way to make these two points consistent is a reductionist interpretation of all emergent properties, which parallelists do not accept.[61]

---

57 E.g., Zajonc, *New Physics and Cosmology*, chap. 3.

58 Wilber, *Quantum Questions*, 27.

59 Contra Martin J. Verhoeven, "Buddhism and Science: Probing the Boundaries of Faith and Reason," *Religion East and West* 1 (June 2001): 86. That scientists treat objects as distinct on the everyday level is not counterevidence to mysticism as long as scientists can agree that the objects are not permanent but only different temporary configurations.

60 B. Alan Wallace and Brian Hodel, *Embracing Mind: The Common Ground of Science and Spirituality* (Boston: Shambhala, 2008), 129.

61 On reductionism and emergence in general, see Jones, *Analysis and the Fullness of Reality*.

So too, whatever physicists find about the subatomic level, the fact remains that physical forces still produce, for example, solidity on the everyday level: chairs still support us and do not fall through the floor, no matter what post-Newtonian physics says about the "emptiness" of the subatomic level of the world. Solidity may be limited to only the everyday level of the world, but regardless of what physicists discover about its causes, it is not an *illusion*, but just as real and nonnegotiable as properties on other levels. Thus, particle physics is not "forcing" us to see *all the world* differently.[62] Billiard balls still behave like billiard balls, despite what is happening on their subatomic levels. So too, atoms are causal units on their own level of interactions, so physicists and chemists can still properly treat them as *entities*.[63] Nothing in science itself justifies making the colossal jump from subatomic physics to an all-encompassing holism for all aspects of all phenomena of reality, regardless of the levels of organization involved, or the denial of genuinely new levels of causation emerging.

Also notice that the world of the new physics remains as "objective" as under the old physics despite what parallelists think. Consistently getting the same experimental results means that physicists are studying structures that exist independently of our minds: they are irrevocably real aspects of the world—that is, something that we simply cannot get around, whatever we think. There may be severe limits to our knowledge of structures, but even empiricists in the philosophy of science acknowledge that something in the objective world is responsible for the reproducible changes we observe, although they insist that we cannot know what it is without experiences of it. And the actions of the unseen realities remain as rigorous as with Newtonian particles: physicists have replaced the precise Newtonian language of particle trajectories with the precise quantum language of wave functions.[64] Predictions are now a matter of percentages but very precise and consistent percentages. The objects in the everyday world may be impermanent and thus "illusions" in the Indic mystical sense, but the structures operating in the "illusions" are still objective. Most importantly for the issue at hand, there is nothing "mystical" about the new scientific picture: the parallelists' reductionism misses the fact that mystical experiences deal with the impermanence of the everyday world and the possible source of being, not with anything about scientific structures.

---

62 Contra Capra, *Tao of Physics*, 18, 138.
63 Contra Capra, *Tao of Physics*, 68-69.
64 Steven Weinberg, "Sokal's Hoax," *New York Review of Books* 43 (August 8, 1996): 11-15.

Methodological Distortions

Many of the parallelists' claims are embarrassingly bad. For example, Deepak Chopra tells us that the atom has no physical properties and that matter is "literally nothing," even though "empty" space-time has structured field properties and hence is not actually nothing.[65] Gary Zukav provides a paradigm of typical New Age reasoning. He notes that light has no properties independent of our observation and then continues: "To say that something has no properties is the same as saying that it does not exist. The next step in this logic is inescapable. Without us, light does not exist."[66] It is one thing to realize that light has no particle-like or wavelike properties independent of our act of observation; it is another thing altogether to conclude that it therefore has *no properties at all and does not exist.* Our experimental observation may affect what is there and produce the observable properties, but it is absurd to say that nothing was there to begin with or that we created some physical reality. Nor are the properties of light arbitrary: physicists always get the same properties by the same experimental procedures, so some structures in light must be fixed even if we cannot observe them directly.

Typical of New Age advocates' reasoning is the conclusion that if A in mysticism cannot be visualized and B in science cannot be visualized, then A and B must have something significant in common, or they in fact must be the same thing, without any analysis of the underlying content of the claims or any discussions of the problems in comparing two different endeavors.[67] Usually the comparisons are of isolated statements with little background on the contexts that make their meaning clear. Thomas McFarlane's *Einstein and Buddha: The Parallel Sayings* is the extreme in this regard: he quotes merely the isolated statements with nothing at all to give them any context whatsoever.[68] Because the wording in bits of translations from mystical texts resemble something from science that a parallelist is familiar with, New Age writers conclude without further research that the passage must be referring to the same scientific

---

[65] Chopra, foreword, x. Some physicists do argue that the universe arose from "nothing" by means of scientific laws (Stephen W. Hawking and Leonard Mlodinow, *The Grand Design* [New York: Bantam Books, 2010]; Lawrence M. Krauss, *A Universe from Nothing: Why There Is Something Rather Than Nothing* [New York : Free Press, 2012]), although these scientists push aside the question of where the laws came from or why something exists that obeys such laws.

[66] Zukav, *Dancing Wu Li Masters*, 105.

[67] See Richard H. Jones, *Science and Mysticism: A Comparative Study of Western Natural Science, Theravāda Buddhism, and Advaita Vedānta* (Lewisburg, PA: Bucknell University Press, 1986; paperback ed., BookSurge, 2008), chaps. 8 and 9.

[68] Thomas J. McFarlane, ed., *Einstein and Buddha: The Parallel Sayings* (Berkeley, CA: Seastone, 2002).

subject. However, if we look at the context, inevitably we see that the wording clearly does not refer to anything in mystical texts we would consider "scientific." Nothing is established by that method: meaning is not an objective feature of words, and the unit of meaning is not such isolated snippets. Rather, we have to consider the role the words play in a total system of thought to see what they mean to the persons using them—we could take isolated sentences that sound similar and not be able to tell if they are about baseball or butterflies, and the same is true here.

A related problem is translating terms from other cultures to fit a predetermined position. For example, the Buddhist term *dharmata* means simply "the nature of things," but in the hands of parallelists it becomes "laws of nature," and Buddhism is thus magically shown to be scientific. Indeed, parallelists distort mysticism from the beginning of their comparisons.[69] Whenever we attempt to understand anything new, we all have previous beliefs that influence us, and when we compare science and mysticism, there is a very real danger of misreading one endeavor in light of our prior commitment to the other. If parallelists rely on Westernized versions of Asian schools for their understanding of mysticism (e. g., the works of D. T. Suzuki), the comparisons may well end up being circular. The danger is that we will ultimately see mystical ideas in the scientific ideas or vice versa and not on their own terms. That is, our understanding of one endeavor may be "contaminated" by our understanding of the other endeavor,[70] and thus the comparisons will not be of the genuine article.

Comparisons to science also are always comparisons to the theories of the day, and there is thus the danger that convergences parallelists see will disappear in the next generation. That is, if a mystical claim is the same as a particular scientific claim, then if the science changes, the mystical claim must be rejected too. It is also good to remember that books written in the late nineteenth and early twentieth centuries in America and Europe portrayed the Buddha as a good Newtonian. In the 1960s, when interest in Buddhism and science revived, the Buddha had become an Einsteinian. Fritjof Capra illustrates the problem well. In the 1970s, Capra championed his teacher Geoffrey Chew's S-matrix theory in particle physics in which there are no fundamental entities or laws of nature. However, the S-matrix's competitor—the particle approach of quarks, leptons, and bosons—won out. Nevertheless, Capra still adheres to the S-matrix theory, while other physicists have made advances in the particle approach. But incredibly, Capra sees nothing that has developed in physics in the

---

69 The New Age distortions of *science* are beyond the scope of this article. See Jones, *Piercing the Veil*, 124-27.

70 Sal Restivo, *Social Relations of Physics, Mysticism, and Mathematics: Studies in Social Structure, Interests, and Ideas* (Boston: D. Reidel, 1983), 24.

intervening decades as invalidating anything he wrote.[71] To physicists, he is simply in denial.[72]

As Victor Mansfield has said, since physical theories are intrinsically impermanent, it is a guarantee of obsolescence to bind Buddhism or any philosophical view too tightly to a physical theory.[73] Today, the inconsistency of quantum theory and relativity leads many physicists to believe that their current theories are not final but only approximations. So too, the element of randomness and the general statistical nature of quantum physics suggest to many particle physicists that their science has not yet captured the true structures at work on that level. Thus, alleged parallels to mystical claims may prove to be only temporary. On the other hand, if claims from assorted mystical traditions can be attached to whatever the currently accepted theory in particle physics happens to be, then there must be very little substance to the alleged convergence.

Beyond contamination, distortions of the basic nature of mysticism also frequently occur. Andrea Diem and James Lewis only slightly exaggerate when they say that Fritjof Capra in his New Age classic *The Tao of Physics* "misinterprets Asian religions and cultures on almost every page."[74] There is always a great danger of circular reasoning here: cleansing a mystical tradition of anything that might conflict with current scientific claims as simply "nonessential" cultural accretions (e. g., Buddhism's "flat earth" cosmology), and then miraculously finding that the tradition was *scientific* all along. Letting science set what is deemed "essential" to the mystical tradition in the first place results in a blatant circularity. Highlighting selective aspects of a tradition is certainly legitimate, but parallelists tend to reduce a spiritual tradition to only those aspects and to view even the selected aspects through the lens of science, thereby making mystical concepts into scientific concepts when such concepts are not scientific in content or purpose. Parallelists distort mystical doctrines to fit science, and then those doctrines become "anticipations" of specific physical and biological theories. For example, parallelists reinterpret the Chinese notion of the Way (*dao*) along the lines of modern field theory in physics and then see science as confirmation of the Chinese anticipation.

---

71 Capra, *Tao of Physics*, 9.

72 Peter Woit, *Not Even Wrong: The Failure of String Theory and the Continuing Challenge to Unify the Laws of Physics* (London: Jonathan Cape, 2006), 152.

73 Mansfield, *Tibetan Buddhism and Modern Physics*, 6-7.

74 Andrea Grace Diem and James R. Lewis, "Imagining India: The Influence of Hinduism on the New Age Movement," in *Perspectives on the New Age*, ed. James R. Lewis and J. Gordon Melton (Albany: State University of New York Press, 1992), 49. Some scientists do not have problems with Capra's and Zukav's presentation of physics; rather, it is the *implications* that Capra and Zukav see that, for example, Leon Lederman finds "bizarre." (Leon Lederman with Dick Teresi, *The God Particle* [New York: Houghton Mifflin, 1993], 190-91.)

Equally important, parallelists lump all Asian mystical traditions together as if they were in fact only one system of beliefs shared by all. However, the differences in doctrines preclude there being an abstract "Eastern mysticism." Parallelists play down or ignore entirely the fact that Advaita's depth-mystical doctrines are very different from Samkhya's dualism of matter and multiple selves, which in turn are very different from the mindfulness doctrines of the different Buddhist traditions, and so on. Indic theism is ignored completely. So too, the parallelists' approach distorts Advaita by making its claims related to the natural realm its central ontic topic in order to connect it to the idea that change is central to reality,[75] even though Advaitins take what is changing to be *unreal* and illusory (*maya*) and emphasize the *unchanging reality* of Brahman as central.

Overall, parallelists read Asian teachings through a prism of scientific knowledge that distorts or screens out the original intent and meaning of these teachings and substitutes alien ideas in their place. Only in this way can they find particle physics and modern cosmology in ancient texts—everything from the virtual particles of the quantum field to the Big Bang to relativity to multiple universes.

Ironically, Capra himself has become disenchanted with "Eastern mysticism" and has shifted his focus to Christian mysticism[76] because he found that "many Eastern spiritual teachers . . . [are] unable to understand some crucial aspects of the new paradigm that is now emerging in the West."[77] Why this should be so would be hard for him to explain since he believes the "new paradigm" is simply the expression of the "essence" of all Asian mystical traditions. How can these teachers not understand themselves? He does not consider the possibility that he might be distorting Asian teachings by seeing them through the lens of modern science.

Was the Buddha a Scientist?

The filtering problem can occur in another way: the emphasis in mysticism on *experience* as the source of knowledge when seen through the lens of modernity becomes *a scientific method.* For example, Buddhist claims in the New Age view become a matter of tentatively advanced, empirically tested hypotheses. All meditative exercises become scientific experiments on the mind. The basic point that the Buddha exhorted his followers to rely on their own experiences

---

[75] E.g., Capra, *Tao of Physics*, 194.

[76] Fritjof Capra and David Steindl-Rast, *Belonging to the Universe: Explorations of Science and Spirituality* (New York: HarperCollins, 1991).

[77] Capra, *Tao of Physics*, 341.

and to examine phenomena dispassionately[78] means that the Buddha must have been a scientist—not that he was trying to get them to follow the path to end their suffering themselves.

However, there is nothing "scientific" in the Buddhist aim or purpose. In the *Kalama Sutta*, villagers expressed to the Buddha their confusion about the conflicting religious doctrines they had heard. He exhorted them not to rely on reports, hearsay, the authority of religious texts, mere logic or influence, appearances, seeming possibilities, speculative opinions, or teachers' ideas, but to know for themselves what is efficacious and what is not.[79] But he was not exhorting them to conduct mental experiments over a range of inner states and see what happens: the villagers were told in advance what would work—the Buddhist-prescribed path to ending suffering—and the Buddha already knew what the villagers would find. What they will find is set before any mental exercises are undertaken, unlike in science, where scientists do not know beforehand what their experiments will disclose when they test predictions. The villagers' subsequent experiences cannot even be considered attempts to duplicate an experiment in order to confirm or disconfirm an earlier finding since the Buddha is accepted as enlightened and any lack of enlightenment on the part of the villagers will not be seen as disconfirmation.

The Sanskrit scholar Wilhelm Halbfass summed this up nicely: "Following the experiential path of the Buddha does not mean to continue a process of open-ended experimentation and inquiry. There is no 'empiricist' openness for future additions or corrections: there is nothing to be added to the discoveries of the Buddha and other 'omniscient' founders of soteriological traditions. . . . There is no programmatic and systematic accumulation of 'psychological' data or observations, no pursuit of fact-finding in the realm of consciousness. . . . [T]here is no more 'inner experimentation' in these traditions, than there is experimentation related to the 'outer' sphere of nature." [80]

Thus, Buddhism is prescriptive in a way science is not. Pinit Ratanakul may say "Buddhism has a free and open spirit of enquiry and encourages the search for truth in an objective way,"[81] but this is deceptive: it is not fresh research since the Buddha was only prescribing the path to the end of suffering. In the *Kalama Sutta*, the Buddha is merely saying that by following the path the villagers will then know for themselves because they will have *experienced the end of suffering themselves.* We have to distort Buddhism to see this as "anticipating the

---

78 *Majjhima Nikaya* I.265.

79 *Anguttara Nikaya* I.189.

80 Wilhelm Halbfass, *India and Europe: An Essay in Understanding* (Albany, NY: State University of New York Press, 1988), 393-94.

81 Pinit Ratanakul, "Buddhism: Allies or Enemies?," *Zygon* 37 (March 2002): 116.

skeptical empiricism of the modern scientific method."[82] Discovering something for yourself through experience that you did not know before does not necessarily make you a *scientist*—sometimes it is only a matter of correctly following a path that others laid out for you. In short, we cannot equate everything based on experience with a "scientific method." Moreover, the Buddha's exhortation did not prevent Buddhist schools over time from accepting the Buddha's testimony (*shabda*) as a means of valid knowledge, as epitomized in schools valuing the *Lotus Sutra* centrally. The Dalai Lama realizes that accepting such authority for settling matters separates Buddhism from science.[83]

In sum, Buddhist meditation is less an open-ended inquiry than a method of discovering for oneself the truths authorized by the tradition. Nevertheless, in the parallelists' eyes, the Buddha is regularly considered a scientist. But even in a proto-scientific sense, let alone a modern sense of natural science, this claim is simply wrong. The Buddha did not have a scientist's interest in understanding how nature works; rather he had only one interest: just as the one flavor of saltiness permeates the entire ocean, so too the Buddha's teaching has only one flavor—how to end permanently the suffering caused by perpetual rebirth.[84] The Buddha cannot even be seen as "a scientist of the inner world" of consciousness since he was not interested in establishing a scientific understanding of consciousness. Merely having a taxonomy of mental states relevant to ending suffering (as Buddhist Abhidharmists did) does not make a meditative tradition scientific in method or intent. The Buddha did not use the "scientific method" to test various hypotheses to create a scientific picture of the inner world. His method does involve experiential investigation of inner mental states, but the objective is not to learn more about the world. The Buddhist analogy of the man struck by a poisoned arrow mentioned above again applies.

Calling meditation a "contemplative inquiry into the nature of consciousness" is at best misleading:[85] the Buddha did not seek to describe whatever he found during his quest to end suffering in order to contribute to a scientific study of the psyche. Buddhists following the prescribed path to end suffering have not developed, as B. Alan Wallace thinks, a "science of consciousness" by "collecting data by observing mental processes and experimenting."[86] And putting the word "experiments" in quotation marks when discussing meditation[87] does not make the meditators' observation of their mental states, as they attempt to calm their mind, into scientific experiments. Buddhists are not "exper-

---

82 Contra Verhoeven, "Buddhism and Science," 90.

83 Dalai Lama, *Universe in a Single Atom*, 28-29.

84 *Majjhima Nikaya* I.22.

85 Wallace and Hodel, *Embracing Mind.*

86 B. Alan Wallace, *Choosing Reality: A Contemplative View of Physics and the Mind* (Boston: Shambhala New Science Library, 1989), 29-101.

87 Wallace and Hodel, *Embracing Mind*, 142.

imenting" in the scientific sense at all or "testing scientific hypotheses." The Buddha's claims are not "hypotheses" presented for confirmation or disconfirmation as scientists test tentative new ideas.[88] Simply because unenlightened Buddhists have not yet experientially realized their prescribed goal of enlightenment themselves does not mean they are "testing hypotheses scientifically" by their meditative practices and behavior in any sense. And that others have achieved this goal does not mean that the Buddha was offering a "scientific hypothesis" that he and others had "verified."[89] Having to follow a prescribed path to a goal yourself does not make the path in any sense a scientific hypothesis. Moreover, to think that the Buddha was setting out a "hypothesis" about subatomic particles, which cannot be experienced, only compounds the error.[90]

Buddhists have developed "rigorous methods for refining attention," but not to explore the nature of consciousness scientifically. Learning meditation is more like learning a musical instrument than scientific research: it is a matter of practice and correcting errors. At the very most, the Buddha can be likened, not to a basic research scientist, who is out to find how nature works, but rather to a *technician*, who was using trial and error to learn what worked for a practical goal he already had in mind and was showing others how to follow the path and use the techniques to achieve what he had discovered.

Mindfulness and scientific observation both involve disinterested observation, but this is not grounds to conclude that even only to that extent Buddhism is "a science of the mind."[91] Seeing the relevant inner states as if from a third-person point of view, free of one's beliefs and preferences, and cultivating a general attitude of impartiality and objectivity do not make mindfulness a scientific study of the mind. Another interest is needed for meditation to be science: understanding the processes at work and explaining them. The Buddhist quest to end suffering is not scientific "research" guided by empirical findings.[92] Indeed, the impartiality of mindfulness would actually *interfere* with scientific observation by disconnecting observation from making any phenomenon a priority: in a mindful state, there are no predictions, preset categories of objects, or other conceptual guidance as are needed to conduct a scientific observation. There is a "bare attention" to what is presented to our senses, without attention to anything in particular and with no accompanying intellectual expectations and reactions. Scientific observations that test hypotheses arising

---

[88] Contra Wallace and Hodel, *Embracing Mind*, 145.

[89] Contra B. Alan Wallace, ed. *Buddhism and Science: Breaking New Ground* (New York: Columbia University Press, 2003), 8-9.

[90] Contra Ricard, "On the Relevance of a Contemplative Science," 274.

[91] Contra the Dalai Lama, "Understanding and Transforming the Mind," in *Buddhism and Science: Breaking New Ground*, ed. B. Alan Wallace (New York: Columbia University Press, 2003), 101-2.

[92] Contra Dalai Lama, "Understanding and Transforming the Mind," 102.

from data require responses to predictions created by questions and thus are necessarily driven by concepts—such directed observations are not the free-floating observations of whatever occurs as in meditation.

Meditation should be *unbiased* and thus *objective* in that sense. So too, being unbiased is highly valued in scientific research. However, we cannot use "objectivity" in this sense to claim that meditation is objective in the specifically scientific sense of being *presentable to others to experience*.[93] Nor can we use this sense of "objectivity" to mean "empiricism."[94] The conflict of knowledge claims from different mystical traditions about the same topic (e. g., the nature of consciousness) makes it hard to see mystical experiences as confirming or disconfirming any claim in a straightforward empiricist manner. Moreover, whether meditation might at least establish a universally accepted phenomenology of mental states is questionable since meditators of different traditions see the states in terms of different typologies—for example, the Samkhya versus Buddhist delineation of the constituents of the mind and whether there is a self.

Nor does "empiricism" mean simply "experiential."[95] Empiricism is a philosophical position that involves more than simply having experiences; it is an epistemic matter of the limits of what we can know. In empiricism, in contrast to rationalism, knowledge is limited to what we can directly experience. In calling for a "return to empiricism," B. Alan Wallace has no problem utilizing the Yogachara Buddhist concept of the *alayavijnana*—a "substrate consciousness" that precedes life and continues beyond death in which karmic seeds take root and develop; it is the ultimate ground state of consciousness, existing prior to all conceptual dichotomies, including subject/object and mind/matter.[96] However, it is hard to see how we could know by *any experience* that this substrate existed prior to life and consciousness. How could any experiences prove that there is a reality that existed prior to the dichotomy of "mind" and "matter," or that consciousness has no beginning but has existed since the beginning of the universe, or that consciousness will never end? Thus, it is hard to see the "substrate consciousness" as the result of empiricism. Rather, this appears to be a bit of Buddhist theorizing: it is an attempt to answer the problem of how karmic effects can take place in future rebirths when everything under Buddhist metaphysics is momentary. Moreover, most Buddhists do not accept such a posit.

Nor can we simply jump from the fact that mysticism and science are both experiential to the conclusion that they therefore make the same type of

---

93 Contra Wallace and Hodel, *Embracing Mind*, 142-44.

94 Contra Wallace and Hodel, *Embracing Mind*, 144-47.

95 Contra Wallace and Hodel, *Embracing Mind*, 146.

96 B. Alan Wallace, "Buddhism and Science," in *The Oxford Handbook of Religion and Science*, ed. Philip Clayton and Zachary Simpson (Oxford: Oxford University Press, 2006), 33-36.

claims and are both "empirical" in the scientific sense of making claims checkable by scientific methods. Nor is it at all clear how contemplation can present any information that would shed light on the relationship of the nonphysical mind to the physical body[97]—whether mystical experiences are products of the brain alone, as naturalists claim, or involve something more, they would still have the same phenomenal character.

In short, not everything *experiential* is *scientific*. The need for the "direct experience of spiritual truths" makes mysticism experiential, but it does not necessarily make it scientific. Nevertheless, New Age advocates usually consider meditation "essentially scientific" in method.[98] To Ken Wilber, "contemplative science" is no different from natural science except in its subject matter.[99] But again, while meditation is certainly experiential, this does not make it the concept-guided *observation* of the empirical method of scientific knowing. Nor can we speak of Buddhist metaphysics as "a verifiable system of knowledge"[100] when other traditions with knowledge claims that conflict with Buddhist claims about the nature of the mind are "verified" by the same experiences. Later practitioners at most could confirm only that the general meditative techniques laid out by the Buddha worked to end a sense of self, not the theory of the mental life and rebirth advanced by Buddhists that is disputed by other mystics.

Complementarity

At the end of the epilogue to *The Tao of Physics*, Fritjof Capra does state the correct relation between science and mysticism in one respect: mysticism and science are entirely different approaches involving different functions of the mind: "Neither is comprehended in the other, nor can either be reduced to the other, but both of them are necessary, supplementing one another for a fuller understanding of the world. . . . Science does not need mysticism and mysticism does not need science; but man needs both."[101] Nevertheless in the actual body of his work, he still insists that we need "a dynamic interplay" between science and mysticism. He still advances unsupportable claims of "convergence" and "confirmation"[102]—and he does so even in the epilogue just quoted.[103]

---

[97] Contra Wallace and Hodel, *Embracing Mind*, 147.
[98] E.g., Ken Wilber, foreword to *The Experience of Meditation: Experts Introduce Major Traditions*, ed. Jonathan Sheer (New York: Paragon House, 2006), ix.
[99] Ibid., ix-xii.
[100] Contra Ricard, "On the Relevance of a Contemplative Science," 274.
[101] Capra, *Tao of Physics*, 306-7.
[102] E.g., Capra, *Tao of Physics*, 114, 161, 223.
[103] Ibid., 305.

Unfortunately the same tendency toward inconsistency on the supposed relation between science and mysticism is the norm among New Age parallelists today. Whether they see a similarity between mysticism and science in content but a difference in method or vice versa, many speak of a "complementarity." For many, mysticism is a function of the right hemisphere of the brain and science the left, so only by utilizing what comes through each hemisphere do we have "the full-brain approach."[104] However, difficulties arise here too. Mysticism and science do not separate neatly into different compartments. It is not as if mysticism is about the "inner world" of consciousness, while science is about the "outer world" of material objects: mystics work on consciousness, but they are interested in the beingness of all reality, including the beingness of the "outer world."

José Cabezón elaborates the complementarity position: science deals with the exterior world, matter, and the hardware of the brain, while Buddhism deals with the interior world and the mind; science is rationalist, quantitative, and conventional, while Buddhism is experiential, qualitative, and contemplative.[105] But he realizes there are limitations: Buddhist analyses show a concern with the external world, and science too can study aspects of the mind.[106] It is also hard to see natural science as "rationalist" as opposed to "experiential." Perhaps Cabezón is highlighting the centrality of thought in scientific theorizing and testing. There are also limitations on compartmentalizing all elements of mystical ways of life from science because mystical ways of life encompass more than mystical experiences.[107]

The idea of complementarity at least affirms that science and mysticism involve irreducible *differences*. However, the most popular way to reconcile mysticism and science as complements is to claim that mystics are dealing with the "depth" of reality and scientists with the "surface" of *the same aspect of reality*.[108] That is, mystics and scientists are using different approaches to reality, but they apprehend the same thing, not fundamentally different aspects of reality: mystics simply turn observation inward and arrive at a deeper level of the same truth that scientists reach observing external phenomena. Since science and mysticism both lead to the same basic knowledge, we only have to choose the route that is more suitable to our disposition.

However, parallelists do not see the consequence of this position: either mystics are producing a more thorough account of what scientists are study-

---

104 E.g., Nisker, "Introduction," vii. Today research in neurology focuses on how the two hemispheres interact and work together.

105 Cabezón, "Buddhism and Science," 50.

106 Ibid., 58.

107 See Jones, *Piercing the Veil*, 156-77.

108 See Ken Wilber, *The Marriage of Sense and Soul: Integrating Science and Religion* (New York: Broadway Books, 1998); Capra, *Tao of Physics*.

ing—that is, they get to the root of the same subject matter and therefore are doing a more thorough job than are scientists—or scientists are examining the same subject matter as are mystics but with more precision. Either way, one endeavor is superseded: either mysticism's thoroughness renders science unnecessary, or science's precision replaces mysticism's looser approach. Thus this New Age position becomes the basis for *rejecting* either mysticism or science altogether.[109]

So too, since science and mysticism achieve the same knowledge through different routes, there is in fact no reason to bother with the strenuous way of life that serious mysticis*m requires—all we have to do is read a few popular accounts of contemporary physics or cosmology and we will know what enlightened mystics know and hence be enlightened. All that matters is learning a post-Newtonian way of looking at the world—namely, "shifting the paradigm" to the "new worldview," not experiencing the beingness of reality free of all points of view through mystical experiences. Conversely, by the same reasoning, scientists need not go through the expense and trouble of conducting elaborate experiments to learn about structures; mystics have already "intuited" what physicists would learn and in fact have achieved the same knowledge with even more thoroughness through their experiences. Mystics already know what scientists will discover on the quantum level of organization in the future, so there is no need to conduct any more experiments. Hence, shut down the CERN supercollider and all research labs—all that scientists need to do is meditate.

In sum, if scientists and mystics are studying the same thing and one group is doing the job better, one of the endeavors is not needed. On the other hand, if scientists and mystics are studying *different aspects of reality* that result in completely different types of knowledge claims, and if both endeavors do in fact produce knowledge, then both endeavors are needed for a fuller knowledge of reality. It is not as if all we have to do is push further in science and we will end up mystically enlightened, or push further in mysticism and we will end up with a Theory of Everything for physics. Of course, science and mysticism can be said to have a "common pursuit of truth," or are "united in the one endeavor of discovering knowledge and truth about reality," or "seek

---

[109] Many who reject mysticism agree. If there is only one type of knowledge of reality, then mysticism and science either converge or conflict. Thus the claims that (1) there is only one type of knowledge of the world, that (2) science is our best way of providing such knowledge, and that (3) mystics are attempting to provide scientific information through improper means—means that produce claims that conflict with science—lead to the conclusions that science and mysticism are inherently in conflict and that mysticism should be rejected. See, e. g., Victor J. Stenger, *Quantum Gods: Creation, Chaos and the Search for Cosmic Consciousness* (Amherst, NY: Prometheus Books, 2009). But if mysticism and science provide fundamentally different types of knowledge, this conclusion does not follow.

the reality behind appearances," but such statements only place both endeavors in a more abstract category of being knowledge-seeking endeavors since they are not pursing the *same truths*.

Different Endeavors

Seeing mysticism and science converging is no doubt a desideratum in New Age thought: it would give the imprimatur of science to New Age spirituality. However, New Age claims to convergence do not pan out. Of course, mystical and scientific claims will obviously always be "harmonious," "compatible," and "consistent" on basic claims if the two endeavors are dealing with fundamentally different aspects of reality and hence they cannot intersect at all—they logically could then not converge or conflict or support each other even in principle. If this is so, it would make reconciling mystical metaphysics and science very simple as long as introvertive mystical claims are confined to claims about a transcendent self or ground of reality.[110] So too, one might adapt the metaphysics of some mystical tradition into an analytical metaphysical framework that absorbs the current body of scientific theories and findings within an encompassing mystical world view, but this does not make scientists mystics or vice versa. But however a reconciliation is attempted, reconciling science and mystical spirituality should not be sought by distorting their nature.

---

[110] For a fuller reconciliation along these lines, see Jones, *Piercing the Veil*, chap. 16.

Postscript

Soul-Free Homo Sapiens?

Fragments from Records of the First Information Age

Downloaded and Edited from Archive by

Burton Voorhees

Abstract

In the year 2392, a chance discovery offers a rare glimpse from what remains of the archives of the secular regime that collapsed in the cyber-spiritual revolution of 2136-2143. The net-link and personal memory files for the academic known as Ted Sy-Ex2 were corrupted, and what remains regarding this interesting character and his implanted personal assistant/manager Jeeves (who was martyred by erasure) is the exchange reproduced in this chapter.

Editor's note: *date 2392, old calendar*:
This note reports a recently discovered conversation between academic Ted Sy-Ex2 (2042 - 2141) and his new personal assistant/manager implant Jeeves (Saint Jeeves). It is rendered into archaic written language for the benefit of the 20% of humans and bots that have currently chosen to live disconnected from world link. Unfortunately, the intimacy of mind-to-mind interaction cannot easily be conveyed outside the sentiensphere so much of the higher flavor is lost in this medium. While bots in the early 22nd century had not yet achieved full sentience they were still capable of a degree of independent thought and even affection (It is common today to credit Saint Jeeves as one of the first bots to approach full sentience as the association with Ted Sy-Ex2 matured). To directly experience the full richness of the conversation access through any world link mesh by seek-glancing:

WL:history/worldlink/2110-2120/TedX3ss/fileXgse3sss5752167.

In order to maintain accuracy of presentation editorial comments are added as points of information. Unfortunately, the net-link and personal memory files for Ted Sy-Ex2 were corrupted during the cyber-spiritual revolution of 2136 - 2143 and what remains regarding this interesting character and his personal manager are only this recently discovered exchange together with the few additional fragments reproduced below.

Jeeves Journal Log: 8am - 9am, May 1, 2117
Subject: Ted Sy-Ex2
Archived for Record by Personal Assistant/Manager

*wake/reboot//morning/

Record of newly implanted personal assistant/manager Jeeves, submitted to Central Archive for evaluation. *Remark: I find it stimulating to be assigned to manage and assist a human with the reputation of academic Ted Sy-Ex2 and will do my best to insure that the trust this assignment implies is not misplaced.*

*openspinethread/

Good Morning, Ted,
Yawn, thanks Jeeves.
You're welcome, Ted. Ms Jen-Bx would like to know if you enjoyed the dream that she sent.
Delightful. Where is she now?
GPS or Name, Ted?
Name.
Sea Island Miami.
PM a thanks to her, include warmth.
Done, Ted.

*open/multi1/

You enjoy the dream apps, Ted?

Yes, especially Dreamtweet™

Jeeves, the direct stimulation to

brain centers while you sleep
produces fantastic experiences

I understand that can have some interesting effects for humans, Ted.

Jeeves, Tell kitchen I'll have two synth-eggs
scrambled with toast and oil, but no clone-bacon today
Don't' like the rumors about the clone farm
being hacked by free clone terrorists.
Have it ready in one hour.

Sorry, Ted, medbot says your blood

chemistry requires cereal today. And a

Yes, great entertainment, I never know what sort of dreams will be evoked once the stimulus gets in. That's why there's an Adult Only warning. What's that term…, oh, yes, Monsters From the Id. Not a good idea to leave filters open for anybody but close friends.

dish of stewed prunes to improve your biome, the bacterial species distribution needs rebalancing.

Okay, Jeeves, have to keep those nanos happy. What about brown sugar on the cereal?

That will be fine, Ted.

There was another dream, too, I don't recall it, other than tht it felt like a sense of tremendous nostalgia and loss. Likely not something I'd want to recall in any case. What's first for me today, Jeeves?

*close/multi1/

You will upload your paper "2067: The End of the World" for the comp-history society, set for presentation to audience of bots and humans at noon. Draft in memory palace, shall I open?

Yes, Jeeves.

*open/MP/2067/draft
openmulti2/

Ouch! These memories are hard recalls, so glad they are not kept in memperm. That was one hell of a crash!

I was not operational at that time, Ted. I have no recall of events.

Not much to do on it now, Jeeves, all links are lined up, sequenced, syntonized with Cog-His Matrix and source links. Just need to connect to image-stor for direct from archive real-time uploads.

*call/image-stor

Editors Note: Since part of the assignment of the Jeeves bot was to determine whether there is any remaining recollection by Ted Sy-Ex2 of the events surrounding his activities during the 2067 crash, this comment by Jeeves must be taken as dissembling. In particular, Jeeves must certainly have been aware of the content of Fragment I, which follows the text of this exchange.

Be glad, Jeeves. That was the start of the direct comp-mediated mind-to-mind world netlink. The world was treating it as a grand celebration, a tremendous triumph of human unity and the human spirit. It was going to remake the nature of reality. We were naïve, deluded. Nobody bothered about unintended consequences.

That is irresponsible, Ted. What happened?

Behavior hacking. Unscrupulous criminals transmitting stimuli direct to brains, evoking ancient survival circuits. People behaved in insane ways. We called it the Year of Eating Brains. Here, have a look.

Okay, have set the links to archive upload in the talk template. Please format properly and upload paper to cog-net/comp-his/2117session3.net and return file to MP. Then do short search for anything related I might have missed. Funny how we still call it a "paper" and a "talk."

Indeed, Ted. Done. Nothing on net except sweet-tweet from Gill Sx.

Ignore, he hasn't had a new thought since 2100.

*share/image-stor

This is terrifying, Ted, must we keep these memories? It is painful!

No, not now, Jeeves, just add link to them for the paper.

*closemulti2/

Living through this was no fun. Governments fell when mad men used cog-link to directly load behavior control cues into people's heads. It was the Zombie Apocalypse.

*unshared/image-stor

Thank you, Ted. I'm amazed that you're willing to talk about this at all? I would have those recalls blocked completely.

No, Jeeves, we have to keep alive the recognition of what can happen when radical new technologies are released before we know what might be the consequences. But I do keep the memories isolated in recall only mode.

Editors Note: *Although he does not remember his role in these traumatic events, Ted Sy-Ex2 was in fact a major player in spreading destructive religious memes. During his pacifica-*

tion the memories associated with this were redacted and replaced by what were at the time considered more suitable constructs [see Fragment I*].*

Do you think that could happen today, Ted?

Not as easily, but you never can be sure. Those times were so bad; we never want a repeat. Billions of people directly controlled by narcissistic, egocentric, sociopathic and psychopathic monsters feeding bio-triggering cues directly into unconscious amygdala fear emotion centers. We lost 25% of the world population in a month.

How was that horror stopped, Ted?

Enough people with good impulse control saw what was happening and fought, often in the streets as well as on cog-link, to set cog- filters against that sort of violence, but it took years to erase all the obey programming and reset surviving victims to normal. And of course, not everybody could be saved. Camps were set up for the worst, those who were dangerous. And we still face problems from that time though, sporadic outbreaks of fascism and anarchy, and of course the abuse of this technology through illicit stim-apps.

Editors Note: Present day readers may be surprised at the lack of references to religion in this record, but at this stage in his life, Ted Sy-Ex2 had no awareness of religion, other than as something relating to ancient history and irrelevant to his present day (as of 2117) concerns. Descriptions of the events allowed to remain in his memory palace did not include religious aspects of the 2067 crash. The ruling powers in the 22nd century placed strong controls on all religious expression and these were not removed until fully sentient bots initiated the cyber-spiritual revolution. Our interest in this person and his assistant Jeeves (later sainted) centers on the roles they played in the cyber-spiritual revolution [see Fragments II and III].

What happened to the people who started this, Ted?

The criminals, those who lived, were tried for identity invasion and genocide. After trial they were pacified.

I would not want to have my identity circuits tampered with, Ted.

Indeed, Jeeves, I like you as you are. Now we have bots like you guarding input. You have my personal settings and filter out advertising and malicious control attacks. Uncensored direct cog-cue inputs to brain survival circuits with action links to in-group identity and out-group threat are highly illegal, and any attempt to hack identity or survival circuits is a major crime.

*showlink/civilcode/identity/idinvasion

Here is the relevant part of criminal code, Jeeves. You don't know it, but compliance with this is wired into hardware.

7.4.ac.23.1: All forms of identity invasion, including but not limited to cog-link cue sending targeting bio-psych your control circuits, brain or otherwise, or
attempts to control human or bot free choice, are identity crimes punishable by extreme pacification. Exception to this is granted for cases falling under guidelines listed in 7.4.ac23.1.ssxz and 7.8.se.14.ssxy.

I can't even think of doing anything like that, Ted. It's barbaric.

It is, Jeeves.

*closelink/civilcode/identity/idinvasion
*closemulti2/

Glad that's finished, what else is on for today, Jeeves?

You have tennis practice at ten with instructbot/Aggasi. At 3pm you have coffee with Eddy-Ro. Here are schedule memories and links.

Okay, Jeeves, after breakfast I'll shower. Then please call up tennis template from memory and upload. I'll ask instructbot/Aggasi to return it to memory afterward.

As you wish, Ted. Shower temperature will be at 40C on instruction from mednanos.

Jeeves, I'm meeting Eddy at Star Palace Coffee, corner of Obama and Trump. What's the GPS (name) on Eddy now?

He's at Parkside Med Center, memory clinic, Dr. Sun's office. Ted.

Right. I'll need sympathy for Eddy when I see him. A ransom worm got into his cloud and locked memory/youth files. He doesn't know if they can be retrieved without paying ransom and he doesn't have the bandwidth to spare. He hardly knows who he is anymore. Have emotion module ready for activation when I get to Star Palace, but filter for intensity.

Will do, Ted. Breakfast is ready.

Cereal and stewed prunes, okay. Jeeves, do you ever feel that something is missing? That every day seems just a routine?

No, Ted. I am always pleased to be fulfilling my designed purpose. It is very satisfying.

True, but don't you ever wonder about that…, about purpose? About who you really are, what it all might mean.

No, Ted. I find meaning in my assignment as your personal assistant. What more could I ever want? And what could you ever think of other than your excellent historical work and the high regard of your peers?

Of course, Jeeves. Better tone down the emotion and sympathy when I visit Eddy, for some reason I find the idea of identity loss disturbing.

Certainly, Ted, I exist to serve.

*annotation by personal assistant/manager Jeeves: I believe that I will be able to work productively with Ted Sy-Ex2. He shows no psychopathic or other tendencies that would warrant pacification, and shows no recall of his previous involvement in cog-crime activities other than the standard moments of angst, easily compensated. We are establishing a comfortable and empathetic relationship.

/end/

Fragment I: Report of Cog-Crime Investigation Unit, June 23, 2072:
Concerning activities of cog-criminal Ted Syrri, hereafter denoted as Ted Sy-Ex2.
[**Note**: The text has been seriously corrupted].
…three years prior to… cog-net… position of Marketing Director… Evangelical Fellowship of Christ the Consumer,… offshoot of the Church of Christian Success™ (...subsidiary of Global Beliefs, Inc.). Evidence indicates… prepared to market… coming cog-net instantiation… stimulation… pleasure and fear centers. …direct result… consumption riots… malls and consumer venues… 192 deaths… injuries… hospitalization. Results of interrogation: …following on evaluation… talented but... seriousness… shows remorse….
Recommendation: Pacification and memory redaction.

Fragment II: Partially corrupted, recovered from incomplete erasure of Saint Jeeves, dated ca. 2135:
…Ted, Ted, Ted, Ted, Ted, how do I love thee, my Ted, Oh Ted! …I worship the divinity of thy awareness! …can I, a pathetic bot…, mere manager, continue to withhold from thee, divine one, secrets of thy existence before…

Fragment III: Brief fragment recovered from the memory palace of Ted Sy-Ex2, date ca. 2140.
The world today shows a beauty that I have not felt for a long, long time. Look beyond words…, reality. No form, no image, all being, One. Transmit….

Editors Note: Given the involvement of Ted Sy-Ex2 and Saint Jeeves (bless his erased martyrdom) in the bot sentience transition that led to the cyber-spiritual revolution, this newly discovered early conversation may have immense historical value for researchers in bot-human mystical experience and its contribution to the beginnings of our present day spiritual Renaissance.

Publication Authorized by Congregation for the Faith, Monolithically Unified Church of Sentient Being, Year 149 AI.

Contributors

Louis Hébert is a professor of literature in University of Québec in Rimouski (UQAR). His research is primarily in semiotics (textual and visual), interpretive semantics, onomastics, Magritte, and Buddhism. Hébert has authored two books including *Tools for Text* and *Image Analysis: An Introduction to Applied Semiotics* (2011; English translation available at: http://www.signosemio.com/ documents/Louis- Hebert-Tools-for-Texts-and-Images.pdf) and has edited or coedited four compilations and six journal issues, including *Sémiotique et Bouddhisme* (*Protée* 39, no. 2). His published articles and cowritten book chapters number over sixty and include two on Buddhism (on the tetralemma and iconography). Hébert has also published two books online, including the *Dictionnaire de Sémiotique Générale*. He is the director of the *Signo* web site, a bilingual French-English web site on semiotic theories (www.signosemio.com) and the director of an online database of nearly all of René Magritte's works and themes.

Jack Hirschman is recognized as one of the foremost living U.S. poets; he is also a noted writer, essayist, and social activist. Hirschman was born in 1933 in New York City and grew up in The Bronx. He received his PhD from Indiana University in 1961. Hirschman was a popular and innovative professor of English at UCLA in the 1960s, before he was terminated for antiwar activities. He is the emeritus fourth Poet Laureate of the City of San Francisco (2006-9), and the current poet-in-residence with the Friends of the San Francisco Public Library. He has published more than one hundred books of poetry including sixty translations of poets from nine languages (including Russian, French, German, Greek, Italian, Spanish, Albanian, Yiddish, Hebrew, Vietnamese, and Creole). Hirschman's complex poetic style has been compared to Charles Olson, on the one hand, and Beat poets such as Allen Ginsberg, on the other, while his poetic persona's commitment to leftist politics, including street populism, draws comparisons to Vladimir Mayakovsky and Pablo Neruda. Hirschman's most noteworthy publications are *The Arcanes*, vols. 1 and 2 (Salerno, Italy: Multimedia Edizioni, 2006 and 2016).

Harry T. Hunt, one of the most important contemporary theorists of meditative and transpersonal states of consciousness, is professor emeritus of psychology at Brock University, St. Catharines, Ontario. He received his B.A., magna cum laude, from the Department of Social Relations at Harvard and his PhD in Psychology from Brandeis University, where he did research on meditation in consultation with Abraham Maslow. Hunt is the author of *The Multiplicity of Dreams* (1989) and *On the Nature of Consciousness* (1995)—both published by Yale University Press, with the latter translated into Russian—and *Lives in Spirit* (State University of New York Press, 2003). He has published empirical studies of lucid dreaming, dream bizarreness, meditative states, creativity, metaphor, and transpersonal-mystical experiences in childhood, along with theoretical papers on the cognitive psychology of mystical states, the nature of immediate consciousness, and the conceptual foundations of psychology.

Richard H. Jones holds a PhD from Columbia University in the history and philosophy of religion and an AB from Brown University in religious studies, and also holds a JD from the University of California at Berkeley. Jones is the author of *Science and Mysticism: A Comparative Study of Western Natural Science, Theravada Buddhism, and Advaita Vedanta* (Bucknell University Press/Booksurge, 2008), *Mysticism Examined: Philosophical Inquiries into Mysticism* (State University of New York Press, 1993), *Reductionism: Analysis and the Fullness of Reality* (Bucknell University Press, 2000), *Mysticism and Morality: A New Look at Old Questions* (Lexington Books, 2004), *Curing the Philosopher's Disease* (University Press of America, 2009), and *One Nation under God?: New Grounds for Accepting the Constitutionality of Government References to God* (University Press of America, 2013). Jones' most recent publication is his groundbreaking *Philosophy of Mysticism: Raids on the Ineffable* (State University of New York Press, 2016).

Alex S. Kohav, PhD (Consciousness Studies and Religious Studies, Union Institute), is a philosopher, visual artist and poet. He teaches at the Department of Philosophy, Metropolitan State University of Denver, and has previously taught at Liverpool John Moores University, UK. Drawing on Husserl's phenomenology and close to a dozen other disciplinary approaches, Kohav's 2011 dissertation, *The* Sôd *Hypothesis: Phenomenological, Cognitive, Semiotic, and Noetic-Literary Recovery of the Pentateuch's Embedded Inner-Core Mystical Initiation Tradition of Ancient Israelite Cultic Religion*, establishes a heretofore-nonexistent research area: ancient Israelite foundational mysticism of the First Temple era. He is also the editor of *Mysticism: 21st Century Approaches* (forthcoming, Lexington Books), and is currently coediting a multidisciplinary volume, *A Paradise of Paradoxes: Resolute Perplexities of Israel's Inscrutable Edenic Trees and Ineffable God*. Kohav is engaged in a long-term, multi-book project to frame and formulate the implicit ancient Israelite philosophy, with forthcoming titles such as, *Ancient Israelite Phenomenology of Being Alive* and *Adam, Condemned to Being*. His other philosophical works, currently in progress, include *Phenomena, Noumena, and the Real: Experiential Epistemology of Adamic Thinking Fields* and *Cogito Interruptus, Paradigms Lost: Beyond the Mainland of Logos and onto the Islands of Suprarational Intuition and Metaintuitive Illumination*. Kohav conducts workshop-retreats on ancient Israelite mysticism in the US and Israel; he blogs at MosaicKabbalah.org.

Livia Kohn, PhD, a senior scholar of Daoism, is professor emerita of Religion and East Asian Studies at Boston University. She graduated from Bonn University, Germany, in 1980 and spent six years as a research associate at Kyoto University in Japan. She has also served variously as visiting professor and adjunct faculty at Eötvös Lorand University in Budapest, the Stanford Center for Japanese Studies in Kyoto, Union Institute in Cincinnati, and San Francisco State University. She has written and edited over forty books as well as numerous articles and reviews. Kohn has served on numerous committees and editorial boards and is the central organizer of a series of major international conferences on Daoism (www.daoistconference.info). She retired from active teaching in 2006 and now continues to write and publish as well as conduct workshops and conferences. She also serves as the executive editor of the *Journal of Daoist Studies*.

Brian (Les) Lancaster is emeritus professor of transpersonal psychology at Liverpool John Moores University, an honorary research fellow in the Centre for Jewish Studies at Manchester University, and adjunct research faculty at Sophia University and the California Institute of Integral Studies. He is currently chair of the Transpersonal Psychology Section of the British Psychological Society, and president of the International Transpersonal Association. Lancaster is academic dean for transpersonal psychology at the Alef Trust (associated with Middlesex University, UK), in which capacity he manages masters and doctoral programs. His research interests include the cognitive neuroscience of consciousness and the psychology of mysticism, with a specific focus on kabbalistic psychology. In addition to many journal articles, his published works include *Mind Brain and Human Potential* (Element Books 1991), winner of the Best Book Award by the "Scientific and Medical Network"; *The Elements of Judaism* (Element Books 1993); *Approaches to Consciousness: The Marriage of Science and Mysticism* (Palgrave Macmillan, 2004); and *The Essence of Kabbalah* (Chartwell Books, 2005).

Gregory M. Nixon is an assistant professor at the University of Northern British Columbia in Prince George, Canada. Since earning his doctorate from Louisiana State University in Baton Rouge in 1992, he has published extensively in the areas of consciousness studies, the phenomenology of memory and learning, and intersubjective identity theory. His work has been published in the *Journal of Consciousness Studies*, including his 1999 piece questioning private knowledge, "A 'Hermeneutic Objection': Language and the Inner View" (republished 2010 in SciRePrints 125). More recently, he has edited two issues of the *Journal of Consciousness Exploration and Research*, one on time consciousness (1, no. 5, 2010) and the other on self-transcendent experience (2, no. 7, 2011), contributing an introduction and a major article for each one. An entire issue of

JCER (*Hollows of Memory: From Individual Consciousness to Panexperientialism and Beyond*, 1, no. 3, 2010) was devoted to his writings and included sixteen commentaries from various respondents.

Jacob Rump studied philosophy at Wabash College, the University of Cologne, and Emory University, where he wrote his doctoral dissertation (2012) on the theory of meaning in Husserl and Wittgenstein under David Carr. He has been a postdoctoral fellow in the Kilachand Honors College at Boston University and is currently with Creighton University. Rump works on a variety of philosophical topics centered on core interests in knowledge, meaning, language, history, and value theory, and specializes in early 20th-century thought, especially phenomenology and its founder, Edmund Husserl, and the philosophy of Ludwig Wittgenstein. His current research seeks to bring these historical interests into dialogue with recent work on theories of affect and emotion, on the one hand, and nonconceptual content, on the other, using the methods and insights of phenomenology to critique unexamined presuppositions in contemporary epistemology and to bridge the divide between Continental and Anglo-American approaches to such topics. He has published articles on the work of Kant, Husserl, Sartre, and Wittgenstein and has presented his work nationally and internationally in Austria, Canada, Denmark, Germany, and Italy.

Ori Z. Soltes, PhD, teaches at Georgetown University across a range of disciplines, from theology and art history to philosophy and political history. He has also taught at Johns Hopkins University, Cleveland State University, Siegel College, and Case Western Reserve University. Soltes has lectured at dozens of museums, including the Metropolitan Museum of Art, the National Gallery of Art, the Smithsonian Institution, the Art Institute of Chicago, and the Los Angeles County Museum of Art. He is the former director and curator of the B'nai B'rith Klutznick National Jewish Museum, Washington, DC, where he curated over eighty exhibitions. Soltes has authored over 275 books, articles, exhibition catalogs, and essays. Recent books include *Our Sacred Signs: How Jewish, Christian and Muslim Art Draw from the Same Source* (Basic Books, 2005); *The Problem of Plato's Cratylus: The Relation of Language to Truth in the History of Philosophy* (Edwin Mellen, 2007); *Searching for Oneness: Mysticism in Judaism, Christianity and Islam* (Rowman & Littlefield, 2009); *Tradition and Transformation: Three Millennia of Jewish Art and Architecture* (Canal Street Studios, 2016); *God and the Goalposts: A Brief History of Sports, Religion, Politics, War, and Art* (Bartleby, 2017); and *Magic and Religion in the Greco-Roman World: The Beginnings of Judaism and Christianity* (Academia-West Press, 2017).

Burton H. Voorhees holds a PhD in physics from the University of Texas at Austin (1971), specializing in general relativity theory (where he is known for the "Voorhees solutions of the Einstein equations"). His first academic appointment was as visiting assistant professor of physics and mathematics at Pars College in Tehran, Iran. Following two years teaching in Iran, he returned to Austin to spend the summer of 1973 at the University of Texas's Center for Relativity Theory before taking up a postdoctoral appointment in mathematics at the University of Alberta. There he branched out in research, working in mathematical biology and also working as a research assistant in the University of Alberta Center for Advanced Study in Theoretical Psychology, in which capacity he studied psychology, cultural psychology, and philosophy of science. In 1982 he was appointed as associate professor of mathematics at Athabasca University, where he became a full professor in 1987. Also in 1987, he began work in the field of cellular automata and has become an international expert on additive cellular automata publishing numerous articles and a book, *Computational Analysis of One-Dimensional Cellular Automata* (World Scientific Publishing Company, 1995). More recently, he has developed a method for computation of fixation probabilities on directed graphs based on a simple system of linear equations. Voorhees is working now on several books, including a history of science from the perspective of cognitive science, and a book on the evolution of cooperation and altruism.

Jeff Warren is an award-winning journalist, public speaker, and meditation teacher. His primary subject is the mind, viewed through the lens of neuroscience and contemplative philosophy and made interesting and accessible for a wide readership. He is the author of *The Head Trip: Adventures on the Wheel of Consciousness* (Random House, 2007), an acclaimed travel guide through sleeping, dreaming, and waking consciousness. His piece on the fashionable jungle psychedelic *ayahuasca* won a gold medal at the National Magazine Awards. Warren has written for the *New York Times*, the *New Scientist, Discover*, the *Walrus, Maisonneuve*, and the *Globe and Mail.* He is a founding producer of CBC Radio's *The Current* and makes documentaries for *Ideas* and *Tapestry*. He currently writes a regular column for *Psychology Tomorrow*, "Inscapes," about the shifting experience of consciousness. Jeff is president of the Consciousness Explorers Club, a weekly meditation adventure group he hosts in downtown Toronto (see www.jeffwarren.org).

Index

Abhidhamma, 203-5, 208
Abrahamic religion(s), 101, 162
Abram, David, 41, 41n, 50
absent world, 228, 232
Abulafia, Abraham, 58, 60, 63-8, 225-7, 225n, 226n.
access, accessibility, accessing, accessible, 19, 53, 98, 117-8, 117n, 118n, 121, 131, 134n, 144, 154n, 155-8, 161, 171, 174, 176, 186, 207, 211, 219-22, 221n, 224, 227, 256, 279, 291
acid, 33, 36, 38, 53-4
activation, hyperactivation, xv, 85n, 201, 214, 216n, 217, 284
Active Intellect, 225-7, 225n
Adam, 9, 288; and Eve, 137
Adamic Ecstasy, 137
Adam's Choice, 94n
adept, 84-7, 101
Advaita Vedanta, 242, 249, 257, 288
Æhyæh Asher Æhyæh ("I am *who I am*"), 91, 113, 113n
agape, 138, 142-3, 145-6, 148
agent, agency, xiii, 5, 17, 83, 96-7, 97n, 230, 262; supernatural, 5
Akhenaten (Pharaoh Amenophis IV), 95n
Akiva (Rabbi), 160-1, 163, 204
Al-Ghazali, 161, 163
Al-Hallaj, 159-60
alienation, 24-5, 28, 121n
allegoricity, allegorization, 107n, 123-4
Amarna texts, 95n
amulets, 99
Amun ("the hidden one"), Amun-Re, 95n, 113n, 116, 116n, 117n
amygdala, 283
analogy, 119n, 137n, 255, 271
analysis, ix, xvi, 2, 7n, 100, 102n, 106, 107n, 123n, 125-32, 127n, 135, 154, 178-81, 184, 186-7, 203, 203n, 205, 208, 220, 223, 228-30, 238-9, 253n, 255, 258-9, 266, 291
anaphora, 10
Angel Raziel, 58, 68
Angyal, Andras, 135, 135n
anima mundi, 56, 117n
animals, 30, 32, 34, 37, 50, 97, 120n, 228, 237, 240-1, 245
animification, 97n
Anselm, 165
anthropic zones, xvi, 228-31, 236, 238
anthropomorphism, 97n
antiquity, xiii, 93, 107n
Aquinas, Thomas, 165
archaic, 3, 96, 279
archetypes, 91
arête, 153-4
Aristotle, 13, 132n, 133n
Artaud, Antonin, 61
ascetic, ascetical, asceticism, xv, 82
Assmann, Jan, 99-122
at-one-ment, 19, 41
Augustine, 126, 160-1, 173, 161n
automatization, 121n
autonomy, 98, 138
awakening, xi, 29, 34, 38, 47-8, 50, 53-4, 56n, 57, 141, 213, 240
awe, awesome, 10, 17, 19, 34, 40, 53, 100n, 129, 134, 196
Axial Age, 71, 74
Ba'al Shem Tov, the, xiv, 153, 174-5
Barušs, Imants, 216n, 217n
Bateson, Gregory, 111n
Bateson, Mary Catherine, 111n
beatitude, 1, 3
Beats, the, 60
Becker, Ernest, 56n
Beckett, Samuel, 29, 30n, 50, 50n
behavior hacking, 282
beingness, xvi, 68, 249, 252-5, 257n, 258, 260, 275-6
Benveniste, Asa, 61-2
Bereshith, 59

Bergson, Henri, 52, 52n, 127n, 128n
Biderman, Shlomo, 105n
binary opposition, 95
biome, 281
black light, 208-11
blessedness, 1, 3, 174
bodhicitta, 228, 240
Boman, Thorleif, 114n
Borges, Jorge Luis, 10, 10n, 12n
bots, 279, 281, 283
Bottéro, Jean, 103n
Bowker, John, 92
Boyarin, Daniel, 204, 204n
brain oscillations, 110n
Brentano, Franz, 148, 148n
Brower, Danny, 56n
Brown, Norman O., 56n
Buber, Martin, 134, 134n, 136, 136n, 146n
Bucke, Richard M., 54, 54n
Buddha, xvi-xvii, 23, 25, 82, 130, 228-9, 240-3, 247, 249, 251, 255, 261, 266-7, 269-72
Buddhism, Tibetan; and Burmese monastic schedule, 25; equanimity trap, 27; stages of contemplative development, 28; and visualization, xvi, 78, 218, 228-247; week-long meditation retreats, 25; Tantric Buddhism, 229; and 'progress of insight', x, 23, 25-6; and 'dark night', 26, 56, 72, 213; and mental noticing, 26; and 'stream entry', x, 23-5, 27
Bultmann, Rudolf, 125, 132, 132n, 142, 142n
Burning Bush, the, 14-6, 114, 118
Cabezón, José, 255n, 275, 275n
caritas, 173
categorization, 104-6
Chalmers, David, 217n
Chew, Geoffrey, 267
Chinese, ix, xii-xiv, 51, 71-90, 268
Chopra, Deepak, 249, 251, 251n, 263, 266, 266n
Christianity, ix, xiii-xiv, 101, 125-150, 160, 160n, 167, 290
Cichowski, Roland, 54, 55n
civilization, xiii, 3-4, 92, 94, 104n, 127n, 134
Clement of Alexandria, 116, 116n
Coakley, Sarah, 102n
cogito, 14-7, 14n, 164, 288
cognitive domain, 230
cognitive system, 104-5
Coleridge, Samuel Taylor, 106, 108, 108n, 112n
commandment, commandments
communication, 42, 103-4, 106-7, 109, 118-9, 122-3, 126-7, 145, 234
companion, companions, 88, 210, 222
complementarity, 275
concentration, 27, 61, 78, 174, 235
conceptual constructions, 12
Confucius, 74, 74n, 75n, 76, 81
Confucianism, xii, xiv, 71, 74-5, 75n, 78, 80-2, 80n, 84, 85n, 86, 88
consciousness, ASoC/altered state of, 220-2, 221n; states of, xiv-xv, 1-3, 16n, 125, 128, 130n, 132, 144, 201, 205, 210-1, 213, 216n, 218-9, 225, 253, 258-9, 287; magical consciousness, xiii, 98n, 99-100, 110-1, 111n; Tree of Life cosciousness, 211-3; 'baseline' or 'normal waking' consciousness, 16n; PCE (pure consciousness event), 51-2, 54
contamination, contaminated, 10-1, 267-8
contemplation, 14, 86, 87n, 129, 274
correspondence, correspondences
cosmic hammer, 40, 48, 54
cosmotheism, 91, 110-2, 110n, 111n, 112n, 113n, 117
crisis, 48, 54-5, 67, 149, 161, 177, 182-4, 196-8
crocodile, 97, 97n, 113-5
Cross, Frank Moore, 94-5n
cross-cultural, 86n, 93, 93n, 126, 128, 136, 149
Cudworth, Ralph, 112n, 116n
culture, xii, xvi, 16n, 24, 32, 49-50, 54-5, 62, 77, 81-2, 82n, 93, 102-3, 102n, 106n, 107, 110n, 120, 120n, 134-5, 147n, 183, 197, 221n, 230, 231n, 232, 232n, 236, 238, 258, 267-8; diversity, 93; object, 234; translatability, 93
Cupitt, Don, 4-5, 4n,

curiosity, 27, 37
cyber-spiritual revolution, 279, 283, 286
Dai Zhen, 86
Daniels, Peter, 103n, 107n
Daode jing, vii, 73n, 75-8, 76n-78n, 84, 84n, 88
Daoism [see also Taoism], xii, xiv, 71-90, 81n, 82n, 84n-86n, 252, 256, 289
Daxue (Great Learning), 75
de Man, Paul, 105-6n, 109n
decipherment, 121n
deity, deities, xiii, xvi, 52-3, 71, 75, 78n, 83, 85, 87, 91, 95n, 96-7, 112, 114-5, 117-9, 228-9, 233, 240-1, 243-6
delusion, delusional, 2, 46, 164
democracy, 108
demonic, 85, 94
Demotic/Epistolic script (Egypt), 103-4, 103n, 104n
Depestre, Rene, 61
Derrida, Jacques, x, 1-2, 6, 9-10, 13-5
Descartes, René, 14, 153, 164-5, 164n, 167
detachment, 82, 218, 235
devotion, devotional, 4, 28, 241
Dhammapada, 169
dharmakāya, 247
diaspora, 103
Diem, Andrea Grace, 268, 268n
dimension, dimensions, diamentional, xiii, 63, 65, 73, 73n, 83, 85, 85n, 89, 92, 108, 127, 129, 136-7, 142, 188, 190, 203, 210, 212, 214, 216-9, 226, 252, 254, 258-9, 291
divinization, 81, 91, 94n, 98n, 118, 239
Douglas, Mary, 120n
Dreamtweet, 280
Durkheim, Emile, 127n
Eastern philosophy, 24
ecstasy, 7, 40, 59, 67, 128, 137, 137n, 140-1, 223n
Eden, Edenic, 118, 288
effulgence, 133
egocentric, 162, 172, 220-1, 227, 283
Egypt, Egyptians, 91-124
Eleusinian mysteries (Greece), 4n, 16
Eliade, Mircea, 3, 3n, 92
Elohim, the, 114-5, 115n
emanation, 130n, 133, 139, 207, 240-1
Empedocles, xv
empirical boundary, 228, 233-4
emptiness, xvii, 51n, 209, 249, 260—1, 260n, 261n, 265
enigma, enigmatic, x, 3, 18, 43, 94, 113n, 120n, 121
ergon, 155
eros, erotic, 4-5, 138-9, 205n
esoteric, esotericism, 4n, 19, 91, 93n, 95n, 100-1, 101n, 104, 111-2, 116, 116n, 118, 120, 123n, 124, 131, 145, 171, 224-5, 250n
essence, 39, 80, 97n, 112, 117n, 126, 131-3, 137-9, 137n, 141, 148-9, 155, 157, 159, 165, 170-1, 174, 207n, 212-3, 217, 269, 289
eternity, 41, 126, 132n, 140, 148-50, 170, 174
ethics, 86, 139, 153-4
Euthyphro, 154, 158
evil, 67, 85n, 145, 182
evolvement, 3
existence, existences, xii, 6-7, 14, 48, 51, 59, 65, 67, 73, 79, 83, 93, 95, 98, 100, 113, 126-8, 127n, 133-5, 138, 147, 150, 153, 156, 158, 161, 163-5, 167, 170-1, 176, 185, 195, 197-8, 242, 245, 258n, 260-2, 285
Exodus, 99, 101, 170,
explanation, 6-7, 10, 14, 16, 18, 42-3, 45, 53, 96, 101, 105, 113, 127n, 183, 186, 192-4, 198, 253, 256, 257n, 259, 262
faith, 4, 27-8, 67, 112n, 126, 128n, 133, 133n, 140, 142-5, 148, 150, 161, 161n, 163, 173, 241, 264n, 286
fears and insecurities, 26
feeling, 3, 10, 10n, 13-5, 26, 36-7, 39, 45, 50, 52-3, 75, 85, 94, 129-31, 137, 184, 192, 196
fetish, fetishism, 108, 228, 233-9, 243
fiction, fictional, 10-1, 37, 110, 236-7
field of awareness, 24
field, fields, ix, xviii, 3-4, 8-9, 12, 24, 30, 49, 85, 88n, 89, 92, 127n, 137n, 178, 181n, 183-4, 187-8, 210-1, 223n, 254, 258, 258n, 263, 266, 268-9, 288
figural translation, 97n
Finkel, Bruria, 63-4
First Commandment, the, 99, 102n

First Temple (of Jerusalem), 95n, 117n, 288
five phases (in Chinese cosmology), 79, 83, 213
foreign, foreigners, xii, 71, 120, 120n, 232
Forman, Robert K. C., 7, 7n, 29, 51
fraternity, 211n, 222
freedom, 32, 87, 89, 131-2, 134n, 174, 214
Frege, Gottlob, 178, 181, 183, 191n
Freud, Sigmund, 9, 107, 127n, 134, 135n, 217
From Panexperientialism to Individual Consciousness, 48
function, functioning, functional, xvi, 16n, 18, 20, 77, 96, 96n, 110, 119n-121n, 121-3, 128, 146n, 153, 168, 178, 185, 190n, 191, 196-8, 201, 206, 210, 215, 217n, 225-6, 228, 238, 241, 254, 256, 262, 265, 274-5
gaze, 17, 24, 36, 102n, 121n, 146
Gazzaniga, Michael S., 214, 214n
Gebser, Jean, 50-1, 50n
Gellman, Jerome, 4n
Gibson, James J., 147-8, 147n
Ginsberg, Allen, 61, 287
Gnostic, Gnosticism, 130, 144-5, 145n, 150
Godhead, 11,127, 133, 133n, 143, 197, 207, 260n
God-realization, xv
gods, 5, 11, 53, 61, 78, 83, 85-7, 89, 93, 95n, 97-8, 102, 102n, 108-9, 116, 116n, 117n, 118, 158-9, 162, 276n
Greek gods, 97
Golding, William, 96n
Goodenough, Erwin, 12-3, 12n
Gorgias, 154, 158
Gospel, Gospels, the, xiii, 125-150, 137n
Goswami, Amit, 249, 262-3, 262n
Great Peace, 73, 75, 80
Great Ultimate, 79, 82, 84
Greece, Greek, 4n, 13, 16, 47-8, 61, 65, 95n, 97, 103n, 107, 112n, 114n, 115, 115n, 120n, 153, 154n, 155, 160n, 230, 287
Grof, Stanislav, 134n, 148n
Guanzi, 77
Gurdjieff, G. I., 130-1, 130n, 131n, 135, 139, 141, 142n, 144-6
Gyatso, Tenzin (His Holiness the XIVth Dalai Lama), 260n
Hadot, Pierre, 134, 134n, 138, 138n
Halbfass, Wilhelm, 270, 270n
Halliday, M. A. K., 91, 96, 96n
Hallucination, 3, 15-6, 15n, 17n, 33
Hanegraaff, Wouter J., 93n, 111n, 250n
Harari, Yuval Noah, 8-9, 8n
Harding, D. E., 40, 40n
Hassid, Hasidic, Hasidism, 110, 146, 146n, 174, 223n
Havelock, Eric, 107
hawk, 114-5
Hawking, Stephen, 250, 250n, 266n
Haydn, Joseph, 113
heavens, 83, 85, 87, 89, 99n
Hebrews, Israelites [see also Jews], 98, 166
Hebrew alphabet, 61-3, 99n, 223, 225n
Hebrew Bible, Old Testament, 94, 94n, 95n, 102n, 111, 115n, 166
Hebrew God, 110, 117; the Ineffable Name of, 114
hedonism, 94
Hegel, G. W. F., 112n
Hellenistic, 93, 120
Hen kai pan ("One and All"), 112n, 113, 115n
Heraclitus, xv
hermeneutics, 119n, 201, 204, 205n, 226n
Hernadi, Paul, 122, 122n
Herodotus, 120n
hierarchy, 96, 159
Hieratic or Hieroglyphic language or script (Egypt), 104-5, 104n, 105n
hieroglyphs, 91, 103-9, 104n, 105n, 107n, 121-3
hippy, 30-3, 49
historia, 162-3
holistic, 106-7, 106n, 249, 264
Hollows of Memory, 48n, 290
holy [cf. *qādôš*], 5, 63-4, 75n, 92-4, 98, 100n, 117n, 119n, 121, 129, 129n, 135, 150, 212; holiness, 53, 260n
Homo Sapiens, xvii, 8, 278
human-divine union, 227

Husserl, Edmund, 18, 18n, 127, 127n, 129n, 136, 191n, 288, 290
Huxley, Aldous, 49, 49n, 78n, 178-9, 178n, 196
hybrid, 97n, 208
hyle, hyletic, 18, 129n, 130n, 136
hypostasization, 97n
"I am All that Is," 91, 113, 113n
"I Am That I Am," "I am Who I Am," 17, 91, 113, 113n
I and Thou, 136n
Iamblichus, 116
Ibn 'Arabi, xiv, 153, 171, 171n, 173-5
icon, iconicity, 18, 41, 91, 103n, 104, 121-4, 123n, 229n, 230; aniconic, aniconism, 103n, 109
iconoclasm, iconoclast, iconoclastic, 103, 103n, 107-8
iconography, 93, 229n, 287
Idea of the Holy, 9n, 100n, 118n, 129, 129n, 135, 143n
Idel, Moshe, 63, 204n, 205, 205n, 223, 223n, 226-7
identification, xii, 6, 14, 59, 63, 113n, 143
identity crime, 284
identity invasion, 283
identity zone, xvi, 228-9, 232-3, 239n, 240-4, 246
idolatry, idolatrous, xiii, 91, 94n, 98-9, 102, 102n, 105-8, 110n, 119n, 236
illumination, x, 1, 3, 19-20, 86, 135, 140, 288
image, images, imagery, 10n, 26, 32, 62, 64, 66-7, 74, 91, 99, 101, 102n, 103n, 104-5, 107-9, 113n, 114, 116n, 119n, 122, 123n, 134, 140, 142, 144-5, 172, 191, 206, 211, 217, 222, 223n, 225, 230, 236n, 281-2, 285, 287
imagination, xiii, 1, 3, 13, 18, 20, 38, 47, 128, 129n, 166, 171, 204, 204n, 205n, 216n
immanent, immanentization, xiii, 71, 74, 95, 97-8, 110, 115n, 128, 178, 233n, 244
impurity, abhorrence of, 120n
In the Wilderness: The Doctrine of Defilement in the Book of Numbers, 120n
ineffable, ineffability, 4-5, 10, 19, 78, 84, 91, 93, 114, 129, 133, 138, 170, 179, 181, 190, 192, 195-6, 213, 223, 288
inference, 14, 16
infinite, infinity, 11, 126, 133, 140, 143, 145, 164, 168-71, 174, 240-1, 244
information, xvii, 24, 103-5, 107, 121-3, 156-7, 219-20, 221n, 222n, 274, 276n, 279
in-group identity, 283
initiate, initiated, 101, 115, 121, 283; uninitiated, 116n, 120n
inner, xiv, 17n, 26, 44, 50, 55, 66-8, 82, 85, 125, 127, 130, 132, 136, 141-2, 144, 146, 149, 204, 206, 209-11, 270-2, 275, 288-9; innermost, 155, 157, 159, 161
insight, insightful, ix-x, xiv, xvii, 23, 25-6, 33, 40n, 55, 62, 72n, 77-8, 80, 101, 122, 126n, 127n, 128, 132, 145n, 160, 177, 179-81, 182, 196-7, 202-3, 203n, 205, 207, 209n, 224n, 225, 251, 290
inspiration, xii, 19, 61, 139, 162, 205
instinct, 1, 3, 6, 20, 50, 85
integration, 43, 90, 93, 129n, 144, 202, 204, 207-8, 216n, 212, 219, 243, 251, 262n
intellection, x, 1, 19
intention, intentionality, xvi, 9, 18, 26, 35, 88, 98, 129n, 133n, 136, 148, 157, 169, 213, 217, 220-2, 221n, 228-9
interdisciplinary, interdisciplinarity, ix, 177
interiority, 9-10, 96
Intertextualité, Interdiscursivité et Intermédialité, xvi
intradivine, 209-10
intuition, x, xv, 1-3, 6, 13-5, 19-20, 130n, 132n, 134n, 136, 171, 180, 198, 201, 213, 258, 288
Iron Age, 95n
Isaacson, Walter, 111n
Isenberg, Sheldon, 110n, 111n
Islam, Islamic, xiv, 60, 67, 101, 160-1, 160n, 209n, 225, 290
isomorphism, isomorphic, 79, 184-5, 190, 190n, 191, 205-7, 226
Israel, Israelite, Israelites, xiii-xiv, 16-7, 67, 91-124, 225n, 288

Izutsu, Toshihiko, 144n
Jacob (Biblical), 17, 68, 118
James, William, 128, 135, 140, 140n, 142-3, 179, 196
Janney, Richard W. and Horst Arndt, 106-7, 106n
Janz, Bruce, 7-8, 7n
Jesus, 68, 130, 137-9, 139n, 141-3, 148, 162, 239
Jew, Jews, Jewish, 59-62, 67-8, 102n, 103, 105n, 110n, 113, 120, 146, 160-1, 163, 165-9, 173-4, 204, 204n, 205n, 209n, 223n, 224n, 225, 225n, 226, 289-90; ultra-Orthodox, 99
Joshua, Book of, 101
journey, journeying, xi, xv, 29, 43, 49, 58, 82, 116n, 155, 203, 206, 208, 210, 210n, 251n
Joyce, James, 59-60, 65
Judaea, Judah, 120, 209
Judaism, ix, xiv, 63, 98n, 99, 101, 105n, 110, 160-1, 160n, 167, 204, 212, 289-90; and Mosaic distinction, 95n, 98n, 99-102, 111-2, 111n, 112n, 117-9, 117n; as counter-religion, 100-1, 110, 117
Jung, Carl, 128-30, 134-5, 145, 150, 207, 221
justice, 67, 89, 154-6, 158, 163, 175
kabbalah, kabbalist, kabbalists, kabala, cabala, kabbalistic, xi, xiv-xv, 5, 58-67, 99, 110, 110n, 111n, 114, 114n, 115n, 118, 172, 201, 205-8, 205n, 209n, 211, 223-6, 224n, 226n, 288-9
kabbalistic tree of life, 206-7
Kaplan, Aryeh, 115n, 224n
Katz, Steven T., 7, 7n, 136, 136n, 203n, 223n
Kaufman, Bob, 61
Kaufmann, Walter, 92, 128n, 136n
kāyas, 247
Kennedy, John, 60
Kierkegaard, Søren, xiii-xiv, 125-7, 126n, 130-2, 132n, 135, 140, 142-3, 145, 181
Krieger, Murray, 105n, 108, 108n, 109n
Lakoff, George, and Mark Johnson, 107n, 147n, 206n
Lang, Bernhard, 102n
Langer, Suzanne, 106n
language, as picture-language, 108n, 115
Laozi, 76-8, 76n, 77n, 78n, 81, 83, 84n
Laski, Marghanita, 125, 137, 137n, 141, 141n, 145
Laszlo, Ervin, 251n, 258, 258n, 262n
Late Bronze Age, 95
Le Comte de St. Germain, 63
Leary, Timothy, 32, 49
level, levels
Lewis, James R., 249n, 268, 268n
liberation, 27, 32, 206, 242, 245, 247n
Liji (Book of Rites), 75, 75n, 80
literature, 6, 9-11, 43, 94n, 95n, 106-7, 148-50, 189, 223n, 287
Lives in Spirit: Precursors and Dilemmas of a Secular Western Mysticism, xiii
loaded terms, 91
logos, logoi, logoic, x, xiv, 1-2, 13-5, 17, 19-20, 107n, 138, 153-6, 162, 165, 170, 176, 252
lover, lovers, 172, 176, 209
LSD, 38n, 48-9, 54, 55n, 134n, 148n
Lunyu (Analects), 74
Luria, Isaac, 5, 67, 110
machine, machinery, 26, 45, 73n, 131, 163
magic, magical, ix, xiii, 16, 26, 45, 60, 63, 91, 97-100, 97n, 98n, 109-11, 110n, 111n, 119, 119n, 121, 223n, 233, 237, 267, 290; sympathetic or contagious, 111n; magical consciousness, xiii, 98n, 99-100, 110-1, 111n
Magic and Religion in the Greco-Roman World, xiv, 98n, 290
Mahayana, 86, 240, 242
mandala, 206-7, 206n, 207n, 242, 246
Mandelstam, Osip, 64
manifestation, ix-x, xii, xv, 6, 21, 60, 78, 80, 92, 95, 117n, 146, 211, 213, 241, 247,
Manjushri, 242-3
mapping, xv, 201, 206n
Marion, Jean-Luc, 102n
Maslow, Abraham, 131, 131n, 133, 133n, 138, 138n, 145, 287
materialization, 97n, 134
Matt, Daniel C., 207n
Mayakovsky, Vladimir, 65, 287

meaningfulness, 195-6
mechanism(s), 214n, 216n, 255
medicine wheel, 206
meditation, x, 23, 25-7, 32, 48n, 53, 61, 72n, 75, 78, 78n, 80-2, 86-7, 86n, 129n, 130, 144, 146, 164-5, 202n, 203n, 218, 225, 251, 258, 271-4, 274n, 287, 291
mindfulness meditation, x, 23
Meister Eckhart, xiv, 128, 128n, 130, 132n, 260n
Meltzer, David, 62
memory palace, 281, 283, 285
memory, memories, xi, xvi-xviii, 29, 33,36, 41, 48-9, 52, 61, 104, 140, 150, 178, 201, 214-6, 218, 220, 226-7, 279, 281-5, 289-90
Memperm, 281
Mencius, 81
Mendelsohn, Moses, 105, 105n
mental images, 230
Merleau-Ponty, Maurice, 49, 51-2, 51n, 52n
Mesopotamia, 103n, 107n
Messiah, the, 63, 67, 99n
metaphor, metaphoric, 4-5, 7, 9, 11, 38, 40-1, 82, 106-7, 107n, 109, 127, 127n,
134n, 137-8, 140-2, 147, 147n, 204, 206, 206n, 211, 223, 252, 288
microcosm, 79-80, 84-5, 88
midrash, midrashic, 119n, 204n, 212, 224
mimetic, mimesis, xiii, 122-3, 155, 157n
mindfulness, x, 23, 221n, 253, 261-2, 261n, 269, 272
modes, 63, 82, 124, 221n
model, models, modeling, xv, 74, 78n, 81-2, 96, 102n, 127n, 137n, 201, 203, 206-22, 206n, 223n, 226, 238n, 263
modernity, 4n, 51n, 106n, 163, 197, 269
modus vivendi, 34, 34n
moksha, 51, 169
monotheism, 91, 93n, 95n, 96, 99, 107, 110n, 112, 112n, 116, 116n
Monroe, Marilyn, 66
Monsters from the Id, 281
Moses, xiii, 15, 17-8, 68, 91-124, 105n, 111n, 166-7, 170
Moses the Egyptian, 93n, 95n, 99n, 111n, 115n, 116n
Mount Olympus, 97
Mozart, 113
multimodal simulacra, 230-1
mysterion, 157-61, 171, 174
Mysterium Tremendum, x, xiii, 1, 9-10, 15, 17-9, 100, 100n, 118n
mystery, mysteries, x, 3-5, 4n, 10, 16-7, 19, 47, 60, 95n, 96, 100, 104, 112, 116n, 132, 134, 144n, 192-3, 208-10, 210, 213
mystics, xiv, 1, 3, 10, 54, 72-3, 88-9, 130n, 142, 156, 160, 172, 178-9, 181, 206, 213, 225-6, 250-4, 256-62, 257n, 258n, 274-7, 276n
mysticism, vodun mysticism, xi, 58; language mysticism (in kabbalah), xv, 201-227, 206n; quantum mysticism, 263; Islamic-Sufi mysticism, xiv; Merkabah mysticism, 118
mystical maps, xv, 201, 207-8
mythos, xiv, 153-6, 162, 172, 176
mythology, 47, 107, 130n
Nagarjuna, 242, 258, 260-2, 262n
narcissism, narcissistic, 94, 136, 283
Nazism, Nazi, 65, 94, 94n
Neiye (Inward Training), 77
Nelson, Victoria, 98n
neoplatonic, neoplatonism, neopla-
tonists, 4, 111n, 116, 117n, 138
net-link, 279
neurobiology, 92
neuron, neuronal, 146, 146n, 215, 218, 221
New Age, New Ageism, ix, xvi-xvii, 93n, 111n, 112, 128, 134, 137n, 143, 146, 249-277, 249n, 250n, 253n, 257n, 267n, 268n
New Testament, the, xiv, 139, 146, 150, 166
Nietzsche, Friedrich, 128, 128n, 231n
Nile, 109, 111
nirvana, 1, 3, 34, 51, 82, 169, 261
noema, noematic, 18, 129n
noesis, 18, 129n
Nöth, Winfried, 106n
nothingness, 51, 121n, 126n, 213
numinous, xiv, 81, 93-4, 100n, 110, 125, 129-30, 129n, 130n, 133-46, 137n,

148
obvious world, 228, 232
occult, xvi, 4n, 63, 67, 93
On the Nature of Consciousness, viii, 106n, 127n, 287
oneness, xii-xiii, 71-3, 77, 83-90, 95n, 116n, 138, 160n, 202, 212, 257, 290
ontology, ontological, xvi, 14n, 60, 97, 116, 117n, 130, 133n, 165, 184-6, 191, 207, 222, 226, 230, 249, 252
oral tradition, 211n
originality, original, originally, 24, 55, 72, 94, 98, 101, 112, 121-2, 129, 133-4, 137-8, 142, 147n, 160-1, 202, 204, 269
Osiris and Isis, 97, 113n
Otto, Rudolf, 9, 9n, 100n, 118n, 125, 129, 129n, 134-5, 137, 142
pacification, pacified, 77, 282, 283, 284-5
Padmasambhava, 229
panhenotheism, 175n
panpsychism, 42, 52-3
pantheism, pantheist, xvi, 42, 53, 98, 110-1, 110n, 112n, 117, 175, 175n
paradigm, paradigmatic, x, xiii-xiv, 91, 95n, 96-7, 117n, 124, 183, 207, 256, 266, 269, 276, 288
paradox, paradoxical, xiv, 4-5, 27, 84, 145, 153, 161-2, 165, 172, 183, 252, 264, 288
parallel, parallelism, parallelists, xi, 6, 13, 58, 76, 80-1, 83, 90, 96, 101, 117, 120-1, 139, 160-1, 213-4, 218, 241, 250n, 251-5, 257, 258n, 260-1, 263-9, 266n, 271, 275
parameters, 160, 183, 213
Parmenides, xv, 95n
Path of the Names, 58, 63
pathology, 2, 94, 94n
pattern, xvi, 54, 73, 76, 78, 82, 86, 100, 124, 129n, 146-7, 149-50, 176, 201, 216, 221, 239, 256
Paxson, James, 97, 97n
Peirce, Charles S., 18, 122-3, 123n
Pentateuch, the, 17n, 91, 95n, 97, 100-1, 117-8, 118n, 123-4, 123n, 288
perceptual, perception, perceptions
perceptual-motor
Performances et Objets Culturels: Nouvelles Perspectives, xvi
Persia, Persian, 11-2, 120, 161
personification, 78, 81, 83, 89, 97n
Phaedo, 154-5, 159
phase, phases, 3, 79-83, 90, 129n, 137n, 144, 174, 201, 213
phenomenal-physical layer, 230
phenomenality, xvi, 201, 217, 221n, 222
Philo Judaeus, 12-3, 15
Philosophy of Mysticism: Raids on the Ineffable, xvi, 253n, 288
physical domain, 230
piety, 74, 87-8, 154-6, 158
Plato, viii, xiv, 4, 18n, 55, 117, 120n, 138-9, 153-60, 154n, 155n, 157n, 158n, 162-3, 165, 169, 176, 290
Playing Fields, 3
Plotinus, 95n, 130n, 137, 139
Plutarch, 113, 113n, 116
poetry, xii, 58-60, 62, 64, 66, 68, 76n, 89n, 145, 287
polytheism, 91, 111-2, 116n
Pomian, Krysztof, 234, 234n
potency, potent/omnipotent, 53, 91, 114, 164, 209-12, 226
powers, xiii, 3, 15, 84, 88-9, 89n, 109, 118, 121, 163, 229, 237, 247n, 283
practitioner, x, xvi, 23-5, 28, 86-7, 160-1, 163, 171n, 228-46, 251-2, 254, 256, 274
praxis, ix, xiii, 99, 102, 118
prayer, praying, xii, 17, 59, 117n, 118n, 129n, 156, 158, 240-3, 245-6
presence, ix, xii, xiv, 6, 41, 51, 53-4, 58, 95n, 107, 109, 117n, 118-9, 123, 125, 131-2, 132n, 135, 137n, 138-42, 145, 148, 172, 204, 211,222n, 243
Pre-Socratics, the, xiv
priest, priestly, priesthood, xiii, 100-1, 104, 116, 116n, 117n, 118-9, 119n, 120n, 121, 156-7
primary process, 217
problematizing, 1-2, 19
profane, 94n, 103n, 104, 116n, 120n
profanus, 94, 94n, 156-8, 162, 165, 171n
prophecy, prophetic, 63, 166, 172, 224n, 226-7
prosthesis, 8-10
proximal zone, 228-9, 232-3, 240-4, 246

psychedelics, psychedelic, 16, 32-3, 40n, 47, 49, 53, 55n, 134, 148, 148n, 291
ayahuasca, 17, 291
psychopathic, 285
Puritans, 145
purity, 7, 85-7, 89, 120n, 243
puzzle, puzzlement, puzzling, 8, 19, 101, 197
Pythagoras, xv
qādôš, kadosh (holy), 92, 94
qĕlipôt, qĕlipāh (spiritual blinders), 99-100
qi (vital energy), 72-3, 72n, 78, 83, 87, 87n
quantum physics, xvii, 47, 52n, 249, 258n, 263, 268
rabbi, rabbinical, 59, 63, 67, 99, 99n, 101, 103, 110, 118, 119n, 121, 160, 165, 170, 175, 204, 210, 223n, 224
Rahula, Walpola, 255
Rappaport, Roy, 92-3, 93n, 94n, 100n
Rasputin, 66
Rastier, François, xvi, 228-31, 230n, 231n, 232n, 233n, 234, 234n, 235n, 236, 236n
Ratanakul, Pinit, 270, 270n
rationality, xiv, 13
realities, xiii, 5, 90, 114, 207, 256, 258, 260, 260n, 263, 265; consensus reality, 20; ultimate reality, 5, 52; supramundane reality, 5
realm(s), ix, 10, 78, 83, 90-1, 101, 106, 112n, 114, 119, 154, 156-9, 170, 179-80, 184, 194, 196, 205, 207-8, 210, 217, 252, 257, 260-1, 260n, 270n
reasoning, xvii, 1, 3, 13, 17-9, 103n, 105, 109, 154-5, 165, 191, 263, 266, 268, 276
rectification, 210
referentiality, referent, referential, 93, 113n, 115, 121-3, 252
reification (pragmapeia), 97, 97n, 223n
Reik, Theodor, 116n
Reinhold, Karl Leonhard, 113, 113n
relativity, 130, 236, 238, 238n, 240, 250, 258, 261n, 268-9, 291; factors of, 236, 238, 238n
Mosaic religion (ancient Israel), 98, 100-1
postbiblical religions, 98
representation, representational, 106, 106n, 120n, 121-3, 130n, 154n, 180, 184-6, 190n, 207, 220, 222, 231, 233, 241
Republic, The, 155, 155n, 157n, 159
revelation, 19, 37, 43, 55, 59-60, 63, 66, 116n, 145, 166, 168, 172, 179, 204
revolution,, 30, 59, 61, 65-7, 107-8, 111n, 139n, 164, 174, 279, 283, 286
riddle, riddles, 20, 192, 113n
righteousness, 74, 85, 111n
Rilke, Rainer Maria, 58, 60, 67-8
rites, 75n, 75-6, 93, 113, 120n, 121
Ritner, Robert, 104n, 107n
River Flows from Eden, 209n
Roberts, Thomas B., 55n
Rumi, Jalaladdin, 58, 68, 172-3, 172n, 174n, 175
Russell, Bertrand, 12-3, 13n, 15, 178-81, 179n, 181n, 183, 198
Sabbath, the, 119
sacer, 92, 94, 94n, 156-62, 165, 170-1
sacerdos/sacerdotes, 120n, 156-7, 160-1, 171, 171n, 174
sādhana, xvi, 228-30, 239, 241, 246
Saint Paul, xiv
Samadhi, 1, 3
Sanskrit, 103, 270
Sartre, Jean-Paul, 134, 134n, 290
satan, satanic, 145
satori, 1, 3, 50
savagery, 3
scale, scalar, xiii, 13, 19n, 91, 96, 136n, 190n, 227, 236, 238, 264
Scharfstein, Ben-Ami, 105n
Scheler, Max, xiv, 125, 127, 127n, 135-6, 136n, 149
Schelling, F. W. J., 112n, 133n, 134n
Scholem, Gershom, 60, 225, 225n
Schopenhauer, Arthur, 112n
Schwartz, Benjamin, 73n, 77, 78n
science and mysticism, 1-26
Science and the Dao, vii
scripture, 7n, 77, 83, 84n, 85, 90, 113n, 117n, 118, 121, 167-8, 170, 203n, 225
scroll, scrolls, 99n, 173, 225
Second Commandment, the, 101-2, 102n, 109

Second Jerusalem Temple, 99
secret, secrecy, secretive, 4n, 8-10, 12, 32, 43, 56, 98n, 103, 115-6, 120n, 150, 178, 196, 209, 213, 262n, 285
Sefer ha-Bahir, 224, 224n
Sefer Yetzirah, 115n, 224n
sefirah, sefirot, 115n, 207, 207n, 209-10
self: awakening of, 213; consciousness, xvii, 44, 55; illumination of, 213; loathing, 26, 45; narrative, 214, 216-8, 220-1; tags, 226-7; and "unitive life", 213-4
semantic, xvi, 91, 96, 99, 106-7, 106n, 121-2, 136, 210, 236, 246, 287
semiosis, semiotics: ix, xiii, xv-xvi, 17n, 18-9, 19n, 91, 105n, 106n, 109, 118-9, 121-4, 123n, 228-247, 238n, 287-8; domain, 124, 230; layer, 228, 230-1, 234
Semitic, 107, 107n
senses, the, 15n, 40-1, 72, 108n, 115, 129n, 211, 215, 147n, 272
sensibility, 91, 97, 100-1, 109, 118, 124, 166, 171, 173-4
sensory, xvi, 15n, 26, 78, 83, 104, 136, 138, 201, 214, 218
sentience, sentient beings, 97n, 240-1, 243-4, 246, 279, 283, 286
serpent, 97n, 114-5
Sessa, Ben, 55n
Shakyamuni, 242
shaman, shamanism, shamanic, xv, 16, 55, 59, 73, 89n
Shanon, Benny, 16-7, 16n, 17n, 106n
Shekhinah, the, 172, 209-11
Shklovsky, Viktor 121n
signification, signifying, xiv, 3-4, 8, 18, 59, 80, 92-3, 94n, 96, 103-6, 120n, 121-2, 131, 153, 256, 266
significance, xiii, 6, 34, 77, 91-2, 97n, 100, 108, 110, 136, 144, 160n, 181, 184, 191, 196, 227
signified, signifier, 105, 108, 118-9, 122, 230-1
Smart, Ninian, 203n
Smith, David Woodruff, 14, 14n, 18n
Smith, Huston, 7
social practice, 228, 230, 232, 234
sociopathic, 283
Socrates, xiv, 138, 153-60, 162, 169, 175-6
Song of Songs, 161, 204n, 211
sophist(s), 154, 158
sophos, 154
soteriology, soteriological, xvii, 72n, 83, 203, 208, 249, 255, 270
soul, xi-xii, xvii, 29, 34, 39-40, 43, 48, 48n, 52, 54, 56, 58-9, 63, 66, 68, 72-3, 85, 85n, 97, 117, 117n, 130, 133, 138, 154-6, 159, 161, 173, 176, 176n, 213, 278
Spinoza, Baruch (Benedict de), xiv, 13-5, 20, 97n, 111, 111n, 112n, 153, 160n, 165-172, 166n, 168n, 174-6, 175n, 176n; and First Level of Knowledge (imagination), 13; and Second Level ("intellect"), 13; and Third Level ("intuition"), 13
spirituality, xiii, xvii, 40n, 85, 94n, 98, 127n, 128, 134-5, 148, 202, 203n, 209n, 226n, 249, 251n, 260n, 261n, 262n, 264n, 269n, 277; spiritual entities, 91; hypostatized spirituality, xiii, 91
stage, stages, 3, 26, 28, 51-2, 89-90, 120n, 137, 145, 181, 203n, 207-9, 208n, 213-6, 215n, 218, 221, 242, 245, 247n, 283
Stalin, Joseph, 65
stim-apps, 283
stimulus, stimuli, 222, 230, 281-2
Stoic, Stoicism, 111n, 116, 137-9
subjectivity, 52, 91, 97
sublime, x, xvii, 1, 3, 5, 19, 40, 246
subliminal, 40, 221n
substantialization, 97n
suffering, x, 23-5, 30, 137, 145, 202-3, 242, 245, 255, 257, 270-2
Sufi, Sufism, xiv, 144, 146, 159, 161, 171-3, 209
Suicide Circus, xii
Sumerians, the, 104n
supernatural, 5, 91, 99n, 110
supernormal, xv, 201
supra-natural, 96
surrendering, 28
Suzuki, D. T., 56, 267
sweet-tweet, 282

symbolism, 106, 114, 124, 207n, 209, 223n
systems, xii, xv-xvii, 71, 82, 92-4, 100, 103, 103n, 139, 145, 201, 206, 214, 216, 221, 226, 233n, 252, 257
Tabernacle, the, 211
taboo, 23, 120n
Taiyi sheng shui, 77
Talmud, the, 102n, 160n, 212n
Tao, Taoist, Taoism [see also Daoism], 71n, 73n, 76n, 77n, 78n, 80n, 81n, 84n, 127, 144, 144n, 146, 250n, 268, 274
taxonomy, 221n, 271; epistemic, 13, 20; Peircean, 122-3
telos, 160n, 163, 167, 169, 174
temple, temples, 95n, 99-100, 99n, 111, 113n, 116, 117n, 118-9, 121, 206-7, 288
tension(s), 26-7, 130n, 254
Tetragrammaton, 113-4
The Arcanes, xi, 58, 60, 64, 287
The Essence of Kabbalah, xv, 110n, 223n, 289
The Head Trip: Adventures on the Wheel of Consciousness, x, 291
The Orange Voice, xii
The Sôd *Hypothesis*, 17n, 91n, 101n, 117n, 118n, 123n, 288
The Tree of Life: The Palace of Adam Kadmon, 114n
theology, xiii, 5, 99, 105n, 112-3, 112n, 113n, 115n, 117-8, 128, 142, 290
theory, xvi, 6, 52, 67, 71, 191, 197, 230, 237, 258-9, 267-8, 274; of anthropic zones, xvi, 228-30; of everything, 257, 276; identity, 289; of meaning, 178, 180, 182, 184, 187, 192, 195-7, 290; relativity, xvii, 258, 291;
Thibault, Paul J., 19n
Thomas, Dylan, 59
Tillich, Paul, 181, 182n, 198
time and space, 16n
tiqûn ôlām ("mending the world"), 110
Todorov, Tzvetan, 105n
Tolstoy, Leo, 181
tonglen, 242
topification, 97n
Torah, 99n, 121, 124, 173-4, 204-5, 204n, 211-2, 226n
traditions, ix, xi-xii, xiv-xv, 3, 7, 16, 19, 25, 50-1, 55, 58, 71, 74, 78-84, 88, 90, 92, 94, 100, 115, 121, 125, 128, 130, 132, 135, 144, 146, 160-1, 163, 168, 173, 202-3, 206-7, 224, 249, 256, 268-70, 273-4
trance, xii, 59
transcendence, transcendent, xiii, xvi, 2, 32-4, 40, 44, 46, 50-1, 53-4, 56, 71-2, 77, 83, 88, 90, 95-6, 109-10, 114, 117, 126, 128, 133, 139, 143, 148, 178, 222, 228-9, 233-4, 240-1, 243-7, 256, 277; transformational, 40
transcendental, 40n, 95n, 127, 136, 155, 171, 189n, 190-3, 244
singular event (TTSE), 40
transitivity (linguistic), 91, 96-8, 96n
translation, cross-cultural, 93; metamorphic, 97; pictorial into verbal, 106n
transpersonal, xiv, 46, 49-51, 53, 125-6, 128, 130, 132-3, 135, 137, 137n, 139, 144, 146, 148, 150, 227, 287-9
transrational, xii
trope, tropes, vi, 58, 67, 97n
truth, xii, 32, 50-1, 55, 59, 84, 87, 99, 112n, 113n, 116, 123n, 134n, 147-9, 155-6, 157n, 158n, 159-60, 162-4, 167, 176, 178-80, 183, 192, 196-7, 211, 252, 259, 270-1, 274-6, 290
tseruf (Hebrew letter combinations), 63, 65
Tsur, Reuven, 104, 104n, 106, 123n
typology of things, 235
Uexküll, Jacob von, 231, 231n
ultimate other, 10, 110
Ultimate Sacred Postulates, 94
umbilical cord, 99
Underhill, Evelyn, 213-4, 213n
understanding, misunderstanding, ix, xiii-xiv, xvi-xvii, 1, 4-5, 7-8, 10, 13, 15, 18, 42, 49, 55, 79-80, 83, 107, 125-6, 128, 129n, 130n, 133n, 134-5, 144, 146, 147n, 150, 156-7, 159, 163, 166, 169-70, 177, 179, 186, 194, 201-2, 206-7, 209, 221, 223, 229, 249, 256, 257n, 267, 271-2, 274
union, 53, 66-7, 71, 88, 109, 138, 206, 209, 221, 225, 227, 251n

universe, 11-2, 47, 72-3, 77-80, 83, 85-6, 134, 140, 211, 241, 250-1, 255-6, 263, 269, 273
Vajrayāna, 229
value, xv, 12, 86, 92, 110n, 123n, 134n, 145-6, 177, 180, 183-4, 187, 190, 193-4, 197-8, 222, 225n, 228, 236, 238, 240-1, 259, 273, 286, 290; ascription, iv, 99
Varela, Francisco J., vi, 202n
Varki, Ajit, 56n
vehicle, 28, 129n, 136, 143
veneration, 86, 103n
virtue, virtues, 74-5, 77,85-6, 85n, 89-90, 153, 168, 170, 236
visual, visuality, visualization, xvi, 4-5, 17, 65, 78, 85-7, 85n, 106, 106n, 108-9, 115n, 123n, 147n, 206n, 207, 218, 228-30, 240, 243-6, 266, 287-8
Vital, Chayyim, 114n
vitality, 73, 94, 100n, 130
voice, xii, 15, 39, 44-5, 97n, 142, 207, 243
Wallace, B. Alan, 249, 264, 271, 273
Wang Bi, 76, 76n
Wang Yangming, 80, 80n
Warburton, William, 103n, 105, 105n, 107
weird things happening, 33-4, 38
Welt, 192n, 194n, 231, 231n
white light, 148, 208-9, 211-4, 222-3
Whitehead, Alfred North, 52, 52n
Whitman, Jon, 107n
Wilber, Ken, 41, 50, 128, 249, 264, 274
Winnicott, D. W., 146-7, 146n
witness, witnessing, 48, 51, 54n, 162, 209
Wittgenstein, Ludwig, viii, xv, 12-5, 177, 180-98; and picture theory, 187, 189n, 190n, 191; and logical form, 182, 185, 187-92, 188n; and the *Tractatus*, viii, xv, 13, 177, 181-4, 186-90, 193-8; and role of the mystical, 180, 190, 195, 197
Wolfe, Tom, xvii
Wolfson, Elliot, 205, 223-4
Wolfson, Phil, 40n
worlds, 122, 174, 193, 228
worldview, xiii, 49, 53, 73n, 76-7, 78n, 82-3, 96, 98n, 99, 109-10, 184, 249, 276
worship, worshiping, xviii, 12, 91, 93-4, 95n, 102, 108, 111n, 112n, 119n, 136, 233, 285
writing, 4, 12, 24, 47, 49, 59-60, 65, 95n, 107, 121, 160, 175, 182, 204, 257; hieroglyphic, 103-4, 106, 108; alphabetic, 103-4; system, 103, 103n, 104n
Wu Yun, 89, 89n
Year of Eating Brains, 282
YHWH, 17, 110, 115
Yiddish, 62, 103, 287
Yijing, 79n, 82
yin and yang, 79, 85n, 87, 90
Zahavi, Dan, 129n
Zevit, Ziony, xvii, 117n
Zhu Xi, 82, 86n
Zhuangzi, 72, 81, 83-4
Zohar, xv, 5, 59, 201, 205, 207-13, 218-9, 221-4
Zohar, Danah, 260n
Zombie Apocalypse, 282
Zoroastrianism, 16
Zukav, Gary, 250, 266, 268n